The Best

PHOENIX & TUCSON

An impertinent insiders' guide

By Don and Betty Martin

Second edition

DISCOVERGUIDES • *Las Vegas, Nevada*

BOOKS BY DON AND BETTY MARTIN

Adventure Cruising • 1996
Arizona Discovery Guide • 1990, 1996
Arizona in Your Future • 1991, 1997, 2003
The Best of Denver & the Rockies • 2001
The Best of Phoenix & Tucson • 2001
The Best of San Francisco • 1986, 1990, 1994, 1997, 2002, 2005
The Best of the Gold Country • 1987, 1992
The Best of the Wine Country • 1991, 1995, 2001, 2005
California-Nevada Roads Less Traveled • 1999
Hawai'i: The Best of Paradise • 2003, 2005
Inside San Francisco • 1991
Las Vegas: The Best of Glitter City • 1998, 2001, 2003
Nevada Discovery Guide • 1992, 1997
Nevada in Your Future • 2000, 2004
New Mexico Discovery Guide • 1998
Northern California Discovery Guide • 1993
Oregon Discovery Guide • 1993, 1999
San Diego: The Best of Sunshine City • 1999, 2002
San Francisco's Ultimate Dining Guide • 1988
Seattle: The Best of Emerald City • 2000
The Toll-free Traveler • 1997
The Ultimate Wine Book • 1993, 2000
Utah Discovery Guide • 1995
Washington Discovery Guide • 1994, 2000

Library of Congress Cataloging-in-Publication Data
Martin, Don and Betty —
The Best of Phoenix & Tucson
Includes index.
1. Phoenix and Scottsdale, Arizona—description and travel
2. Tucson, Arizona—description and travel

ISBN: 0-942053-36-2

COVER DESIGN • **Vicky Biernacki**, Columbine Type and Design, Sonora, Calif.
KOKOPELLI ILLUSTRATIONS • **Bob Shockley**, Mariposa, Calif.

JUST THE BEST; NOT ALL THE REST

This is a different kind of guidebook. Instead of saturating readers with details on everything there is to see and do in Arizona's two metropolitan centers, the authors have sifted through their hundreds of lures and selected only the ten best in various categories. It is more than a mere book of lists, however. Each listing is a detailed description, with specifics on location, hours and price ranges.

Further, there is plenty from which to choose. *The Best of Phoenix & Tucson* offers Ten Best lists in nearly fifty different categories. It is thus a great resource for visitors with limited time, visitors with lots of time and residents who'd like to make new discoveries about their communities.

A guidebook that focuses only on the best must, by its very nature, be rather opinionated. Some would even suggest that it's impertinent. Further, many readers may not agree with the authors' choices, which is part of the fun of reading this book.

This is another in a series of "Ten Best" city guides by Don and Betty Martin, winners of a gold medal in the prestigious Lowell Thomas Travel Writing Competition. Check your local book store for these other titles:

The Best of San Francisco
The Best of Denver & the Rockies
Hawai'i: The Best of Paradise
Las Vegas: The Best of Glitter City
San Diego: The Best of Sunshine City
Seattle: The Best of Emerald City

These and other *DISCOVERGUIDE* titles also are available on line at *amazon.com, bn.com* and *borders.com.*

Keeping up with the changes

Arizona is—by percentage, at least—the second fastest growing state in the Union, after Nevada. Most of this action is happening around its two metropolitan centers, Phoenix-Scottsdale and Tucson. If you discover something afresh during your sun country visit, or if you catch an error in this book, let us know. Contact us if you find that a taqueria has become a parking lot or the other way around.

DISCOVERGUIDES
P.O. Box 231954
Las Vegas, NV 89123-0033

CONTENTS
PART I: PHOENIX & SCOTTSDALE

1 Metro Arizona
An unauthorized history — 14
Getting there and about — 18
Our ten favorite Phoenix-Scottsdale moments — 21

2 Visitor lures
The ten very best attractions — 26
The next Ten Best attractions — 32
The Ten Best things to do in Phoenix-Scottsdale — 37
The Ten Best attractions beyond Phoenix-Scottsdale — 44

3 Grazing Arizona
The Ten Very Best restaurants — 53
The Ten Best specialty restaurants & cafés — 58
The Ten Best Hispanic restaurants — 63
The Ten Best other ethnic restaurants — 67

4 Pillow talk
The Ten Best resorts — 73
The Ten Best hotels & inns — 79

5 Proud paupers: A budget guide
Frugal fun: The Ten Best free or cheap attractions — 84
The Ten Best cheap eats — 88
The Ten Best cheap sleeps — 92

6 Nightside
The Ten Best performing arts centers & groups — 96
The Ten Best nightspots — 99
The Ten Best watering holes — 102

7 Romance and other primal urges
The Ten Best places to snuggle with your sweetie — 108
The ten most romantic restaurants — 111

8 Credit card abuse
The Ten Best shopping malls — 116
The Ten Best specialty stores — 121

9 Odd ends: Assorted bits and pieces
Getting physical: The Ten Best walks and bike routes — 126
The Ten Best viewpoints and photo angles — 136
The Ten Best specialty guides to the area — 140
Easy listening: The Ten Best radio stations — 142

10 Beyond Phoenix
The Ten Best side trips — 144

PART II: TUCSON & SURROUNDS

11 The Old Pueblo
Finding Arizona's Spanish roots — 155
An unauthorized history — 156
Getting there and getting about — 158
Our ten favorite Tucson moments — 160

12 Discovering Tucson
The ten very best attractions — 165
The next Ten Best attractions — 172

13 Tucson dining
The Ten Very Best restaurants — 180
The Ten Best specialty restaurants & cafés — 185
The Ten Best Hispanic restaurants — 189
The Ten Best other ethnic restaurants — 193

14 Lodging & dude ranching
The Ten Best resorts — 199
The Ten Best guest ranches & small inns — 204

15 Affordable Tucson: A budget guide
Frugal fun: The Ten Best free attractions — 210
The Ten Best cheap eats — 214
The Ten Best cheap sleeps — 218

16 Nightfall
The Ten Best performing arts groups — 222
The Ten Best nightspots — 224
The Ten Best watering holes — 227

17 Being spendy
The Ten Best malls and shopping areas — 231
The Ten Best specialty stores — 235

18 Bits & pieces: Assorted odds and ends
Tucson's ten most intimate places — 239
Getting physical: The Ten Best walks, hikes & bike routes — 243
The Ten Best viewpoints and photo angles — 251
Tucson's Ten Best specialty guides — 255
Easy listening: The Ten Best radio stations — 257

19 Beyond Tucson
The Ten Best side trips — 259

NOTE: The beginning of the Tucson section of this book is tabbed in black so readers can thumb quickly to it.

TWO CITIES IN THE SUN

They bask in the heart of America's sunbelt—two of the largest and most popular vacation communities in the Southwest. Even though they're both Arizona desert cities, they are quite different in character.

Phoenix is the younger and yet the larger of the two—faster paced, faster growing and possibly more brash. Tucson is more historic, wise with age and more attuned to its past. It grows more slowly than upstart Phoenix and most of its residents prefer it that way. Phoenix is entrepreneurial spirit and mostly Anglo; Tucson is old money, with a rich Hispanic heritage.

They do have one thing in common—an abundance of visitor lures drawing millions of people each year. And since Phoenix and Tucson are just over a hundred miles apart, many visitors call on both cities as part of an Arizona vacation.

And therein lies a problem: By dividing their time between two large cities, and perhaps nipping off to the Grand Canyon, most visitors find that there's simply too much to do, too many places to see.

Who has time to explore every corner of Phoenix and Tucson; to find their best attractions, their finest museums, their grandest desert parks, the best restaurants, the fanciest resorts, the liveliest cantinas?

As a matter of fact, we do. We're the authors of *Arizona Discovery Guide,* a comprehensive guidebook to the Grand Canyon State, and *Arizona In Your Future,* a detailed relocation guide. Each of these books has generous chapters on Phoenix and Tucson. Through the years of doing the initial research and then revising these volumes, we've explored every museum and other attraction in these cities and their suburbs. We've dined at numerous restaurants, prowled splendid desert resorts and sipped fine *añejo* tequila at not a few cantinas. And in researching this book, we returned again for more exploring, noshing, prowling and sipping.

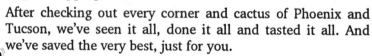 After checking out every corner and cactus of Phoenix and Tucson, we've seen it all, done it all and tasted it all. And we've saved the very best, just for you.

Don & Betty Martin
Hanging out at Mission San Xavier, Tucson

IS SUMMER A BUMMER IN THE SUNBELT?

Obviously, Phoenix and Tucson are primarily fall-through-spring destinations, since summer is often hotter than the hinges of Hades. Tucson is slightly cooler than Phoenix because its elevation is nearly 1,300 feet higher. The average July high in Phoenix is 104.4 degrees; in Tucson, it's 100.

However, to use that old chamber of commerce cliché, it's a dry heat. A summer vacation in the Sunbelt isn't really such a bad idea, since hotel and resort rates are slashed by fifty percent or more. The hot season for cool room bargains runs from June or July through August. Rates at the posh resorts in Phoenix, Scottsdale and Tucson can drop from a peak season high of $300 to as little $100 in summer. Golfers will be pleased to know that green fees and golf cart rentals also are greatly reduced.

Even in mid-summer, mornings are usually comfortable and evenings cool off rather quickly, since there are no large bodies of water to retain the heat. Plan outdoor activities in the early morning and evening. Unlike mad dogs, Englishmen and occasional visitors from North Dakota, don't go out in the noonday sun. Many restaurants in Phoenix and Tucson, including those at resorts, have outdoor seating. A leisurely meal during a warm Arizona evening—with moon and stars above—can be a particularly pleasant experience.

If you do venture forth at midday, virtually everything is air conditioned—malls, museums and most attractions. Or you can head for a water park or take a side trip to higher ground, such as Sedona out of Phoenix or Tombstone out of Tucson. Or simply sit neck deep in the resort swimming pool or lie in the shade, frosted margarita in hand. With those great room rate reductions, you should be able to afford one of the Sunbelt's nicest resorts.

Sizzling summers don't seem to bother the state's residents, since about eighty-five percent of them live in desert climes, well below the cooler elevations of northern and eastern Arizona.

Humidity, not heat alone, causes the greatest distress on a hot day. It slows surface evaporation from your skin, which is nature's cooling device. Climatologists use a scale called a "discomfort rating" to measure perceived temperatures at various humidity levels. It works like a wind chill factor in reverse. At very low humidity, a 100-degree temperature has a discomfort rating of ninety degrees or less. If the mercury hits 115 and the humidity is forty percent, the discomfort factor spirals to 151, which would make survival outdoors impossible. Fortunately, that combination never occurs in the Arizona desert.

According to figures released by the Metropolitan Tucson Convention & Visitors Bureau, Tucson has a lower discomfort rating than Atlanta, New Orleans, St. Louis, Houston or—sorry about this, Mickey—Orlando. (The bureau calls it a "comfort rating," wanting to keep a positive spin on things.)

We live in another hot place—Las Vegas—and we function quite comfortably in 100-degree-plus temperatures. On the other hand, during trips to the soggy tropics, we've wilted at eighty-five degrees because of the humidity.

HOT WEATHER TIPS

If you do decide on a summer visit to Phoenix or Tucson, follow these steps to keep your cool when the weather's not:

1. Avoid dehydration by drinking plenty of water. And we mean *plenty*. A gallon a day will keep heatstroke away, particularly if you're doing a lot of walking or hiking in Phoenix or Tucson desert parks.

2. On very hot days, avoid sweet drinks or alcohol, which speed up dehydration. Besides, you chubby little rascal, a typical twelve-ounce soft drink contains about twelve teaspoons of sugar!

3. Don't take salt tablets, despite what they told you in boot camp. Salt causes you to retain water, and you want to perspire. That's what keeps you cool. And *THAT'S* why you should drink lots of water, to keep plenty of fluid circulating through your system.

4. Don't exert yourself on a hot day. Your body will lose more fluid than you can replace.

5. Wear light colored, loose and reflective clothing—preferably cotton or linen. Avoid nylon and polyester, since these fabrics don't "breathe" and this traps body heat against your skin.

6. If you must be outdoors in the heat, dip your shirt or blouse in water frequently. The garment's evaporation, along with that from your body, will help keep you cool.

7. Use sunscreen with a high PABA content; it ranges from five to thirty-three percent (which is a virtual sunblock). Even if you're working on a tan, use sunblock on sensitive areas, such as your lips, nose and don't forget the tops of your ears. If you have a bald pate, remember to protect that, preferably by wearing a hat instead of a sun visor. In case you're curious, PABA stands for para-aminobenzoic acid and no wonder people use the acronym! A few people are allergic to PABA; if a rash appears, try something else.

8. Bear in mind that suntan lotion will rinse off when you swim or perspire, so re-lather yourself after swimming or exercising.

9. Always wear a broad brimmed hat or visor outdoors. It'll shade your eyes and protect them from sun glare and shield your face from sunburn. There's some evidence that sun glare may be a cause of cataracts. The *vaqueros* knew what they were doing when they created the sombrero.

10. If you spend a lot of time outdoors, some specialists recommend getting a careful, light tan. Moderately tanned skin will resist sunburn—up to a point. You can still get singed from prolonged exposure. Get your tan very slowly, limiting your initial exposure to a few minutes a day. Do your tanning in the morning or very late afternoon when the sun's rays are less direct.

Be careful as you baste yourself in the sun; you may doze off and get too much exposure. Incidentally, clouds don't block all the sun's ultraviolet rays. Also, reflections from sand, pool decks or water can intensify burning. Wet T-shirts may look rather fetching on the right bodies, yet they offer little sun protection, despite their cooling effect.

If you do get burned, ease the pain with a dip in the pool or a cool shower, then use one of those over-the-counter anesthetic sprays. Antihistamine will relieve the itch. That's right; the same stuff that you take for the sniffles. Keep your skin out of the sun until it's fully healed.

Avoiding "heat sickness"

Heat exhaustion and its lethal cousin heatstroke are real dangers on hot summer days. Both are brought on by a combination of dehydration and sun. Signs of heat exhaustion are weariness, muscle cramps and clammy skin. The pulse may slow and you may become unusually irritable. If left untreated, heat exhaustion can lead to deadly heatstroke. The skin becomes dry and hot, the pulse may quicken and you'll experience nausea and possibly a headache. Convulsions, unconsciousness, even death can follow.

At the first sign of heat sickness, get out of the sun and into the shade. Stay quiet and drink water—plenty of water. If you're near a pool, faucet or stream, douse your face and body with water, and soak your clothes to lower your body temperature quickly.

HOW TO TALK LIKE AN ARIZONAN

The people of Phoenix and Tucson speak perfectly good English and in many cases, Spanish. However, as you explore these cities and their surrounds, you'll frequently hear words of native and Hispanic origin that may be strange to your ear. We've prepared a list of some of terms you'll likely encounter, with their pronunciation. Many are names of places you may visit while exploring Arizona. This guide was prepared with aid of Brian C. Catts of the University of Arizona's Office of Public Service, and borrowed from our *Arizona Discovery Guide.*

Ajo *(AH-hoe)* — A town in southern Arizona; the word means "garlic" in Spanish.

Anasazi *(Ana-SAH-zee)* — Prehistoric Southwest tribe; the name means "the ancient ones."

Athabaskan *(A-tha-BAS-kan; "a's" are pronounced as in apple)* — Canadian native tribe; some migrated south to become Arizona's Navajos and Apaches.

Canyon de Chelly *(du SHAY)* — A national monument on the Navajo Reservation.

Canyon del Muerto *(MWAIR-toh)* "Canyon of Death," a ravine adjacent to Canyon de Chelly.

Carne *(CAR-nay)* — Meat; you'll see this reference on many Mexican restaurant menus, such as *carne asada.*

"Cerveza fria, por favor" *(Sehr-VE-sa FREE-ah, por fah-VOR)* — "Bring me a cold one, please."

Chinle *(Chin-LEE)* Navajo town; the gateway to Canyon de Chelly.

Chiricahua *(Cheer-i-COW-wa)* — Southeastern Arizona Apache tribe made famous by Cochise and Geronimo's rebellions.

Cholla *(CHOY-ya)* — Large family of Arizona cactus.

Colorado *(Coh-lo-RAH-doh)* — Red.

Gila *(HEE-la)* — A river in southern Arizona.

Guadalupe Hidalgo *(Wa-da-LU-pay Hee-DAL-go)* The treaty ending the Mexican War, signed in 1848.

Havasupai *(Hah-vah-SOO-pie)* — "Blue-green water people" who occupy beautiful Havasu Canyon; also called Supai.

Hohokam *(Hoe-hoe-KAHM)* — Prehistoric tribe occupying Southern Arizona about 200 to 500 A.D.; means "those who have gone."

Huachuca *(Hwa-CHOO-ka)* — Army fort in southern Arizona with an historic museum; also the name of a mountain range.

Hopi *(HOE-pee)* — Arizona native tribe, probably descended from the Anasazi.

Hotevilla *(HOAT-vih-la)* — Hopi village on Third Mesa. The name means "skinned back" or cleared off.

Hualapai *(HWAL-a-pie or WAH-lah-pie)* — Western Arizona tribe; the name means "pine tree people."

Huevos Rancheros *(WHEY-vose ran-CHER-ohs)* — Popular Hispanic breakfast with eggs and picante sauce.

Javalina *(Ha-va-LEE-na)* — Wild boar.

Kiva *(KEE-vah)* — Rounded clay-coated fireplaces in pueblo style homes; also outdoor ovens. Traditionally, the *kiva* was a ceremonial pithouse.

Kykotsmovi *(Kee-KOTS-mo-vee)* — Hopi administrative center, on Third Mesa below Oraibi, also called New Oraibi. It means "the place of the mound of ruins."

Lantilla *(lan-TEE-yah)* — Traditional pueblo style ceilings of tightly packed and sometimes interwoven twigs and small branches supported by log beams; often used in resorts as decorator features.

Maricopa *(Ma-ri-KOH-pah)* — A name given to the Pipa tribe, which shares a reservation with the Pima. Also the county that encloses greater Phoenix.

Mescalero *(Mess-kah-LAIR-o)* — Arizona-New Mexico Apache tribe. The name is Spanish, referring to mescal cactus, a traditional food source.

Moenkopi *(Mu-en-KO-pee)* —Third Mesa Hopi village; "place of running water."

Mogollon *(MUGGY-yon)* — Ancient tribe occupying eastern Arizona about 200 to 500 A.D. The Mogollon Rim is the abrupt southern edge of the Colorado Plateau in Arizona.

Mohave *(Mo-HA-vay)* — Western Arizona place name, referring to a native tribe and a county. Spelled "Mojave" in California.

Navajo *(NAH-VAH-hoe)* — America's largest native tribe, descended from the Athabascan band of Canada.

Ocotillo *(O-co-TEE-yo)* — Spiny-limbed desert bush with red blossoms at the tips.

Oraibi *(Oh-RYE-bee)* — Hopi settlement on Third Mesa; the name means "place of the Orai stone."

Paloverde *(PAW-lo-VAIR-day)* — Desert tree distinctive for the green bark of its limbs.

Papago *(PAH-pa-go)* — Spanish word for "bean eaters," referring to a Southern Arizona tribe, which has since re-adopted its traditional name of "Tohono O'odham"; see below.

Pima *(PEE-mah)* — Central and southern Arizona tribe. The name was a Spanish mistake. When questioned by early explorers, they responded *"Pi-nyi-match,"* which means "I don't understand." The Spanish thought they were identifying themselves.

Quechan *(KEE-chan or KAY-chan)* — Native tribe near the Yuma area.

Saguaro *(Sa-WHA-roh)* — This first Arizona word most visitors mispronounce. The saguaro is the large heavy-armed cactus prevalent throughout the Sonoran Desert. Its blossom is Arizona's state flower.

San Xavier *(Sahn Ha-vee-YAY)* — Mission south of Tucson; some locals pronounce it *Ha-VEER.*

Sichomovi *(si-CHO-MO-vee)* — Hopi settlement on First Mesa; means "a hill where the wild currants grow."

Sinagua *(Si-NAU-wa)* — Ancient north central Arizona tribe; lived in the area about 900-1000 A.D. It comes from the Spanish words *sin agua*—"without water."

Shungopovi *(Shung-O-PO-vee)* — Hopi settlement on Second Mesa; means "a place by the spring where tall reeds grow."

Tanque Verde *(tawn-ka VAIR-day)* — An area and a noted guest ranch east of Tucson. The name means "green tank" or "green pool."

Tempe *(Tem-PEE)* — A city east of Phoenix.

Tohono O'odham *(To-HO-no ah-toon)* — Traditional Papago and Pima tribal name; it means "people of the desert who have emerged from the earth."

Tubac *(TU-bahk)* — Arizona's first presidio, south of Tucson.

Tumacacori *(Too-mawk-ka-COR-ee)* — Spanish mission several miles south of Tucson.

Tusayan *(TU-sigh-yan or TUSSY-yan)* — Sinagua ruin near Desert View in Grand Canyon National Park; also a town outside the south entrance station.

Verde *(VAIR-day)* — Spanish for "green."

Yavapai *(YA-va-pie)* — Central Arizona tribe. The name's origin is unsure; it might mean "crooked mouth people" or "people of the sun."

PART I
PHOENIX & SCOTTSDALE
OF SUNSHINE, SALONS AND SALOONS

The sprawling Valley of the Sun is Arizona's most popular fall-through-spring vacation destination. Further, it is the state's metropolitan center, home to six of ten Arizonans. It's actually called the Salt River Valley, although that sounded a bit astringent for tourist promoters, so they gave it a more appealing name.

Twenty-two communities occupy this huge 9,000-square-mile basin, although the vast majority of visitors head for Phoenix and Scottsdale. Each offers its own attractions, restaurants and resorts, and tourists inevitably sample both communities.

Phoenix and Scottsdale once were separated by empty desert and by personality. Phoenix was the wanna-be big bird, rising from the abandoned irrigation canals of a former Hohokam settlement. Scottsdale started as a farming community and evolved into a deliberately rustic Western resort town.

The founders of Phoenix wanted to create the largest, most prosperous metropolitan center in the American Southwest. It has been done, almost to an extreme. This big bird is the Southwest's largest city and the sixth largest in America.

Scottsdale sought only to be laid back and charming, a kind of dusty Western community without all that pesky dust. It called itself "The West's most Western town," which it never really was. No cattle herds were ever stampeded down its main street and the James boys never robbed one of its banks. However, it certainly has become appealing as a Western style resort town.

When Phoenix went galloping off in all directions a few decades ago, little Scottsdale feared it would be trampled in the annexation stampede. So town fathers went on a land grab of their own. Inevitably, the two towns collided, each annexing up to the other's border. In the merging, Scottsdale lost more than Phoenix gained. It lost its rural charm while gaining shopping malls and car dealerships. Still, it has managed to retain its rustic Western-Spanish style downtown, while upscale resorts nudge its outskirts. Or rather, the outskirts nudge the resorts.

Today's Phoenix is gloss and glitter and glass highrises and fine museums, Rattlesnakes in baseball uniforms and *nouveau* dining salons. Scottsdale is urban cowboy, opulent desert resorts, Western saloons—and *nouveau* dining salons. They're both great places to visit.

So come West, young man, and bring the family.

Chapter One

METRO ARIZONA

PHOENIX RISING...AND RISING...

By the time he gets to Phoenix, Glen Campbell once sang, she'll be risin'. The song was about a girl left in an unmade bed after her lover headed out the door to return no more. However, every time I hear that song—which is rarely these days—I think of *Phoenix* rising.

I first got to Phoenix in pursuit of a girl, not to flee from one. Some decades back, I dated a pretty young accordion teacher in southern California. Then, at her parents' urging, she relocated to Phoenix. Undaunted, I made frequent trips there—to her parents' dismay. We spent weekends exploring this fine desert city and rustic next door Scottsdale. We saw operettas at a theater in urban Phoenix, drank margaritas in a Scottsdale cantina and played tag in cactus gardens that separated the two communities.

In the years since, things worked out much better for Phoenix and Scottsdale than they did for us. Phoenix has definitely risen, taking Scottsdale up with it. My former lady friend's modest apartment on Indian School Road has disappeared beneath the giant footprint of a highrise office complex. Our cactus patch playground has vanished beneath the asphalt of a new car dealership.

13

Unlike Francine and me, Phoenix and Scottsdale are now one. They have been joined postpartum, like mismatched Siamese twins, to become the largest population center in the Southwest. Arizona lures twenty-five million visitors a year and half of these wind up in Phoenix-Scottsdale. The two cities outdraw the Grand Canyon and they're the America's second most popular winter tourist destination, after Las Vegas.

And while Glitter City has the world's largest collection of gaming resorts, Phoenix-Scottsdale boasts the globe's most highly rated desert getaways. No other sunbelt tourist spot has as many AAA Five Diamond and Mobil Five Star resorts. A recent Zagat survey of frequent travelers rated Phoenix-Scottsdale as the nation's top hotel destination.

The merged cities also have hundreds of restaurants, dozens of museums and other attractions. And as if this weren't enough, they are part of a vast metropolitan sprawl called the Valley of the Sun or—if you prefer—the Salt River Valley. Beyond Phoenix-Scottsdale, visitors can discover another twenty cities with more attractions, museums, restaurants and resorts.

So, how can one possibly find—in the space of a vacation—all of the worthy attractions and the best resorts and restaurants in this vast Salt River Valley of the Sun? Obviously, one can't.

What one can do is use the Phoenix-Scottsdale section of this book to discover the very best that the valley has to offer.

In the next chapter, we shall take you by the hand and lead you—with very detailed directions—to the ten very best attractions in Phoenix and Scottsdale. We'll then follow with the next Ten Best attractions, the Ten Best things to do and the Ten Best lures beyond Phoenix-Scottsdale.

In subsequent chapters, the lists just keep coming—The Ten Best restaurants in assorted varieties, the Ten Best hotels and resorts, the Ten Best places to play after dark, the Ten Best places to hike and bike, and so on...

First, however, we'll tell you something of Phoenix and Scottsdale's past. Then we'll help you find your way around this crowded metropolitan sprawl. That's no easy task in a salty valley entwined by hundreds of miles of streets, highways and freeways—a valley that's home to more than half the registered vehicles in Arizona.

An unauthorized history

The Year 2000 census revealed that Phoenix had a population of 1.3 million, with another 1.7 million in the rest of the Valley of the Sun. How did this once dusty desert basin attract so many people? And in a state with one of America's largest native populations, a state that once was part of Spain and then Mexico, why were the communities of the Valley of the Sun built primarily by Anglos, for Anglos?

In two words: Gringo promotion.

Phoenix didn't just happen. At least not the way Tucson happened because of a mission settlement, Denver happened because of a gold strike and Salt Lake City happened because Brigham Young was chased out of Illinois and needed a place to park his wives.

Phoenix was a deliberate plan from the beginning, born not of historical coincidence but of land developers wanting to water the desert, grow crops and sell city lots. These planners and promoters where white American businessmen. Writes Bradford Luckingham in *Phoenix: The History of a Southwestern Metropolis* (University of Arizona Press, © 1989):

As the Anglos assumed power, they utilized Mexicans as an underclass to help them achieve their goals, including economic growth. Having achieved a dominant position...Anglos acquired more wealth, influence and prestige; and from these positions of strength, they dictated the terms of ethnic arrangement, which invariably found the majority of Mexicans and Mexican Americans living on the wrong side of the tracks.

Others suffered discrimination as well, such as the Chinese who settled here in the 1880s after working on the railroads. During this same period, discriminatory ordinances were passed against native people to control their "behavior."

However, the Phoenix of today is as racially integrated as any American city, with many minorities—notably Mexican Americans—holding important social, economic and political positions. This is not to suggest that it's a rich ethic stew like San Francisco or Seattle. Phoenix more resembles its big city neighbors of Denver and Las Vegas, with a predominately white population.

In the beginning

This Anglo city of the desert began with the arrival of an odd couple—a former Union Army officer named John Y.T. Smith and a hard-drinking Confederate Army deserter named John William Swilling. They didn't arrive together and there is no record of them having re-fought the Civil War in a barroom or elsewhere. Smith arrived in 1866 and began harvesting wild hay to sell to the Army's Fort McDowell, twenty miles northeast of the valley. Swilling came a year later and saw the valley's great farming potential.

Until their arrival, this valley freshened by the Salt River had been virtually ignored during the great Westward migration. The last permanent residents had been an ancient Hohokam tribe that diverted water from the river and raised crops. They built more than 250 miles of canals, the most elaborate pre-Colombian irrigation system in all the Americas. After occupying the land for more than a thousand years, they mysteriously vanished into the desert around 1400 A.D. Drought or disease or warfare may have driven them from the valley, and their ancestors are likely the Tohono O'odham people of central and southern Arizona. *Hohokam* is a Tohono O'odham expression for "gone away" or "perished."

Jack Swilling formed the Swilling Irrigating and Canal Company to clean out old Hohokam canals and build new ones. By 1868, fifty people were living in the new settlement and they began casting about for a name. Either Swilling or an educated Englishman named Darrel Duppa came up with the idea of "Phoenix," since the town was rising from the Hohokam settlement, as the legendary bird rose from its own ashes. The new town prospered slowly, although Swilling didn't prosper at all. He died a penniless alcoholic several years later in the Yuma Territorial Prison, while awaiting trial on robbery charges.

Other developers and canal diggers arrived and the town plodded along. Unlike many Western boomtowns, early Phoenix apparently was a rather boring place. A reporter observed in the 1870s:

We are...a very sober, industrious people, and we have been, at least the greater part of us, hard at work putting in our crops and taking care of them.

And so the Phoenix bird slowly germinated in the desert. It became the seat of the newly-formed Maricopa County in 1871, allegedly after Anglo citizens bribed several native people to pose as Mexicans and vote in the election. Native folks, of course, weren't allowed to vote. As this Gringo town grew, it took on a rather New England look. Brick and woodframe Victorian style buildings began replacing the earlier "unsightly and useless 'dobies." (They were neither, of course, for adobes provided better protection from summer heat and winter chill, and to live in an adobe these days is quite fashionable.)

The railroad came to town in 1887 and Phoenix began taking on the pace of a roadrunner instead of a desert tortoise. Two years later, its citizens wrestled the territorial capital from venerable Prescott, and the city's future was assured. On St. Valentine's Day, 1912, chubby President William Howard Taft signed the bill making Arizona the last of the forty-eight contiguous states. The capital, of course, would remain in Phoenix.

SCOTTSDALE'S FOUNDER ARRIVES

Meanwhile, Army chaplain Winfield Scott had arrived in the area in 1888. He bought a section of land on the northeast side of the valley and—with the aid of his brother George—started a fruit ranch. Scott traveled about the West, promoting the attributes of central Arizona and conducting Baptist revival meetings, while his brother stayed home and tended the oranges. In 1894, he platted the town of Orangedale which later became Scottsdale.

Hardly the wild Western town that it later pretended to be, early Scottsdale was as dry as the surrounding desert. Its citizens formed the Arizona Territory's first Anti-Saloon League. By the turn of the last century, it contained about a hundred residents and not one drop of Demon Rum.

The rest of Phoenix-Scottsdale's history reads like the history of the American West, only duller. The Valley of the Sun prospered with the completion of the Roosevelt Dam Project in 1911, which brought an assured water supply. It struggled through the Depression, prospered again with the arrival of military bases during World War II and fairly boomed in the postwar years when household air conditioning became common.

With air conditioning came high tech industries and tourism. These set the pattern for the Phoenix of today, with those industries ranking first and second in the local economy. Agriculture has slipped far down the list.

Retirement also is a major Valley of the Sun industry. The world's first planned senior community—Youngtown—was built west of Phoenix in 1954. Del E. Web, who earlier had been the contractor for Bugsy Siegel's Fabulous Flamingo in Las Vegas, started his first Sun City adjacent to Youngtown in 1960. (The story goes that Web became nervous when the Flamingo project fell behind schedule. Siegel assured him: "Don't worry, we only kill our own." It was a prophetic comment. The hotel opened in 1946 behind schedule and over budget and six months later, Siegel was assassinated by the mob. Web went on to become the world's leading developer of retirement communities.)

A SECOND REBIRTH

If Phoenix had a rather boring past, it certainly is enjoying an exciting present. Toward the end of the last century, a multi-billion-dollar renewal project turned the aging downtown area into a cultural showplace and events center. Among its elements are the Herberger performing arts center, Phoenix Symphony Hall, Civic Plaza and Convention Center, Bank One Ballpark, America West Arena and a business, shopping and dining complex called Arizona Center. Phoenix is more into progress than preservation. However, city fathers have saved a few historic buildings in Heritage Square, which also is home to the new Arizona Science Center and Phoenix Museum of History.

Although Phoenix is the nation's sixth largest city, its downtown area is quite compact; all of those new facilities are within walking distance. With its public plazas and parks, it's an appealing urban center.

However, downtown Phoenix still lacks the dynamic pulse of cities such as San Francisco or New York. A busy business hub during office hours, it's rather quiet at night and on weekends, and very few people live downtown. There are three areas where life does thrive after dark—Arizona Center, kept lively by its restaurants and bars; the Symphony Hall-Convention Center area on event nights; and the America West Arena and Bank One Ballpark area, which obviously jumps on game nights. Otherwise, urban Phoenix seems almost deserted after dark. One could shoot a cannon up Central Avenue at midnight and hit only an occasional Toyota.

Most of the restaurants, nightspots and certainly the resorts are in the suburbs and in next-door Scottsdale. Phoenix is not a single urban city but more a collection of suburban communities. This is the style of many Western American cities, which didn't reach full bloom until after the invention of the automobile. And this permitted—even encouraged—low density development. The California dream also was the Phoenix dream: A plot of land with an orange tree and barbecue in the back yard.

To again quote from Bradford Luckingham's *Phoenix: The History of a Southwest Metropolis*:

Though it was seen as an "anticity" by critics, particularly those from older urban America, admirers called the sprawling, multicentered metropolis the urban form of the future. The popularity of the new form attracted hordes of newcomers to Phoenix; the "anticity" became part of the lure.

Whatever its odd makeup, Phoenix is the second fastest growing city in America, after its rowdy smaller sister Las Vegas. This intriguing urban scatter sprinted into the new millennium like the roadrunner with Wile E. Coyote on its tail. And it's not looking back.

Getting There

Located near southern Arizona's geographic center, Phoenix is an easy reach. It's served by major highways, rail and one of the nation's busiest airports.

By highway • Interstate 10 approaches Phoenix from the west and merges with north-south I-17 just northeast of the downtown core. It does an abrupt ninety-degree turn, heads east toward Tempe, then swings south. The Superstition Freeway, U.S. 60, branches off I-10 in Tempe and goes through Mesa and well beyond. The north-south Squaw Peak Freeway links downtown with the resort areas of Scottsdale and Paradise Valley.

Motorists approaching from the northwest—Las Vegas and Kingman—can cut off dozens of miles by taking U.S. Highway 93 to Wickenburg and then U.S. 50 into Phoenix. These are mostly two-lane roads although they're rather fast and they travel through some interesting desert country. Wading through the sprawled outskirts of Sun City, Peoria and Glendale is rather slow, however. Some prefer to head east from Sun City on Bell Road and pick up I-17 north of Phoenix.

By air • Phoenix Sky Harbor International Airport, three miles southeast of downtown, is served by twenty-three U.S. and foreign carriers with more than a thousand arrivals and departures each day; (602) 273-3300. (*www.phxskyharbor.com*)

PHX is home base to America West Airlines and a major hub for Southwest Airlines. Other carriers include AeroMexico, Air Canada, Alaska Airlines, American, American Trans Air, British Airways, Continental, Delta and its Skywest shuttle, Frontier, Mesa (a regional Arizona carrier), Midwest Express, Northwest/KLM, Scenic Air, Sun Country, Sunrise Airlines, United and USAir.

All major **rental car** agencies serve the airport and **SuperShuttle** provides airport transfers to downtown; (602) 244-9000.

By rail • Amtrak serves Phoenix from a terminal at 401 W. Harrison, with trains west to Yuma and Los Angeles and east to Tucson, Chicago and New Orleans; call (800) USA-RAIL.

By bus • Greyhound provides service from two outlying terminals—2115 Buckeye Road, (602) 389-4200; and 2647 W. Glendale Ave., (602) 246-9855. Or call (800) 231-2222.

GETTING ABOUT

Phoenix is an easy city to learn. Although its sheer sprawl can be intimidating, it's mostly laid out in a precise north-south and east-west grid. In the downtown area and immediately beyond, most streets are named for U.S. Presidents; Washington is the axis street. Central Avenue is the dividing north-south thoroughfare. Numbered avenues parallel it to the west and numbered streets are to the east. For the most part, addresses coincide with numbered streets and avenues. (For instance, the 300 block of west Van Buren starts at Van Buren and Third Avenue.)

Converging freeways form a convenient box around the city's downtown core, providing easy access. Interstate 17 passes just to the south, then takes a ninety-degree turn north to skim the western edge of downtown. I-10 crosses the northern edge of downtown and then turns sharply south. Although not directly linked by freeway, Scottsdale is an easy reach from downtown Phoenix. Go north on the Squaw Peak Freeway and then east on Thomas Road or Indian School Road. The heart of town is cradled by Thomas, Indian School, Scottsdale Road and 76th Street.

NOTE: It's essential that you pick up a current map before beginning your exploration of the Valley of the Sun. Freeway construction is an ongoing—and probably never ending—program, and you'll need to keep up with the latest routings. Many surface streets are disappearing under new freeways.

Local bus service • Phoenix Transit provides bus service. The inexpensive downtown area shuttle (DASH) runs every few minutes through the urban core, weekdays from 6:30 a.m. to 5:30 p.m., with extended links to the state capital complex from 11 to 2. Other service runs throughout the Valley of the Sun, often linking with bus systems in surrounding communities. For long term visitors, monthly bus cards and discounted DASH tokens are available. The transit information number is (602) 253-5000.

Motel, hotel and resort shopping • Many motels are clustered along Van Buren, mostly east of downtown. Most are modestly priced although some—particularly on East Van Buren toward the airport—are rather scruffy. Other motels hover around I-10 and I-17 off-ramps.

Several first class hotels are in downtown Phoenix and most of the luxury resorts are northeast of downtown, tucked into the foothills of rugged desert mountains around Scottsdale and Paradise Valley.

Sightseeing ● The area's attractions are divided between Phoenix and Scottsdale. Most of the museums are in Phoenix while the Scottsdale area tilts toward Western lures like cowboy cookouts, saloons and a pretend western town called Rawhide. However, it also has most of the area's better art galleries. Phoenix museums are focused in the downtown area or just north across I-10. Many are within walking distance of one another. We link several together in "The best walk route" in Chapter Nine, page 127.

THINGS YOU SHOULD KNOW
About Phoenix and Arizona in general

Visitor services ● The Greater Phoenix Convention & Visitors Bureau is at One Arizona Center, 400 E. Van Buren, Suite 600, Phoenix, AZ 85004-2290; (877) CALL-PHX (225-5749); (602) 254-6500 or (602) 252-5588 for recorded information. (*phoenixcvb.com*). Other offices are downtown at 50 North Second Street and in Biltmore Fashion Park at 24th Street and Camelback Road.

The bureau issues winter-spring and summer-fall editions of the free *Greater Phxplorer* visitor guide. That's a silly name although it's full of useful information about attractions, activities, annual events, transportation, lodging, restaurants, shopping and such.

Area codes ● The code for metropolitan Phoenix is (602); Scottsdale, Tempe, Mesa, Chandler and eastern suburbs are (480); and Sun City, Glendale, Peoria and other western valley cities are (623). All of the rest of Arizona is (520). However, that area code soon may Tucson's only, with another for the rest of the state.

Time zone ● Arizona is in the Mountain Time Zone and it doesn't switch to daylight saving time, except on the Navajo Reservation. From April through October, Arizona clocks match Pacific Daylight Time.

Time and weather checks ● Call (602) 265-5550.

Is likker quicker? ● Unlike some neighboring states—Utah and Colorado come to mind—Arizona doesn't have any really strange liquor laws. Alcohol is readily available, although Sunday is slightly blue, with no package sales before 10 a.m. Otherwise, liquor can be sold— by the drink or bottle—daily from 6 a.m. to 1 a.m. Legal drinking age is twenty-one. Beer, wine and hard liquor can be sold in supermarkets, drug stores and liquor stores. Sales aren't state controlled, so prices aren't rigged. A law prohibits drinking liquor in public from its original container and most public parks allow only beer. That seems discriminatory, although park officials mostly are trying to discourage glass containers, so bring your beer in cans and your wine in a *bota*.

Drinking and driving • Arizona has very tough DUI laws. Motorists are presumed drunk with a blood alcohol level of .10 and they can be cited at lower levels if their driving ability is impaired.

OUR TEN FAVORITE VALLEY OF THE SUN MOMENTS

When you spend extended time in an area, seeking the very best that it has to offer, you encounter special moments and fascinating places that say in your memory. Here are ten things that made Phoenix, Scottsdale and surrounds particularly memorable, listed in no particular order of preference. You'll find further mention of these places and activities in the upcoming Phoenix-Scottsdale chapters; check the index for their listings.

1 *WATCHING AN ARIZONA SUNRISE FROM DOBBIN'S LOOKOUT* • *In South Mountain Park and Preserve, in southern Phoenix at the end of Central Avenue. Park gates are open from 5:30 a.m. until 10 p.m. GETTING THERE: From downtown, start south on First Avenue, which blends into Central Avenue and leads directly into the park after about eight miles. Then follow the scenic drive up to Dobbin's Lookout.*

Although it doesn't have a very romantic name, Dobbin's Lookout high up South Mountain is a fine place for watching the sunrise, as first light dances over the Valley of the Sun far below. On a clear morning, you can almost see the entire valley from this perch. It's also a nice vantage point for watching the sun go down and the lights come up over the great sprawl. A winding five-mile road leads from the park entrance to the lookout. Or you can hike the Holbert Trail to the lookout during daylight.

2 *STARTING THE DAY WITH AN ICED LATTE IN ARIZONA CENTER* • *Arizona Center's Central Gardens is between the office towers and the shopping complex. GETTING THERE: Arizona Center is on the northeastern edge of downtown Phoenix, bounded by Van Buren, Third, Fillmore and Fifth streets.*

A pretty sunken garden at Arizona Center—busy with palm trees, flower patches and ponds—is one of our favorite Phoenix places. We like to start the day with an iced caffé latte, sitting on one of the park's benches, watching downtown Phoenix come awake. It's a pleasant place to relax, with soft piped-in music accompanied by the twittering of real birds. The caffé latte? There's a Starbucks in Arizona Center, just a short stroll away.

3 *SITTIN' ON A HAY BALE AT RAWHIDE* ● *Rawhide Western town, 23023 N. Scottsdale Rd., Scottsdale; (280) 502-1880. Daily 11 to 10. GETTING THERE: From downtown, take the Squaw Peak Freeway north about fourteen miles to Bell Road and go east less than five miles to Scottsdale Road. Follow it north just under four miles; Rawhide is on the right.*

Wait! There's more to it than just sitting on a bale of hay in this pretend cowboy town. It's buying a margarita at an outdoor stand, finding a bale of hay, sitting and listening to a cowboy combo sing "Cool Water" or "Little Joe, the Wrangler." Now those are *real* cowboy songs. What's the difference between cowboy music and country music? In the first, they sing about cowboys and their horses; in the second, they sing about pickup trucks and faithful dogs and unfaithful women.

4 *WALKING ALONG SCOTTSDALE CIVIC CENTER MALL* ● *East side of Old Town, between Indian School Road and Brown Avenue. GETTING THERE: Go north on the Squaw Peak Freeway and then east on Indian School Road, cross Scottsdale Road, then go south briefly on Brown Avenue.*

Scottsdale Civic Center Mall, known by locals as the Scottsdale Greenbelt, is one of the most inviting parks in the Valley of the Sun. This wide two-block swatch of lawns, fountains, patios, mature trees and bronze statuary extends two blocks east from Old Town Scottsdale. It's a pleasant place to stroll, removed from the tourist excess of Old Town. Benches and picnic tables invite lingering. Several restaurants and cafés line its edges and most have outside tables. The Scottsdale Historic Museum, Scottsdale Center for the Arts and Museum of Contemporary Art are mall occupants as well.

5 *CATCHING A PRE-SEASON BALLGAME* ● *Cactus League baseball during March. For a rundown on which teams play where, see Chapter Two, page 40.*

Well of course it's great to go to Bank One Ballpark and see the Arizona Diamondbacks in action during the baseball season. It's equally fun—perhaps more—to catch one of the many Cactus League exhibition games during March spring training in the Valley of the Sun. The games are more casual and less stressed as the players work off their winter fat. The stadiums are small and ticket prices are a fraction of the cost during regular season play. Those small ballyards get you close to the action, even in the cheap seats.

Seven major league teams take their spring training in the valley. Which brings up a curious question. Since Bank One Ballpark is the

Arizona Diamondbacks' home field, where do *they* go for spring training? For some odd reason, they go down to Tucson, nearly a hundred miles south.

6 *HAVING LUNCH AT EL PEDREGAL* • *el Pedregal Festival Marketplace, Scottsdale Road at Carefree Highway; (480) 488-1072. Bakery Café is open from mid-morning through late afternoon; (480) 488-4100. (www.elpedregal.com) GETTING THERE: It's about thirty miles northeast of downtown, on the border between Scottsdale and Carefree. Follow the Squaw Peak Freeway about thirteen miles to Bell Road, then go east less than five miles to Scottsdale Road and north twelve miles toward Carefree. The marketplace is on the right.*

An attractive courtyard forms the centerpiece of the curiously designed el Pedregal Festival Marketplace. It's a pleasant place to relax with a light lunch from the adjacent Bakery Café. A free-form pool is home to brightly colored Japanese *koi* and occasional transient ducks. Signs request that you not share your lunch with them. The ducks and resident sparrows will try to convince you otherwise. After we've lunched, we like to browse through el Pedregal's shops, many of which are galleries featuring Western and native peoples' arts and crafts. A branch of the famous Heard Museum is located in el Pedregal as well.

7 *STROLLING THE GROUNDS OF THE BOULDERS RESORT* • *In Carefree, off Tom Darlington Road. GETTING THERE: The resort is just beyond el Pedregal (above).*

The Boulders resort and el Pedregal, separated by a brief swatch of desert, comprise one of our favorite settings in the Valley of the Sun. The opulence of the Boulders and the whimsy of el Pedregal provide pleasing contrast. After lunching in the marketplace courtyard, we like to stroll over to the Boulders and amble through its lush desert gardens and past its green swatches of golf course. We then explore the main lodge and pause for a drink at the handsome Southwest style lounge off the Lantilla restaurant. To reach the resort, walk to the north side of el Pedregal and follow an extension of Carefree Highway east to a lift gate. (Guests in cars need a code to activate the gate, although pedestrians can walk through.)

8 *SIPPING A MARGARITA AT THE HYATT REGENCY SCOTTSDALE RESORT LOBBY BAR* • *7500 E. Doubletree Ranch Rd., Scottsdale; (480) 991-3388. (www.hyatt.com) GETTING THERE: Drive north on Freeway 101 to exit 43, then go west on Via de Ventura, which becomes Doubletree Ranch Road. About three miles from the freeway, turn north into the resort complex.*

The Hyatt's huge lobby bar spills into a great open space between the lower lobby and the resort's elaborate pool complex. Cocktail tables sit beside cascading fountains and beneath swaying palms. In addition to the main service bar inside the lobby, a special bar is set up outdoors Wednesday through Saturday evenings. The barkeep has an interesting selection of gins, vodkas and tequilas. Margaritas are a specialty and our favorite is a margarita on the rocks with Herradura tequila and Grand Marnier. Drink in hand, we adjourn to a table beside the fountain and beneath a palm, lean back and enjoy the opulence of one of the area's finest resorts.

9 *HAVING A DINNER UNDER THE STARS AT LON'S* • At *the Hermosa Inn, 5532 N. Palo Cristi Rd., Paradise Valley; (602) 955-7878. GETTING THERE: Take any major northbound street from downtown to Lincoln Drive, go east to 36th Street and turn south. It becomes Palo Cristi Road and the inn is at the corner of Stanford Road.*

Although the Southwest style Lon's restaurant is handsome within, its most attractive dining area is under the stars on a flagstone patio beside a courtyard fountain. Old style lanterns with scented oil light the tables and wood fires crackle in portable *horno* ovens placed about the patio. Lon's is one of the area's most romantic restaurants, part of an historic inn that dates back seven decades.

10 *WATCHING AN ARIZONA SUNSET FROM THE COMPASS LOUNGE* • *On the twenty-fourth floor of the Hyatt Regency at 122 N. Second St., Phoenix; (602) 252-1234. GETTING THERE: The Hyatt is downtown between First and Second streets.*

Arizona is famous for its cloud-painting sunsets, and the best place to watch the sun sink over Phoenix is from the Hyatt Regency's Compass restaurant cocktail lounge. The restaurant and lounge make a complete revolution every fifty-five minutes. During that almost-hour, you can watch the sun slip below distant hills, then enjoy the drama of a million lights gradually winking on throughout the Valley of the Sun. There is a small gamble involved; the rotating lounge may have rotated east as the sun sinks into the west. But never mind; the awakening lights of the valley below are still impressive.

Chapter Two

VISITOR LURES
BEING A SUN-BAKED TOURIST

Not everyone comes to the Valley of the Sun just to get a tan, sip margaritas at poolside and play golf—although those are certainly pleasant ways to spend a vacation. Although it fortunately lacks a major theme park, the greater Phoenix area provides a fine selection of attractions, from world class museums to parks, botanical gardens, zoos and historic sites.

Most of its attractions and activities reflect the flavor of the Southwest. You'll find no medieval jousting tournaments or fake alpine villages here. The lures of this sun-drenched valley speak of the desert, Arizona's native people and the history of the city and its surrounds.

The attractions of the Valley of the Sun, like the valley's communities, are not only numerous but widely scattered. A visitor on a one or two-week vacation will be hard pressed to see all that the area has to offer, while still finding time for sunbathing, margaritas and golf. So how can one possibly choose the best museums and attractions to visit? Obviously, by thumbing through the pages of this book. And how did we choose the very best? By visiting every single one of them, and by being quite opinionated.

We list the best lures in packages of ten—the Ten Best attractions in and near Phoenix and Scottsdale, the next Ten Best attractions, the Ten Best things to do in the Valley of the Sun, and the Ten Best lures in surrounding communities.

GETTING THERE: Since this is a huge metropolitan-suburban region—covering more area than greater Los Angeles—we provide detailed driving instructions to each attraction. And since we need a starting point, we launch you from the downtown area or from major freeways. You'll need a detailed city map to survive museum-hopping and sightseeing in this large and complex area.

NEVER ON MONDAY: The first working day of the week is blue Monday for museum fans, since many are closed that day. However, most of the larger ones, such as the Heard and Arizona Science Center, are open daily. Also, some smaller attractions close their doors in summer—usually from May through September or October—or they reduce their hours.

☺ **KID STUFF:** This little grinning guy marks attractions that are of particular interest to pre-teens.

NOTE: Items marked with ❖ are listed elsewhere in this book; check the index for page numbers.

PRICING: Since prices frequently change, we use dollar sign codes to indicate the approximate cost of adult admission to various attractions and activities: *$* = under $5; *$$* = $5 to $9; *$$$* = $10 to $14; *$$$$* = $15 to $19; *$$$$$* = $20 or more. And you already know that prices are almost always less for seniors and kids.

THE TEN VERY BEST ATTRACTIONS

It was no great challenge to select the very best attraction in the Valley of the Sun. Phoenix is the proud possessor of the Heard, one of the finest native peoples museums in America. After we herd you to the Heard, we list the next Ten Best attractions in alphabetical order. Thus, there are no losers in this book, only winners and runners-up.

1 **THE HEARD MUSEUM** ● *2301 N. Central Ave., Phoenix; (602) 252-8840, 252-8848 (recorded information) and 252-8344 (shop and book store). (www.heard.org) Daily 9:30 to 5; Ironwood Café open 9:30 to 3:30. Major credit cards; $$. GETTING THERE: The museum is just under two miles north of downtown, at the corner of Central and Monte Vista.*

The Heard is *huge*, with permanent and changing exhibits in eleven different galleries and courtyards, all contained within in a rambling Spanish style complex. Although it dates back to 1929, this treasury of native cultures is a modern facility. With more than 32,000 objects to draw from, its staff exercises artistic discipline in keeping displays both simple and topical. Every exhibit is designed to interpret and inform. This is a living museum as well as a repository of the past. Entering the Southwest style courtyard, you may see a Hopi working on a kachina doll or a Navajo weaving on an ancient loom. A herd of happy school children might be pulverizing corn on *metate* grinding stones.

Your first stop should be the Sandra Day O'Connor Gallery, which provides a quick study of the museum's history and its founders, early Phoenix developers Dwight and Maie Heard. They collected artifacts from all over the world—some are on display here—although their main focus was Southwest native culture. From here, head for the Native Peoples of the Southwest Gallery. Among its many excellent exhibits is a collection of nearly 500 Hopi kachina dolls donated by the Fred Harvey Company and the late Barry Goldwater. Another major gallery has a display called "We Are!" with exhibits of the past and present lives of Arizona's twenty-one native tribes. Other galleries focus on native art, artifacts and sculptures, and the Southwest's history and geology. The Museum Shop and Bookstore has an excellent selection of books, crafts and curios.

2 *ARIZONA SCIENCE CENTER • 600 E. Washington Street in the Heritage & Science Park, Phoenix; (602) 716-2000. (www. azscience.org) Daily 10 to 5. Major credit cards; $$; combined admission to the Science Center and planetarium or theater, $$$.*

You can spend several hours in this facility, which is one of the finest such centers west of the Rockies. However, avoid the place on school days or you'll spend most of the time waiting your turn to play with its many hands-on exhibits. The center has four floors of science displays, plus the Dorrance Planetarium and the Flinn Theater, which shows Imax and Omnimax films. A science store with some really cool stuff and a food court complete this extensive complex.

The center is busy with computer-activated programs and hands-on exhibits. You can draw harmless "lightning" to your palm, generate solar energy, test your reaction time, determine how you handle stress, activate an artificial hand and view a living brain via videos of CAT scans and other imaging devices. Particularly fascinating—or maybe gross—is a 3-D voyage through a man's body, using a photo-imaging process first developed here. If you must, you can learn how a zit is formed, and you'll be happy to learn that your brain has a million times more neurons than a cockroach's.

3 *ARIZONA STATE CAPITOL MUSEUM • 1700 W. Washington St., Phoenix; (602) 542-4675. (www.lib.az.us/museum) Weekdays 8 to 5. During the January-May legislative session, it's open until 8 on Thursday evenings and 10 to 3 Saturday. Tours weekdays at 10 and 2;*

free. GETTING THERE: The capitol building is just west of downtown, rimmed by Jefferson and Adams streets and Seventeenth and Eighteenth avenues.

This museum virtually *is* the state capitol building. Many of its rooms have been given over to exhibits while most of the business of government is conducted elsewhere on the capital campus. Once occupying a large open space, the distinctive copper-domed capitol is now crowded by those other structures. Approaching the old capitol's main entrance from Seventeenth Avenue, you'll pass between the new Senate Building on the left and the House Building on the right, and these are directions, not political judgments. The capitol was undergoing major—and frequently delayed—renovations as we researched this book, so you may or may not see all of its exhibits. These include senate and house chambers restored to their appearance when Arizona achieved statehood in 1912, several artifacts from the U.S. Arizona sunk at Pearl Harbor, the restored office of Arizona's first governor, George W.P. Hunt, and the office of the Secretary of State.

A display in the Secretary of State's office runs an intriguing parallel to a recent bit of elective history. Remember that business in Florida during the 2000 presidential election? The 1916 gubernatorial election between incumbent Hunt and challenger Thomas E. Campbell was so close that both refused to concede. Each man rustled up a judge willing to swear him in. When a court ruled that Campbell had won after a recount, Hunt refused to leave office and had to be forced out. Then after Campbell had been governor for eleven months, a final recount and a State Supreme Court ruling declared Hunt the winner by forty-three votes and he regained his throne.

The best way to see the capitol's offerings is to take stairs or an elevator to the fourth floor mezzanine, where you can stare up to the dome and dizzily down to a huge state seal embedded in the main floor. From here, work your way downward, viewing exhibits along the way. Once you've done that, walk east through Wesley Bolin Memorial Park, which is busy with statues and war memorials. If you walk far enough, you'll wind up at the Arizona Mining & Mineral Museum at Washington and Fifteenth.

4 **DESERT BOTANICAL GARDEN** • *1201 N. Galvin Parkway, Phoenix; (602) 941-1225. (www.dbg.org) Daily 7 to 8 May through September and 8 to 8 the rest of the year; gift shop 9 to 5; café 8 to 4. Major credit cards; $$. GETTING THERE: The garden is about six miles east of downtown in Papago Park. Take Van Buren Street east to Galvin Parkway and turn north, or go east on I-10 and Freeway 202 and take the Van Buren exit.*

This fine botanical garden will even appeal to folks who wouldn't know mesquite from mistletoe. It appears at first glance to be a consolidation of the desert flora that grows wild just beyond its borders.

However, its plant selection reaches considerably beyond the Southwest. A good many of the globe's thousands of varieties of cactus are represented in this large garden, which sprawls over several acres. The plants are labeled, so one can tell a north African *euphorbia resinsera* from an *opuntia tesajo* of Baja California.

A paved Desert Discovery Trail winds through the garden and smaller trails branch off to special exhibits such as a cactus house, succulent house and the Sonoran Desert Trail. Particularly interesting is the Desert House, an environmentally-attuned dwelling using the latest active and passive technology to save fuel, water and other resources. There's even a family in residence so energy and water consumption can be measured. They don't do tours, however, so don't bother to knock. Public exhibits are in the garage and in an adjacent information center. Here, visitors can learn how to conserve water, energy and other resources.

5 HALL OF FLAME MUSEUM OF FIREFIGHTING ● *6101 E. Van Buren St., Phoenix; (602) 275-3473. (www.hallofflame.org) Monday-Saturday 9 to 5 and Sunday noon to 4; guided tours daily at 2. MC/VISA/AMEX; $$. GETTING THERE: From downtown, follow Van Buren Street about six miles east to Papago Park and cross Galvin Parkway; the facility is on your right, just past Phoenix Municipal Stadium.*

Every kid whose pulse is quickened by the shriek of a siren and the red flash of a fire engine will love this place. It's the world's largest museum of firefighting equipment, exhibiting ranks of nicely restored hand-drawn pumpers, hook-and-ladder rigs and other smoke-chasing classics. Nearly 100 fire engines are on display, from a 1725 English hand pumper to 1960s ladder and chemical trucks. A couple of nineteenth century rigs are mobile pieces of art, with scroll work, rosettes and dainty brass lanterns with cut glass lenses; they were used mostly for parades.

The extensive collection also includes a Hall of Heroes devoted to firemen who have saved fire victims and in come cases lost their own lives. Other displays include badges, helmets and uniforms, lithographs, drawings and photos of firemen in action. A cinema shows films of famous fires and firefighting techniques. A recent addition, the Wildland Firefighting Gallery, features equipment and rigs used in battling wildfires.

6 HERITAGE SQUARE ● *Sixth Street and Monroe, a block east of Phoenix Civic Plaza; (602) 262-5029.*

Part of the Heritage & Science Park, Heritage Square features an architectural taste of yesterday Phoenix—ten structures dating from the late nineteenth to early twentieth centuries. They're gathered around an attractive patio garden, shaded by an imposing curved-wood lath house. Surprisingly, all but one of the old buildings is in its original location. The square is more than a collection of historic structures, however. It often hosts art exhibits and other special events, and it presents a farmers' market every Thursday.

These are some of the square's more interesting buildings and their present functions: **Rosson House**, a three-story 1886 brick home is open for guided tours on the half hour, 10 to 3:30 Wednesday-Saturday and noon to 3:30 Sunday, **$**; (602) 262-5072 or (602) 262-5029 for recorded information. The **Bouvier-Teeter House**, an 1899 Midwestern style bungalow, contains a Victorian tearoom serving sandwiches and other light fare. It's open for lunch daily except Monday, and on Friday and Saturday evenings; (602) 252-4682. The **Arizona Doll and Toy Museum** occupies the Stevens House, a 1901 bungalow. Exhibits include American, English and Japanese dolls, advertising symbols such as the Campbell Soup kids and the Crackerjack sailor. It's open Tuesday-Sunday 10 to 4, **$**; (602) 253-9337.

7 PHOENIX MUSEUM OF HISTORY ● *105 N. Fifth Street, Phoenix; (602) 253-2734. Monday-Saturday 9 to 5 and Sunday noon to 5; $. GETTING THERE: It's in the Heritage & Science Park on the east side of downtown.*

This nicely done museum traces Phoenix from its earliest days as a farm settlement along ancient Hohokam canals to its development as the Southwest's largest city. Exhibits include examples of Hohokam and later native pottery and baskets, a display on the making of adobe bricks, relics from an early Phoenix general store and exhibits concerning frontier soldiers and cowboys. Particularly interesting are a stuffed ostrich from an early attempt at ostrich farming in the area, and a curious steam-powered high wheeler bicycle that was exhibited at the 1884 Arizona Territorial Exposition in Phoenix. A turn-of-the-last-century mock-up living room reflects the city's dual personality, displaying Victorian furniture and a Navajo rug.

ZOO NOOZ

The Valley of the Sun has three wildlife parks, perhaps more than any other metropolitan area. While none are awesome, the Phoenix Zoo listed below is the largest and the best. The other two are Wildlife World Zoo northwest of Phoenix in Lichfield Park and Out of Africa, northeast of town near Fountain Hills. Both are listed near the end of this chapter, in the "Ten Best attractions beyond Phoenix-Scottsdale."

8 PHOENIX ZOO ● *455 N. Galvin Parkway, Phoenix; (602) 273-1341. (www.phoenixzoo.org) Daily 9 to 5 Labor Day through April, 7:30 to 4 the rest of the year. Major credit cards; $$$. GETTING THERE: The zoo is in Papago Park, just south of the Desert Botanical Garden.*

This well-kept zoo is certainly one of the valley's Ten Best attractions. It has a fine animal collection and its staff tries hard to make it interesting and educational for its visitors, sponsoring informational programs, animal encounters and other special activities. Perhaps it tries *too* hard, offering gimmicks such as a Safari Train, mule-drawn wagon rides, and a photo gallery that places folks next to digital animals. Vendors sell big bags of designer popcorn, which encourages kids to do what signs tell them not to do—feed the animals. Many zoos are shying away from such gimmickry, focusing more on pure animal behavior and species preservation.

This is the largest privately owned nonprofit zoo in the country. Covering more than a hundred acres of lumpy desert, it's populated by 7,600 critters representing 400 species. It focuses on warm-weather animals—no polar bears or penguins in this desert—and it has earned a reputation for helping preserve endangered desert dwellers such as the Arabian oryx. Thick vegetation makes this a botanical garden as well as an animal park, and lakeside shade ramadas provide welcome refuges on hot days. Although the zoo exhibits animals from around the world, our favorite section is the Arizona Trail, where one can see critters that lurk in the state's variable terrain. In a nocturnal exhibit, you'll see such creatures of the night as the black-footed ferret and—ugh!—a giant and very hairy desert scorpion.

9 PUEBLO GRANDE MUSEUM AND ARCHEOLOGICAL SITE • 4619 E. Washington Street, Phoenix; (602) 945-0901. (www.pueblogrande.com) Monday-Saturday 9 to 4:45, Sunday 1 to 4:45; ruins trail closes at 4:30. MC/VISA; $; free on Sundays. GETTING THERE: It's about five miles east of downtown. Follow one-way Jefferson Street, which blends into Washington, then turn right into the complex just past the airport entrance. Or take I-10 and Freeway 202 and follow directional signs.

It can be said that this is where Phoenix began. Now surrounded by the growing city, this archeological site once was a major Hohokam community. The settlement of about 1,500 people was supported by a canal system that was partially excavated by the city's first white settlers in the 1800s. Outlines of some of the original dwellings have been excavated and a fine little museum at the visitor center describes what life was like for the first Phoenicians.

Focal point of the settlement is a "platform mound" the size of a football field, which has been partially excavated. It may have been the domain of village leaders, a holy place or simply an observation platform. A ruins trail takes visitors atop the mound, then on to a reconstructed pit house and an above-ground adobe dwelling of a later era. The original village, occupied from about 700 to 1450 A.D., extended as much as a mile to the northeast.

10 *TALIESIN WEST* • *12621 Frank Lloyd Wright Blvd., Scottsdale; (480) 860-2700. (www.franklloydwright.org) Bookstore-Visitor Center daily 8:30 to 5:30. One-hour Panorama Tour every half hour, 9:15 to 4:15 November through April; MC/VISA; $$$. Other more in-depth tours available; call (480) 860-8810. Tours less frequent in summer. GETTING THERE: From downtown, take Squaw Peak Freeway north fourteen miles to Bell Road and go east 9.5 miles. (Bell becomes Frank Lloyd Wright Boulevard at Scottsdale Road.) At the junction of Cactus Road and Taliesin Drive, go north on Taliesin to the complex.*

The former winter home and studio of America's foremost architect, Taliesin West is an intriguing mix of concrete and stone that seems fused to the desert instead of rising above it. The complex sits on a 600-acre alluvial fan, sweeping down from the McDowell Mountains. Frank Lloyd Wright came here from Wisconsin in the 1930s to create a teaching center for his concept of "organic architecture." His designs involved the repeated play of geometric forms. Natural materials were used to embody nature, man and architecture. Taliesin West is mostly triangular, with red sandstone, concrete wedges and desert stone. After his death in 1959, the Frank Lloyd Wright Foundation was created to continue his school. It also sponsors public programs, including seminars on art, architecture and Wright's philosophy.

The Panorama Tour takes visitors over landscaped terraces and courtyards and past a drafting studio where students are learning the Wright stuff. Visitors see the Cabaret Theater, Music Pavilion, Seminar Theater and Wright's private office. Architectural drawings and models by Wright and his students are displayed in the Kiva conference center.

THE NEXT TEN BEST ATTRACTIONS

Phoenix and Scottsdale have so many interesting lures that it's impossible to contain them within a single list of ten. So we've come up with "A" and "B" lists. These attractions are certainly worthy of a pause if you have sufficient time.

1 *PHOENIX ART MUSEUM* • *1625 N. Central Ave., Phoenix; (602) 257-1880 or (602) 257-1222 (recorded information). (www.phxart.org) Tuesday-Sunday 10 to 5 (Thursday until 9); closed Mondays and holidays. MC/VISA; $$. GETTING THERE: The museum is at the northeast corner of Central and McDowell Road, about a mile north of downtown.*

The American West, contemporary art, old world classics and the art of Asia provide an interesting mix for Phoenix's large and versatile art museum. The galleries are spacious, with one flowing into the next instead of being boxed into individual rooms. Among its permanent collections are Western American, early European and American, Asian and Spanish Colonial art; plus costume displays and decorative arts. Particularly interesting is the Thorne Miniature Gallery of finely detailed dollhouse-sized rooms of European and American homes from the 1800s through the 1920s. Also intriguing is the Gilbert Stuart portrait of George Washington that appears on the dollar bill.

The museum's changing exhibits range from Frank Lloyd Wright drawings to Rodin sculptures to Ansel Adams photos to Norman Rockwell paintings. Founded in the 1950s, it's the Southwest's largest art museum, with more than 160,000 square feet of exhibit space. Facilities include a lecture hall, restaurant, an inter-active hands-on children's gallery and two art reference libraries.

2 *ARIZONA HALL OF FAME MUSEUM • 1101 W. Washington St., Phoenix; (602) 225-2110. (www.lib.az.us) Weekdays 8 to 5; free. GETTING THERE: It's on the south side of Washington near Eleventh Street, about half a mile east of the capital complex.*

This museum's most appealing features are the building and its surroundings—a handsome brick 1908 Carnegie Library in a spacious tree-shaded park. Only two exhibits are permanent—the Arizona Woman's Hall of Fame and some interesting cast-from-life statues representing typical people of the state's past. This cast of characters includes a Harvey Girl from the Fred Harvey Company, a rancher, a black Buffalo Soldier of the U.S. Cavalry, a miner, a woman's suffrage leader and a World War II Navajo code-talker. (They were used as communicators in the Pacific because Navajo was one of the few languages the Japanese couldn't understand.)

Exhibits in the Arizona Women's Hall of Fame include the state's most famous ladies—Sandra Day O'Connor, the first woman appointed to the U.S. Supreme Court; and Jane D. Hall, Arizona's first elected woman governor. Elected in 1998, she is part of an exhibit concerning the most "womanized" state government in American history, which had a lady governor, secretary of state, attorney general, treasurer and superintendent of public instruction.

3 *ARIZONA MINING & MINERAL MUSEUM • 1502 W. Washington St., Phoenix; (602) 255-3791. (www.admmr.state.az.us) Weekdays 8 to 5 and Saturday 11-4; free. GETTING THERE: The museum is at Washington and Fifteenth Avenue, on the northeastern end of a park mall that extends from the capital complex.*

This museum reflects Arizona's role as one of America's leading mining states, with displays focused primarily on the mining side of minerals. It's housed in a former Shrine Temple whose Mideastern façade is still evident. Upon entering, visitors first see life-sized bronzes of modern miners. Beyond, a large room is busy with mining and mineral exhibits—mockups of mines, mining tools, core samples and hundreds of kinds of minerals and fossils. It also offers displays of turquoise, both raw and shaped into the popular Navajo jewelry.

A recent addition, having nothing to do with mining or minerals, is a cluttered collection of native artifacts, odds and ends, family and political memorabilia and photos donated to the museum by Rose Mofferd. The lady with the beehive hairdo was Arizona's longtime secretary of state, then she became its first woman governor when Evan Meacham was drummed out of office in 1988. She retired after completing Meacham's term, deciding not to run for election.

4 *COSANTI* • *6433 Doubletree Ranch Road, Scottsdale; (480) 948-6145. (www.cosanti.com) Monday-Saturday 9 to 5 and Sunday 11 to 5; small donation requested. Major credit cards accepted at the gallery. GETTING THERE: Drive north on Freeway 101 to exit 43, then go west on Via de Ventura, which becomes Doubletree Ranch Road. Cosanti is about four miles from the freeway, on the south side of Doubletree Ranch near the corner of Invergorden.*

Paolo Soleri is an architectural visionary working on an environmentally idealistic city called Arcosanti, sixty-eight miles north of Phoenix. Cosanti is his home, workshop and art gallery in Paradise Valley, north of Scottsdale. Here, he and his students create Soleri bronze and ceramic bells, wind chimes and other decorator items whose sales help finance Arcosanti. Like his city of the future, Soleri's Cosanti studio has an extra-terrestrial look with pre-cast concrete freeform shapes. It suggests melted geometry, with a kind of doughy primitive appearance. Yoda would feel right at home here. The complex includes a gallery of sculptures and other artwork by Soleri and his students, a sales shop and a small foundry. On weekdays, visitors can watch artists at work.

5 *DEER VALLEY ROCK ART CENTER* • *3711 Deer Valley Rd., Phoenix; (623) 582-8007. (www.asu.edu/clas/anthropology/dvrac) Tuesday-Saturday 9 to 5 and Sunday noon to 5 October through April; and Tuesday-Friday 8 to 2, Saturday 9 to 5 and Sunday noon to 5 the rest of the year; $. GETTING THERE: Drive north on I-17 about eighteen miles, take exit 217-B and follow Deer Valley Road about two miles west.*

Operated by Arizona State University's Department of Anthropology, this 47-acre site preserves more than 1,500 petroglyphs in the Hedgpeth Hills. A quarter-mile interpretive trail takes visitors past the 'glyphs, or one can arrange for a guided tour. These petroglyphs were inscribed from 700 to 10,000 years ago on the black, tumbled basaltic rocks of an ancient lava flow. The interpretive trail travels along the base of a steep hillside, and the primeval graffiti occupies hundreds of the rocks above. Exhibits at the visitor center focus on the petroglyphs and area plant and animal life.

NOTE: Since most of the 'glyphs are several dozen yards from the path, a pair of binoculars will be useful. They can be rented at the visitor center. Also, come before late afternoon; otherwise, you'll be squinting into the lowering sun.

6 *ENCANTO PARK • Fifteenth Avenue and Encanto Boulevard, Phoenix; (602) 261-8993. Boat rentals, (602) 254-1520. Enchanted Island Amusement Park open Wednesday-Friday 10 to 4 and Saturday-Sunday 10 to 8; closed Monday-Tuesday. GETTING THERE: The park is about two miles northeast of downtown. Take any primary street north, then go west on Encanto Boulevard and turn north into the park.*

Encanto is Spanish for "enchanted," which may be too generous a description for this pleasant swatch of green. However, this is the area's most attractive urban park. Most of the Valley of the Sun's parklands are desert mountain preserves and while they're dramatic, they don't have the more traditional park facilities. Encanto's features include a golf course, large lake with boat rides, swimming pool, food courts, kiddie amusement park, and tennis, handball and racquetball courts. Large shade trees, some nearly as old as Phoenix, provide lots of shelter from the noonday sun. A water channel meanders from a central lake, forming several islands and providing fun watercourses for boaters. One can even catch trout by purchasing an "urban fishing license" at the boathouse; a state license isn't required.

This is an inexpensive place to play. Boat rentals and food and drink prices are modest, and a round of golf is cheaper here than at most other valley courses. If you have toddlers in tow, take them to the little amusement park called Enchanted Island. Admission is free and ride prices start at less than a dollar. Even if you're kidless, you might like to stop by and admire—or ride—its classic 1948 carousel. Booths at Enchanted Island sell inexpensive picnic fare—everything from fried chicken to corn dogs. Shaded lakeside picnic tables are nearby.

7 *HYATT REGENCY NATIVE PEOPLES EXHIBITS • In the Hyatt Regency Scottsdale Resort at 7500 E. Doubletree Ranch Rd., Scottsdale; (480) 991-3388. (www.hyatt.com) GETTING THERE: Drive north on Freeway 101 to exit 43, then go west on Via de Ventura, which becomes Doubletree Ranch Road. About three miles from the freeway, turn north into the resort complex. If you're coming from Scottsdale, go north on Scottsdale Road, then briefly east on Doubletree Ranch and north into the resort.*

One of the area's most opulent resorts also is home to a fine exhibit of native peoples arts and crafts. The Hopi Learning Center to the right of the main entry features changing exhibits of Hopi culture and history. It's an "open museum" without set hours, although a docent—usually a tribal member—is on hand most days from 9 to 5 to answer questions and discuss the exhibits. Particularly interesting is an interactive computer video program "hosted" by Kevin Cosner called *Five Hundred Nations,* with historical and contemporary data on America's various tribal groups.

The Hyatt's native peoples exhibits aren't limited to its museum. Fine examples of art are scattered throughout the hotel. They include bronzes, pottery, paintings and artifacts, mostly from Southwest native tribes, with a few rare pre-Colombian pieces. The collection also features several Frederick Remington bronzes and fine examples of Mexican folk art.

8 MYSTERY CASTLE ● *800 E. Mineral Rd., Phoenix; (602) 268-1581. Thursday-Sunday 11 to 4 October through June; closed July through September; $. GETTING THERE: The "castle" is near the entrance South Mountain Park. From downtown Phoenix, take Central Avenue about eight miles south, then go east briefly on Mineral Road to Seventh Street.*

San José, California, may have Sarah Winchester and her Winchester Mystery House, although Phoenix offers a close rival. Boyce Luther Gulley arrived in Phoenix early in the last century, hoping to cure his tuberculosis. Between other construction projects, he spent fifteen years—from 1930 until his death in 1945—building this rambling stone mansion as a fantasy project for his daughter, Mary Lou. She still lives there and personally conducts tours through this interesting sprawl of a castle.

The three-story, 8,000-square-foot structure contains eighteen rooms, three fireplaces, sundry stairways and hallways and even a wedding chapel. It's furnished with Southwest antiques and assorted other odds and ends. Boyce built his mansion mostly of native stone, although he also utilized petroglyphs (a practice that would be frowned upon today), adobe, old car parts and a cement mixture that included goats' milk.

9 SALT RIVER PROJECT HISTORY CENTER ● *1521 Project Dr., Tempe; (602) 236-2723. Weekdays 9 to 4; free. GETTING THERE: It's in the Salt River Project headquarters off Washington Street, adjacent to the Hall of Flame Museum of Firefighting. From downtown, follow Van Buren Street about six miles east to Papago Park and cross Galvin Parkway; the facility is just beyond.*

Displays in the lobby and adjacent History Room of the Salt River Project administrative center focus on efforts to bring water to the Valley of the Sun shortly after the turn of the last century. Exhibits, artifacts and videos trace the history of valley water usage from the

Hohokam canals through the construction of Roosevelt Dam to modern water delivery methods. Exhibits also focus on the centennial of the Salt River Project and native artifacts discovered during recent escavation for a generating site.

10 *THE SCOTTSDALE MUSEUM OF CONTEMPORARY ART* • *7374 E. Second St., Scottsdale; (480) 994-ARTS. (www.scotts-dalearts.org) Tuesday-Wednesday 10 to 5, Thursday-Saturday 10 to 8; closed Sunday and Monday. MC/VISA; $$. Museum store open Tuesday-Wednesday 10 to 5, Thursday-Saturday 10 to 8 and Sunday noon to 5. GETTING THERE: Go north on the Squaw Peak Freeway and then east on Indian School Road about seven miles to Scottsdale Road. Continue two more blocks to Civic Center Boulevard, turn right and go two blocks to Second Street.*

Since art is in the eye of the beholder, visitors' eyes will behold strange and fascinating things in this leading-edge museum. The main gallery is adjacent to the Scottsdale Center for the Arts, and other exhibits occupy the center's lobby and mezzanine. You'll find interesting constructions, odd shapes, artistically fuzzy photos, things that glow in the dark and things that glow in the light. Some of these are striking; others are just strange.

Particularly impressive, hanging in the art center's lobby, is artist Dale Chihuly's dazzling chandelier of twisted teardrop red, yellow and orange glass pendants. It could be a giant cluster of chilis or the inverted head of Medusa or tongues of soft fire. Less brilliant yet equally fascinating is "Skyspace," a large walk-in elliptical chamber fused to the side of the main museum building. It was designed by artist James Turrell, who likes to work with the quality of light. One is supposed to sit quietly in the chamber and stare through an oval at a small patch of pure, isolated sky.

THE TEN BEST THINGS TO DO
IN PHOENIX-SCOTTSDALE

There's always something to do here. You can poke about souvenir shops, attend a ballgame, pretend to be a cowboy or train to be a real one, and even visit a curious Chinese "island."

1 *PROWL OLD TOWN SCOTTSDALE'S SHOPS AND WALK THE MALL* • *Old Town Scottsdale is bounded by Scottsdale and Indian School roads, Brown Avenue and Second Street. For information, contact Downtown Scottsdale Partnership Inc., 7044 E. Fifth Ave., Scottsdale, AZ 85251; (480) 947-6423. (www.downtownscottsdale.com)*

For walking tours, contact the Scottsdale Historical Society at (480) 946-0394 or (480) 945-4499. GETTING THERE: Go north on the Squaw Peak Freeway and then east on Indian School Road about seven miles to Scottsdale Road. You're on the northern edge of Old Town.

Old Town is where Scottsdale began. It's also where it nearly lost its old West charm as the village exploded into a city. A merchants' group has tried to rescue the downtown area by preserving its old buildings in an historic district. They've more or less succeeded, although Old Town offers more hoopla than history. It's busy with souvenir shops, boutiques, T-shirt shops, galleries, restaurants and cafés. This is where tourists come for their Kokopelli wind chimes and refrigerator magnets. Although most of the shops sell souvenirs, Old Town has a few good art galleries. Many are along a long two-block stretch of Main Street from Scottsdale Boulevard to Goldwater Boulevard; see Chapter Eight, page 121. For an interesting mix of Southwestern art, artifacts and tourist trinkets, check out the several ❖ **Gilbert Ortega** shops in Old Town. The largest are at the corners of First Street and Brown Avenue, and Main Street at Scottsdale Road.

❖ **Scottsdale Civic Center Mall** provides a pleasing contrast to Old Town's tourist excess. It's a wide swatch of lawns, fountains, patios, shady trees, statuary and picnic tables, extending two blocks east from Old Town. Several restaurants and cafés line its edges. It's also home to the small Scottsdale Historic Museum, the ❖ **Scottsdale Center for the Arts** and the **Museum of Contemporary Art.**

2 *TAKE YOURSELF OUT TO A BALLGAME* ● *The area's major outlets for sports and other tickets are Dillard's at (480) 503-5555, Ticketmaster at (480) 784-4444 and Tickets Unlimited at (602) 840-2340.*

A sports fan alert: Phoenix is one of the few cities in America with all four major league franchises. Further, tickets to the games usually are available, except when the Cardinals are hot. You can even get Cardinal tickets if you're willing to over-pay, since scalping isn't illegal in Arizona. Here's where to catch ballgames:

ARIZONA CARDINALS ● Formerly the St. Louis Cardinals, this National Football League team moved to Phoenix in 1988. It plays at Arizona State University's Sun Devil Stadium, although the team and city are building a new ballyard that may be completed by the time you arrive. *FOR TICKETS: (602) 379-0102.*

ARIZONA DIAMONDBACKS ● This National League Western Division expansion team started playing baseball in 1998 in Bank One Ballpark; see page 39. *FOR TICKETS: (888) 777-4664 or (602) 514-8400. (www.azdiamondbacks.com)*

PHOENIX COYOTES ● Phoenix is a long way from Winnipeg and it's considerably warmer. The National Hockey League's Winnipeg Jets made the trip south in 1996 to become the Phoenix Coyotes. They play in America West Arena where, even on the hottest days, the ice doesn't melt. *FOR TICKETS: (480) 563-7825*

PHOENIX SUNS ● The city's oldest major league franchise, the National Basketball Association's Phoenix Suns emerged as an expansion team in 1968. Its home court is America West Arena. *FOR TICKETS: (602) 379-SUNS.*

3 **TOUR THE D'BACK BALLYARD** ● *Bank One Ballpark; (888) 777-4664 or (602) 514-8400 for tour information $$. Tours at 10:30, noon, 1:30 and 3 Monday-Saturday in the off-season and on non-game days; and at 10:30 and noon on days with evening game; no tours on Sundays. (www.arizona.diamondbacks.mlb.com) GETTING THERE: Bank One Ballpark is on Jefferson Street downtown, between Fourth and Sixth streets.*

Two nice things happen when people take the Bank One Ballpark tour—they get to see one of America's most modern baseball stadiums, and the money goes to Arizona Diamondback charities. Tour tickets, which needn't be reserved, are sold at one of the ticket windows at the rear of a plaza between the ballpark and an adjacent parking structure. Visitors gather in the "Rotunda"—the main entrance—then are taken to many of the park's features. They see luxury boxes, the visitors' dressing room and the home team's dugout, and they get to stand on the edge of the playing field. All the while, tour guides regale their flock with statistics. The $353 million facility has 650 video monitors so fans needing a hot dog won't miss a pitch; and it has eighty-one food venues ranging from traditional 'burgers and beer to shaved ice and sushi, plus several full-service restaurants. The wealthy can rent luxury boxes with twelve to twenty-eight seats for a mere $85,000 to $125,000 a season—beer and 'burgers not included. The park even has a game-view swimming pool, which you and thirty-five good friends can rent for $5,000 a game. Bank One Ballpark has a telescoping roof, not to keep out the rain but to drive out the heat. A massive air conditioning system can drop the temperature by thirty degrees.

And here's a statistic we really appreciated: Although the best seats in the house cost $70, about 350 non-reserved seats are sold two hours before game time for a dollar each.

4 **PLAY COWBOY IN RAWHIDE** ● *23023 N. Scottsdale Rd., Scottsdale; (280) 502-1880. Daily 11 to 10; shorter summer hours. MC/VISA. General admission $$; additional charges for Wild West Show and other activities and rides. (www.rawhide.com) GETTING THERE: From downtown, take the Squaw Peak Freeway north about fourteen miles to Bell Road and go east less than five miles to Scottsdale Road. Follow it north just under four miles and you'll see Rawhide on the right.*

CACTUS LEAGUE: THE BOYS OF SPRING

Shouts of "play ball!" have echoed from southern Arizona every March since 1947 as the boys of summer become the boys of spring for Cactus League baseball action. The Valley of the Sun is the focal point for spring training, hosting seven major league teams; another three play in Tucson.

Fans like the informality and vigor of Cactus League baseball, and the intimacy of the small stadiums. It's baseball played with enthusiasm, gusto and mistakes; the way we played as kids on sandlots. Fans like the ticket prices, too—under $15 for the best seats in the stands.

Many people come to Arizona specifically to watch these exhibition games, particularly "Snowbirds"—retired fall-through-spring visitors. A survey during the 1990s showed that three-fourths of spring training ticket-buyers were from out of state.

Tickets for Cactus League games are available a few days in advance, and often on the day of the game at the respective ballparks. Dillard's sells tickets for several Cactus League teams; call (480) 503-5555. For others, dial the numbers listed below. Most games start at 1:05. **For information: *www.baseballarizona.com.***

Who plays where: Valley of the Sun

Anaheim Angels play at Tempe Diablo Stadium at 2200 W. Alameda Dr., Tempe; (602) 438-9300; *www.angelsbaseball.com.*

Chicago Cubs play at HoHoKam Park at 1235 N. Center St., Mesa; (480) 964-4467; *www.cubspringtraining.com.*

Milwaukee Brewers play at Maryvale Baseball Park, 3600 N. 51st Ave., Phoenix; (623) 245-5500; *www.milwaukeebrewers.com.*

Oakland A's play at Phoenix Municipal Stadium, 5999 E. Van Buren St., Phoenix; (602) 392-0217; *www.oaklandathletics.com.*

San Diego Padres play at the Peoria Sports Complex, 16101 N. 83rd Ave., Peoria; (623) 878-4337; *www.padres.com.*

San Francisco Giants play at Scottsdale Stadium, 7408 Osborn Rd., Scottsdale; (480) 990-7972; *www.sfgiants.com.*

Seattle Mariners also play at the Peoria Sports Complex; (623) 878-4337; *www.mariners.com.*

Tucson

Arizona Diamondbacks play at Tucson Electric Park, 2500 E. Ajo Way; (520) 434-1111; *www.azdiamondbacks.com.*

Chicago White Sox also play at Tucson Electric Park; (520) 434-1111; *www.whitesox.com.*

Colorado Rockies play at the Qwest Sports Complex at Hi Corbett Field, 3400 Camino Campestre; (520) 327-9467; *www.coloradorockies.com.*

"Happy trails to you," sings a recorded Roy Rogers as you step into this pretend Western town. If you ever spent Saturday afternoons at the movies, watching old Republic Studios Westerns, this place will bring back memories. Like all good spoofs, Rawhide doesn't take itself too seriously. It's a pretend Western town for wanna-be cowboys, with all the gimmicks. *Faux* false front stores stand behind boardwalks along a dusty main street. Folks can ride horses or a mechanical bucking bull, hitch a ride on the Butterfield Stage, pan for gold, shop for cowboy and Indian souvenirs and chow down on a serious steak or a simple hotdog. There's never a dull moment here—gunfights, jailbreaks, the arrival of the Pony Express, the departure of the Butterfield stage, Mexican folkloric dancers and native dancers. The Wild West Show—at an additional cost—has lots of ropin', ridin', trick shootin', buffalo ridin', bull whip crackin' and more.

Rawhide is a wholesome family place where the worst you'll hear during assorted entertainments is "dang my britches." Although it's mostly a place for kids, moms and dads aren't forgotten. They can buy walk-away margaritas, sit on hay bales and listen to real live cowboy singers. Happy trails, indeed.

5 *LEARN TO BE A REAL COWBOY* • *Arizona Cowboy College, Lorill Equestrian Center, 30208 N. 152nd St., Scottsdale, AZ 85255; (888) 330-8070 or (480) 471-3151. (www.cowboycollege.com) Six-day sessions in spring and fall. Rates are around $1,500, including all equipment, plus food and camping gear during a four-day roundup.*

Dude ranches and cowboy theme parks such as Rawhide are designed to give Arizona visitors a Western experience without the sweat, dusty discomfort or the abilities needed to be a *real* cowboy. Arizona Cowboy College is quite the opposite, offering wanna-be wranglers a six-day course in cowboy skills. Think of it as *City Slickers* without cameras, makeup, studio lights or a snarling Jack Palance. Students learn how to ride, rope, wield a branding iron, shoe horses and herd cattle.

Attendees take two days of intensive training at the Lorill Equestrian Center, then they spend four days taking part in a roundup on a working cattle ranch. Just like the real cowpokes, they herd cattle, go after strays, cut out calves and brand them. They camp out at night, eat beef and beans and even sing cowboy songs around a campfire.

6 *PADDLE TEMPE TOWN LAKE* • *Downtown Tempe, just south of and parallel to the Red Mountain Freeway. Tempe Beach Park is open 5 a.m. to midnight; lake access is sunrise to sunset. Boat rentals available from Rio Lago Cruise, (480) 517-4050. Rental office open Sunday-Thursday 10 to 6 and Friday-Saturday 10 to 8; MC/VISA/AMEX. GETTING THERE: Follow directions to the Hall of Flame Museum (above, page 29), then continue southeast on Mill, which crosses the lake after* *just over a mile. Go right onto Rio Salado Parkway for a block, then right again onto Ash Street and right yet again into the parking lot of Tempe Beach Park.*

Since the completion of Roosevelt Dam nearly a century ago, the Salt River is dry most of the year. Tempe officials recently brought a two-mile stretch back to life with a pair of dams to create a basin they call Tempe Town Lake. Its main activity center is Tempe Beach Park, on the south shore between Mill and Ash avenues. The lake is closed to swimming, although folks can rent sit-upon kayaks, paddleboats and canopied electric boats from Rio Lago Cruise. Paddling about the lake can provide exquisite relief on a hot day. And to really get heat relief, rent two boats and start a water fight. A multi-use recreational trail follows the lake's shoreline. Lakeside shops, restaurants and entertainment venues are planned for the future.

7 TAKE A GAMBLE AT A TRIBAL CASINO ● *Casino Arizona, Freeway 101 and McKellips Road; (480) 850-7777. (www.casinoarizona.com) GETTING THERE: Follow I-10 and Freeway 202 about twelve miles east from Phoenix, then go north a mile on Freeway 101. Take the McKellips Road exit half a mile east, turn left onto 92nd Street and left again to the casino.*

The Federal Indian Gaming Act permits native people to operate casinos on reservations, once details are worked out with the host state. Arizona has a good many of these and some are near Phoenix and Scottsdale, which border on the Fort McDowell and Salt River Indian communities. They don't measure up to Nevada standards; a typical Indian casino would fit into a Las Vegas resort's swimming complex.

However, Casino Arizona, opened in late 2000 by the Salt River Pima-Maricopa Indian Community, is rather attractive. A front courtyard is formed by Stonehenge type monoliths linked by glass brick walls, with a fountain as a centerpiece. The casino interior has a pleasing Southwest décor, accented by native peoples art and artifacts. It offers the usual gaming devices, a race book (dog and pony betting only), a card room, bingo parlor, gift and souvenir shop, several dining areas and a showroom that books noted performers. The Eagles Nest Restaurant serves lunch and dinner buffets and a Sunday brunch, plus individual menu items. The attractive Cholla Restaurant is a cozy retreat serving Southwestern and other American fare.

8 ATTEND A SCOTTSDALE-STYLE FARMER'S MARKET ● *At the Borgata, Scottsdale Road between McDonald and Malcolm drives, Scottsdale; (480) 998-1822. Every Friday from 1 to 6, October through April. GETTING THERE: The center is about two miles north of Old Town on the west side of Scottsdale Road.*

What's a "Scottsdale style" farmer's market? It's an outdoor market where croissants outnumber cucumbers. Although you can buy produce here, this is mostly a crafts and prepared foods fair, with more food than crafts. Which is fine, since most of the food vendors offer samples of their wares. Dozens of vendor stalls fill the Borgata's main plaza and spill into its smaller corridors. The market has a couple of produce and plant stalls, although you'll find mostly specialty mustards, creative breads, inventive salsas and even designer chocolates. You can sip wine samples or buy it by the glass or bottle. Vendors also sell beer, soft drinks, hot dogs and other snack foods. Find a seat at one of the courtyard tables, listen to live music and enjoy this distinctly Southwest-suburban version of a farmer's market. And never mind that the cucumber selection is rather limited.

9 *VISIT CHINA IN PHOENIX* ● *Chinese Culture Center, 668 N. 44th St., Phoenix. GETTING THERE: Drive east from downtown on I-10 and Freeway 202, take the 40th-44th offramp (exit 2), and turn south onto 44th Street. The center is a couple of blocks down on the right.*

Phoenix doesn't have a Chinatown, since its few Asian residents are scattered throughout the valley. However, it does have a large Chinese cultural center, complete with temple style architecture and curled-up eves. It's easy to spot, standing like a lone Asian sentinel in an area razed in recent years for redevelopment. Although it's more commercial that cultural, the center does have several faithful reproductions of historic Chinese gates and pavilions. Bronze plaques explain their significance.

The rest of the center is comprised of shops, restaurants and a large Asian supermarket with a takeout, bakery and deli. This is where you go for your tofu, potsticker wrappers, bamboo shoots, *kimchee* and shrimp paste—which is definitely an acquired taste. (Despite my wife being Chinese, I haven't yet acquired it.) Although most of the businesses are Chinese, one of the larger restaurants is Japanese—Ichi Ban Sushi Buffet.

10 *SAMPLE OLD MEXICO IN GUADALUPE* ● *Town of Guadalupe, southeast of downtown Phoenix. GETTING THERE: Take southbound I-10 twelve miles to Baseline Road (exit 155), go east two blocks and then turn south onto Priest Drive; it becomes Avenida del Yaqui as it enters Guadalupe.*

We begin this listing with a quick qualifier. Guadalupe is a scruffy, dusty community and you'll likely feel more comfortable visiting there in the daytime than at night. Then why go at all? Because this small community surrounded by more progressive suburbia is an authentic slice of old Mexico. Its street names are Spanish, its shops are mostly Mexican and its centerpiece is an old whitewashed Spanish colonial style church on a large, dusty plaza. You'll feel as if you've slipped across the border when you drive its streets.

Touring Guadalupe is simple. Drive slowly down Avenida del Yaqui and you'll soon see **Mercado Mexico** on your right. It's a large Mexican import shop whose shelves are jammed with pottery, terra cotta figurines, Mexican blankets, piñatas, hand-blown glass and more. The merchandise spills into a side yard and adjacent shed. Prices here are rather modest, although not as cheap as in Mexico, and there's no haggling. A sign says: "Please don't ask for Mexican prices. This is Guadalupe, USA." A block beyond, near the corner of Calle Sonora, you'll see ❖ **Filito's Café**, which has very inexpensive food. **Flores Bakery** is adjacent, offering Mexican pastries, baked goods and Hispanic groceries. Continue down Avenida del Yaqui to Calle San Angelo, turn right and you'll see the handsome yet austere **Our Lady of Guadalupe** church rising above its dusty plaza. On feast days and on Cinco de Mayo (May 5), you'll likely see processions and traditional dances on the plaza.

THE TEN BEST ATTRACTIONS BEYOND PHOENIX-SCOTTSDALE

The Valley of the Sun sprawls over 1,000 square miles and contains more than sixty percent of Arizona's people. It shelters eight of the state's ten largest cities. Although most cities beyond Phoenix and Scottsdale aren't tourist destinations, they contain some of the valley's most interesting lures. It's certainly worth driving a few miles to see one of Arizona's finest museums, an outstanding collection of vintage fighter aircraft, a pair of small animal parks and more.

Navigational tip: Before striking out, you may want to create a driving tour by plotting locations of these attractions on an area map.

1 *MESA SOUTHWEST MUSEUM* ● *53 N. MacDonald St., Mesa; (480) 644-2230. (www.ci.mesa.az.us) Tuesday-Saturday 10 to 5 and Sunday 1 to 5; closed Monday. MC/VISA; $$. GETTING THERE: The museum is in downtown Mesa, a block north of Main Street. From Phoenix, take I-10 and then Freeway 202 east about twelve miles. Go just over a mile south on 101 Freeway, then east into downtown Mesa on Main Street; MacDonald is about 3.5 miles from the freeway exit.*

Mesa Southwest rivals the Heard as the finest museum in the area. Further, it's one of the finest in the entire state. Cleverly, in this Valley of the Sun, the main exhibit begins with Ole Sol, focusing on the sun and the formation of its universe. From there, "time travelers" pass through a nicely done gem and mineral exhibit and arrive at "Dinosaur Mountain," an imposing display of life-sized animated creatures on terraces of a large red rock formation. Occasional "cloudbursts" send streams coursing down the terraces and into a pool below. Several other skeletons and reconstructions of dinosaurs reside in nearby Dinosaur Hall.

Other exhibits include "Dineh: Life and Cultures of the Navajo," mockups of several territorial prisons, a Sonoran Desert walk, plus artifacts from Arizona's Spanish colonial period. Moving on to contemporary times, a really fun exhibit, "Arizona and the Movies" focuses on the many films shot here. Visitors can view a 1930s Western classic, *Arizona* with William Holden and Jean Arthur and—through clever computer gimmickry—put themselves in the film. Movie posters and production stills recall the many movies and film sequences that were shot here, from uncounted "B" Westerns to *The Return of the Jedi*, *Indiana Jones* and Tom Cruse's *Days of Thunder*. Another museum exhibit points out that Arizona's first real cowboys were the *vaqueros* of Mexico. They were the source of such familiar American cowboy regalia as the wide- brimmed hat, lariat, chaps and saddle horn.

2 *ARIZONA HISTORICAL SOCIETY MUSEUM* • *1300 N. College Ave., Tempe; (480) 929-0292. (www.tempe.gov/ahs) Monday-Saturday 10 to 4 and Sunday noon to 4; free. Gift shop open Monday-Saturday 10 to 4; MC/VISA. GETTING THERE: From downtown Phoenix, use the same approach as for Pueblo Grande (page 31), then continue 3.5 miles into Tempe and turn north onto College Avenue.*

Although this museum is in Tempe, it focuses more on the history of Arizona than its host city. The most interesting exhibit is in the Foundations Gallery. Life-sized terra cotta figures represent the types of people most significant to the state's history—a Tohono O'odham basketmaker, an Apache warrior youth, a Mexican miner, a U.S. cavalryman, a Mormon mother and her child, a cattleman, a Chinese entrepreneur and a Midwestern land developer. Other major exhibits feature Roosevelt Dam and the resultant agricultural industry, motorsport racing in Arizona and the state's hometown role in World War II. Among the displays are mock-ups representing Arizona's two types of wartime prison camps—a Japanese-American relocation camp and a German prisoner of war camp that was located in Papago Park.

3 *ARIZONA STATE UNIVERSITY CAMPUS* • *The Visitor Center is at the southeast corner of the campus at Apache Boulevard and Rural Road. It's open weekdays 9 to 4:30; (480) 965-3633. GETTING THERE: Go east on Freeway 202 to exit 7 and head south on Scottsdale Road. It becomes Rural Road and the visitor center is about a mile from the freeway.*

Green lawns shaded by palms and other subtropical plants create a parklike setting for ASU's imposing gathering of brick buildings. Although not the state's oldest university—that honor belongs to Tucson's University of Arizona—ASU is the largest, with a student enrollment approaching 50,000. The campus centerpiece is Grady Gammage Memorial Auditorium at the corner of Apache Boulevard and Mill Avenue. It's a dramatic sandstone pink structure of circles within circles designed by Frank Lloyd Wright; the effect is a bit like a masonry circus tent. Nearby is the university's arts complex, with another circular building that mimics the Gammage.

Start your visit at the visitor center, housed in a squat, copper-colored geodesic dome. Pick up a campus map that will direct you to attractions and visitor parking areas. Among the lures you'll want to see are the **Art Museum** and various galleries in the **School of Fine Arts building**, (965-ARTS); the **Anthropology Museum** on the north side of Tyler Mall, (965-6224); the **Gallery of Design** in the College of Architecture and Environmental Design building, (965-6384); the **Museum of Geology** south of University Drive, (965-7065) and the adjacent **Center for Meteorite Studies**, (965-3576). Other worthy stops are the **Planetarium** in the Physical Science Center, (965-6891); the **Sports Hall of Fame** in the Wells Fargo Arena, (965-3482); and of course, the ❖ **Grady Gammage Memorial Auditorium**, (965-4050), ASU's main performing arts center. If campus strolling works up a thirst or an appetite, head for the **Memorial Union**, (965-5728), which has cafés, a campus shop and even a bowling alley and movie theater.

4 *CAREFREE & CAVE CREEK* ● *These two small towns are about thirty miles northeast of downtown Phoenix. GETTING THERE: Follow the Squaw Peak Freeway about thirteen miles to Bell Road, then go right (east) less than five miles to Scottsdale Road and left (north) twelve miles to Carefree.*

A short drive north will take you from the metropolitan sprawl of Phoenix into an imposing terrain of massive boulders, rocky ridges and profuse desert gardens. You'll encounter two small towns that have almost nothing in common except the first letters of their names and their locations in this striking desert setting. Carefree is an excessively cute planned residential community dating only from 1959. Cave Creek is a deliberately funky Western town and some would say that it's a little scruffy. Populated with false-front stores, cowboy saloons and steak houses, it dates from the 1870s when gold was discovered in the rough hills nearby. Both communities are more than a thousand feet higher than Phoenix and thus somewhat cooler—something to keep in mind if a heat wave hits.

A brief loop drive will take you past the highlights of these dissimilar desert towns. Heading north on Scottsdale Road, watch on your right for the curiously designed ❖ **el Pedregal Festival Marketplace**. Beyond el Pedregal, as you cross the junction of Carefree Highway, Scottsdale Road becomes Tom Darlington Road. A short distance north, watch for a sign indicating the elegant ❖ **Boulders Resort,** up a desert lane to your right. (Ask for a guest pass at the entry kiosk.)

After visiting the Boulders, continue on Tom Darlington Road into **Carefree,** with its elegant homes bunkered into rocky desert hills. The town seems to have been planned by a brochure writer. Its streets have silly names like Wampum Way, Easy Street, Ho Hum Road, Tranquil Trail and Lucky Lane. (We'd be embarrassed to use our return address on our mail.) Carefree's main claim to fame, other than inane street names, is the ❖ **world's largest sundial.** Its 62-foot-long copper-clad arm casts a solar shadow over a giant clock face that's part of a circular garden. One advantage of this sundial is that it's always correct, since Arizona never switches to daylight saving time. To reach this curiosity, turn right onto Wampum Way and follow it to Sundial Circle.

Return to Tom Darlington, continue past Carefree's trendy shops and desert homes and turn left at a stop sign onto Cave Creek Road. The funky look and attitude of **Cave Creek** begins almost immediately. As you drive, watch for names such as the Horny Toad Restaurant, the Buffalo Chip Saloon, Crazy Ed's Satisfied Frog and Nacho Mamma's Restaurant. (We really like the last one; think about it for a moment.) If you want to learn more about this area, pause at the **Carefree-Cave Creek Chamber of Commerce** on the right at 6710 Cave Creek Rd.; (480) 488-3381. It's open weekdays 9 to 4.

In mid-Cave Creek, you'll encounter the corny and scruffy **Frontier Town** on your left, with shops and cafés in weathered false front buildings. The Western style **Crazy Ed's Satisfied Frog** packs in the tourists and slumming Phoenicians, particularly on weekends. Its adjacent **Black Mountain Brewery** often features live entertainment in its beer garden.

Pressing through town, watch for signs on the left directing you to the **Cave Creek Museum** at 6140 E. Skyline Drive. Although not professionally done, it has some interesting exhibits and it avoids the clutter of many small town archives. In addition to historic displays in the main building, the complex includes the 1948 Black Mountain Community Church, some rusting mining equipment and a 1920s "tubercular cabin" of the type used by TB patients who came to this area for its dry air. The museum is open Wednesday-Sunday 1 to 4:30, October through May, (480) 488-2764.

Cave Creek Road leaves its funky namesake town and travels through more rocky desert. Several nice homes appear among dramatic hillside forests of saguaro (*sa-WHAR-oh*) cactus, suggesting that Cave Creek is becoming more upscale, like its trendier neighbor. However, we doubt if it will ever have a Tranquil Trail. A few miles south, Cave Creek Road intersects with Carefree Highway. You can accomplish a loop by following it east to el Pedregal, or continue south on

Cave Creek Road. At Beardsley Road, which at press time was under construction as a Freeway 101 extension, you can go west to I-17 and return to Phoenix.

5 CHAMPLIN FIGHTER MUSEUM • *4636 Fighter Aces Dr., Mesa; (480) 830-4540. (www.champlinfighter.com) Daily 10 to 5 mid-September to mid-April and 8:30 to 3:30 the rest of the year. MC/VISA; $$.. GETTING THERE: From downtown Phoenix, go east and northeast on I-10 and Freeway 202, take the McKellips exit and continue east just under seven miles to the airfield.*

If you've ever fantasized flying a fighter plane—in a Sopwith Camel with silk scarf fluttering, or streaking through the sky in a P-38 or Sabrejet—you'll want to spend a lot of time here. This is the world's largest collection of fighter aircraft, with more than thirty-five mostly airworthy planes from World War I through Vietnam and beyond. Most of the World War I craft are precise replicas, although the later planes are originals. Among stars of the collection are a German 109E Messerschmitt, British Spitfire, Curtis P-40 Warhawk with the Flying Tiger shark's teeth on its cowling, P-52 Mustang and P-38 Lightning, all from World War II; and three Russian MiGs from the Korea and post-Korea era. My favorite is a replica of the world's first combat aircraft—a 1914 German Rumpler Taube fabric-winged observation plane. It streaked along at seventy-four miles an hour and the pilot's only weapons were hand-lobbed grenades.

The museum has thousands of other bits of aviation memorabilia—weapons, flight gear, medals, dramatic oil paintings of fighters in action and one of the original engines from Howard Hughes' "Spruce Goose." The "Hall of Aces" features photos and write-ups about 700 of America's top fighter pilots. (My old Marine Air Wing commander, Colonel James N. Cupp, is honored on this wall.)

6 COMMEMORATIVE AIR FORCE—ARIZONA WING MUSEUM • *2017 N. Greenfield Rd., Mesa; (480) 924-1940. Daily 10 to 4. MC/VISA; $$. GETTING THERE: Follow directions above for the Champlin Fighter Museum. The Confederate Air Force Museum is at the southwest corner of Falcon Field, with its entrance off Greenfield.*

Originally called the Confedrate Air Force, this group of mostly former pilots collects, restores, displays and occasionally flies historic military aircraft. Although the name seemed harmless enough, the "Confederates" yielded to pressure a few years back and settled on a politically correct and bland new title. The Arizona unit has some of the finest planes of any of the CAF's various "wings." Its pride and joy is a restored and operational B-17 Flying Fortress, the *Sentimental Journey*, with leggy Betty Grable painted on its fuselage. Visitors can tour this grand old aircraft (for a small fee) and even book flights (for a larger fee). It's not always here since it is taken on tours to other aviation museums. Other aircraft in the Arizona Wing collection include a C-26 Invader that saw action in World War II, Korea and Vietnam; a rare Heinkel HE-111 Blitz Bomber; and a B-25 Mitchell.

7 *OLD DOWNTOWN GLENDALE* • *Glendale Avenue between North 57th Avenue and Grand Avenue. For information: Glendale Office of Tourism, 5800 W. Glenn Dr., Suite 140, Glendale, AZ 85301; (623) 930-4500. (www.tourglendaleaz.org) Visitor Center open Monday-Saturday 10 to 5. GETTING THERE: Glendale is northwest of downtown Phoenix. Follow Grand Avenue about nine miles, then just before it angles across Glendale Avenue, turn right onto 51st Place. If you overshoot, make a hard right onto Glendale Avenue.*

While most valley communities seem preocuppied with progress, Glendale is more focused on preservation. The city was founded in 1892 and much of the downtown area retains that look, with tree-lined brick sidewalks, gas lamps and old fashioned storefronts. A five-block section of Glendale Avenue is busy with antique shops and small cafés. In another section just to the north called Historic Catlin Court, several small Craftsman style homes have been turned into boutiques and galleries, with a particular focus on folk art and crafts.

A one-mile stroll will take you past some of Glendale's historic charms. Even if it's a hot day, the streets are tree-shaded and most of its old storefronts have sidewalk canopies. Look for a parking place shortly after turning off Grand Avenue. Head for the **Visitor Center** by cutting diagonally through **Murphy Park** from City Hall at Glendale Avenue near 59th Avenue. From here, follow 58th Drive into the **Historic Catlin Court shopping district.** To loop through the district, walk a block west to 59th Avenue, a block north to Myrtle Avenue, then two blocks east to 58th Avenue.

Two museums are in the area. The **Marty Robbins Glendale Exhibit** occupies a small cottage at Myrtle and 58th, open Tuesday-Saturday 10 to 5; (623) 847-7047. Robbins was a Glendale native. At the corner of 58th and Glenn Drive, check out the **Bead Museum**, open Monday-Saturday 10 to 5 and Sunday 11 to 4; (623) 931-2737.

Continue back to Glendale Avenue and turn left (east). Walking along the north side of the avenue, you'll encounter several antique shops. The largest is **Mad Hatter's** at 5734 Glendale, with dozens of antique stalls on the main floor, mezzanine and second floor. Continue to 54th Avenue and cross to the south side of the street for the **Cerreta Candy Company** factory; (623) 930-9000.

Return west along Glendale Avenue. **Auntie Em's Miniatures and Smilin' Jack's Pedal Cars** at the corner of Glendale and 57th is a combined shop featuring miniature figurines, doll houses and such, plus all sorts of old fashioned kiddie pedal cars. Half a block further, note the bronze statue of **Bill Nebeker**, who typified the territorial sheriffs of early Arizona. It's in front of the Glendale City Court Building. Just beyond is **Parkside Eatery**, a restaurant with outdoor tables in a shady ally. A few doors down is **Kimberly Ann's Victorian Ice Cream Parlor,** near the corner of 58th Avenue. This brings you back to your starting point.

8 OUT OF AFRICA • *9736 N. Fort McDowell Rd., Fountain Hills; (480) 837-7779. (www.outofafricapark.com.) Tuesday-Sunday 9:30 to 5 October through May; Wednesday-Friday 4 to 9:30 June through September; then Saturday 9:30 to 9:30 and Sunday 9:30 to 5 the rest of the year. Major credit cards; $$$$. GETTING THERE: Take Freeway 202 north and east into the Fort McDowell Mohave-Apache Indian Community; the route becomes the Beeline Highway when the freeway ends above Mesa. Just beyond the junction of Fort McDowell Road, turn right and follow signs. Total distance from downtown Phoenix is about twenty-eight miles.*

This is the smallest and most congested of the Valley of the Sun's three animal parks. By congested, we mean that the cages are rather small and packed closely together. This probably is better for visitors than animals, since folks can see the critters almost eye-to-eye. It's also the valley's most friendly and intimate zoo, since its main attraction is close contact between animals and their handlers. The best show is the "Tiger Splash" in which handlers, big cats, bears and other critters slosh about in a pool. It looks like wonderful hot weather fun. Unfortunately, visitors can't join in. Most of the park's critters are big kitties—lions, tigers, leopards and cougars, plus a few exotic birds, monkeys and other smaller animals. Out of Africa was started by two animal enthusiasts who became so intrigued with people-big cat relationships that they turned their research project into a public attraction.

9 *PIONEER ARIZONA LIVING HISTORY MUSEUM* • *Off Pioneer Road at I-17, Phoenix; (623) 465-1052. Tuesday-Sunday 9 to 5. MC/VISA; $$. Light fare served at the Pioneer Café. GETTING THERE: Drive about thirty miles north of Phoenix on I-17 and take Pioneer Road (exit 225) briefly west. From the Cave Creek-Carefree area, take the Carefree Highway west to I-17 and then go north to the Pioneer Road interchange.*

More than twenty structures—originals or reconstructions—comprise this outdoor museum, which has been an ongoing project since 1956. It's a sampler of Arizona buildings from its earliest Spanish days through statehood. The site is rather disconnected, with structures randomly scattered, and it could use some sprucing up. However, it's worth the drive north, or certainly worth a pause en route to or from Phoenix. Some structures, such as a turn-of-the century brick bank and a wood frame Victorian, are nicely furnished. The 1881 adobe sheriff's office and jail looks right out of *Rio Bravo.* You expect John Wayne to step outside and confront the bad guys. Also interesting are a working blacksmith shop, a chink-log 1880s schoolhouse and an adjacent log "teacherage" where the school ma'arm lived in relatively austere discomfort. The museum's largest structure is an 1870s brick opera house where Lilly Langtry once sang. Furnishings are rather sparse although it's a fun place when periodic "mellerdrammers" are presented.

10 **WILDLIFE WORLD ZOO** ● *16501 W. Northern Ave., Litchfield Park; (623) 935-WILD. (www.wildlifeworld.com) Daily 9 to 5. No credit cards; $$$$. GETTING THERE: Drive west on I-10 about twenty miles to exit 124; start north on Cotton Lane, then shift to the right to Loop 303 and follow it about five miles to Northern Avenue. Turn right on Northern and then right again into the parking lot.*

The term "appealingly scruffy" occurred to us as we toured this rural zoo. It's rather dusty—even the parking lot—so you might want to avoid it on windy days. However, the grounds are thickly landscaped and quite pleasant. Wildlife World was started as a private breeding farm for unusual animals in 1975 and opened to the public in 1984. Although it isn't as large as the Phoenix Zoo, it has a good number of critters. The brochure claims the largest variety in Arizona, with more than 250 species of animals and birds. Some are on islands in the middle of small moats; others live in reasonably roomy corral-sized enclosures and a few occupy smaller cages. An old fashioned carousel, a miniature train ride and petting zoo make this a popular stop for families. Although this is hardly a world class zoo, we saw a fair number of unusual critters, from large rodents called agouti to a slender-tailed meerkat, a member of the mongoose family. We also saw Peruvian guinea pigs which—if you ever visit Peru—might be served to you for lunch.

Chapter Three

GRAZING ARIZONA

PHOENIX-SCOTTSDALE'S BEST RESTAURANTS

One cannot possibly go hungry in the Valley of the Sun. At last count, there were more than 2,400 restaurants here. Still, Phoenix is not a dining mecca to rival cities such as San Francisco, Seattle, New Orleans, New York and—yes—Las Vegas. The Zagat dining survey apparently has decided that the nation's sixth largest city doesn't rate its own book. Phoenix-Scottsdale shares space—albeit the largest space— with New Mexico and the rest of Arizona in Zagat's *Southwest Top Restaurants* survey.

Still, the Phoenix-Scottsdale area does have several outstanding restaurants, particularly in the upscale resorts. It even boasts a few celebrity chefs, and we don't mean imports such as Wolfgang Puck and Roy Yamaguchi, although both have restaurants in the valley. Ranked high among local celeb chefs is James Beard Foundation nominee Rox-Sand Scocos of RoxSand and Michael Hoobler of T. Cooks. The Phoenician resort recently hired top chef James Boyce to bring even more luster to one of America's most honored restaurants, the AAA Five Diamond and Mobile Five Star Mary Elaine's.

Incidentally, as you seek out interesting restaurants, are you suffering confusion over fusion? Some generations ago, a chef named Alice Waters created a new American food movement at her Berkeley restaurant called Chez Panisse. Her idea was simple—get fresh local ingredients, spice them creatively and cook then lightly. Food critics called it American *nouveau* and then came other versions—American regional, Southwest *nouveau* and how about regional *nouveau* and American with Pacific Rim accents and American-Mediterranean? As the new schools of cooking became more diverse and therefore more similar, foodies finally came up with a catch-all name—American fusion. That sounds a bit too nuclear for us; we prefer the term contemporary American. That's really a catch-all because it simply means what's happening now. And good things are happening in the Phoenix-Scottsdale dining arena.

Although the top restaurants can be expensive, the Valley of the Sun also is a relatively cheap place to dine, primarily at many of its ethnic restaurants. This area doesn't have the ethnic diversity of San Francisco or New York, although it does have many Hispanics. This is certainly reflected in the valley's restaurants. There are so many good Hispanic cafés that we created a special category for them. A few, such as La Hacienda at the Fairmont Scottsdale Princess, are quite elegant and pricey. However, most Latin cafés are inexpensive. For really cheap dining—Hispanic and otherwise—turn to Chapter Five, page 88.

PRICING: Dollar sign codes indicate the price of a typical dinner with entrée, soup or salad, not including drinks, appetizers or dessert: *$* = less than $10 per entrée; *$$* = $10 to $19; *$$$* = $20 to $29; *$$$$* = "Did you say you were buying?"

The Ten Very Best Restaurants

With 2,400 restaurants in the Valley of the Sun, how could we possibly select the very best? Obviously, by being quite arbitrary. However, we did not make our choices by thumbing through the Yellow Pages, nor did we place much faith in local tourist publications, whose listings are paid for. To narrow our choices, we consulted a variety of sources, including Zagat and other non-commercial restaurant guides, travel guides that don't charge for listings, AAA and Mobil ratings, endorsements by local food critics, and our own dining experiences.

Our choices range from upscale resort restaurants to free-standing and shopping center cafés, and from long-time establishments to *nouveau* places on the block.

1 MARY ELAINE'S • *Fifth floor of the Phoenician, 6000 E. Camelback Rd., Scottsdale; (480) 941-8200. (www.thephoenician.com) French with contemporary American accents; full bar service. Dinner Monday-Saturday; closed Sunday. Major credit cards; $$$$. GETTING THERE: The resort is about ten miles northeast of downtown Phoenix, just north of Camelback Road between 44th and 64th streets on the western edge of Scottsdale.*

The highest rated restaurant in Arizona and one of the most honored in America certainly deserves the spot atop our list. Mary Elaine's was rated tops in a recent Zagat survey, and it is the recipient of both the AAA Five Diamond and Mobile Five Star awards. It's a study in European opulence with soft colors, museum quality art works, plush floral carpeting, scalloped drapes, mirrored columns and glittery chandeliers. Perhaps equally impressive is the view, through window walls to the swimming complex and lushly landscaped grounds of the Phoenician and beyond to the Valley of the Sun. Expect to pay for this almost excess of understated elegance; entrée prices range into the fifties. Chef James Boyce's creative offerings change frequently, although you may encounter roasted turbot, pan-seared New Zealand john dory, swordfish with bacon polenta or caramelized sea scallops.

2 CRESCENT MOON • *At Four Seasons Resort Scottsdale at Troon North, 10600 E. Crescent Moon Dr., Scottsdale; (480) 515-5700. (www.fourseasons.com) Italian and contemporary American; full bar service. Breakfast, lunch and dinner daily. Major credit cards; $$$. GETTING THERE: From downtown, take the Squaw Peak Freeway north fourteen miles to Bell Road and go east less than five miles to Scottsdale Road. Drive north to Pinnacle Peak Road (just beyond Rawhide) and go east briefly, then go north on Pima Road and east on Alma School Parkway. Shortly after passing the turnoff to Pinnacle Peak Patio, turn left onto Crescent Moon Drive.*

That's Italian? The Four Seasons Resort in the rocky desert mountains of north Scottsdale rivals the Boulders as the area's most striking pueblo style retreat. Yet its Crescent Moon restaurant serves not Southwestern but contemporary Italian fare, along with some American entrées. The view from here is simply stunning—rock-strewn desert gardens, the rocky spire of Pinnacle Peak and the distant lights of Phoenix. Prices are surprisingly affordable for such a setting, starting in the high teens. Food fans can choose between a handsome dining room with light woods and a curving stone wall around a *kiva* style oven, or a patio open to that awesome view. The creative fare includes *gnocchi a la bolognese*, oven roasted chicken piccata, braised lamb shank, New York strip steak, and striped bass with butternut squash. Whole wheat crust pizzas are a specialty.

3 DIFFERENT POINTE OF VIEW • *At the Pointe Hilton Tapatio Cliffs Resort, 11111 N. Seventh St., Phoenix; (602) 866-7500. (www.pointehilton.com) American contemporary; full bar service. Dinner nightly. Major credit cards; $$$$. GETTING THERE: The Pointe Hilton resort is about twelve miles north of downtown on the southeast corner of Seventh Street and Thunderbird Road. The fastest route is via I-17 to Thunderbird and then about three miles east to Seventh.*

Sitting dramatically at the highest point of the Pointe Hilton resort, this restaurant with an odd name provides a striking view of far-away Phoenix, framed through rough-hewn mountains. Reached by a steep and winding road from the main resort—don't try to walk it—the restaurant has a Mediterranean look with tile roof and beige stucco walls. A curving stairway reaches the dining room, which is almost austere, as if its designers didn't want to distract from the view. A cocktail lounge-jazz club occupies a lower floor; both it and the dining room have outside decks. The restaurant's changing menu offers a typically contemporary mix of creative American cookery. Some recent examples were Maine lobster and scallops, rack of lamb with basil garlic persillade, Chilean sea bass, roast chicken with whipped potatoes, and tenderloin of pork with candied pancetta glaze.

4 THE GOLDEN SWAN • *Hyatt Regency Scottsdale Resort, 7500 E. Doubletree Ranch Rd., Scottsdale; (480) 991-3388. (www.hyatt.com) American with Southwest accents; full bar service. Dinner nightly and Sunday brunch. Major credit cards; $$$$. GETTING THERE: Drive north on Freeway 101 to exit 43, then go west on Via de Ventura, which becomes Doubletree Ranch Road. About three miles from the freeway, turn north into the resort complex. If you're coming from Scottsdale, go north on Scottsdale Road, turn east onto Doubletree Ranch and then north into the resort after less than half a mile.*

The Hyatt Regency's signature restaurant comes with impressive credentials. *Condé Nast Traveler* rated the Golden Swan as one of the Southwest's top five restaurants and *Travel-Holiday* magazine listed it among its "Outstanding Restaurants of the World." And we rate it doubly—as one of our Ten Very Best, and as the valley's most romantic restaurant (Chapter Seven, page 112). This gorgeous restaurant flows onto a patio rimmed by a floral planter wall alongside the Lagoon, one of the resort's many "water fixtures." A section of the restaurant reaches into the Lagoon itself—to a sunken seating area nearly surrounded by water. The food and service are as pleasing as the setting. Among its innovative entrées during our last visit were marinated pork tenderloin with pancetta and roasted garlic, chicken baked in red clay and stuffed with corn bread pudding, grilled lamb chops glazed with jalapeño honey mustard, and lime grilled shrimp and scallops. The portions are very generous, but do save room for créme brûlee.

5 LANTILLA RESTAURANT • *At The Boulders Resort, 34631 N. Tom Darlington Dr., Carefree; (480) 488-2090. (www.wyndham.com/luxury) American with Southwest accents; full bar service. Breakfast and dinner Monday-Saturday, plus Sunday brunch. Major credit cards; $$$$. GETTING THERE: The Boulders is about thirty miles northeast of downtown Phoenix, on the border between Scottsdale and*

Carefree. Follow the Squaw Peak Freeway about thirteen miles to Bell Road, then go east less than five miles to Scottsdale Road and north twelve miles toward Carefree. The resort entrance is on the right, beyond el Pedregal Marketplace, after Scottsdale Road has changed its name to Tom Darlington Road.

Dining is a special event—and an expensive one—at this opulent resort's main restaurant. The décor might be described as "upscale pueblo," with a fascinating log webwork held up by a massive tree trunk and interlaced with small twigs to create its namesake *lantilla* ceiling. A similar ceiling enhances the adjacent and very comfy cocktail lounge. The Lantilla's frequently changing menu is more straightforward and less contrived than at the valley's trendy "fusion" restaurants. You may encounter—always well prepared and beautifully presented—fare such as herb crusted rack of lamb, roast stuffed chicken breast, pan-seared sea bass and venison loin. The menu always features a couple of "Golden Door" health conscious entrées, named for the resort's full service spa.

6 **THE MARQUESA** • *At the Fairmont Scottsdale Princess, 575 E. Princess Dr., Scottsdale; (480) 585-4848. Spanish-Mediterranean; full bar service. Dinner nightly, plus Sunday brunch. Major credit cards; $$$$. GETTING THERE: From downtown Phoenix, go north about fourteen miles on the Squaw Peak Freeway and take Bell Road less than five miles east to Scottsdale Road. Head north briefly and turn east onto Princess Drive.*

The AAA Five Diamond Marquesa exudes elegance from its old world Spanish décor to its splendidly crafted and artfully presented fare. The look is exquisite, with crystal chandeliers, plush curved booths, high-backed chairs and ornately carved woods. Walls are graced with museum quality oil paintings. The Marquesa earned the second highest food rating in the *Zagat Survey of Southwest Top Restaurants* and it has been rated number one by many local foodies. Despite its ethnic roots and the overall Spanish theme of its host resort, the food isn't typically Spanish. Continental *nouveau* might be a more apt description for fare such as marinated rack of lamb and pomegranate glazed chicken. The *flan* is outstanding and at the Marquesa's lofty prices, it should be.

7 **RANCHO PINOT** • *In the Lincoln Village Shops at 6208 N. Scottsdale Rd., Scottsdale; (480) 367-8030. Contemporary American with Southwest accents; full bar service. Lunch and dinner Tuesday-Saturday. GETTING THERE: Lincoln Village is about two miles north of downtown Scottsdale on the west side of Scottsdale Road, between Rose Lane and Lincoln Drive, just beyond the Borgata. The restaurant is in the rear of the shopping complex, off a plaza behind Stewart Anderson's.*

Hard to find and easy to like once you've found it, Rancho Pinot is an appealing suburban cowboy kind of place. It's on the rim of a shady plaza, removed from the rumble of Scottsdale Road traffic. The restaurant essentially is one large room whose walls are hung with Western paintings and photos, and mounted trophies of rare desert critters such as jackalopes. The skeleton of a saguaro forms an interesting centerpiece. Outside, the simple façade is done in Southwestern salmon and turquoise, accented by glass bricks and large windows. An open kitchen with a blazing hickory oven issues innovative entrées. Local organically grown and pesticide-free ingredients are used when available. The menu changes monthly, so you may or may not find fare such as pork tenderloin marinated with bay leaf, quail on soft polenta, yellowtail with caper-lemon aioli, mesquite grilled lamb chops or oven-roasted vegetables with risotto-wheatberry cake. Among its noteworthy desserts and créme brûlet, bittersweet chocolate with dried cherries, and créme fraiche ice cream.

8 **RESTAURANT HAPA** • *Lincoln Village Shops at 6204 N. Scottsdale Rd., Scottsdale; (480) 998-8220. Contemporary American; full bar service. Dinner Monday-Saturday; reservations essential. Major credit cards; $$$ to $$$$. (www.restauranthapa.com) GETTING THERE: It's near Rancho Pinot; see above.*

What's happening at Hapa? A smash hit when it was opened by James and Stacey McDevitt a few years ago, Restaurant Hapa has changed hands. New owner Margarita Lopez Walker is adding a front dining patio and a walk-in wine and cheese cellar. The menu may have taken on spicier Hispanic-Mediterranean tones inspired by Margarita by the time you arrive, although the McDevitt's executive chef Graham Mitchell remains. So you may or may not experience what the Zagat Survey described as "orgasmic" entréss such as grilled tenderloin of veal with crispy sweetbreads, miso marinated Chilean sea bass or grilled Hawaiian swordfish with cilantro-scented Jasmine rice or seared Muscovy duck breast with roasted sweet potatoes.

9 **ROXSAND** • *In Biltmore Fashion Park at the corner of Camelback Road and 24th Street; (602) 381-0444. Contemporary American; full bar service. Lunch through dinner daily. MC/VISA, AMEX; $$$. GETTING THERE: Take the Squaw Peak Freeway north about three miles to Highland, go east less than a mile to 24th and then north to Camelback. The shopping center is at the northeast corner of 24th and Camelback Road.*

Noted Valley of the Sun chef RoxSand Scocos creates tasty health-conscious fare, using mostly locally grown and organic products. Everything is produced in house, including desserts and breads. And the restaurant is smoke-free. "Contemporary American" doesn't quite describe her creative cuisine, since she likes to add Mediterranean, Mexican or Asian accents. A house specialty is air dried duck with pistachio onion marmalade, served with buckwheat cakes. Other interesting offerings include rack of lamb with dijonaise sauce; Alaskan king salmon with couscous, curried remoulade sauce and lemongrass vinaigrette; and quesadillas with Mexican herbs and corn-stuffed pablano chili. She also produces some interesting pizzas. If her fare is complex, her two-level restaurant's décor is simple—severely modern black and white, accented with contemporary art.

10 *T. COOK'S • At the Royal Palms Resort, 5200 E. Camelback Rd., Phoenix; (602) 808-0766. Contemporary Mediterranean; full bar service. Lunch Monday-Saturday, plus Sunday brunch; dinner nightly. Major credit cards; $$$ to $$$$. GETTING THERE: The inn is about ten miles northeast of downtown Phoenix on the north side of Camelback Road between Arcadia Drive and 56th Street. The restaurant is off the resort's central courtyard.*

Beamed ceilings, wrought-iron chandeliers, coarse brick walls and warm woods provide a rustically elegant setting for T. Cook's. It's the culinary centerpiece of the small and attractive Spanish-Mediterranean style Royal Palms Resort. The restaurant has been featured in *Bon Appétit; Gourmet Magazine* called it "one of America's top tables"; and *Food & Wine Magazine* rated it as the best Phoenix-Scottsdale Restaurant. The fare is contemporary with spicy Spanish and Tuscan accents. Among Chef Michael Hoobler's "signature dishes" are roasted duck breast with artichoke, peppers and sun-dried cherries; mussels sautéed in Chardonnay thyme broth; Mediterranean *paella*; grilled prawns and vegetables with potato risotto cake; and pit-roasted chicken.

THE TEN BEST SPECIALTY RESTAURANTS AND CAFÉS

Our specialty choices are a mixed feedbag, ranging from specific kinds of food to outdoor lunch spots to the best view restaurant. They are thus listed in no particular order.

1 *THE BEST COWBOY STEAK: Pinnacle Peak Patio • 10426 E. Lomax Rd., Scottsdale; (280) 585-1599. (www.pppatio.com) Western American; full bar service. Dinner Monday-Saturday and lunch through dinner Sunday; Major credit cards; $$$$. GETTING THERE: From downtown, take the Squaw Peak Freeway north about fourteen miles to Bell Road and go east less than five miles to Scottsdale Road. Follow it north to Pinnacle Peak Road (just beyond Rawhide) and go east briefly, then turn north on Pima Road, east on Alma School Parkway and west on Jomax Road. (Watch for Pinnacle Peak Patio signs.)*

The Scottsdale area is noted for touristy cowboy steak houses and two are particularly popular—Pinnacle Peak Patio and Riata Pass Steakhouse. Both are part of pretend frontier towns and both serve decent steaks, along with a few other hardy American dishes. They're darlings of the tour bus set and they feature cowboy entertainment along with their grub. Of the two, Riata Pass is more historic, descending from an 1882 roadhouse, although Pinnacle Peak is more fun. Since the Peak opened in 1957, the house policy is to cut off the necktie of any dude foolish enough to wear one. So of course, legions of diners have arrived with sacrificial neckwear to become part of the game. Thousands of snipped ties hang from the ceiling of the main dining room like an inverted forest.

None of this tomfoolery guarantees a decent meal, although the food actually is quite good. There's no fusion, no *nouveau* and no snobby sommeliers. At Pinnacle Peak, cheerful servers dressed like cowboys and cowgirls bring two-pound steaks with all the fixin's to happy tourists and occasional locals. In-house microbrews such as Cowgirl Blonde and Barbwire Brown are served, along with hard likker and a limited selection of wines.

2 BEST NON-COWBOY STEAK: Harris' Restaurant •

3101 E. Camelback Rd., Phoenix; (602) 508-8888. (www.harrisrestaurantphx.com) American; full bar service. Lunch weekdays and dinner nightly. Major credit cards; $$$ to $$$$. GETTING THERE: Harris is on the south side of Camelback Road, at the corner of 30th Street.

Occupying opposite end of the beef pendulum is the elegant Harris' Restaurant, housed in a classic *ranchero hacienda* with a tile roof and Spanish arch windows. It has one of the area's most handsome dining rooms, with a flickering fireplace, beam ceilings with carved corbels, white nappery and tufted leather booths. Harris' is the venue for serious beefeaters; no cutesy raspberry purée and air-dried tomato fusion fare here. The menu features eight versions of mesquite grilled steak, from New York sirloin to petite filet. Among other offerings are steak and lobster, prime rib, lamb and veal chops, grilled calf's liver, pan crusted sweetbreads, breast of chicken and a few seafood dishes. Locals rave about Harris' martinis. Precede dinner if you dare with a Stoly martini and steak tartar. And when you settle back and listen to the tuxedo-clad pianist playing jazz, you'll know this ain't no cowboy steak house.

3 THE BEST BARBECUE: El Paso Bar-B-Que Company •

8220 Hayden Rd., Scottsdale; (480) 998-2626. Full bar service. Lunch through dinner daily. Major credit cards; $$ to $$$. GETTING THERE: It's in the Village at Hayden shopping center on the west side of Hayden between Via de Ventura and Royal Palm Road. From Phoenix, take Free-

way Loop 101 north about seven miles to Indian Bend Road (exit 44). Go west 1.5 miles to Hayden, then north 1.5 miles, cross Via de Ventura, then turn left into the shopping center at mid-block. Other El Paso restaurants are at 4303 W. Peoria Ave., Glendale, (623) 931-2438; 1641 Stapely Dr., Mesa, (480) 507-7400; and 4921 E. Ray Rd., Ahwatukee, (480) 705-5050.

Old El Paso never looked this good. These are among the area's most appealing designer Western restaurants, done with chubby adobe walls and room dividers, flagstone tile floors, peeled log columns and wrought iron trim. A trellised patio at the Hayden Road branch has an inviting gas fireplace, nice for those rare chilly evenings. A specialty at Old El Paso is no-bean barbeque chili with smoked brisket cubes, cheddar cheese and red onions. Other featured items are smoked salmon and grilled prawns. Typical barbecue items include babyback ribs, brisket dinner, smoked chicken, pulled pork, Andouille sausage platter and slow-smoked beef ribs.

4 **THE BEST SEAFOOD RESTAURANT: Steamers Genuine Seafood** ● *In Biltmore Fashion Park at the corner of Camelback Road and 24th Street; (602) 956-3631. (www.steamersgenuineseafood.com) Full bar service. Lunch through dinner daily. MC/VISA, AMEX; $$$. GETTING THERE: Take the Squaw Peak Freeway north about three miles to Highland, go east less than a mile to 24th and then north to Camelback. The shopping center is at the northeast corner of 24th and Camelback.*

Since Phoenix is a long way from salt water, the only seafood restaurants worth their salt have fresh fish flown in daily. Steamers is one of several doing so, and we like its location on the second deck "restaurant row" at Biltmore Fashion Park. The dining room is quite eye-appealing, with light woods, brocaded booths and scalloped drapes. However, we prefer our fish outside, above the nicely landscaped grounds of this upscale shopping complex. Among its kitchen creations are sesame-miso seared Chilean sea bass, pepper crusted sea scallops, pumpkin seed crusted salmon and seafood jambalaya. If you prefer less contrived fish fare, the daily menu features a choice of what's been flown in—generally albacore, halibut, salmon, swordfish or sea bass.

5 **THE BEST VIEW RESTAURANT: Compass Restaurant** ● *On the 24th floor of the Hyatt Regency at 122 N. Second St; (602) 252-1234. American; full bar service. Lunch Friday-Saturday and Sunday brunch; dinner nightly. Major credit cards; $$ to $$$. GETTING THERE: The Hyatt is downtown between First and Second streets.*

While the Compass Room hasn't won many culinary awards, it easily wins first prize for its outstanding view of the vast sprawl of Phoenix and beyond. And since few surrounding highrises are higher, the vista is virtually unobstructed. The view also is pleasing within, since the restaurant was remodeled and redecorated in late 2001, featuring a smart modern look. While there are more creative kitchens in the valley, the Compass serves rather tasty food, dancing from American to continental fare, such as seared salmon, pork saltimbocca, fresh seafood, lamb and prime rib.

6 THE BEST BREAKFAST CAFÉ: First Watch • First and Washington streets in downtown Phoenix, (602) 340-9089; 61 W. Thomas Road just off Central, Phoenix, (602) 265-2092; and 4422 N. 75th Street at Camelback Road, Scottsdale, (480) 941-8464. Breakfast through mid-afternoon daily; no alcohol. MC/VISA, AMEX; $.

We often start our Phoenix days at the downtown First Watch, since it's one of the few city center cafés serving breakfast. This local chain features traditional breakfasts such as omelettes, French toast, pancake and Belgian waffles. The menu also tilts seriously toward healthy fare, with cholesterol-free eggs, fruit bowls and a "Health Nut Scramble." This is a blend of egg whites, mushrooms, peppers, tomatoes and low fat cheese, served with an English muffin and fresh fruit. Our favorite is the fresh fruit crepe with seasonal fruit and topped with low-fat strawberry yogurt, cinnamon and sugar. This chilly breakfast is particularly tasty on a warm summer morning. The First Watch cafés are bright and cheery little establishments with light woods, drop lamps, potted plants and ceiling fans. They're smoke free and most have outside tables.

7 THE BEST POWER LUNCH PLACE: Sam's Café • Lower level of Arizona Center at 455 N. Third St. (near Van Buren); (602) 252-3545. Also in Biltmore Fashion Park at Camelback and 24th Street, (602) 954-7100; and at 10010 N. Scottsdale Road near Mountainview, (480) 368-2800. American-Southwest; full bar service. Lunch through late evening Monday-Saturday and lunch through dinner Sunday. Major credit cards; $$ to $$$.

The downtown business community likes to do lunch at Sam's in the Arizona Center. More stylish than its simple name, it's a handsome Southwest theme restaurant overlooking a landscaped swatch called Central Gardens. The best seats on warm days—and aren't they always in Phoenix?—are on a dining patio above the garden. We like to sit beneath umbrella tables at the outer edge, next to a cascading "linear fountain" that forms a wet proscenium. The menu wanders from Southwest to contemporary American, with fare such as grilled vegetable *paella*, applewood smoked pecan salmon, chicken piccata and chili-rubbed sirloin. Modestly priced and quite tasty are its Mexican and Southwest tortilla-wrapped things, such as chicken chili rellenos, beef fajita wraps and smoked chicken quesadillas.

8 *THE BEST PIZZA PARLOR: Pizzeria Uno* • *Lower level of Arizona Center at 455 N. Third St. (near Van Buren); (602) 253-3355. Full bar service. Lunch through dinner Tuesday-Sunday; closed Monday. Major credit cards; $ to $$.*

History and prejudice rule this selection. When we wrote the first edition of *The Best of San Francisco* nearly two decades ago, we were startled to discover that a Chicago-based restaurant chain served the best pizza in the city. And San Francisco is *famous* for its pizzas! In sampling several pizza parlors around Phoenix and Scottsdale, we still found none better than Pizzeria Uno, creator of the original Chicago deep dish, brick oven-fired pizza. Our favorite pizza from our favorite pizza parlor is the Numero Uno special with sausage, pepperoni, mushrooms, onions, peppers and chunky tomatoes. It comes in its own deep dish skillet, still sizzling from that brick oven.

Pizzeria Uno's interior is typical Chicago style, done in warm wood and brick, yet with a few Western accents such as an old Roy Rogers movie poster and framed photos of cowboy heroes and villains. Outdoor tables front on Arizona Center's main promenade.

9 *THE BEST COFFEE STOP*

Yes, we mean coffee "stop," not coffee shop. Iced latte, espresso or other specialty coffees can be quite refreshing on a warm Phoenix day. The area doesn't have a lot of coffee venues, and in fact two downtown places closed since we did the first edition of this book. However, there are still three establishments where you can get your designer coffee fix—the ubiquitous Starbucks at the northeast corner Adams and Central, Jacquee's in Renaissance Square at the southwest corner of the same intersection, and Einstein's Cafe in the Hyatt Regency at the corner of Adams and Second Street East. Our caffeine of choice is caffé latte, which we sipped several times at each of the three places. And the winnah is:

Jacquees Espresso Gourmet Deli • *In the Renaissance Center at 40 N. Central, corner of Adams; (602) 252-0000. Early morning to late afternoon.*

The caffé latte at Jacquees achieves that delicate balance between smoothness and a hearty coffee flavor. It was this smooth taste than won our tastebuds over from Starbucks and Einstein's. Jacquees is a popular light breakfast and lunch stop for the downtown business crowd, offering bagels, toast, muffins, scones, sandwiches, salads and quiche. Although there are no seats within the deli, patrons can perch at tables in the adjacent Renaissance foyer, and here's a nice touch: Each is adorned with a bud vase. Or one can adjourn to the parklike plaza, with gurgling fountains, tables and benches.

10 *BEST VEGETARIAN VENUE:* **Green Leaf Café** •
*4426 N. Nineteenth Ave., Phoenix; (602) 265-5992. No alcohol; lunch
and dinner Monday-Saturday; closed Sunday. MC/VISA; $$ to $$$.
GETTING THERE: It's in a small strip mall on the west side of Nineteenth, just south of Campbell Avenue. From downtown, go 1.5 miles
northwest on Grand Avenue and then 2.5 miles north on Nineteenth.*

This is a disarmingly charming little storefront café with white
walls, ceiling fans, potted plants and brocaded linens. Like any good
vegetarian venue, it uses tofu, portabella mushrooms and eggplant to
give substance to its dishes. Many of its entrées have a Mideastern accent, such as *merzh* (grilled eggplant stuffed with onion, garlic, tomatoes and feta cheese) and *falafel* coquettes with assorted vegetables.
The restaurant isn't strictly vegetarian. Although it uses no beef, you
can order many of its dishes with chicken or shrimp. Quite tasty is a
gyro platter of lamb with Persian spices and feta. If you need to stock
up on your health foods and super vitamins, Arizona Health Foods
store is next door.

THE TEN BEST HISPANIC RESTAURANTS

A city whose population is twenty-five percent *Latino* obviously has
a good selection of Hispanic cafés. They range from high end Southwest *nouveau* restaurants often found in resorts to simple mom and
pop cantinas. Our selections reach beyond Mexican cafés to include a
cross section of Hispanic tastes. We don't list franchise operations
founded by restaurant management school graduates; sorry about
that, Chevy's. We do include one chain, Blue Burrito Grille, although
it's based in Phoenix.

Latino restaurants are as widely scattered as Hispanics in the Valley
of the Sun, although a good number are along south Central Avenue, a
large Mexican community just below downtown. However, we found
the very best Hispanic restaurant at one of the leading resorts:

1 *LA HACIENDA* • *At the Fairmont Scottsdale Princess, 575 E.
Princess Dr., Scottsdale; (480) 585-4848. Spanish-Mediterranean; full
bar service. Dinner nightly, plus Sunday brunch. Major credit cards; $$$
to $$$$. GETTING THERE: From downtown Phoenix, go north about
fourteen miles on the Squaw Peak Freeway and drive east less than five
miles on Bell Road to Scottsdale Road. Head north briefly and turn east
onto Princess Drive. La Hacienda is on the far western side of the resort.*

Hacienda, indeed! With its corbeled beam ceilings, richly carved
woods, thick columns adored with art and artifacts, flagstone floors
and brocaded chairs, this restaurant suggests the oversized dining

room of a wealthy Spanish *don*. And you can dine like a *don*. The menu is Spanish-Mediterranean with contemporary touches, such as breast of chicken with charred poblano cream, charbroiled rack of lamb with pumpkin seed crust, grilled filet mignon with corn and portobello salsa, and baby sea bass and rock shrimp with toasted almond-tomato sauce.

2 ARRIBA MEXICAN GRILL • *1812 E. Camelback Rd., Phoenix; (602) 265-9112. (www.arribamexicangrill.com) Mexican and Southwestern; full bar service. Lunch through dinner daily. Major credit cards; $$. GETTING THERE: Arriba is near the northeast corner of Camelback and Eighteenth Street. Also at 17211 N. 79th Avenue in Glendale; (623) 878-5777.*

If you prefer upbeat *Latino* to mom and pop Mexican, stop by this lively grill. It's a busily decorated place with brightly painted wall murals, Mexican doodads, potted plants and tequila and beer posters. A sunken cantina is a popular gathering spot each evening from 4 to 6, when margaritas are offered for a dollar. The food is inexpensive for such an attractive place. Although the menu is mostly Mexican, Southwestern accents are evident in several dishes featuring the legendary—and burning hot—New Mexico Hatch chilis. Among them are carne adobada (marinated pork), adobada burritos and Hatch chicken with diced green chilis. Arriba's dishes are rated from one to three chili peppers. Have a pitcher of water or plenty of *cervesa* handy if you go for three-chili items such as the Hatch chili rellenos or steak Tampico. If you prefer somewhat milder fare, try the steak or chicken picado or chimichanga plate.

3 BLUE BURRITO GRILLE • *Outlets at 31189 Camelback in the Biltmore Plaza, (602) 955-9696; 3815 N. Central near Clarendon, (602) 234-3293; 4622 E. Cactus at Tatum, (602) 787-2775; and 7318 E. Shea Blvd., Scottsdale, (480) 951-3151. Also in Chandler and Mesa. (www.blueburrito.com) Mexican; full bar. Lunch through dinner daily; some branches serve lunch only. Major credit cards; $ to $$.*

These cheerful, simply attired cafés feature both walk-up and full table service, which is usually at the bar. They're the best of several regional Mexican food chains, offering monster burritos at modest prices, along with chimichangas, tacos, enchiladas and fajitas, plus some interesting salads. Our favorite is the fish burrito with grilled cod, shredded veggies and white cilantro sauce. If you're starving, try the trademark Big Blue Burrito, sufficient for two ordinary people or one NFL lineman. The cafés use only canola oil, with no lard or MSG, and they have several "heart smart" entrées. They also serve margaritas using 100 percent agave tequila. Most outlets have shaded patios—nice places for burrito munching and tequila sipping on warm days.

4 **LOS DOS MOLINOS** • *8646 S. Central Ave., Phoenix; (602) 243-9113. Santa Fe Mexican; full bar service. Lunch through dinner Tuesday-Sunday; closed Monday. Major credit cards; $ to $$. GETTING THERE: It's just under six miles south of downtown, at the corner of Euclid Avenue.*

Although this restaurant is several miles from downtown in a mostly Hispanic neighborhood, gringos flock here for its hearty lunches and dinners. So much so that the small dining room can be rather chaotic. The food has a Southwest tilt—not *nouveau* but Santa Fe—since one of its founders is a native New Mexican. If you want to learn what *real* New Mexico food is like, try one of the *adovada* dishes—pork with red or green chili sauce. Among its renditions are *adovada* burritos, enchiladas and ribs. Other specials are seared shrimp Veracruz, garlic shrimp and chili rellenos. The kitchen also produces— always on order and never pre-prepared—the usual enchiladas, tacos, tamales and burros. Meals are served with tortilla chips, red and green salsa and a large pitcher of ice water, which you will need. Nothing is mild since the restaurant uses New Mexico Hatch chilis. It occupies a bougainvillea-splashed hacienda; walls are painted with New Mexican murals over which are tacked colorful doodads that give it a cheerful-funky look. Incidentally, *los dos molinos* means "two chili grinders," named for keepsakes given to the owners by their two grandmothers.

5 **MACAYO'S MEXICAN KITCHEN** • *Several in the area, including 4001 N. Central Avenue at Clarendon in Phoenix, (602) 264-6141; in the Desert Sky Mall at 7829 W. Thomas Road in Phoenix, (623) 873-0313; and 11107 N. Scottsdale Road in Scottsdale, (480) 596- 1811. Mexican; full bar service. Lunch through dinner daily. Major credit cards; $ to $$.*

Local foodies may drop their forks when we include the colorfully tacky Macayo's chain in our Ten Best Hispanic list. But ya gotta admit these places are lively and fun, and the food's ample, tasty and very in-expensive. There's not much original on the menu—the usual tacos, burritos, chimichangas and such—although what we've tasted has been just fine. And Macayo serves one of the best burritos in the val-ley. They're stuffed with meat, with no rice or bean fillers, and they're seared on the griddle to give the sheltering tortillas a nice crispy finish.

Macayo's was established in 1945 by Woody and Victoria Johnson (Woody Johnson is Hispanic?), and the chain is now run by their two sons and a daughter. The restaurants Macayo have all the trimmings of a typical Mexican-American café—gaudy colors, friendly and saucy waitresses, mariachi music and entrees ample enough to sink your boat. Some have lively—well noisy—cantinas adjacent to their dining rooms.

6 **MATADOR** • *125 E. Adams St., Phoenix; (602) 254-7563. Spanish-Mexican-American; full bar service. Breakfast through late evening daily. Major credit cards; $$ to $$$. GETTING THERE: It's downtown at the corner of Adams and First Street.*

Despite the *Latino* name, Matador offers a mix of Hispanic and Gringo food. The décor is as eclectic as the menu, with matador paintings on the walls and *faux* Tiffany drop lamps. It has seating indoors and out, and its next-door cantina is a lively downtown nightspot. The mostly-Mexican menu features steak or chicken picado, beef or chicken fajitas, chimichangas and chili colorado or verde. American dishes include steak, calves liver, fried chicken and shrimp. This also is your place if you like Mexican-style breakfasts. It has several types of breakfast burritos, *meneudo, huevos rancheros, chorizo* with eggs and other spicy wake-up fare.

7 **MIA AMIGO'S MEXICAN GRILL** • *Lower level of Arizona Center at 455 N. Third St. (near Van Buren); (602) 256-7355. Several other locations in greater Phoenix. Mexican; full bar service. Lunch through dinner daily. MC/VISA, AMEX; $$ to $$$.*

This attractive designer Mexican restaurant is cheerfully done with light wood booths over which dangle cute chili drop lamps. We like the fact that Mia Amigo's folks make their own tortillas and chop their own salsa, assuring tasty freshness. Mia Amigo's specialties are sizzling chicken, steak or pork fajitas or *combinacions* thereof. A particularly tasty featured item is Baja chicken—grilled breasts with a spicy sauce, spinach, mushrooms and avocados. Other menu selections include *pollo asada, carne asada*, chimichangas, enchiladas and a very good tortilla soup.

8 **OLD TOWN TORTILLA FACTORY** • *6910 E. Main St., Scottsdale; (480) 945-4567. Southwestern; full bar service. Dinner nightly. Major credit cards; $$ to $$$. GETTING THERE: It's at the corner of Main and 69th Street, about three blocks west of the Old Town shopping district.*

Two things are misleading about the name. It's not quite in Old Town and it's not a tortilla factory, but an attractive restaurant featuring creative Southwest fare. Locals like this cafe, which occupies a renovated 1933 hacienda in a quiet neighborhood. Most visitors miss it because it's several blocks west of tourist-busy Old Town. The dining room is pleasantly done in Mexican-territorial style, with candle-lit tables and framed historic photos of early Arizona on warm orange walls. However, most people head for the spacious courtyard, shaded by orange trees. The fare is much more interesting than the usual tortilla-wrapped things, although those are available. Among menu items are Chilean crusted sea bass, red chili grilled pork chops, orange tequila glazed swordfish, blackened mahi mahi and pepperjack stuffed chicken breasts.

9 PEPIN RESTAURANTE ESPAÑOL • 7363 E. Scottsdale Mall, Scottsdale; (480) 990-9380. Traditional Spanish; full bar service. Lunch Tuesday-Saturday, dinner Tuesday-Sunday; flamenco shows Tuesday, Friday and Saturday; Latin dance Friday and Saturday; closed Monday. Major credit cards; $$$ to $$$$. GETTING THERE: It's on the south side of Scottsdale Civic Center Mall, two blocks east of Old Town.

This appealing restaurant provides a broad sampler of old Spain, from its menu to its flamenco entertainment. The look is traditional as well, with low Spanish arches and spiral vine-entwined columns, bright floral wall designs and an occasional bullfight painting. Like most restaurants on the Scottsdale greenbelt, it has an outside dining area. Pepin offers an extensive selection of hot and cold *tapas* (Spanish-style appetizers) and dinner entrées such as aged beef and Gulf shrimp in cheese sauce, braised veal shank simmered in red wine, and rabbit in wild herb sauce. Among its specialties are several types of *paella*—chicken, seafood or vegetarian.

10 TEE PEE • Tee Pee Tap Room is behind Bank One Ballpark at 602 E. Lincoln near Seventh Street, (602) 340-8787; and Tee Pee Mexican Food is at 4144 E. Indian School Road near 41st Street, (602) 956-0178. Mexican; full bar service. Lunch through dinner daily. MC/VISA, AMEX; $ to $$.

The valley's two Tee Pees have different personalities. The Tap Room suggests a sports bar with Mexican accents and Tee Pee Mexican Food is a comfortable and cozy family restaurant. Both serve hearty meals at very reasonable prices. This isn't Mexican *nouveau*; it's traditional fare such as burros (or burritos, if you prefer), tacos, flautas, chimichangas and such, plus a few spicy specials. Our favorite here is the mildly spiced chicken burro with lots of shredded chicken, cheese and pinto beans; it's served beside a bed of crunchy shredded lettuce. We like the Tap Room because of its Mexican sports bar ambiance.

THE TEN BEST OTHER ETHNIC RESTAURANTS

As noted above, the Valley of the Sun isn't exactly an international melting pot. It has no large ethnic neighborhoods other than Mexican. However, it does have a modest selection of interesting internationally-flavored restaurants. We list them alphabetically by ethnicity.

1 CHINESE: Mr. C's • 4302 N. Scottsdale Rd., Scottsdale; (480) 941-4460. *Full bar service. Lunch and dinner daily. Major credit cards; $$. GETTING THERE: The restaurant is a few blocks north of Old Town, on the southwest corner of Scottsdale Road and Sixth Avenue.*

Mr. C—Bobby Cheng—draws from the far corners of China to provide an interesting mix of mild Cantonese and spicy Szechuan and Mandarin fare. Among the tasty items on his large menu are batter-fried shrimp with walnuts and loquats, prawns with hot chili sauce, crystal prawns with vegetables in white wine sauce, Peking duck, spicy Mongolian lamb, and lobster with hot chili sauce. He also offers the usual noodle soups and rice dishes. The restaurant is cozy and almost elegant, with a crystal chandelier at the entrance and subdued track lighting in the main dining room. Curved banquettes are accented by lacquered wood cases containing Chinese artwork.

2 EUROPEAN: Peter's European Café • 7158 E. Fifth Ave., *Scottsdale; (480) 421-1902. (www.petervamos.com) Wine and beer. Lunch Monday-Saturday and Sunday brunch; dinner nightly. GETTING THERE: The restaurant is on the northwest corner of Scottsdale Road and Fifth Avenue, a few blocks north of Old Town.*

One of the area's more charmingly cute cafés, Peter's serves an interesting mix of middle European and contemporary American dishes. The restaurant and the menu are the creation of Peter Vamos, who fled to America from communist Hungary in the 1970s. He became a nationally known pianist and then decided to go into the restaurant business. His corner café is a cheerful little place, with tables set beneath walls splashed with European countryside murals. More tables spill outside, shaded by a sidewalk overhang. Among his kitchen offerings are risotto with roasted fennel, linguine with wild mushroom pasta and pan-seared peppercorn salmon. From the Hungarian side of the menu comes *palacsintas* (stuffed crepes), paprika chicken breasts, beef goulash and Transylvania goulash with sauerkraut.

3 FRENCH: Coup des Tartes • 4626 N. Sixteenth St., Phoenix; (602) 212-1082. *Wine and beer. Dinner Tuesday-Saturday. Major credit cards; $$$ to $$$$. GETTING THERE: The restaurant is about four miles northeast of downtown Phoenix, on the west side of Sixteenth, near Highland Avenue and just south of Camelback Road.*

A simple stucco cottage—two joined cottages in fact—belie the old world charm of the valley's best French restaurant. Two small dimly-lit dining rooms are separated by an equally cozy dining patio. Tables are set with crisp white nappery, votive candles and fine crystal, and Parisian theatrical posters add splashes of color to the walls. Chef Lionel

Geuskens changes his menu frequently, based on what's available and perhaps on his mood of the moment. His creations often have Mediterranean or Mideastern accents. Recent examples were lemon-garlic chicken with oven-roasted tomatoes, *farfalle* with artichoke hearts and mint in a garlic cream sauce, pork tenderloin with fig demi-glace and feta mashed potatoes, and spice-rubbed lamb shank with dried fruits.

4 GERMAN: Bavarian Point Restaurant • *4815 E. Main St., Mesa, (480) 830-0999. Full bar service. Lunch through dinner daily. Major credit cards; $$ to $$$. GETTING THERE: Take U.S. 60 (the Apache Freeway) east from I-10 to exit 185, follow Greenfield Road north about two miles to Main Street, then go right (east) about half a mile. The restaurant is in the eastern end of a small strip mall.*

You'll have to travel a few miles out of Phoenix to get the best German food in the valley. While a couple of Germanic restaurants have closed since we produced the first edition of this book, Bavarian Point has survived for nearly two decades. It's not dark and somber German, but light and cheery in a folksy sort of way, with natural knotty pine walls, fabric-covered drop lamps and an occasional beer stein. The fare is mostly basic Bavarian, including assorted *schnitzels*, veal *cordon bleau*, paprika chicken and *wurst phanne* (Polish sausage, bratwurst and knockwurst with sauerkraut). However, the menu gets a bit creative, offering several seafood dishes, including salmon in wine sauce with bay shrimp, and fried orange roughy with capers.

5 GREEK: Bacchanal Greek Restaurant • *3015 E. Thomas Rd., Phoenix; (602) 224-9377. Full bar service. Dinner Tuesday-Saturday; open late Friday and Saturday. MC/VISA; $$ to $$$. GETTING THERE: It's about two miles north and three miles east of downtown, in a small shopping complex at Thomas and 30th Street.*

This isn't a typically elaborate Greek-American restaurant with *faux* Parthenon columns and Herculean statues. Bacchanal is rather simple—essentially a large room with a painted Greek mural on one wall. However, it's a fun place, with belly dancing and other live entertainment. You can even buy inexpensive plates to break as part of a Greek dancing custom. The food is reasonably priced and includes such traditional bites as *capama* (lamb in tomato sauce), *moussaka* (eggplant, potato and meat sauce with cheese), shrimp Korfu with feta cheese and spicy tomatoes, and chicken or shrimp shish kebab.

6 INDIAN: A Jewel of the Crown • *7373 Scottsdale Mall, Scottsdale; (480) 949-8000. Full bar service. Lunch and dinner Tuesday-Sunday; closed Monday. Major credit cards; $$ to $$$. GETTING THERE: It's adjacent to Pepin Restaurante Español (page 67) on the south side of Scottsdale Civic Center Mall.*

A recent Scottsdale Center for the Arts culinary festival awarded a "best of show" to the spicy fare of this attractive restaurant. The menu is traditional East Indian, with such peppy offerings as assorted *tandooris* (clay oven baked meats) and *kormas* (meat or chicken chunks cooked with onion, nuts, spices and cream or yogurt), plus several spicy curry dishes. Jewel of the Crown also features *biryanis* (bastami rice dishes) and several vegetarian entrées. Baked-to-order breads are a specialty. We like the restaurant's simple décor—a few ornamental screens and wall hangings. It sits right on the Scottsdale greenbelt, with tables inside and out.

7 **ITALIAN: Maria's When in Naples** • *7000 E. Shea Blvd., Scottsdale; (480) 991-6887. Full bar service. Lunch weekdays and dinner nightly. Major credit cards; $$ to $$$. GETTING THERE: The restaurant is in Scottsdale Promenade, between 70th and 71st streets. From downtown Scottsdale, take Scottsdale Road about six miles north to Shea. Go west for a block and a half, then turn north into the center midway between 70th and 71th.*

This is the area's best Italian restaurant because it's family run and serves classic old world fare, with no *nouveau* gimmickry. The menu reads like an Italian cookbook, with entrées such as veal scallopine sautéed in lemon-butter sauce; eggplant and mozzarella Parmigiana for vegetarians; and classic cioppino with mussels, clams, shrimp, scallops, calamari and fresh fish. All pastas are made in-house; try the traditional gnocchi, lasagna or spaghetti, or specialties such as linguine with garlic-sautéed baby clams, and ravioli stuffed with lobster. This is an attractive place, with murals of Italian coastal scenes set in arched brick niches, potted plants, white linen tablecloths and a huge vase of paper flowers as a centerpiece. Vincenzo and Maria Ranieri emigrated from Italy in 1956 and started their restaurant in 1991.

8 **JAPANESE: Sushi on Shea** • *7000 Shea Blvd., (480) 483-7799. Wine and beer. Dinner nightly. Major credit cards; $$ to $$$. GETTING THERE: The restaurant is in Scottsdale Promenade, between 70th and 71st streets. See directions for Maria's above.*

If you knew sushi like I knew sushi—having spent two years in Japan—you'll want to seek out this trendy Japanese *moderne* restaurant. The valley's best raw fish and sticky rice creations are prepared on order at a large sushi bar. If cold fish and rice with hot green mustard isn't your idea of a compete meal, you can order traditional Japanese dishes such as chicken or beef teriyaki, tempuras, *shabu shabu* (rice noodles with thinly sliced steak) and several noodle dishes. While the faithful prefer seating at the open sushi bar, one can adjourn to tables along smoked-glass walls of this large restaurant, or dine on a narrow porch outside.

9 *PAN-ASIAN: Roy's of Scottsdale* ● *7001 N. Scottsdale Rd., Scottsdale; (480) 905-1155. Full bar service. Lunch through dinner daily. Major credit cards; $$ to $$$. GETTING THERE: Roy's is in the Scottsdale Seville center at the corner of Scottsdale Road and Indian Bend Road, just over three miles north of downtown Scottsdale. From the Phoenix area, go north on the Pima Freeway and then west at exit 44 on Indian Bend.*

Roy Yamaguchi has come a long way since opening his first restaurant in Honolulu in 1988—all the way to Phoenix, Denver and points east. A fast-rising celebrity chef, he blends Japanese, Thai, Chinese, Polynesian, French and Italian cuisine into a kind of tropical polyglot. Foodies call it Pacific Rim or Pan-Asian fare. Yamaguchi's culinary creativity has won an impressive number of awards. The James Beard Foundation picked him as "Best Chef in the Pacific & Northwest" in 1993; his Honolulu restaurant received Hawaii's highest Gault Millau rating; and Roy's Kahana Bar & Grill was picked as Maui's most popular restaurant by the Zagat survey. Examples of his polyglot-in-paradise fare are lemon grass chicken breast, Mongolian grilled rack of lamb, blackened ahi with soy mustard butter sauce, and roasted banana pork loin. The restaurant has a pleasing Polynesian-Japanese modern look with light woods and floral accents.

10 *SOUTHEAST ASIAN: Malee's on Main* ● *7131 E. Main St., Scottsdale; (480) 947-6042. Thai; wine and beer. Lunch Monday-Saturday and dinner nightly. GETTING THERE: The restaurant is on "gallery row" in Old Town Scottsdale, at Main near Marshall Way.*

The look is Old Scottsdale and the restaurant owner is American. The only thing Thai about Malee's is the food, which is excellent. And it should be. Dierdre Fawcett's chef is Panee Plabsett, whose culinary training began with her father, who once cooked for Thai royalty. Among her specialties are hot Burmese prawns with garlic sauce; "tropical pineapple" with shrimp, scallops, minced chicken and pineapple chunks, simmered in coconut curry sauce; five-spice pork; roast duck sautéed in coconut milk and stir fried in hot Thai curry; and a lively seafood stew of shrimp, squid, fish and scallops with Thai herbs in a red curry sauce. This is but a sampler; the huge magazine-size menu contains more than eighty-five items. Diners can sup in the simple adobe style restaurant with Southwestern art hung on its soft orange walls, or in an outside patio which is essentially a pleasantly landscaped alley.

Chapter Four

PILLOW TALK
THE BEST PHOENIX-SCOTTSDALE LODGINGS

The Valley of the Sun shelters more upscale desert resorts than any other region in America. Nearly a dozen of these cactus-rimmed retreats have earned four to five AAA diamond ratings and/or an equal number of Mobil star awards.

Such elegance doesn't come with moderate prices; expect to pay at least $200 a night for the more modest accommodations in these desert retreats. Higher end suites reach into the thousands. Even if the prices are a bit beyond your budget, these resorts are worth a visit. They're so elaborate that they have become attractions within themselves. Stop by for lunch, cocktails or dinner and explore their opulent facilities and lush landscaping. Some of these vacation havens have specific lures, such as the Hopi Learning Center at the Hyatt Regency Scottsdale, the museum quality art in the Phoenician and the fine native and Western art and artifacts in the Camelback Inn. At two resorts—The Boulders and Four Seasons Scottsdale—the main attraction is the setting. They're nestled into a stunning landscape of boulder strewn hills and desert gardens.

If you're willing to contend with summer heat, perhaps you can afford the rates at one of these upscale resorts. Prices drop dramatically between June and September—often by more than half. Bear in mind, however, that summer temperature can top 110 degrees. Such extremes are survivable if you're sitting in the shade and sipping a frozen margarita, or skimming down a waterslide at a resort swimming lagoon. Also, mornings and evenings are quite comfortable in summer, even on the hottest days. And you know what local tourist promoters say: It's a *dry* heat.

We've chosen our Ten Best lodgings in two categories—resorts and hotels. Most of our selected properties are in open desert settings, although a few are in urban Phoenix and Scottsdale. It's often difficult to separate the resorts from the hotels, since both may offer extensive vacation amenities. A simple definition is that resorts have more facilities and activities, generally including a golf course, and they're often on very large swatches of land, sheltering themselves from the Valley of the Sun's suburbia.

PRICING: Dollar sign codes indicate room price ranges for two people, based on high season (fall through spring) rates: **$** = a standard two-person room for $99 or less; **$$** = $100 to $149; **$$$** = $150 to $249; and **$$$$** = $250 or more.

THE TEN BEST RESORTS

We considered several candidates for the best resort in the Valley of the Sun—the legendary Arizona Biltmore and Camelback Inn, the Fairmont Scottsdale Princess, Hyatt Regency Scottsdale and the Phoenician. However, none can match the luxury and splendid setting of our final choice.

1 *THE BOULDERS RESORT* ● *P.O. Box 2090, Carefree, AZ 89377; (800) 553-1717 or (480) 488-2090. (www.wyndham.com/luxury) A luxury resort with 160 casitas and villas, each with a kiva style fireplace, private patio, refreshment center and other amenities. Major credit cards; $$$$. GETTING THERE: The resort is about thirty miles northeast of downtown Phoenix, on the border between Scottsdale and Carefree. Follow the Squaw Peak Freeway about fourteen miles to Bell Road, then go east less than five miles to Scottsdale Road and north twelve miles toward Carefree. The resort entrance is on the right, beyond el Pedregal Marketplace, after Scottsdale Road has changed its name to Tom Darlington Road.*

There is no other Sunbelt resort quite like the Boulders. It's in a class by itself with its many amenities, handsome pueblo style architecture and particularly its dramatic setting among massive granite boulders and lush desert gardens. The buildings blend so well with this striking setting that they almost seem to have grown there, along with the saguaro cactus and flame-tipped ocotillo. Lodgings are in casitas and two to three-bedroom villas; all are carefully placed among those giant pebbles and desert shrubbery. The main lodge personifies the pueblo theme, with softly rounded corners, earth tones and museum quality native art. Particularly striking are the Lantilla restaurant (page 56) and its adjacent lounge. Octagonal ceilings are held up by massive tree trunks, with a complex webwork of logs radiating outward.

Although the Boulders is small for a major resort, with only 160 units, it offers every kind of amenity—two eighteen-hole golf courses, two swimming pools and a full service spa, exercise room, tennis courts and a trail system through its 1,300 acres. Available guest activities include nature walks, conducted hikes, horseback riding, rock climbing and biking. The Boulders has several dining areas—indoors and out—including the Lantilla. For shopping, el Pedregal Marketplace is a short stroll away. Added in late 2001 was the Golden Door Spa, with a fitness room, its own pool and even a cooking demonstration center.

The Boulders has won many awards, including a rare AAA Five Diamond rating. *Andrew Harper's Hideaway Report* has named it America's best resort for thirteen straight years, and it's rated as one of the country's top golf resorts by *Golf Magazine*.

2 **ARIZONA BILTMORE RESORT & SPA** • *2400 E. Missouri Ave., Phoenix, AZ 85016; (800) 950-0086 or (602) 955-6600. (www.arizonabiltmore.com) A legendary 39-acre resort with 620 elegantly decorated rooms and casitas, all with full amenities. Major credit cards; $$$$. GETTING THERE: Take the Squaw Peak Freeway north about three miles to Highland, go east less than a mile to 24th and then north about half a mile. Turn right onto Missouri and follow it into the resort complex.*

One of America's grand old retreats, the Arizona Biltmore set the standard for desert resorts when it was opened in 1929. Although glossier properties have since been built, none quite matches the money-eyed elegance of the valley's first true destination resort. For more than seventy years, it has survived the stock market crash, depression, recession and wear. To keep pace with those newer resorts, its current corporate owners completed a $50 million facelift in the 1990s. The concrete block exterior—unchanged in the renovation—has the stern look of a citadel, softened by the lush landscaping that surrounds it. Unlike the rustically cheerful look of the area's other legendary inn, the Camelback, the Biltmore has more of a hard-edged opulence with its fortress-like façade and grand interior spaces with muted fall colors.

Of course the Biltmore has all the amenities, including several swimming pools, a kids' play area, tennis courts, two eighteen-hole golf courses, an eighteen-hole putting green, a spa and fitness center, and several restaurants and shops.

A common misconception is that the Biltmore was designed by Frank Lloyd Wright. In fact, it was created by one of his former draftsmen, Albert Chase McArthur. Ironically, Wright was a bit down on his luck at the time and McArthur called in his former boss as a consultant. The legendary architect's main contribution was the design and placement of the unusual fluted concrete blocks that give the main building its citadel look. To learn more about this historic resort, check out its "hall of history," lined with framed newspaper clippings and magazine articles and photos of the rich and famous who have stayed here. That list includes every U.S. President since Herbert Hoover, although George W. Bush hadn't made it by press time. The corridor is off the south side of the main lobby. Follow signs to the Biltmore Grill then turn left into a hallway just short of the restaurant entrance. Other displays of early Biltmore memorabilia and some fine pieces of native art are placed randomly throughout the hotel.

3 *CAMELBACK INN MARRIOTT* • *5402 E. Lincoln Dr., Scottsdale, AZ 85253; (800) 24-CAMEL or (480) 948-1700. (www.marriott.com) An historic 454-unit resort with TV/movies, phones, dataports and voice mail; honor bars and safes; some units with kitchens and private pools. Major credit cards; $$$$. GETTING THERE: The resort is north of Lincoln Drive between Scottsdale Road and Tatum Boulevard. From Phoenix, go north six miles on the Squaw Peak Freeway to exit 6, then east on Lincoln for about seven miles. From downtown Scottsdale, go north about 2.5 miles on Scottsdale Road, then west briefly on Lincoln Drive.*

This is "where time stands still," says a sign at the entrance to another of the valley's most historic resorts. A clock adjacent to the sign always reads 12:25, although no one we spoke with knew when or why it stopped at that moment. The resort was founded in 1936 by Jack and Louise Stewart, and the main lodge exudes an old money ambiance, with Southwest architecture, coarse whitewashed adobe interior walls, tile floors, Navajo rugs and leather chairs. Despite its age, the Camelback is impeccably maintained and deserving of its AAA Five Diamond award, one of only three in the Valley of the Sun. Surrounded by lush landscaping splashed with brilliant bougainvillea, the resort is terraced into a gentle slope opposite its namesake mountain. Its Navajo Restaurant and several of its lodgings units have views of this famous landmark. Another restaurant, the Chaparral, overlooks the main pool deck. The resort's many amenities include a golf course, three swimming pools, tennis courts and hiking trails. A large gift shop and art gallery offers an extensive selection of native and Western style giftwares. A tiny rock chapel in front of the main lodge displays a few historic plaques concerning the resort.

4 *FAIRMONT SCOTTSDALE PRINCESS* • *7575 E. Princess Dr., Scottsdale, AZ 85255; (800) 344-4758 or (480) 585-4848. (www.fairmont.com) An opulent 650-unit resort on 450 acres. All rooms have TV/movies, video games, multiple phones with computer ports, voice mail and honor bars; some have FAX machines. Major credit cards; $$$$. GETTING THERE: From downtown Phoenix, go north about fourteen miles on the Squaw Peak Freeway and follow Bell Road less than five miles east to Scottsdale Road. Head north briefly and turn east onto Princess Drive.*

This large Southwest style resort with lavishly landscaped gardens is a rare double winner of the AAA Five Diamond award—one for the resort and another for its Marquesa restaurant. If AAA awarded diamonds for golf, the Princess probably would win a third. Its two eighteen-hole courses are the site of the annual Phoenix Open. The opulent low-rise resort is built as a series of lushly landscaped courtyards that shelter patios, fountains and pools. A dramatic focal point in the central courtyard is a large fountain, with water cascading down terraced block walls to a lower level and eventually into one of its swimming lagoons. Hispanic art works, marble columns, richly carved woods, flagstone tile floors, oversized wicker chairs and spacious breezeways give the Princess the aura of a sophisticated Spanish coastal resort.

The rich southern European look carries into its most noted restaurant, the Marquesa (page 56), with an elegant Spanish décor, and La Hacienda Restaurant (page 63) has a similar visage of old Spain.

5 *FOUR SEASONS RESORT SCOTTSDALE AT TROON NORTH* • *10600 E. Crescent Moon Dr., Scottsdale, AZ 85255; (480) 515-5700. (www.fourseasons.com) A striking 210-unit resort with kiva fireplaces, TV/movies, videogames, CD players, voice mail, honor bars and safes. Major credit cards; $$$$. GETTING THERE: From downtown, take the Squaw Peak Freeway north fourteen miles to Bell Road and go east less than five miles to Scottsdale Road. Drive north to Pinnacle Peak Road (just beyond Rawhide) and go east briefly, then turn north on Pima Road and east on Alma School Parkway. Shortly after passing the turnoff to Pinnacle Peak Patio, turn left onto Crescent Moon Drive.*

Yes, the name is strange. However, Troon North (not true north) nearly rivals the Boulders for its setting among the rocky desert peaks of northern Scottsdale and its old Southwest design. Its lodgings are fashioned like classic New Mexican pueblos, multi-terraced with thick adobe walls. The pueblo look continues in the main resort building, with heavy log beam and *lantilla* ceilings. Set in lush desert gardens at the base of the rocky upthrust of Crescent Peak, Troon North enjoys one of the most impressive resort settings in America. The even more imposing Pinnacle Peak is just to the west and Troon Mountain—from

whence comes the resort's odd name—stands nearby. Although the resort is relatively small, it has most of the amenities of the area's larger
properties—four tennis courts, a swimming complex, fitness center
and spa, three restaurants and access to the Troon North Golf Course.

Our favorite spot here is the Lobby Bar veranda overlooking Troon
Mountain, Pinnacle Peak and far-away Phoenix. It's a grand place to sit
with a margarita (no salt please) and watch the sunset. The dining
patio of the Crescent Moon (page 54) has the same view.

6 *HYATT REGENCY SCOTTSDALE RESORT* ● *7500 E.
Doubletree Ranch Rd., Scottsdale, AZ 85258; (800) 55-HYATT or (480)
991-3388. (www.hyatt.com) A luxury resort with 493 rooms, suites and
casitas. All have TV/movies, honor bars, voice mail, phones with dataports and other amenities. Major credit cards; $$$$. GETTING THERE:
Drive north on Freeway 101 to exit 43, then go west on Via de Ventura,
which becomes Doubletree Ranch Road. About three miles from the freeway, turn north into the resort complex. From downtown Scottsdale, go
north on Scottsdale Road, turn east onto Doubletree Ranch and then
north into the resort after less than half a mile.*

Stunning desert gardens, a large swimming lagoon and an outstanding collection of native peoples' art are the jewels of the Hyatt
Regency. This showplace at the historic Gainey Ranch has all the elements of a desert vacation: A large Water Garden with several pools,
spas and a sandy beach; plus twenty-seven holes of golf, tennis, cycling, desert hiking and four restaurants. It's one of the valley's most
opulent resorts and—in our estimation—deserves more than the Four
Diamond rating awarded by AAA.

If the $300-plus room rates are beyond your budget, at least stop
by to admire the opulence of this fine hideaway. Particularly interesting is its extensive native peoples' art collection and the Hopi Learning
Center (page 36). Visitors can browse its lushly landscaped grounds,
admire the striking Fountain Court with its lily pads and fountains,
have lunch or dinner in the adjacent Golden Swan Restaurant (page
55), or pause for a drink at the Hyatt Regency Lobby Bar (page 102).

7 *THE PHOENICIAN* ● *6000 E. Camelback Rd., Scottsdale, AZ
85251; (800) 888-8234 or (480) 941-8200. (www.thephoenician.com)
A 654-unit resort with rooms featuring safes, honor bars, multiple
phones with dateports and voice mail. Major credit cards; $$$$. GET-
TING THERE: The resort is about ten miles northeast of downtown Phoenix. It's just north of Camelback Road between 44th and 64th streets on
the western edge of Scottsdale.*

The only Valley of the Sun resort with something of a checkered
past, the Phoenician was built by Savings and Loan mogul Charles
Keating. His empire disintegrated and he wound up in federal prison,
although the Phoenician survived the financial fires and remains one

of the area's premiere resorts. Its main building appears to be a bit austere—a linear grid that's terraced into the slopes of Camelback Mountain. Most of the elegance is inside—a splendid study in marble, crystal chandeliers and museum quality artwork. The rooms—box-like from without—are opulently decorated, featuring rattan furniture, Berber carpets and oversized bathrooms. The hotel's grounds are lavishly landscaped and the vast parklike entry is particularly impressive.

The Phoenician has some of the area's best restaurants, notably Mary Elaine's, named for Keating's wife, which many sources—including this one—rate as the area's finest (page 53). Also impressive is the main lobby bar with a rather knavish name, the Thirsty Camel. Spilling onto a wide terrace with an open flame as its centerpiece, it offers fine views over the landscaped pool deck and beyond to the great scatter of Phoenix. Resort amenities include twenty-seven holes of golf and a putting green, tennis courts, seven swimming pools, the area's longest waterslide, a health spa, playground, volleyball and basketball courts, bowling green and a two-acre cactus garden with interpretive paths. The Phoenician also has one of the area's larger shopping galleries.

8 POINTE HILTON SQUAW PEAK RESORT ● *7677 N. Six-teenth St., Phoenix, AZ 85020; (800) 876-4683 or (602) 997-2626. (www.pointehilton.com) A 563-unit resort with casitas and two-room minisuites; TV movies, dual phones with dataports and voice mail, video games and honor bars. Major credit cards; $$$$. GETTING THERE: The resort is about 6.5 miles north of downtown Phoenix. Take the Squaw Peak Freeway north to exit 6, go west briefly on Glendale Avenue and then north on Sixteenth. The resort is on the right.*

This large vacation retreat is within walking distance of a busy commercial area along Sixteenth Street, yet its extensive grounds are rather isolated, reaching into foothills near Squaw Peak. The landscaping is quite elaborate, not desert flora but palm trees, flowers and turf. The resort is built in a series of sheltered courtyards; two of them enclose swimming pools. A much more extensive swimming lagoon, the Western-theme River Ranch, features water slides and a meandering water course. Resort amenities include three restaurants, spas, saunas, an eighteen-hole golf course, tennis courts, exercise room and stables.

9 POINTE HILTON TAPATIO CLIFFS RESORT ● *11111 N. Seventh St., Phoenix, AZ 85020; (800) 876-4683 or (602) 866-7500. (www.pointehilton.com) A 585-unit all-suite resort with TV movies, dual phone lines with dataports and voice mail and stocked refrigerators. Major credit cards; $$$ to $$$$. GETTING THERE: The resort is about twelve miles north of downtown on the southeast corner of Seventh Street and Thunderbird Road. The fastest route is via I-17 to Thunderbird (exit 210) and then east about three miles to Seventh.*

This Spanish-Mediterranean style retreat is cantilevered into mountains slopes north of downtown Phoenix. The two-story atrium lobby is an appealing space, with polished tile floors, light carved woods and coarsely textured walls. The rooms of the steeply terraced resort are linked by walkways and elevators. One of the few level areas in this tilted retreat encompasses a large swimming lagoon called The Falls, with a forty-foot waterfall, a water slide and a large free-form pool. The resort's amenities include a spa, fitness center, tennis courts, nearby golf course, riding stables, steam rooms and three restaurants, including the Different Point of View; see page 55.

10 *THE WIGWAM RESORT ● 300 Wigwam Blvd. (P.O. Box 278), Litchfield Park, AZ 85340; (800) 327-0396 or (623) 935-3811. (www.wigwamresort.com) A luxury 331-unit resort with rooms and suites in Arizona territorial style casitas; TV movies, videogames, voice mail, safes and honor bars. Major credit cards; $$$$. GETTING THERE: The resort is on the west side of the Valley of the Sun in Litchfield Park. From Phoenix, take I-10 west to exit 128, follow Litchfield Road north about three miles, go right three blocks on Wigwam Boulevard, then turn left into the resort.*

Another of Arizona's legendary desert retreats, the Wigwam began in 1918 as a lodge for visiting executives of the Goodyear Tire and Rubber Company, which had opened a plant here. A decade later, it became a public resort and Litchfield Park's upscale shopping and residential areas grew up around it. With similar architecture, the town in fact appears to be an extension of the resort.

Far from the dramatic desert mountains that mark the valley's east side resorts, the AAA Four Diamond rated Wigwam has created its own sanctuary of gardens, lawns and fountains. The décor is early Arizona territorial, rustic and yet opulent. *Lantilla* ceilings and cowhide chairs are contrasted by modern furnishings, light woods and muted colors. Both classic and modern Southwest artwork graces the public areas and guest rooms. Lodgings are in casitas that rim a large pool complex. They're gorgeously decorated with Southwest themes; some have stone fireplaces and spa tubs. The resort's amenities include two restaurants, fifty-four holes of golf and a putting green, pools with spas and waterslides, a kids playground, tennis courts and stables.

THE TEN BEST HOTELS & INNS

Phoenix isn't noted for world-class hotels since visitors are drawn more to its desert resorts. However, our top choice—while small—will rival most major urban hotels for amenities and service. This list includes hotels and smaller inns, many of which are mini-resorts. Some are new and modern, others—nicely maintained—date back to the Valley of the Sun's earliest resort days.

1 **RITZ-CARLTON** • *2401 E. Camelback Rd., Phoenix, AZ 85016; (800) 241-3333 or (602) 468-0700. (www.ritzcarlton.com) A luxury 281-room hotel with TV movies, multiple phones, dataports and voice mail, honor bars and safes. Major credit cards; $$$. GETTING THERE: Take the Squaw Peak Freeway north about three miles to Highland, go east less than a mile to 24th, then north briefly to Camelback Road. Turn right onto Camelback and then immediately left to the hotel.*

The valley's most opulent hotel, the Ritz-Carlton sits—appropriately—in the area's most upscale shopping and business district. It's adjacent to Camelback Esplanade and across from Biltmore Fashion Park. The hotel is a study in Old World opulence, with marble or carpeted floors, cabinets with displays of fine china, museum quality art, beaded crystal chandeliers, wall sconces and textured wallpaper. Particularly elegant is the wood paneled bar simply called The Club. The nearby Bistro 24 restaurant, featuring American and continental cuisine, has laminated hardwood floors, bowl chandeliers and European style furnishings. The hotel's amenities include a swimming pool, fitness center, spa and meeting rooms.

2 **DOUBLETREE GUEST SUITES AT GATEWAY CENTER** • *320 N. 44th St., Phoenix, AZ 85008; (800) 800-3098 or (602) 225-0500. (www.doubletreehotels.com) A 242-unit hotel with microwaves, refrigerators, two TV sets, speaker phones, high speed internet connections and wet bars. Major credit cards; $$ to $$$. Prices include a breakfast buffet. GETTING THERE: The hotel is in the Gateway Center office complex near Sky Harbor International Airport. Take 44th Street north from the airport to Gateway Center near Van Buren Street; the complex is on the left.*

This attractive midsize hotel is convenient for air travelers and it has sufficient amenities to provide a home away from home, since all units are two-room suites with microwaves and refrigerators. The large lobby has a pleasing Western-modern theme and an adjacent courtyard is nicely landscaped, with a burbling fountain. A swimming pool is just beyond. Other amenities include a sauna, spa, exercise facility and meeting rooms. The Belvedere Restaurant is adjacent.

3 **CHAPARRAL SUITES** • *5001 N. Scottsdale Rd., Scottsdale, AZ 85250; (877) 495-2191 or (480) 949-1414. (www.chaparral-suites.com) A 311-unit all-suite hotel with TV movies, video games, wet bars, microwaves and refrigerators. Major credit cards; $$$. Rates include cooked-to-order breakfast. GETTING THERE: The hotel is at the northeast corner of Scottsdale Road and Chaparral Road, about a mile north of downtown Scottsdale.*

Built around a landscaped swimming pool courtyard, this Spanish style four-story hotel is near Scottsdale's shops and galleries. Among its offerings are a dining room, two swimming pools, spa pools, fitness room, tennis courts, gift shop, business center, evening cocktails and meeting rooms.

4 *DOUBLETREE PARADISE VALLEY RESORT • 5401 N. Scottsdale Rd., Scottsdale, AZ 85250; (800) 222-TREE or (480) 947-5400. (www.doubletreehotels.com) A 387-unit resort hotel with TV, phones with dataports and voice mail, honor bars and private balconies or patios. Major credit cards; $$$. GETTING THERE: The resort is at the southeast corner of Scottsdale Road and Jackrabbit Road, just over a mile north of downtown Scottsdale.*

Tall palms and a fountain with a bronze sculpture of galloping horses mark the entry to this 22-acre resort. The low-rise hotel is built around a large, nicely landscaped courtyard with two swimming pools, hot tubs and a putting green. Its amenities include two restaurants with indoor and outdoor dining, a cocktail lounge, tennis and racquet-ball courts, spa and fitness club, saunas and meeting rooms.

5 *HERMOSA INN • 5532 N. Palo Cristi Rd., Paradise Valley, AZ 85253; (800) 241-1210 or (602) 955-8614. An historic thirty-five unit inn with TV, honor bars and phones with voice mail. Major credit cards; $$$ to $$$$. GETTING THERE: Take any major northbound street from downtown to Lincoln Drive, go east to 36th Street and turn south. It becomes Palo Cristi and the inn is at the corner of Stanford Road.*

Sitting on the edge of Paradise Valley, this handsome hacienda style inn seems remote from the hustle of suburban Phoenix, yet it's only minutes away. One of our favorite small inns, it was built in the 1930s as the home, studio and guest ranch of noted cowboy artist Lon Megargee. Many of his paintings grace its walls. The look is classic pueblo, with rough-hewn doorway lintels, wood accents, textured adobe walls and beam ceilings. Lush desert landscaping, cool lawns and brilliant splashes of bougainvillea create a striking effect. The inn's villas and casitas are individually decorated and many have *kiva* fireplaces and private patios. Lon's, the inn's highly regarded restaurant, serves Southwest fare; see page 113.

6 *HILTON SCOTTSDALE RESORT & VILLAS • 6333 N. Scottsdale Rd., Scottsdale, AZ 85250; (800) 528-3119 or (480) 948-7750. (www.merv.com) One and two-bedroom suites and villas, some with washers and dryers, spa tubs and private patios. Major credit cards; $$$ to $$$$. GETTING THERE: The resort is on the southeast corner of Scottsdale Road and Lincoln Drive, about two miles north of downtown Scottsdale.*

Owned by Merv Griffin and operated by Hilton, this Grecian style hotel has an attractively spacious lobby. Its rooms and suites rim courtyard enclosing a landscaped garden and free-form pool. Among its amenities are a wading pool, spa and sauna, steam room, fitness room, tennis courts, beauty salon, meeting rooms and two restaurants. Griff's Restaurant is particularly appealing, with a mural of a red rock canyon scene and blue Plexiglas lighting fixtures suggesting clouds.

7 *HYATT REGENCY PHOENIX* ● *122 N. Second St., Phoenix, AZ 85004; (800) 233-1234 or (602) 256-0801. (www.hyatt.com) A 24-story hotel with 667 rooms and forty-five suites; TV movies, dual phones with voice mail and data ports. Major credit cards; $$$$. GETTING THERE: The Hyatt Regency Phoenix is downtown between First and Second streets.*

While not as awesome as many Hyatt's Regency, this downtown hotel has the company's signature atrium lobby. It towers seven stories—not from the ground floor but from a mezzanine lobby. It's decorated with wonderfully whimsical humanoid rabbit "trapeze artists" that appear to scamper and swing about. One peers over a railing to the lower lobby while several others form a "human" pyramid. Columns supporting the atrium are bedecked with multi-colored native peoples' designs. The largest of the city's few downtown hotels, the Hyatt is well located, opposite Phoenix Civic Plaza and Symphony Hall. Its most impressive feature is the Compass Restaurant (page 60) and small cocktail lounge, which revolve every fifty-five minutes, providing a slowly unraveling panorama of the surrounding city. The Compass is reached by a glass elevator that skims the wall of the seven-story atrium lobby then emerges dramatically into thin air, crawling up the outside of this 24-story hotel. The Hyatt's amenities include a café and deli, business center, pool, spa, exercise room and two gift shops.

8 *ROYAL PALMS HOTEL & CASITAS* ● *5200 E. Camelback Rd., Phoenix, AZ 85018; (800) 672-6011 or (602) 840-3610. (www. royalpalmshotel.com) An historic 116-unit resort hotel with TV, videogames, honor bars and phones with dataports and voice mail. Major credit cards; $$$$. GETTING THERE: The inn is about ten miles northeast of downtown Phoenix, on the north side of Camelback between Arcadia Drive and 56th Street.*

A cobbled, palm-lined lane leads from busy Camelback Road to the hushed elegance of one of the valley's more attractive small resorts. Set in the gentle foothills of Camelback Mountain, this elegant hideaway was built in 1926 as a mansion for New York financier Delos Cooke. The look is classic Spanish Mediterranean with tile roofs, rough textured walls, beam ceilings, carved woods and ceramic tile accents.

The main lodge and several casitas enclose a landscaped courtyard and tiled fountain. Strolling about the grounds, one encounters cozy niches and hidden gardens. It seems difficult to believe that the busy outside world is less than a block away. The resort's amenities include a clubby library, swimming pool, tennis courts and a fitness center. Rooms are individually decorated and some have fireplaces and private patios. T. Cook's Restaurant (page 58) serves Mediterranean fare.

9 *SOUTHWEST INN AT EAGLE MOUNTAIN • 9800 N. Summer Hill Blvd., Fountain Hills, AZ 85268; (800) 992-8083 or (480) 816-3000. (www.southwestinn.com) A 42-unit inn with spa tubs, gas fireplaces and other amenities. Major credit cards; $$$ to $$$$. Rates include an extended continental breakfast and daytime snacks. GETTING THERE: From Phoenix, take I-10 and Freeway Loop 202 east and then northeast; it becomes the Beeline Highway after about twelve miles. Continue eleven miles northeast on Beeline to Shea Boulevard, and turn left toward Fountain Hills. Just beyond the town, go left onto Eagle Mountain Road into a planned community and follow signs to the inn.*

Tucked into cactus-covered hills northeast of Phoenix, Southwest Inn is a rarity—an AAA Four Diamond property without a restaurant or extensive resort amenities. What it does offer, at relatively modest prices, is large rooms and suites in several pueblo style buildings, a golf course, swimming pool and lots of privacy. The attractive complex is landscaped with desert flora, except for the cool green of the adjacent golf course. Its large rooms have spa tubs for two, gas fireplaces and private decks or patios.

10 *WYNDHAM BUTTES RESORT • 2000 Westcourt Way, Tempe, AZ 85282; (800) WYNDHAM or (480) 225-9000. (www.wyndham.com) A 353-unit hotel with TV movies, videogames, honor bars, and phones with voice mail and data ports. Major credit cards; $$$ to $$$$. GETTING THERE: Drive south and east on I-10, take 48th Street exit 150, go south about half a mile and turn left into the resort.*

The Buttes sits in the saddle of a rugged hill that emerges rather suddenly from the flatlands between southeast Phoenix and Tempe. Architects have taken full advantage of this lofty perch, designing a dramatic curving red sandstone main building and adjacent restaurant, which are fused into this rocky promontory. Raw stone forms the wall behind the registration desk, creating a striking effect. Two swimming pools are several stories below the main hotel, tucked into a small ravine and linked by a swim channel. The only drawback to this lofty perch is that the I-10 freeway is but a stone's throw away, although its sounds are muffled in most of the complex. Its Top of the Rock restaurant provides imposing views, and is rated as one of the area's ten most romantic dining spots in Chapter Seven, page 115.

*Being poor is no
disgrace but it's no
great honor, either.*
— Will Rogers

Chapter Five

PROUD PAUPERS
A BUDGET GUIDE

This chapter is for budget-minded folks seeking inexpensive places to play, eat and sleep. It begins with the area's Ten Best attractions that are either free or have only token admission fees. This list is followed by inexpensive restaurants and motels.

NOTE: Items marked with ❖ are listed elsewhere in this book; check the index for page numbers.

FRUGAL FUN: THE TEN BEST FREE OR CHEAP ATTRACTIONS

These lures are a mixed bag, ranging from some of the valley's better museums and historic sites to its more interesting parks and recreation areas. Our choices extend beyond Phoenix-Scottsdale to include other Valley of the Sun communities. Most of these attractions are featured elsewhere in this book, with page references for their main listings.

☺ **KID STUFF:** The little grinning guy indicates attractions that are of particular interest to pre-teens.

1 **HERITAGE SQUARE** • *In the Phoenix Heritage and Science Park at Sixth Street and Monroe; (602) 262-5029. GETTING THERE: The park is just east of downtown, immediately beyond Civic Plaza and the Phoenix Convention Center.*

Our favorite budget attraction provides an historical architectural sampler of Phoenix. This nicely landscaped park has ten structures dating from the late nineteenth to early twentieth centuries. Many of these historic homes are open to visitors; some are free and some charge token fees; one is an appealing tearoom. The square also hosts art exhibits and special events, and it presents a farmers' market every Thursday. The Heritage and Science Park also is home to the ❖ Arizona Science Center and the ❖ Phoenix Museum of history, both featured in Chapter Two.

2 **ARIZONA HISTORICAL SOCIETY MUSEUM** • *1300 N. College Ave., Tempe; (480) 929-0292. (www.tempe.gov/ahs) Monday-Saturday 10 to 4 and Sunday noon to 4; free. Gift shop open Monday-Saturday 10 to 4; MC/VISA accepted. GETTING THERE: From downtown Phoenix, use the same approach as for Pueblo Grande (below), then continue another 3.5 miles into Tempe and turn left (north) onto College Avenue. The museum soon appears on your left.*

Although it's in Tempe, the overall focus of this museum is on the state, with emphasis on the Valley of the Sun. Exhibits include life-sized figures representing types of people most significant to the state's history, the building of Roosevelt dam, agricultural and ranching industries, and the valley's role in World War II. Oddly, it was home to both a Japanese-American relocation camp and a German prisoner of war compound. See Chapter Two, page 45.

3 **ARIZONA STATE CAPITOL MUSEUM** • *1700 W. Washington St., Phoenix; (602) 542-4675. (www.lib.az.us/museum) Weekdays 8 to 5. During the January-May legislative session, it's open until 8 on Thursday evenings and 10 to 3 Saturday. Tours weekdays at 10 and 2; free. GETTING THERE: The capitol is west of downtown, rimmed by Jefferson and Adams streets and Seventeenth and Eighteenth avenues.*

With most state offices moved elsewhere, Arizona's copper-domed capitol has become an interesting museum of the state's political history. Many of its rooms, such as the senate and house chambers, have been restored as they were when Arizona became the lower forty-eight's final state in 1912. Exhibits in assorted rooms and corridors focus on Arizona's march to statehood, the construction of the capitol building, and the battleship U.S.S. Arizona that was sunk during the

Japanese attack on Pearl Harbor. For more details on the capitol and its surrounding campus, see Chapter Two, page 27.

4 **THE BEAD MUSEUM** • 5754 W. Glenn Dr., Glendale; (623) 931-2737. (www.thebeadmuseum.com) Monday-Saturday 10 to 5 and Sunday 11 to 4; $. GETTING THERE: To reach Glendale, follow Grand Avenue about nine miles, then just before it angles across Glendale Avenue, turn right onto 51st Place. If you overshoot, make a hard right onto Glendale Avenue. Go a block east to 58th Avenue, turn left and the museum is a block away at 58th and Glenn.

Moved here from Prescott in 1999, this intriguing museum features 100,000 beaded items, from prehistoric jewelry and other artifacts to modern beadwork. A timeline traces the history back 30,000 B.C. The museum has permanent and changing exhibits, and it hosts classes, lectures and tours. Folks can buy their own beaded items at Accent on Beads, the museum store.

5 **DEER VALLEY ROCK ART CENTER** • 3711 Deer Valley Rd., Phoenix; (623) 582-8007. (www.asu.edu/clas/anthropology/dvrac) Tuesday-Saturday 9 to 5 and Sunday noon to 5, October through April; and Tuesday-Friday 8 to 2, Saturday 9 to 5 and Sunday noon to 5 the rest of the year; $. GETTING THERE: Drive north on I-17 about eighteen miles from Phoenix, take exit 217-B and follow Deer Valley Road about two miles west.

This site preserves more than 1,500 petroglyphs in rough lava-strewn hills north of Phoenix. A short interpretive trail takes visitors past the Valley of the Sun's largest collection of 'glyphs, and a fine little exhibit center has displays on the region's early people and area flora and fauna. See Chapter Two, page 34.

6 **ENCANTO PARK** • Fifteenth Avenue and Encanto Boulevard, Phoenix; (602) 261-8993. Boat rentals, (602) 254-1520. Enchanted Island Amusement Park open Wednesday-Friday 10 to 4 and Saturday-Sunday 10 to 8; closed Monday-Tuesday. GETTING THERE: The park is about two miles northeast of downtown. Take any primary street north, then go west on Encanto Boulevard and turn north into the park. ☺

This "enchanted" park deserves a spot on our frugal list for a couple of reasons. Obviously, admission to the park itself is free. Further, its many facilities are quite inexpensive. These lures include a public golf course with modest green fees, a lagoon complex with boat rides and a kiddie amusement park with free admission and inexpensive rides. Even the amusement park's food venues are cheap. It's a refreshing change from the inflated prices charged captive audiences at many attractions. See Chapter Two, page 35.

7 *HYATT REGENCY NATIVE PEOPLES EXHIBITS* ● *In the Hyatt Regency Scottsdale Resort at 7500 E. Doubletree Ranch Rd., Scottsdale, AZ 85258; (480) 991-3388. (www.hyatt.com) GETTING THERE: Drive north on Freeway 101 to exit 43, then go west on Via de Ventura, which becomes Doubletree Ranch Road. About three miles from the freeway, turn north into the resort complex. If you're coming from Scottsdale, go north on Scottsdale Road, turn east onto Doubletree Ranch and then north into the resort after less than half a mile.*

It certainly can be said that the Valley of the Sun's more elaborate resorts are attractions unto themselves. And while room rates start around $300 and restaurant entrées reach to $30 and beyond, there is no charge to prowl about these opulent retreats. Most don't even charge for parking. Our favorite "attraction resort" is the Hyatt Regency Scottsdale, which has an excellent native peoples' and Southwestern art display. Particularly appealing is the Hopi Learning Center off the main lobby, with exhibits about Arizona's most historic tribal group. Anthropologists—and the Hopi themselves—believe they're descended from the ancient Anazasi. See Chapter Two, page 36.

8 *PUEBLO GRANDE MUSEUM AND ARCHEOLOGICAL SITE* ● *4619 E. Washington St. (44th Street), Phoenix; (602) 945-0901. (www.pueblogrande.com) Monday-Saturday 9 to 4:45, Sunday 1 to 4:45; ruins trail closes at 4:30. MC/VISA; $; free on Sundays. GETTING THERE: It's about five miles east of downtown. Follow one-way Jefferson Street, which blends into Washington, then turn right into the complex just past the airport entrance.*

The true roots of Phoenix can be viewed at this fine archeological dig and museum. This was the site of a large Hohokam community whose canal system was re-excavated centuries later by the area's first white settlers. Exhibits include a partially excavated "platform mound" that was the village's center, and furnished reconstructions of ancient adobe dwellings. See Chapter Two, page 31.

9 *SOUTH MOUNTAIN PARK & PRESERVE* ● *Park gates open daily 5:30 a.m. to 10 p.m.; visitor center open 9 to 5 Monday through Saturday; closed Sunday; (602) 534-6324. (www.ci.phoenix.az.us/parks/hikesoth.html) GETTING THERE: From downtown Phoenix, start south on First Avenue, which blends into Central Avenue and leads directly into the park after about eight miles.* ☺

South Mountain is one of America's largest municipal parks, covering nearly 17,000 acres. Its attractions include miles if hiking and cycling trails winding through lush cactus gardens, several picnic areas and a fine visitor center focused on the area's flora, fauna and geology.

A highway spirals up to ❖ Dobbin's Lookout near the mountain's crest, offering a fine view of the valley. At 2,330 feet, it's one of the highest points in the valley reachable by car.

10 *FOUNTAIN HILLS & McDOWELL MOUNTAIN RE-GIONAL PARK • About twenty-five miles northeast of Phoenix. The Fountain Hills Chamber of Commerce phone number is (480) 837-1654; the McDowell Mountain Regional Park number is (480) 471-0173. GET-TING THERE: To reach Fountain Hills, take I-10 and then Freeway 202 north and then northeast; the route becomes the Beeline Highway. Continue to Shea Boulevard, then go west briefly into Fountain Hills. For the regional park, drive four miles north from Fountain Hills on McDowell Mountain Road and turn left.* ☺

The attractive town of Fountain Hills has a curious claim to fame—the world's tallest fountain. Located in the middle of a small lake, the geyser spurts 560 feet into the air for fifteen minutes, every hour on the hour from 10 to 9. It doesn't operate on windy days, since gusts could bathe a good number of this city's 10,000 residents. To find the fountain, turn right from Shea Boulevard onto Saguaro Boulevard on the eastern edge of town and follow it about a mile.

Just beyond Fountain Hills is 21,000-acre McDowell Mountain Regional Park. This gently hilly preserve has fine desert gardens and miles of cycling and hiking trails. Mountain bikers will like the fourteen-mile rollercoaster McDowell Mountain Competitive Path, located to the left, just past the main park gate. Cyclists feeling less challenged can ride the preserve's asphalt roads. The park also has a campground and several picnic areas. See Chapter Nine, page 135.

THE TEN BEST CHEAP EATS

We define "cheap eats" as restaurants where you can get a filling meal for less than $8. We're talking about dinner, not a light lunch. We don't include popular franchise fast food joints, although most can fill you up with greasy 'burgers and over-salted fries for well under our price ceiling. Eating at MacDonald's or Taco Bell isn't a true dining experience; these places are more into marketing than providing healthy food for their customers. We've never cared much for plastic dinosaurs or cartoon characters with our meals.

Although we ignore these takeouts, some of our selections are walkups where the fare is prepared to order. It will come as no surprise that many of our budget selections are ethnic restaurants, particularly Hispanic ones. Few gringo cafés come within our price range. Although inexpensive cafés—often Mexican or Asian—are scattered throughout the valley, we've limited our choices to downtown or other areas where visitors are likely to congregate.

1 **BLUE BURRITO GRILLE** • *Outlets at 31189 Camelback Road in the Biltmore Plaza, (602) 955-9696; 3815 N. Central Avenue near Clarendon, (602) 234-3293; 4622 E. Cactus Road at Tatum, (602) 787-2775; and in the Shea Scottsdale East Shopping Center at 7318 E. Shea Blvd., near Harkins 14 Theaters, (480) 951-3151. Also in Chandler and Mesa. (blueburrito.com) Mexican; full bar service. Lunch through dinner daily; some open for lunch only. Major credit cards.*

Our favorite budget dining venue also makes our list of the Ten Best Hispanic restaurants in Chapter Three, page 64. The food is prepared to order, it's very tasty and served in cheerful surroundings. Many of Blue Burrito's dishes—including its trademark burritos—qualify for our budget list, since most are under $6. If you're with a companion and you're both poor and hungry, order the Big Blue Burrito. Priced under $8, it's more than ample for two, leaving sufficient funds within the budget for a drink. Our favorite drink here is China Mist iced tea with a touch of raspberry, great for a hot Phoenix day. Actually, our favorite is the grille's excellent margarita on the rocks, although that—coupled with a burrito—exceeds our $8 limit.

2 **BAJA FRESH** • *Central and Adams downtown, (602) 256-9200; 1615 E. Camelback Road at the corner of 16th Street, (602) 263-0110; and 39th Street at Thomas Road, (602) 914-9000. (www.bajafresh.com) Mexican; no alcohol. Lunch through dinner weekdays, lunch through midafternoon weekends. MC/VISA.*

The brochure says "No microwaves, no can openers, no freezers, no lard and no MSG," and we're inclined to believe it. Although this is a chain with outlets in several states, everything at Baja Fresh *is* fresh, or at least freshly prepared. You can get a hefty burrito, quesadilla, taco, steak or chicken taquito or tostada well below our budget limit, with room for a side of nachos, salad, Spanish rice or beans, plus a small soft drink. Combo plates of fajitas or tacos also fall within our price guidelines. Bajas Fresh are cheerfully decorated places, and most have outside seating.

3 **FILITO'S** • *8400 S. Avenida del Yaqui, Guadalupe; (480) 839-5814. Mexican; no alcohol. Breakfast through early dinner daily. No credit cards. GETTING THERE: Take southbound I-10 twelve miles to Baseline Road (exit 155), go east two blocks and then turn south onto Priest Drive; it becomes Avenida del Yaqui. Filito's is a few blocks down on the right, at the corner of Calle Sonora.*

This may be the cheapest Mexican restaurant in the valley. And while the old village of ❖ Guadalupe is decidedly scruffy, Filito's is relatively neat and clean. It's a takeout, with seating in a small air conditioned dining room and at outside tables. Virtually everything here is well below our price limit. Individual tacos, enchiladas, quesadillas and such are so cheap that you can get two or three for under $8. Fish, shrimp or chicken dinner platters were just over $5 when we last noshed here. In addition to Mexican fare, Filito sells American 'burgers and ice cream specialties.

4 KIRIN WOK ● *15 W. Jefferson St., Phoenix; (602) 252-3884. Japanese-Chinese; no alcohol. Lunch through early dinner weekdays; lunch only weekends; closed Sundays. GETTING THERE: The wok is on the south side of downtown, between First and Central avenues.*

If you don't mind eating early—Kirin Wok closes weekdays at 6— you can have a healthy and inexpensive Japanese or Chinese dinner at this small, prim place opposite Patriot's Square. And it's within a short stroll of downtown hotels and businesses. Within our dining budget are substantial meals such teriyaki chicken with rice and veggies, shrimp and veggie bowls, Hawaiian orange chicken, *gyoza* (Japanese dumplings) and chow mein.

5 KOKOPELLI MEXICAN GRILL ● *1949 E. Camelback Rd. (at 20th Street), Phoenix; (602) 279-9302. Mexican; beer. Lunch through early dinner Monday-Friday and lunch to late afternoon Saturday; closed Sunday. Major credit cards. GETTING THERE: It's on the back side of Camelback Colonnade Shopping Center, near Fry's Food and Drug.*

Not a mom and pop beanery, Kokopelli is a prim little takeout decorated with large silhouettes of its namesake character. The fare is basic Mexican, yet with a health-conscious tilt. It features several low cholesterol "heart smart" entrées. The costliest item on the menu was under $6 when we last checked and most were under $5. That leaves room for chips with salsa or guacamole, plus a soft drink. The food is what you'd expect for a Mexican takeout—burritos, fajitas, tacos and taco salads. Among its specialties are fish tacos and a shredded beef and serrano pepper wrap called *barbacoa.* Kokopelli has tables indoors and out.

6 LA PALOMA MEXICAN FOOD ● *519 W. Thomas Rd., Phoenix; (602) 266-1423. Mexican; no alcohol. Midmorning through dinner daily. GETTING THERE: This small takeout is just north of downtown between Fifth and Sixth avenues, in a small strip mall opposite St. Joseph's Hospital.*

If you're near downtown and hungry and your wallet's lean, a short drive north will deliver you to one of the Valley of the Sun's most inexpensive Mexican cafés. It's a simple walk-up with a few tables; portions are ample and everything is remarkably cheap. Further, it offers a surprisingly large selection for such a small diner, with twenty-five different combination plates. They include a chicken burrito with rice and beans, beef or chicken tostada, a pair of tacos with rice and beans, four beef or chicken flautas, chili relleno and a beef or chicken taco with rice and beans, shrimp with rice and beans, pork loin with rice and beans—and the list goes on. All of these combo meals are well under $10. Assorted burritos, tacos, enchiladas and tostadas *ala carté* are less than $5.

7 **LUCKY CHINESE RESTAURANT** • *7050 S. Central Ave., Phoenix; (602) 276-5486. Chinese; wine and beer. Lunch through dinner daily. MC/VISA. GETTING THERE: It's about five miles south of downtown, at the corner of Fremont.*

This simple Chinese café offers some of the cheapest meals in town, particularly its lunch and dinner buffets. It also has several combination dinners between $5 and $6, leaving extra change for a drink. These are filling meals, including an egg roll and fried rice. Don't expect fancy décor at these prices. Sitting in the middle of an Hispanic neighborhood, Lucky occupies a small hacienda with a spartan interior. Tables are Formica and walls are almost bare, except for a few Chinese and Mexican artifacts.

8 **PASTABILITIES** • *17 E. Monroe St, Phoenix.; (602) 254-4500. Italian; no alcohol. Weekdays mid-morning to early evening; closed weekends. MC/VISA. GETTING THERE: It's in downtown Phoenix between First Street and Central Avenue, opposite Bank One tower.*

Although it's mostly a pizza parlor, this small downtown café also features several hearty "pasta bowls" with different kinds of pastas, meats and sauces. Its pizzas come in creative versions such as spicy veggie, Western barbecue and "Garlic Lovers." Another tasty curiosity at Pastabilities is a pizza salad platter. Many of these dishes fit within our price range. This establishment is popular with locals and has won "Best of Phoenix" awards as the top pizza parlor and the best downtown lunch spot.

9 **PONCHO'S** • *7202 S. Central Ave., Phoenix; (602) 276-2438. Mexican; wine, beer and margaritas. Lunch through dinner daily. Major credit cards. GETTING THERE: It's about five miles south of downtown, at the corner of Fremont, opposite Lucky Chinese Restaurant (above).*

No mom and pop beanery, Pancho's is surprisingly cute and cozy for an inexpensive café. It has Spanish tile accents, Moorish arches and artifacts tucked into wall niches. It also has an attractive cocktail lounge in back and a takeout up front near the main dining room, for those who need to run and eat. Among this restaurant's remarkably inexpensive combo dinners are a taco, tostada and enchilada; taco, enchilada and beans; and enchilada, tostada and rice. It also features very inexpensive luncheon specials.

10 *SOUTH CHINA BUFFET* • *4517 Seventh Ave., Phoenix; (602) 279-2787 or (602) 279-2788. Chinese; full bar service. Lunch through dinner daily. Major credit cards. GETTING THERE: The café is on the east side of Seventh Avenue, between Minnezona and Campbell, about four miles north of downtown.*

Bright, airy and neat as a pin, this small Chinese restaurant offers remarkably inexpensive lunch and dinner buffets. When we last checked, the dinner buffet was just under our $8 limit, with a choice of more than a dozen dishes, a large salad bar and a soft drink. Items include seafood combo, egg fu young, beef with squash and filet of fish. South China has a weekend seafood buffet from lunch through dinner for the same low price as weeknight dinners. In addition to the buffets, you can order individual entrées off the menu; most are under our price limit. They range from mild Cantonese to spicy Szechuan dishes.

THE TEN BEST CHEAP SLEEPS

Phoenix hotel and motel rooms are moderately priced for a major city and a popular tourist area, and they're *really* cheap during the summer, as we've already noted.

Still, the Valley of th Sun *is* a major tourist area, and rooms at most nicer motels go for $100 or more during the fall through spring high season. It's difficult to find a clean room for less than $60 a couple, which is our criteria for "cheap sleeps." We did find a few at this price, and three are downtown, including our favorite. However, one of our downtown selections—the good old YMCA—doesn't really cater to vacationing families. We found most of our cheap sleeps in the suburbs, and we chose only lodgings that were well maintained and reasonably clean, with easy freeway access.

If you don't mind a little scruffiness, there are several low priced motels along east Van Buren near the airport, and others along Grand Avenue, which runs northwest from downtown. However, none met our criteria for cleanliness and many are rather poorly maintained.

1 *BUDGET LODGE MOTEL* • *402 W. Van Buren St., Phoenix, AZ 85003; (602) 254-7247. Major credit cards. GETTING THERE: It's near the heart of downtown, at the corner of Fourth Avenue.*

Our favorite budget lodging, from where we researched the Phoenix portion of this book, is surprisingly clean and tidy for a low priced motel. It has room phones, TV movies, small refrigerators and microwaves, plus a swimming pool. The location is excellent—within walking distance of downtown attractions and restaurants. Its weekly rates are quite affordable for vacationing families.

2 **BUDGET INN MOTEL** • *424 W. Van Buren St., Phoenix, AZ 85003; (602) 257-8331. Major credit cards. GETTING THERE: The motel is near the heart of downtown, at the corner of Fifth Avenue.*

Like Budget Lodge above, this is a well-kept motel with TV movies, phones, refrigerators and microwaves. It also has weekly rates.

3 **COMFORT INN** • *255 N. Kyrene Rd., Chandler, AZ 85226; (480) 705-8882. Major credit cards. Rates include a continental breakfast. GETTING THERE: The motel is about fifteen miles southeast of downtown Phoenix. Take I-10 exit 160 and follow Chandler Boulevard 1.5 miles, then go briefly north on Kyrene.*

This 70-unit motel has a quite a few amenities for its modest prices—phones with data ports, TV movies, radios and a swimming pool. Some units have microwaves and refrigerators.

4 **MOTEL 6** • *Fifteen in the Valley of the Sun; call (800) 4-MO-TEL-6 for specific locations. (www.motel6.com) Major credit cards.*

Motel 6's feature the usual spartan but clean rooms, with phones and cable TV. Some have swimming pools and guest laundries.

5 **SELECT SUITES** • *4341 N. 24th St., Phoenix, AZ 87016; (800) 827-8704 or (602) 954-8049. (www.selectsuites.com) MC/VISA, DISC. GETTING THERE: It's about five miles northeast of downtown. Take Squaw Peak Freeway exit 3, go less than a mile east on Indian School Road and then briefly north on 24th Street; it's on the right.*

This nice complex has daily, weekly and monthly rates for studios and one and two bedroom units. Although nightly rates exceed our budget limit, weekly and monthly rates on some of the studios are within our range. Units have phones, microwaves and refrigerators and dishes; larger ones have full kitchens. Amenities include two pools and a spa, barbecues and picnic tables, an exercise room, laundry facilities and covered parking.

6 **STUDIO 6** • *Two in the Valley of the Sun; major credit cards; (800) 4-MOTEL-6. Deer Valley Studio 6 is at 18405 N. 27th Ave., Phoenix, AZ 85053; (602) 843-1151. GETTING THERE: It's about fifteen miles north. Take I-17 exit 214 and go west briefly on Union Hills to 27th Avenue; the motel is on the west side. Tempe Studio 6 is at 4909 S.*

Wendler Dr., Tempe, AZ 85282; (480) 414-4470. GETTING THERE: It's just southeast of Sky Harbor airport. Take I-10 exit 155, go west briefly on Baseline Road and then north on Wendler Drive.

These are extended stay studio units operated by Motel 6, with weekly rates that are within our budget range. They have fully equipped kitchens, cable TV and room phones with voice mail, plus coin laundries.

7 **SUPER 8 MOTEL** ● *8130 N. Black Canyon Hwy., Phoenix, AZ 85051; (602) 995-8451. Major credit cards. GETTING THERE: It's about six miles northwest of downtown. Take I-17 exit 206 and follow Northern Avenue briefly west to the frontage road, which is Black Canyon Highway. The motel is just to the north.*

This 120-unit motel has room phones with data ports, TV movies, a swimming pool, spa and coin laundry. Some rooms have microwaves and refrigerators.

8 **TRAVELERS INN** ● *5102 W. Latham St., Phoenix, AZ 85043; (602) 233-1988. Major credit cards. GETTING THERE: The motel is about seven miles west of downtown. Take I-10 exit 139 and go briefly south on 51st Avenue to Latham Street, then west.*

This 126-unit motel has phones with data ports and voice mail, TV movies, a pool, spa and coin laundry. A restaurant is adjacent. Some units have radios and refrigerators.

9 **TRAVEL INN NINE MOTEL** ● *201 N. Seventh Ave., Phoenix, AZ 85007; (602) 254-6521. MC/VISA. Major credit cards. GETTING THERE: It's a block south of Van Buren Street, just west of downtown.*

Travel Inn is less expensive than Budget Lodge and Budget Inn above, although it's not as well maintained. Rooms have TV and phones and the motel has a pool.

10 **YMCA** ● *350 N. First Ave., Phoenix, AZ 85003; (602) 253-6181. GETTING THERE: The "Y" is in the heart of the downtown area, between Van Buren and Fillmore.*

The rooms aren't fancy, the potties are down the hall and the TV is in a common lounge. However, the "Y" has the cheapest room rates in town—under $30 a night when we last checked. It also has very affordable weekly rates. Rooms are clean and they come with or without running water and/or phones. The "Y's" major plus is that it's well located, within a short walk of downtown attractions and restaurants.

All the world's a stage,
And all the men and
women merely players.
They have their exits
and entrances,
And one man in his
time plays many parts.
— **William**
Shakespeare

Chapter Six

NIGHTSIDE
CULTURE, CLUBS & PUBS

Is there life after dark in Phoenix? Well, of course! Although the downtown area doesn't match the vitality of cities such as San Francisco, Chicago or New York, it has a rather upbeat evening scene, thanks primarily to three relatively recent developments.

As the result of a multi-zillion dollar renovation program in the last two decades, downtown Phoenix offers two serious cultural venues—Symphony Hall and the Herberger Theater, plus a lively nightlife scene at Arizona Center and—while this isn't quite cultural—two downtown sports centers, Bank One Ballpark and America West Arena.

Beyond these three areas, urban Phoenix is rather quiet after the last office worker has fled to the suburbs. And it is in those suburbs—and in the valley's desert resorts—that much of the after dark action occurs. Thus, many of our choices of nightclubs, pubs and such are rather scattered.

Overall, the Valley of the Sun is quite active culturally. With its rich mix of performing arts centers, art galleries and museums, it was ranked in 2001 as the fifteenth top arts destination in America by *AmericanStyle* magazine.

NIGHTLIFE SOURCES ● The *Arizona Republic* publishes "The Rep," a tabloid sized weekly entertainment guide, and the East Valley-Scottsdale *Tribune* prints a similar tab called *Get Out.* Both are included in Thursday newspapers, and individual copies of *Get Out* can be found on news racks around town. An alternative newspaper, *Phoenix New Times,* also appears on Thursdays, available free at news racks. All three blanket the local entertainment scene, with listings of performing arts groups, sports events, movies, restaurants and anything else that might draw one from house, hotel, resort or motel. The *New Times,* with its provocative liberal editorial slant and salty classified ads, is the most interesting of the three.

GETTING TICKETED • The area's major tickets-by-phone sources are Dillard's Box Office, (480) 503-5555; Ticketmaster, (480) 784-4444; and Tickets.com, (888) 464-2468. All three sell tickets for both cultural and local sports events. ASU Public Events Box Office sells tickets for just about everything happening at the Grady Gammage Auditorium and elsewhere on campus; (480) 965-3434. About twenty ticket vendors are listed in the Phoenix Yellow Pages, including some speculators who buy, sell and mark up ticket prices. Scalping isn't illegal in Arizona, except immediately outside the venues.

NOTE: Items marked with ❖ are listed elsewhere in this book; check the index for page numbers.

THE TEN BEST PERFORMING ARTS CENTERS AND GROUPS

Phoenix offers a diverse cultural scene, much of it focused in Symphony Hall and the Herberger Theater Center near Civic Plaza downtown. Other major performing arts venues are the Scottsdale Center for the Arts on Scottsdale Civic Center Mall and—our favorite—the Grady Gammage Memorial Auditorium on the campus of Arizona State University in Tempe.

Our Ten Best cultural selections start with performing arts venues, then finish with the area's best performing arts groups.

THE BEST PERFORMING ARTS CENTERS

1 GRADY GAMMAGE MEMORIAL AUDITORIUM • *On the Arizona State University campus at Gammage Parkway and Mill Avenue, Tempe; (480) 965-3434. GETTING THERE: Drive south and then east past the airport on I-10 and take University Avenue (exit 151-A) about 4.5 miles east to the ASU Campus. Turn south on Mill Avenue and the auditorium arrives shortly, on the left.*

The Gammage is both a visual and a cultural treat. The last major building designed by Frank Lloyd Wright, this dramatic curving showpiece of circles within circles was completed in 1964, then the interior was renovated and modernized a few years ago. Although it's on the

ASU campus, the 3,000-seat Gammage is a cultural center for the entire Valley of the Sun community. It books touring Broadway shows, local productions and presentations from ASU performing arts departments. With a massive organ and excellent acoustics, this is a fine place to hear a concert. Tours of the theater are conducted from 1 to 3:30 during the academic year. The Gammage was named in honor of the ASU president who had asked Wright to design it. Ironically, both men died before ground was broken and its construction was supervised by Wright's Taliesin West disciples.

2 **HERBERGER THEATER CENTER** • *222 E. Monroe (between Second and Third streets); (602) 254-7399 and (602) 252-8497 for the box office.*

Six resident companies keep Phoenix's "second theater" (after Symphony Hall) jumping with more than 500 performances a year. How can so many groups share a single stage? They don't. The Herberger has two performance venues, the 815-seat Center Stage and the more intimate 333-seat Stage West. Both are steeply tiered so patrons are never far from the action.

The center is home to Actors Theatre of Phoenix, (602) 253-6701 and 252-8497 for the box office; Arizona Jewish Theatre Company, (602) 264-0402; Arizona Theater Company, (602) 256-6899 and 256-6995 for the box office; Ballet Arizona, (602) 381-0184 and 381-1096 for the box office; Center Dance Ensemble, (602) 844-2788; and Childsplay, a group that does creative dramas and comedies for adults and children; (602) 350-8101.

3 **ORPHEUM THEATRE** • *203 W. Adams St., Phoenix; (602) 252-9678 and (602) 262-7272 for the box office. Guided tours by reservation. GETTING THERE: The Orpheum is on the southwestern edge of the downtown area, at Adams and Second Avenue.*

The city's most historic theater, the 1,400-seat Orpheum was opened in 1929 as a venue for vaudeville and assorted other amusements. The ornate Spanish Baroque building faded with the passing decades and was closed in the 1980s. The city took over the tired old showplace, floated a $14.2 million bond issue and restored it to its original splendor. Re-opened in 1997, it hosts traveling shows, concerts, ballets, top stars and area theater productions. It's one of Phoenix's most handsome buildings, with an elaborate frieze of Grecian style comedy and tragedy masks.

4 **PHOENIX SYMPHONY HALL** • *225 E. Adams St., Phoenix; (602) 262-6225; (602) 262-7272 for the Civic Plaza box office and (602) 495-1999 for Phoenix Symphony Orchestra box office. GETTING*

THERE: Symphony Hall is on the eastern edge of downtown, part of the Civic Plaza and Phoenix Convention Center complex. It's opposite the Hyatt Regency at Second and Adams.

Built in the 1990s as home field for the Phoenix Symphony Orchestra and Arizona Opera, Symphony Hall is one of the state's most attractive concert halls. Its spacious lobby is bedecked by massive crystal chandeliers, and plush, steeply tiered seats can accommodate 2,600 patrons. In addition to the symphony orchestra and opera, it hosts pop concerts, big-name performers and assorted other cultural events.

5 SCOTTSDALE CENTER FOR THE ARTS ● *7380 E. Second St., Scottsdale; (480) 874-4610; tickets (480) 994-ARTS. (www.scottsdalearts.com) GETTING THERE: The center is east of Old Town Scottsdale, on the eastern edge of Civic Center Mall, at the corner of Civic Center and Second Street.*

The Valley of the Sun's finest multiple arts complex, the Scottsdale Center houses a performing arts theater, the ❖ Scottsdale Museum of Contemporary Art and an excellent arts and museum shop. The facility was completed in 1999 as the cultural hub of Scottsdale. The theater hosts the Scottsdale Symphony Orchestra, Phoenix Symphony Chamber Orchestra, traveling shows and international performers, plus assorted drama, musical, dance and ballet groups.

THE BEST PERFORMING ARTS GROUPS

6 PHOENIX SYMPHONY ORCHESTRA ● *455 N. Third St., Suite 390, Phoenix; (602) 495-1117; tickets (602) 495-1999. Performs at Symphony Hall.*

Our favorite performing arts group, the Phoenix Symphony has lightened up in recent years to appeal to broader musical tastes. The 75-member orchestra presents pops concerts as well as classics. Doc Severinsen has served as its pops conductor for two decades. Concerts often spotlight particular performers or styles of music, and some are even preceded by lectures to help get the audience in tune. With these efforts, it has become one of the nation's most respected symphony orchestras, and has hit Billboard charts with several CDs and cassettes. Founded more than half a century ago, the Phoenix Symphony also provides music for Arizona Opera, Ballet Arizona and the Phoenix Boys Choir.

7 ACTORS' THEATER OF PHOENIX ● *112 N. Central Ave.; Phoenix; (602) 253-6701; tickets (602) 252-8497. Performs at the Herberger Theater Center.*

After playing at assorted venues around town, Actors' Theater has found a permanent home at the Herberger, performing on Stage West. It was established in 1982 and presents at least five shows a season, ranging from classic to quirky. It has done abridged Shakespeare, straightforward contemporary dramas and *avant garde* productions, living up to its motto of "off-center and off-Broadway."

8 *ARIZONA OPERA COMPANY* • *4600 N. Twelfth St., Phoenix; (602) 266-7464. Performs in Symphony Hall.*

This ambitious company presents operas in both Phoenix and Tucson, with its local season running from October to March. It offers mostly classic opera and its reputation for elaborate costuming and staging has made it one of America's most honored and fastest growing opera companies. In addition to productions in Arizona's two major cities, it presents Richard Wagner's complete cycle of *Ring of the Nibelung* each year in Flagstaff. (Having suffered through the entire cycle several years ago, I can understand why it is sent out of town.)

9 *ARIZONA THEATER COMPANY* • *502 W. Roosevelt St., Phoenix; (602) 256-6899; tickets (602) 256-6995. Performs at the Herberger Theater Center.*

The state's most acclaimed professional drama group, Arizona Theater has companies in both Phoenix and Tucson. It presents six shows a year in each city. Productions range from classic and contemporary dramas to musicals and works by new playwrights. The group was established in Tucson in 1966 as the amateur Arizona Civic Theater, then it went professional in 1972, and started a second company in Phoenix in 1978.

10 *BALLET ARIZONA* • *3645 E. Indian School Rd., Phoenix; (602) 381-0184; tickets (602) 381-1096. Performs at the Herberger Theater, Symphony Hall, Orpheum Theater and Grady Gammage.*

Ballet in the desert? Certainly. America's sixth largest city boasts its tenth largest ballet company, established in 1986 and gaining more stature each year. Arizona's only professional ballet troupe, it dances at various venues around Phoenix and—like several other local groups—also performs in Tucson. It presents mostly classical ballet and its annual *Nutcracker* is a high point of the Christmas season.

THE TEN BEST NIGHTSPOTS

Perhaps it's those long, warm evenings. More likely, the Valley of the Sun's nightlife diversity is inspired by the fact that the median age of its three million residents is relatively young. They just like to get out and party after sundown. Many of the valley's nightspots are in Tempe, nurtured by the students of ASU.

Jazz is particularly strong in the Phoenix-Scottsdale area, which prides itself in being both urban and *urbane*. Surprisingly, however, the most popular live music is pure country, a leftover from Arizona's cowboy roots. Rock is strong as well, and the valley produced one of America's top groups—Alice Cooper.

The list below is but a tiny sampler of clubs in the Valley of the Sun. For much longer listings of live music, dance clubs and such, check the "Nightlife sources" on page 95.

1 MARCO POLO SUPPER CLUB ● *2621 E. Camelback Rd., Phoenix, (602) 468-0100; and 8608 E. Shea Blvd., Scottsdale, (480) 483-1900. (www.marcopolosupperclub.com) Dance club and restaurant, open Monday-Saturday. GETTING THERE: The Phoenix club is in Camelback Plaza between 26th and 27th streets. The Scottsdale version is in Pima Crossing center just beyond the 84th street traffic light.*

With all of its glitzy resorts, the Phoenix-Scottsdale area has only one classic swing era supperclub—two, actually; one in each town. Live bands and a small dance floor invite you to trip the light fantastic—although no one says that any more—at these two dapper 1920s style clubs. There's live music most nights, with golden oldies on the music box the rest of the time. Unfortunately, the clubs encourage cigar smoking in their cocktail lounges, so you may want to look elsewhere if this is a problem. The two Marcos Polo also are popular restaurants. And they're quite romantic, with their sleek décor and cozy curved banquettes. For menu details, see page 113.

2 CLUB LEVEL ● *411 S. Mill Ave., Tempe; (480) 967-6655 or (480) 967-7755. Dance club featuring deejay pops and rock Wednesday through Sunday. GETTING THERE: The club is just west of the ASU campus near the corner of Mill and Fifth Street.*

Club 411 is one of the area's top deejay dance pubs, drawing a mostly youthful audience from the nearby ASU campus. Speakers the size of minivans fill this colorful dive with upbeat noise, ranging from hard rock to pops and alternative rock.

3 DIFFERENT POINTE OF VIEW ● *11111 N. Seventh St., Phoenix; (602) 863-0912. Restaurant with dinner nightly and live jazz or other music Wednesday-Saturday. GETTING THERE: The club and restaurant are part of the Pointe Hilton Tapatio Cliffs Resort about twelve miles north of downtown. It's on the southeast corner of Seventh Street and Thunderbird Road, and the fastest route is via I-17 to Thunderbird and then about three miles east to Seventh.*

Many of the valley's resorts feature live entertainment in their clubs and lounges, and this is one of the more appealing. The lounge is on the lower level of the Different Pointe of View restaurant and both provide splendid nighttime views from their high perches. This moderately dressy place features jazz or other easy listening music.

4 **HARRAH'S AK-CHIN CASINO RESORT** • *Highway 347 in Maricopa; (800) 427-7247, (480) 802-5000; entertainment hot line is extension 4544. Oasis Lounge offers a variety of live shows. (www.harrahs.com) GETTING THERE: Head south from Phoenix on I-10, take exit 164 (Queen Creek Road) and go southwest for seventeen miles to the town of Maricopa. The casino is at the town's only stoplight.*

This casino resort's Oasis Lounge hosts both up-and-coming performers and some of the nation's top entertainers such as Tanya Tucker and Steve Wariner. Most of the shows are good-old-boy country and many are free. Tickets for leading performers are moderately priced, starting around $20.

5 **THE IMPROV** • *930 E. University Dr., Tempe; (480) 921-9877. Comedy club; dinner and non-dinner shows Thursday-Sunday. GETTING THERE: The club is in the Cornerstone Mall at University and Rural Road, which is a southern extension of Scottsdale Road.*

The Improv is part of a national chain and thus attracts some of the country's leading touring comics. It also book up-and-comers and locals looking for their first break. Since it's near the ASU campus—within view of Sun Devil Stadium—the audience and the humor are young and contemporary.

6 **MARTINI RANCH** • *7295 E. Stetson Dr., Scottsdale; (480) 970-0500. Serious pub with live entertainment most nights. Open Monday and Wednesday through Saturday; closed Sunday and Tuesday. (www.martiniranchaz.com) GETTING THERE: Stetson Drive is in downtown Scottsdale, off Scottsdale Road just north of Indian School Road. Take Fifth Avenue east from Scottsdale Road; it blends onto Stetson.*

This upbeat, glossy and trendy nightspot features entertainment five nights a week in its downstairs main lounge and upstairs Shaker Room. Despite the "ranch" reference, the music is mostly rock, featuring groups such as Kid Rock and Everclear.

7 **MASON JAR** • *2303 E. Indian School Rd., Phoenix; (602) 956-6271. Primarily hard rock, with live music most nights. GETTING THERE: The club is about three miles northeast of downtown at the corner of 23rd Street and Indian School.*

If you like your rock hard, maybe tinged with heavy metal, head for this loud and excessively upbeat place. You may be the only one there without a pierced body part. And if you are into naval and nostril rings, you'll feel right at home.

8 MR. LUCKY'S ● *3660 W. Grand Ave., Phoenix; (602) 246-0686. Country and Western club; live or canned music most nights. GETTING THERE: The club is near the corner of Grand and 37th Avenue, about five miles northwest of downtown.*

The club's name may sound urban, although Mr. Lucky—J. David Sloan—is one of the valley's senior country performers. His bands have backed the likes of Lyle Lovett and the late Waylon Jennings. He's now the host of one of the area's top country music clubs—the proper place practice your cowboy line dance.

9 RED RIVER MUSIC HALL ● *730 N. Mill Ave., Tempe; (480) 829-6779. Country and Western, with live or recorded music and dancing nightly. GETTING THERE: The music hall is near the corner of Mill Avenue and Washington Street, between Phoenix and Tempe.*

This large red barn of a place is easy to spot, sitting alone just up from the banks of the Salt River. It's the valley's largest country and Western center, featuring live and recorded sounds for listening and dancing. It doesn't limit itself to s---kicking music, however. It also hosts occasional jazz and pops concerts.

10 RHYTHM ROOM ● *1019 E. Indian School Rd., Phoenix; (602) 265-4842. (www.rhythmroom.com) Mostly blues, with some jazz and rockabilly; open nightly. GETTING THERE: The club is about three miles north of downtown, between Tenth and Eleventh streets.*

One of the valley's oldest and best blues clubs, the Rhythm Room features both touring acts and local bands. Host Bob Corritore also presents a Sunday night blues show on local PBS station KJZZ at 91.5.

THE TEN BEST WATERING HOLES

We've never been much for dingy bars, unless they exude character and interesting elbow-bending history. We prefer cheery cocktail lounges with soft conversation and music and possibly a nice view.

1 LOBBY BAR AT THE HYATT REGENCY SCOTTSDALE RESORT ● *7500 E. Doubletree Ranch Rd., Scottsdale; (800) 55-HYATT or (480) 991-3388. (www.hyatt.com) Noon through evening daily. GETTING THERE: Drive north on Freeway 101 to exit 43, then go west on*

Via de Ventura, which becomes Doubletree Ranch Road. About three miles from the freeway, turn north into the resort complex. If you're coming from Scottsdale, go north on Scottsdale Road, turn east onto Doubletree Ranch and then north into the resort after less than half a mile. ❖

One of the neatest things about the valley is that its warm weather encourages people to live—and drink—outdoors. Thus our favorite area cocktail lounge is mostly outside. The Lobby Bar is a great open space between the resort's lower lobby and its elaborate pool complex, with cocktail tables and chairs set beside cascading fountains. Guitarists, marimba players or other musicians perform most evenings. At other times, soothing recorded music issues from hidden speakers and soft lighting and falling water create a romantic mood after sundown.

Cocktail waitresses provide full bar service or you can order custom-made martinis or margaritas at a special walk-up outdoor bar; it operates Wednesday through Saturday. The friendly barkeep has an array of designer gins, vodkas and tequilas, which can be accompanied by curiously innovative mixes. Our favorite libation is a margarita on the rocks made with Herradura tequila and Grand Marnier instead of Triple Sec. We then take our creation to a quiet table beside a rustling fountain, sit and sip and pretend to forget what's happing in the world.

2 AZ 88 • *Scottsdale Civic Center Mall; (480) 994-5576. Midday through evening. GETTING THERE: The mall is immediately east of Old Town Scottsdale. Walk about two blocks through the mall from Brown Avenue and AZ 88 is on the right.*

AZ 88 wins our award—if we were giving one—as the coolest looking cocktail lounge in the valley. The large, open interior is a pleasing study in glass and stainless steel, with distinctive steel planters suspended from the ceiling like modernistic chandeliers. A patio just off the Scottsdale Mall is shaded by dramatically curious red shapes that suggest inverted sea kayaks or giant papaya spears. This is a great place to watch people strolling the mall's attractive greenbelt.

3 ELI'S BAR & AMERICAN GRILLE • *In Scottsdale Promenade at 7000 E. Shea Blvd., Scottsdale; (480) 948-9800. Lunch through late evening daily. GETTING THERE: From downtown Scottsdale, take Scottsdale Road about six miles north to Shea. Go west for a block and a half, then turn north into the center midway between 70th and 71th.*

Eli's is a good example of an upbeat neighborhood bar and grill. It's a large, lively establishment with the requisite TV monitors hung over an island service bar. A couple of pool tables are off to one side. Eli's serves hearty and inexpensive hamburgers, steaks, ribs and chickens and it's noted for its Friday night fish fry. The look is contemporary, with exposed ceiling ducts and a cool, dark décor of black, burnt, orange, hunter green and mauve. It features live music several nights a week, and a really neat Elvis statue stands beside a small bandstand. Like may valley pubs, it has an outside patio.

The Scottsdale Promenade complex is comprised mostly of restaurants and pubs. Two of our recommended dining spots—Maria's When in Naples and Sushi on Shea—are located here; see page 70.

4 FOUR SEASONS LOBBY LOUNGE • *At Four Seasons Resort Scottsdale at Troon North, 10600 E. Crescent Moon Dr., Scottsdale; (480) 515-5700. (www.fourseasons.com) Daily noon through evening. GETTING THERE: From downtown, take the Squaw Peak Freeway north about fourteen miles to Bell Road and go east less than five miles to Scottsdale Road. Drive north to Pinnacle Peak Road (just beyond Rawhide) and go east briefly, then go north on Pima Road and east on Alma School Parkway. Shortly after passing the turnoff to Pinnacle Peak Patio, turn left onto Crescent Moon Drive.*

The Four Seasons' Lobby Lounge and its outdoor terrace offer stunning views of the mountainous, rocky deserts of northern Scottsdale. From the terrace—margarita in hand—one can admire the lush desert flora, the awesome spire of Pinnacle Peak, the rocky ramparts of Troon Mountain and the distant shimmer of Phoenix and the rest of the Valley of the Sun. This is an awesome place to watch Arizona sunsets.

5 FRIDAY'S FRONT ROW SPORTS GRILL • *In Bank One Ballpark at 401 Jefferson St. (Fifth Street); (602) 514-8400. Lunch through late evening.* ❖

There are many sports bars in Phoenix, including the one claiming to be "America's Original" (above). However, Friday's is the only one offering *live* sports action, since it hangs over left field at the home of the Arizona Diamondbacks. Tables are terraced to maximize the view, and the field also is visible from most of the barstools. Friday's requires reservations during games, although none are needed for a drink or meal the rest of the time. Anyone can come up and enjoy a view of the imposing—if empty—ballyard. Like many Phoenix pubs, Friday's also is a restaurant, serving American fare. And it's a good sports bar even if the Diamondbacks aren't playing below, since it has a score of TV monitors tuned to assorted games elsewhere. And of course it's decorated with sports star regalia.

6 GREENHOUSE GRILLE • *Downtown at 139 E. Adams St., near the corner of Second Street; (602) 252-2742. Lunch through late evening daily.*

It doesn't much resemble a greenhouse, although this is one of the more inviting lounges and restaurants in downtown Phoenix. A neon sign offers a subtle invitation: GET IN HERE! The Grille's large front patio provides a view of the passing pedestrian parade while ceiling fans and misters keep things cool and shady. Two large-screen TVs face onto the patio, and the Grille also has an indoor drinking and dining area. This place serves a serious margarita, which arrives over ice in a large tumbler. During nightly happy hour, patrons get two drinks for the price of one. This place features live entertainment Thursday through Saturday.

Bar nibbles include curious nachos using fried wonton skins instead of tortilla chips, plus spicy onion rings, chili poppers and cheese rolls. The Grille also has a full menu, featuring rather tasty American and Mexican fare.

7 *HARRIS'* • *3101 E. Camelback Rd., Phoenix; (602) 508-8888. (www.harrisrestaurantphx.com) Lunch weekdays and dinner nightly at the adjacent restaurant. GETTING THERE: Harris is on the south side of Camelback Road, at the corner of 30th Street.*

The bar in this handsome steak house has the comfortable warm-wood feel of an elegant men's club, yet it is at the same time rather light and cheerful. With beam ceilings, tufted leather booths and a flickering fireplace in the adjacent restaurant, it's a grand place to await lunch or dinner. Or come with no plans to dine. Order a martini—a Harris specialty—lean back and listen to a tuxedo-clad pianist at the baby grand, playing soft and gentle jazz. The bar also offers several wines by the glass and a good selection of single malt whiskies and American bourbons. For details on the adjacent restaurant, see Chapter Three, page 59.

8 *HOOTERS* • *Lower level of Arizona Center at 455 N. Third St. (corner of Van Buren), (602) 495-1234; and 2834 W. Bell Rd. (near 29th Avenue, three blocks east of I-17), (602) 375-0000. Also in Tempe at 501 S. Mill Ave. (near Sixth Street), (480) 967-2222. Lunch through dinner daily.*

Rest assured that your service person at Hooters will be a nubile young lady wearing orange hotpants and a tight fitting, scoop- neck T-shirt, and not a pouting male in gym shorts and tank top. Several years ago, the National Organization for Women tried unsuccessfully to force Hooters to hire men to serve drinks alongside the sexy ladies that have made this chain popular.

Like others in this national chain, the valley's Hooters are harmlessly outrageous, boasting that they are "delightfully tacky yet unrefined." The food is typical sports bar—Philly cheese steak, buffalo wings and other light fare, supported by a long list of beers and wines by the glass. The décor consists mostly of the girls and their pin-ups and logo items, plus TV sets tuned to the latest games.

9 *PAOLA'S WINE BAR* • *In Biltmore Fashion Park at the corner of Camelback Road and 24th Street; (602) 522-2344. (www.fermier.com) Adjacent restaurant open for lunch through dinner. GETTING THERE: Take the Squaw Peak Freeway north about three miles to Highland, go east less than a mile to 24th and then north to Camelback. The shopping center is at the northeast corner of 24th and Camelback.*

Part of Christopher Fermier's Brasserie on the Biltmore Fashion Park's restaurant row, Paola's is *the* place for wine aficionados. Its thick wine list—a book, really—lists 400 choices and nearly a hundred wines by the glass. Although we found them to be a bit pricey—a chronic problem in area restaurants—we can't fault the selections. While the list favors California and France, it also includes interesting choices from Australia, Chile and other wine-producing nations. Sommelier Paola Embry Gross, a wine writer and lecturer, obviously isn't a wine snob. His list has a sense of humor, with categories such as "ABC"—Anything but Chardonnay and Anything but Cabernet. His Pinot Noir selections are described as "satin sheets in a bottle." The adjacent restaurant offers contemporary American cuisine.

10 *TEQUILA GRILL* • *4363 N. 75th St., Scottsdale; (480) 941-1800. (www.tequilagrillaz.com) Lunch Monday-Saturday and Sunday brunch; dinner nightly. GETTING THERE: It's just south of Camelback Road, between Scottsdale and Miller roads near downtown Scottsdale. Turn south from Camelback onto 75th Street, then curve around to the left on Indian Plaza; the restaurant is on your left.*

The valley's best tequila bar also is one of its most striking architectural creations. Slab-stone walls and columns topped by bowl shapes create an imposing exterior look, suggestive of a Frank Lloyd Wright Mayan temple. The interior is equally dramatic, with a circular bar as its focal point. A conical structure suggesting a torch rises skyward from this central bar, topped by metal "flames." The kitchen issues trendy *nouveau* cuisine with Southwest accents. However, we come here to praise its tequila more than its architecture and menu.

First, a brief commentary on the nectar of the agave plant. Serious tequila *aficionados* don't drink José Cuervo Gold, since it's sweetened with sugar cane syrup to suit American tastes. *Real* tequila is made from 100 percent blue agave, and the very best is aged from several months (*reposido*) to several years (*añejo*). The grill's bar pours include Herradura Silver, Sauza Triada and Don Julio Silver. Its margaritas are huge and excellent, served in a glass large enough to comfortably house a goldfish. The only José Cuervos on the premises are several of the firm's classic *añejos*, including the 1800 Collection, which goes for $110 a shot.

*'Tis the land of promise,
romance and health.*
**— A 1907 edition of
Twentieth Century
Phoenix Illustrated**

Chapter Seven

ROMANCE
AND OTHER PRIMAL URGES

Many of the early Western movies filmed in Arizona ended with the hero riding off into a romantic desert sunset—on his horse, and without the heroine. In reality as well as in the movies, early Phoenix wasn't really a very romantic place, since it was founded as a no-nonsense farming community. Scottsdale, too, was established by tillers of the soil. Its romantic Western image came later.

However, by the turn of the last century, the Valley of the Sun was seen as a place of "promise, romance and health," as quoted above. Entrepreneurs saw the potential of this warm valley as a health and vacation retreat, which led to the development of romantic hideaway resorts. The opening of the Arizona Biltmore in 1929 and the Camelback Inn seven years later drew the rich and famous, including glamorous Hollywood film stars.

However, the area wasn't the exclusive domain of the wintering rich. Modest priced hotels and inexpensive auto courts lured the middle class to the Valley of the Sun. Tourist promoters urged chilly northerners to come to the "winter playground of the Southwest" and spend their vacations "among the palms and roses."

Modern desert resorts, both opulent and affordable, provide romantic retreats, with their palm-shaded swimming pools, in-room spas for two and quiet enclaves where a couple can share margaritas and intimate conversation. Today's visitors don't ride alone into the sunset; they sit and snuggle and admire it.

NOTE: Items marked with ❖ are listed elsewhere in this book; check the index for page numbers.

THE TEN BEST PLACES TO SNUGGLE WITH YOUR SWEETIE

Even though the Valley of the Sun is home to three million people, there are still plenty of places to be alone—or at least places where you can ignore those around you. Parks, posh resorts and lonely deserts provide ample opportunity for sweetie-snuggling. Our favorite spot is—good grief!—in the middle of downtown Phoenix.

1 *ARIZONA CENTER'S CENTRAL GARDENS* • *Arizona Center is on the northeastern edge of downtown, bounded by Van Buren, Third, Fillmore and Fifth streets.* ❖

This sunken garden between Arizona Center's office towers and its shopping complex is the most romantic snuggling place in the valley, particularly at night. Soft pathway lighting and strings of lights on palm trunks provide a wonderful atmosphere for getting close. Intimate benches for two invite quiet sitting. Sandy pathways wind through the garden's terraces and past a pretty reflection pool. When not gazing into one another's eyes, you can gaze across that pool and watch the diners and shoppers of Arizona Center. And the nice thing is, with such dim light in the garden, they can't watch you.

2 *MEZZANINE LOBBY OF THE HYATT REGENCY* • *122 N. Second Street downtown, between Monroe and Adams streets.* ❖

The Hyatt Regency Phoenix has two lobbies—one at street level and another on a mezzanine, with a soaring seven-story atrium above. The upper lobby, rarely busy, has several overstuffed chairs and couches and little tables for two. The pair of you can enjoy views across Second Street to Phoenix Civic Plaza, or just sit quietly and enjoy views of one another. If you'd like to lighten this quiet mood, check out the delightful "humanoid rabbit" trapeze artists that appear to be cavorting around this upper lobby. One is peering down to the lower lobby so don't worry; he's ignoring you. But watch that guy on one of the upper balconies; he's about to launch his trapeze.

3 SCOTTSDALE CIVIC CENTER MALL • *East side of Old Town, between Indian School Road and Brown Avenue. GETTING THERE: Go north on the Squaw Peak Freeway and then east on Indian School Road about seven miles to Scottsdale Road. Continue two more blocks to Second Street and go south two blocks.* ❖

There are many inviting places to sit and snuggle in this attractive Scottsdale greenbelt. Our favorite is a tree-shaded sunken brick fountain patio rimmed by gorgeous flower beds and cascading bougainvillea. Sounds great, but how does one find it? From City Hall at the northeast corner of the plaza, walk to the right side of a series of "geyser" fountains, and you'll see the sunken patio on your right. It's adjacent to an outdoor stage with a canvas saddleback roof, and opposite the museum store of the Scottsdale Center for the Arts.

4 DOBBIN'S LOOKOUT • *In South Mountain Park and Preserve. Park gates open daily 5:30 a.m. to 10 p.m.; visitor center open Monday-Saturday 9 to 5; closed Sunday; (602) 534-6324. (www. ci.phoenix.az.us/parks/hikesoth.html) GETTING THERE: To reach South Mountain from downtown, start south on First Avenue, which blends into Central Avenue and leads directly into the park after about eight miles. A five-mile scenic drive leads to Dobbin's Lookout.* ❖

Perched near the top of South Mountain, this lookout with a very unromantic name offers a fine—if often smoggy—panorama of the valley. Expect it to be busy on weekends, although you may find solitude on weekdays, particularly if you arrive at the most romantic times—just before sunrise or sunset. It's a splendid vantage point for watching Ole Sol's first and last rays cast stark shadows over this desert valley. However, since this is a very remote place, you may feel uncomfortable about lingering too long after sundown.

5 ENCANTO PARK • *Fifteenth Avenue and Encanto Boulevard, Phoenix; (602) 261-8993. Boat rentals, (602) 254-1520. GETTING THERE: The park is about two miles northeast of downtown; take any main street north, then go west on Encanto Boulevard and turn north into the park.* ❖

Encanto, which means "enchanted," is Phoenix's largest conventionally landscaped park, with grass, flower beds and trees. Most of the others, like South Mountain, are desert preserves. It is thus a particularly inviting place for lovers, who can snuggle on shady park benches beside a large lagoon, or take a paddleboat-for-two along the lagoon and its slender water channels. To recapture that youthful feeling, ride the old fashioned carousel at the Enchanted Island kiddie amusement park. After all, aren't you lovers feeling like children?

6 **THE LOUNGE AT THE BOULDERS** • *The Boulders Resort, 34631 N. Tom Darlington Dr., Carefree; (480) 488-2090. (www.wyndham.com/luxury) GETTING THERE: The resort is about thirty miles northeast of downtown Phoenix, on the border between Scottsdale and Carefree. Follow the Squaw Peak Freeway about thirteen miles to Bell Road, then go east less than five miles to Scottsdale Road and north twelve miles toward Carefree. The resort entrance is on the right, beyond el Pedregal Marketplace, after Scottsdale Road has changed its name to Tom Darlington Road.* ❖

Now, you two have got to behave yourselves, for this is a very proper place. Just hold hands as you gaze into the *kiva* fireplace in the lounge just outside the resort's Lantilla restaurant. A small couch in front of that firepit is a great place to relax together. If you plan a romantic dinner at the Lantilla (page 112), arrive early so you can enjoy a drink in the lounge. If you don't plan to dine, order a drink and absorb the splendid ambiance of the valley's very finest resort.

7 **THE LOUNGE AT ROYAL PALMS HOTEL** • *5200 E. Camelback Rd., Phoenix; (602) 840-3610. (www.royalpalmshotel.com) GETTING THERE: The hotel is about ten miles northeast of downtown Phoenix, off Camelback Road between Arcadia Drive and 56th Street.* ❖

The Royal Palms is a quite cozy resort, built in the 1920s as a private retreat for wealthy New York financier Delos Cooke. One doesn't need a financier's wealth to enjoy one of the most intimate spots in the valley—the dimly lit cocktail lounge adjacent to T. Cook's restaurant; see page 58. It's called the Cigar Lounge, but hopefully no one will be puffing one when the two of you arrive. Two facing couches are adjacent to a *kiva* fireplace in a quiet corner. Plan on dinner at the restaurant and arrive early for a pre-dinner cocktail in this cozy spot.

8 **THE LAGOON AT THE HYATT REGENCY SCOTTS-DALE RESORT** • *7500 E. Doubletree Ranch Rd., Scottsdale; (480) 991-3388. (www.hyatt.com) GETTING THERE: Drive north on Freeway 101 to exit 43, then go west on Via de Ventura, which becomes Doubletree Ranch Road. About three miles from the freeway, turn north into the resort complex. If you're coming from Scottsdale, go north on Scottsdale Road, turn east onto Doubletree Ranch and then north into the resort after less than half a mile.*

The Hyatt Regency Scottsdale is noted for its elaborate use of water and landscaping, with ten swimming pools, twenty-eight fountains and forty-seven waterfalls, all enhanced by lush plantings. Our favorite place to be alone in this extensive complex is the Lagoon. This quiet oasis is just off the Golden Swan restaurant, yet few people visit it.

Three benches-for-two are tucked among its thick thatch of palms and shrubbery and they're discreetly spaced. While you're here, consider dinner at the adjacent Golden Swan, which we rate below as the valley's most romantic restaurant.

9 TEMPE TOWN LAKE • *Downtown Tempe, just south of and parallel to the Red Mountain Freeway. Tempe Beach Park is open 5 a.m. to midnight; lake access is sunrise to sunset. Boat rentals are available from Rio Lago Cruise, (480) 517-4050. Rental office open Sunday-Thursday 10 to 6 and Friday-Saturday 10 to 8; MC/VISA/AMEX. GET-TING THERE: Take Van Buren Street about seven miles east from downtown Phoenix. In Tempe, it blends south into Mill Street, which crosses the lake. Go right onto Rio Salado Parkway for a block, then right again onto Ash Street and right yet again into the parking lot of Tempe Beach Park. ❖*

Tempe town officials created a community lake by putting a pair of small dams in the bed of the usually dry Salt River. They then created a nice grassy swatch called Tempe Beach Park, with shoreline walks on both sides of the pond. A park concessionaire rents paddleboats. This urban desert lake offers several options for the two of you—sit in the park and stare into the refreshing patch of blue, walk hand-in-hand along the shoreline, or be happy children and play in a paddle boat

10 DESERT BOTANICAL GARDEN • *1201 N. Galvin Parkway, Phoenix; (602) 941-1225. (www.dbg.org) Daily 7 to 8 May through September and 8 to 8 the rest of the year. GETTING THERE: The garden is about six miles east of downtown in Papago Park. Take Van Buren Street east to Galvin Parkway and turn north, or go east on I-10 and Freeway 202 and take the Van Buren exit.*

This fine botanical garden seems a rather public place for snuggling. However, it's generally lightly visited on weekdays and there are many shaded benches where you can sit and admire the fascinating desert flora around you. If you want to escape the few weekday visitors, stroll one of the lesser-trod paths that branch from the main Desert Discovery Trail. Both the Desert Wildflower Trail and Plants & People of the Sonoran Desert Trail offer shade ramadas.

THE TEN MOST ROMANTIC RESTAURANTS IN PHOENIX-SCOTTSDALE

As we noted in the introduction, many of the valley's opulent resorts are attuned to romance. It is thus no surprise that many of our most romantic restaurants—including our favorite—are tucked into these luxurious hideaways.

PRICING: Dollar signs indicate the price of dinner with entrée, soup or salad, not including drinks, appetizers or dessert: **$** = less than $10 per entrée; **$$** = $10 to $19; **$$$** = $20 to $29; **$$$$** = "Did you say you were buying?"

1 THE GOLDEN SWAN • *Hyatt Regency Scottsdale Resort, 7500 E. Doubletree Ranch Rd., Scottsdale; (480) 991-3388. (www.hyatt.com) Southwest cuisine; full bar service. Dinner nightly and Sunday brunch. Major credit cards; $$$$. GETTING THERE: See "The Lagoon at Hyatt Regency" listing above.*

Imagine the two of you dining beside a fountain lagoon, listening to the quiet splash of water and smelling perfume of flowers beside you. A scented oil lamp casts shadows that scamper across the table and dance in your lover's eyes. At the Hyatt Regency's signature restaurant, intimate tables for two line a floral planter wall beside the Lagoon, one of the many water courses in this luxury resort. A section of the restaurant even extends into the lagoon itself—a sunken seating area nearly surrounded by water. The fare is contemporary American with Southwest accents. For more on the restaurant and its menu, see Chapter Three, page 55.

2 CONVIVO • *7000 N. Sixteenth St., Phoenix; (602) 997-7676. Contemporary American; full bar service. Dinner Tuesday-Saturday. Major credit cards; $$$. GETTING THERE: The restaurant is on the Sixteenth Street side of the Squaw Peak Promenade at the northeast corner of Sixteenth and Glendale Avenue. Follow the Squaw Peak Freeway north from downtown, then take Glendale Avenue (exit 6) and go briefly west to Sixteenth.*

Although Convivo is a storefront restaurant in a strip mall, tucked behind a Walgreen's pharmacy, this is indeed a romantic spot. It's small size and simplicity—white nappery, blonde woods and walls adorned with modern art—create a special intimacy. Appropriately, many of its tables are for two, and they're set with fresh flowers tucked into tiny vases. The menu changes frequently, although your romantic dinner might consist of seared Hawaiian ono with avocado-lemon *coulis*, grilled sea bass with roasted tomato-basalmic sauce, grilled chicken breast with pine nut pesto, or pork chops with Port wine sauce and polenta.

3 LANTILLA • *At The Boulders resort, 34631 N. Tom Darlington Dr., Carefree; (480) 488-2090. (www.wyndham.com/luxury) American with Southwest accents; full bar service. Breakfast and dinner Monday-Saturday and Sunday brunch. Major credit cards; $$$$. GETTING THERE: See page 110.*

This is one of the most romantic and most expensive restaurants in the valley, and isn't your companion worth it? We've already praised the adjacent lounge as a cozy place to snuggle before a *kiva* fireplace, so it's quite logical to continue your intimate evening in the restaurant. As you await dinner, study the striking log and *lantilla* ceiling held up by a huge tree trunk, and the museum quality artifacts about the dining room. Gaze out the large windows at the surrounding desert gardens; note the lighted waterfall spilling over massive boulders that inspired the resort's name. You may want to stroll about later. For more on the restaurant and its menu, see Chapter Three, page 56.

4 *LON'S AT THE HERMOSA* • *Hermosa Inn, 5532 N. Palo Cristi Rd., Paradise Valley; (602) 955-7878. Southwest cuisine; full bar service. Lunch Monday-Friday, plus Sunday brunch; dinner nightly. Major credit cards; $$$ to $$$$. GETTING THERE: Take any major northbound street from downtown to Lincoln Drive, go east to 36th Street and turn south. It becomes Palo Cristi Road, and the inn is at the corner of Stanford Road.*

The classic Southwest adobe look of the Hermosa Inn (page 81) is reflected in its intimate dining room, with whitewashed walls, corbeled beam ceilings and Southwest art. If it's a cool evening, choose a table beside a warming *kiva* fireplace. For a romantic dinner under the stars, dine on the flagstone patio, at tables set with crisp white linens. Scented oil lanterns light the tables, and wood fires crackle in portable *horno* ovens placed about the patio. The menu is quite contemporary, offering entrées such as filet mignon over gorgonzola mashed potatoes, seared breast of duck with gnocchi, rack of lamb with poblano mashed potatoes or grilled salmon over white beans with Swiss chard.

5 *MARCO POLO SUPPER CLUB* • *2621 E. Camelback Rd., Phoenix, (602) 468-0100; and 8608 E. Shea Blvd., Scottsdale, (480) 483-1900. (www.marcopolosupperclub.com) Eclectic menu; full bar service. Lunch weekdays at Phoenix location only; dinner Monday-Saturday at both clubs; closed Sunday. Major credit cards; $$ to $$$. GETTING THERE: The Phoenix restaurant is in Camelback Plaza near 26th Street; the Scottsdale version is in Pima Crossing center just beyond the 84th street traffic light.* ❖

If you and your lover want to dance during dinner, plan an evening at one of these dapper 1920s style supperclubs. The décor is cool—dark woods, etched glass and white nappery. Walls are hung with black and white photos of movie and sports stars and other celebs. When a live band isn't playing, you'll likely hear recorded Sinatra or swing era music. Cozy banquettes invite snuggling as you choose from a busy menu that features several pastas, seafood, steaks, chops and some Chinese dishes—presumably in salute to Marco Polo, who wandered there a few centuries ago. The only negative about these supper-clubs is that cigar smoking is encouraged in the adjacent bar, and the stink probably will drift into the dining room.

6 **THE MARQUESA** • *At the Fairmont Scottsdale Princess, 575 E. Princess Dr., Scottsdale; (480) 585-4848. Spanish and continental; full bar service. Dinner nightly, plus Sunday brunch. Major credit cards; $$$$$. GETTING THERE: From downtown Phoenix, go north about fourteen miles on the Squaw Peak Freeway and follow Bell Road less than five miles east to Scottsdale Road. Head north briefly and turn east onto Princess Drive.*

This handsome Spanish style restaurant exudes old world romance with its crystal chandeliers, fine oil paintings and elegant detailing in carved woods and beveled glass. Seating is in plush booths or carved high-backed chairs. With a piano tinkling in the adjacent lounge or soft guitar music floating from hidden speakers, this is indeed a sensual place. And the food—more European *nouveau* than Spanish—is excellent. See Chapter Three, page 56, for menu items.

7 **MARY ELAINE'S** • *Fifth floor of the Phoenician, 6000 E. Camelback Rd., Scottsdale; (480) 941-8200. (www.thephoenician.com) French with contemporary American accents; full bar service. Dinner Monday-Saturday; closed Sunday. Major credit cards; $$$$. GETTING THERE: The resort is about ten miles northeast of downtown Phoenix. It's just north of Camelback Road between 44th and 64th streets on the western edge of Scottsdale.*

One of the area's most honored restaurants, with AAA Five Diamond and Mobil Five Star awards, also is one of its most romantic. All the elements are here—a gracious interior of fine art, plush floral carpeting, scalloped drapes, mirrored columns and chandeliers. The restaurant has a soft feminine touch, which is appropriate since it's named for the wife of Phoenician founder Charles Keating. The view from its fifth floor perch is quite striking, across the resort's lush landscaping to the lights of Phoenix and the valley. However, the most intimate seating is in curved banquettes at the back of the room, away from that vista. Wouldn't you really prefer looking into your lover's eyes? Or perhaps at the check. This is one of the most expensive restaurants in the valley, with entrées ranging into the fifties. To learn what fine fare you get for the price, see Chapter Three, page 53.

8 **OLD TOWN TORTILLA FACTORY** • *6910 E. Main St., Scottsdale; (480) 945-4567. Southwestern cuisine; full bar service. Dinner nightly. Major credit cards; $$ to $$$. GETTING THERE: It's at the corner of Main and 69th Street, about three blocks west of the Old Town shopping district.*

The name doesn't sound very romantic, although that's misleading. This is an attractive restaurant done in Arizona territorial style, featuring creative Southwest fare. The dining room has candle-lit tables and a few are in quiet corners. However, the most romantic part of this alleged tortilla factory is a large courtyard. A fountain whispers at the center, and several orange trees are entwined with white lights. Tables are set with multicolored chipped glass votive candles, the better to flicker into your lover's eyes. For details on the menu, which ventures far beyond smashed beans and rice, see Chapter Three, page 66.

9 *RISTORANTE SANDOLO* • *At the Hyatt Regency Scottsdale Resort, 7500 E. Doubletree Ranch Rd., Scottsdale; (480) 991-3388. (www.hyatt.com) Italian; full bar service. Dinner nightly. Major credit cards; $$$$. GETTING THERE: See "The Lagoon at Hyatt Regency" listing above, on page 110.*

A pistol packin' Mona Lisa won't stir your romantic souls, but how about a singing waiter, or a gondola ride with a singing "sandoleer?" If you're lighthearted about romance, take your significant other to this Italian bistro. Dinner includes a free ride around the resort's extensive water course in a Venetian gondola. The restaurant's Italian décor features whimsical artwork such as variations of the Mona Lisa, including a spaghetti Western version. Ask for a table overlooking the resort's water course and enjoy the view of lush landscaping, fountains and palm trees. And that isn't the voice of the gondolier still ringing in your ears. The Sandolo servers also serenade their patrons. So enjoy the singing and order classic Italian fare such as fettucini Alfredo, chicken parmigiana, beef cacciatore, ossobuco or one of the fresh-made pastas. Sandolo is both romantic and whimsical; note that the pistol packin' Mona is wearing a sly grin.

10 *TOP OF THE ROCK* • *At the Wyndham Buttes Resort, 2000 Westcourt Way, Tempe; (480) 225-9000. Contemporary American; full bar service. Dinner nightly and Sunday brunch. Major credit cards; $$$$. GETTING THERE: Drive south and east on I-10, take 48th Street exit 150, go south half a mile and turn left into the resort.* ❖

This restaurant is more spacious than intimate, with a dramatic circular shape topped by a spiral laced-wood roof suggesting an inverted waffle cone. However, it has one of the valley's best dining views, and therein lies the romance. Settle at a candle-lit table and gaze through floor-to-ceiling windows at the sparkling lights of Phoenix and the Valley of the Sun. An outdoor deck is a fine place to sit and sip cocktails; there, you can add a canopy of stars to the view. While not admiring the vista or one another, you can dine on fare such as *roulade* of turbot and prawns, rack of lamb with spinach and roasted bell pepper stuffing or mesquite grilled coriander salmon.

Chapter Eight

CREDIT CARD ABUSE

SHOPPING UNTIL YOU'RE DROPPING

With three million residents and another twelve million annual visitors, the Valley of the Sun offers shopping in abundance. There is no better place in Western America to abuse one's credit card.

Several large shopping centers are spread about the valley and many are covered malls, in deference to the summer sun. Scottsdale has a fine collection of art galleries and boutiques and Old Town has enough souvenir and curio shops to keep its visitors well supplied with bola ties and Kokopelli refrigerator magnets.

NOTE: Items marked with ❖ are listed elsewhere in this book; check the index for page numbers.

THE TEN BEST SHOPPING MALLS

Most of the area's malls are in the suburbs, since downtown Phoenix is more of a business center than a retail haven. It has only one shopping mall of significance, Arizona Center, which makes our Ten Best list. Beyond downtown, the valley has an interesting mix of malls, from typical shopping centers to trendy collections of boutiques to discount outlet stores.

1 BILTMORE FASHION PARK ● *2502 E. Camelback Rd., Phoenix; (602) 955-8401. (www.shopbiltmore.com) Most stores open weekdays 10 to 9, Saturday 10 to 6 and Sunday noon to 6. GETTING THERE: Take the Squaw Peak Freeway north about three miles to Highland, go east less than a mile to 24th Street, then north to Camelback. The shopping center is at the northeast corner of 24th and Camelback.*

Although not the valley's largest shopping complex, Biltmore Fashion Park is the most stylish, with an impressive array of upscale shops. And it is indeed a park, with thirty-five acres of landscaping set in five theme gardens. Its developers are so pleased with their gardens that they've created a *Botanical Walking Tour* brochure. Copies are available at a visitor center at the mall's west end, which is operated by the Phoenix-Valley of the Sun Convention & Visitor's Bureau. Among the trendy shops lining the mall's garden promenade are Williams-Sonoma, Ann Taylor, Gucci and Neiman Marcus. In keeping with the center's high end theme, anchors are Saks Fifth Avenue and Macy's. Biltmore Fashion Park also has the valley's best cluster of restaurants, all sharing a second level mezzanine at the mall's east end— Christopher's Fermier Brasserie, Che Bella Tuscan Grill and three that are featured in our dining chapter—Sam's Café (page 61), Steamers Genuine Seafood (page 60) and RoxSand (page 57).

2 ARIZONA CENTER ● *In downtown Phoenix, bounded by Van Buren, Third, Fillmore and Fifth streets; (602) 271-4000 or (602) 949-4353. (www.arizonacenter.com) Various hours for shops and restaurants.* ❖

Area residents and visitors come downtown to drink, dine, party and attend concerts and ball games, although they don't do much shopping here. The attractive and nicely landscaped Arizona Center was opened in the 1980s to lure credit card clutchers to Phoenix's urban core. Although it's one of the valley's most popular dining, drinking and entertainment venues, the retail shops haven't done very well. Several stores have closed through the years and the few surviving ones are specialty, clothing and giftware shops and art galleries. With its shift away from retail, this two-level outdoor center has become *the* place to dine and wine, with one of the area's best selections of restaurants and bars. Arizona Center has done much to keep downtown's nightlife scene alive. It also has a large Gardenside Food Court with tables inside and out, and a multi-screen theater complex. One of the center's most pleasing lures is its lushly landscaped ❖ Central Gardens, a favorite for people-watchers and noontime brownbaggers. The food court and two of its restaurants, Sam's Café (page 61) and Lombardi's, have tables overlooking this pretty parkland.

3 *ARIZONA MILLS • 5000 Arizona Mills Circle, Tempe; (480) 491-9700. (www.arizonamills.com) Most stores open Monday-Saturday 10 to 9:30 and Sunday 10 to 7. GETTING THERE: Head south on I-10 to exit 155, take Baseline Road briefly east, then turn north into the parking area.*

Creators of these "Mills"—there are more than a dozen across America—have come up with a simple concept. Build a massive warehouse-sized structure and stuff it with factory outlet stores, smaller shops and boutiques, restaurants and entertainment venues, then color it with a carnival atmosphere. Arizona Mills is where the budget-minded come to shop and sometimes to party. Among its anchors are JCPenny Outlet Store, Oshman's SuperSports, Neiman-Marcus Last Call, Off 5th Avenue by Saks, Virgin Megastore (page 125) and even a Hilo Hattie Store of Hawaii. It also has a multi-screen theater plus an Imax Theater, Gameworks video parlor and a large food court. The mall is *huge*—laid out in a squared circle and divided into several numbered "neighborhoods." Its corridors are busy with kiosks, full-body massage capsules, balloon vendors and caricature artists.

4 *THE BORGATA • Scottsdale Road between McDonald and Malcom drives, Scottsdale; (480) 998-1822. Most stores open 10 to 8. GETTING THERE: Go north on the Squaw Peak Freeway and then east on Indian School Road about seven miles to Scottsdale Road, then north two miles. The Borgata is on the left.*

The Borgata is the Valley of the Sun's handsomest shopping complex. It's styled as a fourteenth century Mediterranean village with weathered brick walls spilling with vines, a pretend watch tower and flagstone walkways. The open-air complex is built around two shady plazas with fountains and tables—inviting places to sit and watch the shoppers pass. There are no major anchors here. The rather small center is comprised mostly of boutiques, jewelry stores, high fashion clothiers and galleries with Western and native art. The Borgata has about forty shops and three restaurants—Mancuso's, the Patio Café with seats off the main plaza, and Café Terra Cotta (Chapter Three, page 54). Appropriate to its upscale aura, the Borgata's store directories are done in cast bronze, like little topo maps. The center hosts a rather urbane farmer's market every Friday afternoon from October through April (page 42), and it's noted for its glittery holiday décor during the Christmas season.

5 *EL PEDREGAL FESTIVAL MARKETPLACE • 34505 N. Scottsdale Rd., Scottsdale; (480) 488-1072. (www.elpedregal.com) Most shops open Monday-Saturday 10 to 5:30 and Sunday noon to 5. GETTING THERE: It's about thirty miles northeast of downtown, on the bor-*

der between Scottsdale and Carefree. Follow the Squaw Peak Freeway about thirteen miles to Bell Road, then go east less than five miles to Scottsdale Road and north twelve miles toward Carefree. The market-place is on the right, at the corner of Carefree Highway. ❖

This wonderfully odd shopping complex suggests a cross between Frank Lloyd Wright architecture and Tune Town. The style is "pueblo whimsy," with softly rounded corners and earth tones, splashed here and there with brilliant swatches of colo. The opulent Boulders Resort (page 73), within a short walk, has a similar pueblo look, although its décor is considerably more subdued. *El pedregal* means "a place with many stones," referring to the massive tumbled boulders that make this area a particularly striking swatch of desert. The center focuses on galleries and specialty shops, many with Western and native themes. Not a large complex, it has about thirty shops and three dining venues. Our preferred lunch stop here is Bakery Café, serving light fare and specialty drinks, which can be taken to tables in the adjacent patio. It's open from breakfast to late afternoon; (480) 488-4100. The Heard Museum has a small gallery here with changing exhibits and a native arts gift shop; (480) 488-9817.

A happening place as well as a shopping place, el Pedregal hosts concerts and other cultural activities, and visitors may encounter an artist at work or a special art exhibit.

6 *FIESTA MALL* • *Southern Road at Alma School Road, Mesa; (480) 833-4121. (www.shopfiesta.com) Most stores open Monday-Saturday 10 to 9 and Sunday 11 to 6. GETTING THERE: Drive east on the Superstition Freeway to Alma School Road (exit 178), go north briefly and then west into the mall.*

This attractive mall has about 150 stores, with Dillard's, Sears, Macy's and Robinsons-May as its anchors. It's on two floors, with the entry at ground level and a second level of shops below. Although this is an older mall, it has been redone with an appealing Southwest décor. If you like to take a daily walk, this is a good place to come on a hot or stormy day, since the format is rather simple. Each of the two levels is laid out in a large square with upper level stores balconied above the lower shops. The mall has a large food court called Cafés at Fiesta, with fourteen takeouts. There's a customer service stand on the mall's west end on the lower level, outside of Dillard's.

7 *PARADISE VALLEY MALL* • *Cactus Road and Tatum Boulevard, Phoenix; (602) 953-2959. (www.westcor.com) Most stores open Monday-Saturday 10 to 9 and Sunday 11 to 6. GETTING THERE: From downtown, go north on the Squaw Peak Freeway about twelve miles, then take Cactus Road (exit 10) east for six miles; the mall is on the north side of Cactus.*

Although this large single level covered mall is a couple of decades old, it has been refurbished to keep pace with newer, flashier shopping centers. While not opulent, it's a comfortable place to shop, with groups of cushioned chairs spaced along the main corridor. This is essentially a middle to upper price range mall, anchored by Robinbsons-May, Sears, Dillard's, JCPenny and Macy's. More than 150 stores, shops and boutiques are tucked among them. You can get a map—or get pointed in the right direction—at a service center just outside Robinsons-May. The mall has a multi-screen theater, a toddlers' area and an attractive food court called Café Paradise, with nearly a dozen take-outs. It has seating on two levels, with a *faux* boulder fountain as a focal point. More tables are on an adjacent outdoor patio. The mall is in the middle of a major shopping area, surrounded by satellite stores such as REI (page 124), Target, CompUSA, ABCO supermarket, Circuit City and Borders Books and Music.

8 SCOTTSDALE FASHION SQUARE • 7014 E. Camelback Rd., Scottsdale; (480) 941-2140. (www.westcor.com) Most stores open Monday-Saturday 10 to 9 and Sunday 11 to 6. GETTING THERE: The mall is half a mile north of Old Town Scottsdale, on the west side of Scottsdale Road. From downtown Phoenix, go north on the Squaw Peak Freeway and then east on Indian School Road about seven miles to Scottsdale Road, then north three blocks to Camelback.

One of the valley's largest covered malls, Fashion Square spreads its 225 shops, boutiques, galleries and restaurants over the intersection of Scottsdale and Camelback roads. It's an impressive facility, with stores on three levels beneath greenhouse roofs. Cascading fountains, courtyards and palm trees provide a pleasing environment for credit card abuse. Particularly interesting is a U-shaped curtain waterfall draping around a stairway near the Grand Rotunda concierge desk. Some of the shopping areas are mingled with the mall's covered parking facilities, which can be confusing for first time visitors. However, it's convenient for regulars, who can park close to their destinations. The mall's anchors are Dillards, Robinsons-May, Nordstrom and Sears. It has eight restaurants, a large food court and a multi-screen theater. Under construction at press time was a new addition called Scottsdale Waterfront. A waterfront in the desert? Stay tuned.

9 SCOTTSDALE PAVILIONS • Indian Bend Road and Pavilions Boulevard, Scottsdale; (480) 933-1626. Stores have various hours. GETTING THERE: From Phoenix, take I-10 and Freeway Loop 202 east, then Loop 101 north about seven miles to Indian Bend Road (exit 44) and go west into the complex.

Occupying land leased from the Salt River Pima-Maricopa Indian Community, Scottsdale Pavilions is not a mall but a major retail district targeting mostly budget to middle-range shoppers. This is your venue if you want to find several major chain stores in one handy place. Among its occupants are Target, Cost Plus, Miller's Outpost, Ross Dress for Less, Sports Authority, Hallmark, Home Place, Toys R Us, Home Depot, Mervyn's, Circuit City and more. It as a large multi-screen United Artist Theater and even a golf course and driving range.

10 SUPERSTITION SPRINGS CENTER • *6555 E. Southern Ave., Mesa; (480) 832-0212. Most stores open Monday-Saturday 10 to 9 and Sunday 11 to 6. GETTING THERE: Drive west on the Superstition Freeway, take Superstition Springs exit 187 briefly north, then go east on Auto Drive into the mall.*

Large, bright and airy with greenhouse skylights, this two-level mall serves the Valley of the Sun's booming east end. It has about 130 stores, with JCPenny, Mervyn's, Dillards, Sears and Robinsons-May as anchors. Like Fiesta Mall, it's on two tiers with the upper section at ground level. The mall is designed to appeal to families, with a desert botanical walk, an old fashioned carousel, a carnival type fun zone called Pocket Change, a multi-screen theater complex and a large food court with eleven outlets. An information counter is on the mall's east end, on the lower level opposite JCPenny.

THE TEN BEST SPECIALTY STORES AND SHOPPING AREAS

What's your specialty? Fine art, tourist trinkets, CDs of Ukrainian folk music or hiking gear for the surrounding mountains? If it exists, you'll find it in the Valley of the Sun. This list contains a mix of specialty shopping areas and specialty stores.

1 THE BEST PLACE TO BUY SOUTHWESTERN ART: *Old Town Scottsdale • A two-block section of Main Street from Scottsdale Road to Goldwater Boulevard. GETTING THERE: Go north on the Squaw Peak Freeway and then east on Indian School Road about seven miles to Scottsdale Road. Turn right and drive two blocks to Main Street.*

Most of Old Town Scottsdale's dozens of shops sell tourist trinkets and T-shirts. However, it also has some excellent fine arts galleries, which focus primarily on Southwestern, native peoples and cowboy art. Several are along two long blocks of Main Street, reaching from Scottsdale Road to Goldwater Boulevard. Landscaped sidewalks flank both sides of Main and several fine bronzes are displayed outside on this "gallery row." Among our favorites along are the Heritage and Legacy galleries, sharing the corner of Main and Scottsdale, with fine selections of Western and native paintings and large bronze pieces;

Trailside Galleries at 7145 E. Main, with a good choice of bronzes and paintings; Joan Cawley Gallery at 7135 E. Main, with some whimsical animal carvings along with Western scenics and sculptures; and Expressions in Bronze Gallery at Main and Marshall, featuring painted bronzes of native people by New Mexico artist Dave McGary.

Two other large galleries flank the entrance to Scottsdale Civic Center Mall at Main and Brown Avenue—Bischoff's at the Park, and another Trailside gallery. Bischoff's is busy with Western, native peoples and Hispanic art, artifacts, books and recordings. Trailside features paintings, bronzes and other sculptures, mostly with Western themes.

2 BEST PLACE TO BUY "TOURIST ART": Gilbert Ortega Arts and Gifts • *Several locations in Scottsdale's Old Town, plus a shop in the Hyatt Regency in downtown Phoenix at 122 N. Second Street; (602) 949-0436.*

Are these Western art galleries or souvenir shops? Certainly. The Gilbert Ortega galleries and gift shops best represent the Southwest style of—well—tourist shopping. The merchandise mix ranges from expensive bronzes and paintings to Western attire to Kokopelli refrigerator magnets. The largest of several Gilbert Ortega shops is on the northwest corner of First Street and Brown Avenue in Old Town. Another big one is around the block at Main and Scottsdale Road. Both brim with Western, native peoples and other Southwest-theme merchandise. The selections include everything from macho Western style furniture to museum quality artwork to leather belts to bola ties and assorted tourist trinkets.

3 THE BEST BOOK STORE: Barnes & Noble Booksellers • *7685 W. Bell Road at 76th Avenue across from Arrowhead Mall, Peoria, (623) 487-9022; 10235 N. Metro Parkway East near 28th Drive and Peoria, Phoenix, (602) 678-0088; 4847 E. Ray Road at 48th Street, Phoenix, (480) 940-7136; and 10500 N. 90th Street at Shea, Scottsdale, (480) 391-0048. Most stores open Monday-Saturday 9 to 11 and Sunday 10 to 10.*

Phoenix doesn't have a huge independent book store such as the Tattered Cover in Denver or Powell's City of Books in Portland. However, it does have four Barnes & Noble outlets. B&N is our favorite chain, not only because it sells a lot of **DiscoverGuides**, but because it is the *compleat* book store. The outlets carry tens of thousands of titles plus a good selection of CDs and cassettes, and they offer cozy cafés and comfortable places to sit among the aisles of books. Like large public libraries, these places invite browsing through the world of literature and music.

4 *THE BEST HEALTHY FOOD STORE: Wild Oats* • *3933 E. Camelback Road at 40th Street, Phoenix, (602) 954-0584; and at 7139 E. Shea Boulevard at Scottsdale Road, Scottsdale, (480) 905-1441. Daily 7 to 10.*

We call these healthy food stores instead of health food stores because they're full service supermarkets that feature—as much as possible—organic and pesticide-free groceries. The stores also have books and magazines on nutrition and natural living, whole grain bakeries, build-in-yourself salad bars and delis. These markets have a few tables near their delis and outside, in case you want to take a healthy lunch or snack break. And if you're one of those no meat, no fish, no dairy health fanatics, this is where you go for your soy yogurt, brown rice and *couscous.*

5 *THE BEST LIQUOR STORE: Sportsman's Fine Wines & Spirits* • *3205 E. Camelback Rd., Phoenix; (602) 955-7730. Monday 10 to 10, Tuesday-Saturday 9 to 10 and Sunday noon to 7. MC/VISA. GETTING THERE: It's in a small mall at the southwest corner of Camelback and 32nd Street.*

Phoenix doesn't have huge liquor stores on the scale of those in California and Nevada, although Sportsman's certainly can satisfy your thirst. It's mostly a serious wine shop with more than 2,500 wines available, including some fashionably overpriced "collectibles." Single malt Scotches and tequilas are other specialties. And if you want to have a wine picnic in one of the nearby desert parks, Sportsman's can provide all the ingredients. It has a small deli that offers made-to-order sandwiches to go with your newly-purchased wine. Or have a snack here, accompanied by sips from the wine tasting bar.

6 *THE BEST STORE FOR COUCH POTATOES: Field of Dreams* • *Scottsdale Fashion Square at 7014 E. Camelback Road at Scottsdale Road, Scottsdale, (480) 874-1100; and 770 Arrowhead Towne Center in north Glendale, (623) 773-2200. Monday-Saturday 10 to 9 and Sunday 11 to 6.*

If you're looking for a gift for the guy who spends Sundays watching all the ball games, these stores can offer some interesting additions to his trophy shelf. They sell autographed sports action photos, posters, baseballs, gloves, footballs, football helmets and other memorabilia from stars past and present. (We were dismayed to note that a baseball autographed by Sammy Sousa fetched a higher price than one signed by Willie Mays.) Although most of the merchandise is sports related, the stores also have autographed movie and TV star photos, posters and other Tinseltown souvenirs.

7 **THE BEST STORE FOR THINKING COUCH POTATOES:**
Discovery Channel Store • *Scottsdale Fashion Square at 7014 E.*
Camelback Rd., Scottsdale, (480) 941-4300; and Chandler Fashion
Square at 3111 W. Chandler Blvd., Chandler, (480) 917-0135.

For those whose TV viewing leans more toward Discovery, A&E
and PBS, this specialty store follows the same "Entertain your brain"
concept as the TV channel. It offers such cerebral items as nature, science and history videos; science books; semi-serious binoculars and
telescopes and intellectual games such as backgammon, chess and a
really cool *New York Times* touch screen electronic crossword puzzle.

8 **THE BEST PLACE TO BUY SOMETHING SENSUOUS:**
Victoria's Secret • *In Arrowhead Town Center, Glendale, (623) 412-*
8225; Biltmore Fashion Park at 2888 E. Camelback Rd., Phoenix, (602)
957-4516; Metrocenter at 9802 N. Parkway East, Phoenix, (602) 944-
0826; Paradise Valley Mall at 4550 E. Cactus Rd., Phoenix, (602) 996-
2890; Scottsdale Fashion Square at 7014 E. Camelback Rd., (480) 990-
7551; and Superstition Springs Center at 6555 E. Southern Ave., Mesa,
(480) 396-3350.

Unmentionables are quite mentionable these days, and Victoria's
Secret has brought new levels of sensual dignity to scanty and sexy underthings. At the start of this century, the firm unveiled a $10 million
Millennium Miracle Bra and thong, studded with 2,000 diamonds and
sapphires. The Millennium came and went apparently with no takers
for the size 34B support bra, so it still may available if you really want
to impress your lady love. And if her cups don't runneth over, the firm
will alter it to fit. Lack the capital for such an uplifting investment?
You can buy her a regular Miracle Bra for considerably less. Victoria's
stores feature a full line of other sexy underthings and outer things as
well. Always with class and never in poor taste, the shops are the best
places in the Valley of the Sun to buy something nice for your lady.
The naughty comes later.

9 **THE BEST STORE FOR OUTDOOR TYPES: REI** • *12634*
Paradise Village Parkway West, Scottsdale, (602) 996-5400. Monday-
Friday 10 to 9, Saturday 10 to 6 and Sunday 11 to 5. GETTING THERE:
From downtown, go north on the Squaw Peak Freeway about twelve
miles, then take Cactus Road (exit 10) east six miles to Paradise Village
Parkway West. Go north briefly, then turn west into Village Center.
There's another REI at 1405 W. Southern Ave., Tempe; (480) 967-5494.

REI means Recreational Equipment International and it's the ultimate outdoor store. Outdoor types will find everything they need in
these warehouse sized stores—tents, sleeping bags, backpacks, fanny

packs, outdoor clothing for all ages and both sexes, camping gear, freeze-dried food and power bars, kayaks, bikes, and winter sports gear (in season). The Paradise Village store has a special section for climbing gear and a small climbing wall to try it out. A mezzanine is busy with outdoor books and maps, with special emphasis on Arizona travel, hiking, mountain biking and river running.

10 THE BEST PLACE TO BUY RECORDED SOUND:

Virgin Megastore ● *In the Arizona Mills mall at 5000 Arizona Mills Circle, Tempe; (480) 413-1700. (www.virginmega.com) Monday-Saturday 10 to 9:30 and Sunday 10 to 7. GETTING THERE: Head south on I-10 to exit 155, take Baseline Road briefly east, then turn north into the parking area.*

If it has been recorded, you'll likely find it in the Valley of the Sun's largest CD and cassette music store. This huge sanctuary of sound has it all—rock, pop, hip-hop, rockabilly, gospel, soul, bluegrass, blues, jazz, country, domestic and international folk, Latin, classical and more. If you'd like to try before you buy, Virgin has dozens of CD listening stations including one for each of the current Top Forty hits. It also has books—mostly relating to music and entertainment, plus videogames, movies on videocassette and DVD, and a café.

*A variety of mere nothings
gives more pleasure than
uniformity of something.*
— **Jean Paul Richter**

Chapter Nine

ODD ENDS
ASSORTED BITS AND PIECES

Do you want to get physical during your visit to the Valley of the Sun? It has miles of walking and cycling paths, plus hiking trails in its desert mountain parks. Or would you prefer a low-key vacation, enjoying the views, taking photos or just listening to your favorite music and reading more about this fascinating area? This chapter consists of assorted lists that don't seem to fit into other lists.

NOTE: Items marked with ❖ are listed elsewhere in this book; check the index for page numbers.

GETTING PHYSICAL: THE TEN BEST WALKS, HIKES AND BIKE ROUTES

The single most dramatic feature of this valley is its rugged desert-mountain topography. Several rocky peaks and ridges rise abruptly from the valley floor, offering stark contrast to the sprawling suburbia that surrounds them. Many are preserved in an elaborate system of public parks covering more than 40,000 acres. No other metropolitan region in America has such a vast area of natural parklands. These are splendid places, with desert gardens, rocky ridges, rugged canyons and sheer cliff faces.

The mountain parks are interlaced with miles of hiking, biking and riding trails. Many of these parks are technically wilderness areas, since plant life has been left relatively undisturbed and development has been limited to trail systems and a few access roads. However, hiking or biking these trails isn't a wilderness experience. Phoenicians love their mountain parks and they keep the trails busy.

A good source of material on outdoor activities in this area and beyond is the **Arizona Public Lands Information Center** at 222 N. Central Avenue in downtown Phoenix, between Van Buren and Monroe; (602) 417-9300. (*www.publiclands.org*). It's open weekdays 8:30 to 4:30. Jointly operated by the Bureau of Land Management, U.S. Forest Service and Public Lands Interpretive Association, it has scores of books, maps and brochures on outdoor lures. Among its offerings is a free *Metropolitan Phoenix Area Bike Ways* map, produced by the Maricopa Association of Governments. It outlines multi-use trails as well as bike paths, so it's useful for cyclists, hikers and walkers.

We list below, in groups of five, our favorite walking/hiking and biking routes, starting each list with our top choice.

THE BEST WALKING AND HIKING ROUTES

We begin with an ambitious stroll around downtown Phoenix. If you're a walker and a Phoenix visitor, we suggest taking this long stroll soon after you arrive to get yourself oriented. From there, we adjourn to the suburbs for recommended walks and hikes in the surrounding desert and its mountains.

1 DOWNTOWN PHOENIX ● *Starting from Heritage & Science Park. About two and a half miles, all level. GETTING THERE: The park is on the eastern edge of downtown, wrapped by Fifth, Monroe, Seventh and Washington streets.*

A group called Downtown Phoenix Partnership, Inc., which seeks to rekindle interest in the city's urban core, has designated a ninety-square-block area as Copper Square. Not really an historic district, it encompasses most of downtown, which contains more modern highrises than historic structures. The name comes from the fact that Arizona produces more copper than all of the other states combined. Some of the early copper millionaires helped finance Phoenix, although the mines were—and still are—elsewhere. The group produces business and dining guides to the area, each with detailed maps that you can use to follow our walking route. These brochures are available at racks throughout downtown, and at visitor centers.

This urban hike weaves an erratic course through Copper Square, starting—appropriately—in one of the town's few historic sites. The walk begins, as we noted above, at the **Heritage & Science Park.** It's home to three major attractions that featured elsewhere in this book: ❖ **Heritage Square** with several historic houses, the **Arizona Science Center** and the **Phoenix Museum of History**.

From Heritage Square, angle north and west across Monroe, passing through the downtown campus of **Arizona State University**. You'll exit at the corner of Fifth and Van Buren, catty-corner from ❖ **Arizona Center,** with its highrise office tower and low-rise shopping, restaurant and entertainment complex. Walk to mid-block between Fifth and Fourth, then angle to the right past the Arizona Center office tower to ❖ **Central Gardens**. It's a lushly landscaped swatch of flower beds, palms and fountains between the tower and the center's shops.

After prowling Arizona Center, exit the southwest corner, go a block south on Third Street and then west on Monroe, passing the ❖ **Herberger Theater Center**. It's home to several area performing arts groups. Then go left (south) onto Second Street to the ❖ **Hyatt Regency,** the city's largest downtown hotel. For a crows-eye view of the Phoenix metrosprawl, step inside and take a glass elevator to the 24th floor Compass Restaurant. After exiting the Hyatt, you may want to cross Second Street to Phoenix Civic Plaza and admire the foyer of ❖ **Symphony Hall** with its mirrored walls and glass chandeliers.

Then wrap around the southeast corner of the Hyatt and stroll west half a block to **Museo Mexicano** at 147 E. Adams. This small archive displays artifacts and changing exhibits concerning the area's rich Hispanic culture. It's open Tuesday-Saturday 10 to 4: (602) 257-5536.

Continue west a block and a half on Adams to ❖ **Renaissance Square** at Central Avenue. An attractive courtyard sits at the base of this highrise office structure. You're now in the heart of downtown, with glass and steel rising all about. Walk two more blocks on Adams to Second Avenue and check out the elaborate façade of the 1929 Spanish Baroque ❖ **Orpheum Theatre** with its ornate *frieze* of comedy and tragedy masks. Walk southward along the east side the theater through a landscaped plaza to the modern **Phoenix City Hall** at the corner of Washington Street and Third Avenue. Its soaring lobby is topped by a galleria style arched glass canopy, held up by steel and concrete columns. From here, continue another block west on Washington past an old federalist style building to the more modern **Phoenix Municipal Court Building.** It's a square rose-colored masonry structure accented by a six-story concave glass façade.

Across the street at Washington and Fourth Avenue is the dramatically stark seven-story **U.S. Federal Court Building** completed in 2001. It resembles a huge box of glass and steel, with a free-standing silo-shaped structure inside. That silo contains the main courtrooms while other offices occupy balconies on the four sides of this great hollow square. Return to Third and Washington and angle to your right into the desert-landscaped **Caesar Chavez Plaza,** which honors the United Farm Workers' leader.

To your left is the **Historic Phoenix City Hall,** with a busy façade best described as Spanish colonial and federalist. Completed in 1929 and still housing some city offices, it's worth a peek for its rose marble interior walls and art deco chandeliers. Note particularly the ornate copper doors on the building's main entrance and elevators. Take one of those old fashioned lifts to the third floor for a look at a **presidential portraits** collection, donated to the city by the Del Webb corporation. The portraits are in three rooms which are usually open to the public—the Ceremonial Room, Community Room and meeting room 301. When we last looked, the most recent portrait was that of George (not W) Bush.

Continue through Caesar Chavez Plaza and cross Jefferson Street to the **Maricopa County Court and Government Complex.** It's not particularly interesting, except for a bronze statue of a rather nude family group in the front plaza. (They lost their clothes in court?) You can catch a bit of lunch here in the building's **Change of Venue Dining Market Place.** Press eastward a block to Jefferson and First Avenue for ❖ **Patriots Square,** where you can enjoy nice skyline views of Phoenix rising. On your right along Jefferson Street are some of the few still-surviving brick and masonry office buildings from yesterday. If you didn't catch lunch at Change of Venue, you'll find several small cafés along here, including **Kirin Wok,** which we recommend for budget dining in Chapter Five, page 90.

From Patriots Square, continue eastward on Jefferson to ❖ **America West Arena,** home to the Phoenix Suns NBA basketball squad and Phoenix Coyotes NHL hockey team. It has a food court, and its Suns Team Shop sells logo items for various teams. Next door is ❖ **Bank One Ballpark,** where the National League Arizona Diamondbacks chase fly balls. The complex includes the Copper Club Restaurant and lounge and one of our favorite pubs, ❖ **Friday's Front Row.** You can view this imposing stadium's interior by taking an elevator up to the pub, which hangs over left field. For a much more detailed look, take a public tour; details are in Chapter Two, page 39.

From the ballyard, cross Jefferson at Fifth Street, backtrack to Fourth and follow steps up to **Phoenix Civic Plaza.** Work northward along the plaza beside the **Phoenix Convention Center,** paralleling Third Street. This elevated plaza is a pleasant place to pause from your stroll. It has several outdoor seating areas that provide nice views of downtown highrises.

Continue along the plaza, shifting to your right to cross a pedestrian bridge over Washington Street, then walk another two blocks and return to earth at Monroe Street. Just to your left at the corner of Monroe and Third Street is the handsome twin-towered **St. Mary's Basilica.** It was established in 1881 and the present structure dates from 1915; it's the oldest Catholic church in the valley. Walk a block east on Monroe and you're right back where you started, at Heritage and Science Park.

2 **SOUTH MOUNTAIN PARK AND PRESERVE** ● *Holbert Trail to Dobbin's Lookout; moderately difficult, about five miles round trip. Park gates open daily 5:30 a.m. to 10 p.m.; visitor center open 9 to 5 Monday-Saturday; closed Sunday; (602) 534-6324. (www.ci.phoenix.az.us/parks/hikesoth.html) GETTING THERE: From downtown Phoenix, start south on First Avenue, which blends into Central Avenue and leads directly into the park after about eight miles. The trailhead is at the far end of the main parking area, reached by turning left shortly after driving through the park entrance gate.*

Covering nearly 17,000 acres, South Mountain is one of America's largest municipal parks. Eighteen hiking and walking trails interlace its rock-strewn, steeply sloping cactus garden terrain. Our favorite is the Holbert Trail, which climbs up through a rocky canyon toward the peak. At a high ridgeline, it intersects with the National Trail that leads all the way to Mexico. Of course, we don't go that far.

The best time to take this hike is early in the morning, since it travels up the west side of that desert canyon for much of the way, and you'll be in shade. The Holbert is marked with numbered posts matched to a trail guide that points out features along the way. This trail begins rather tamely, wandering along the foothills of South Mountain, and then it begins a serious climb up that aforementioned canyon. It takes you into a lush desert garden of saguaro and other cactus, palo verde and mesquite. From February through March, it presents a spectacular floral show of yellow-blooming brittlebush, blue lupine, flame-tipped ocotillo and assorted cactus flowers.

After hiking a couple of miles, you'll see a hole-in-the-rock ridge. A short distance beyond, look for a sign for the Dobbins Extension trail that takes you to Dobbin's Lookout. Sitting just below the mountain's peak at 2,330 feet, it offers predictably impressive valley vistas. A brass "mountain finder" on a raised platform points out natural and manmade landmarks. While the views are nice, they're almost always tinged by smog these days. Also, what solitude you enjoyed on the trail will be lost, since this viewpoint can be reached by the park's winding scenic drive. If you return to the Holbert Trail and continue upward, you'll soon intersect that drive, and a sign marks the Holbert's junction with the National Trail. Just above, you'll see a forest of antennae sprouting from South Mountain's peak.

3 **SQUAW PEAK RECREATION AREA** ● *Squaw Peak Summit Trail, 2.5-mile round trip; very steep and difficult. Park gates open 5 a.m. to 11 p.m. GETTING THERE: Drive north on the Squaw Peak Freeway about five miles, take Lincoln Drive briefly east, then turn north onto Squaw Peak Drive and follow it into the preserve. The nearest parking lot to the trailhead is Summit, the first one on the left.*

Squaw Peak is one of the area's most prominent landmarks—a rugged cone of tilted strata rising abruptly from the suburban desert northeast of downtown Phoenix. The trail to the top, while mercifully short, is the steepest in the Phoenix desert-mountain preserves. Think of it not as a hiking trail, but as a 1.2-mile rough stone staircase. Elevation gain averages a thousand feet a mile and that's *steep*.

The trail is essentially a series of rough stepping stones switchbacking up the southwestern side of the mountain. Up to a thousand people a day chug up this incline. On most weekends, the recreation area's parking lots are filled by early morning, and hikers are so close that they seem almost in lock-step. Except for the switchbacks, the scene resembles those famous Klondike Gold Rush photos of miners struggling up Chilkoot Pass. Start early in the day, both for cooler weather and to avoid the worst crowds.

You'll begin climbing steeply soon after leaving the parking lot, trudging up those switchback stepping stones. You will get a brief respite after three-quarters of a mile as the trail follows a ridgeline. Then it becomes even steeper on the final assault, ending with a scramble up to the mountain's twin peaks, which essentially are rockpiles. Most hikers are satisfied to achieve the west peak. Once there, they choose an outcropping or a cleft and slump down wearily, like exhausted marmots. The hardier—and those with no fear of heights—scramble to the even more rough-hewn and slightly higher east peak.

The views are awesome from either promontory—a dizzying 360-degree sweep of the valley. The vista is more impressive than from Dobbin's Lookout, since Squaw Peak is in the heart of the valley, closer to downtown highrises and other landmarks.

4 DESERT FOOTHILLS SCENIC DRIVE • *From el Pedregal Festival Marketplace to Ashler Hills Road. About three miles round trip; level with gentle dips. GETTING THERE: Follow the Squaw Peak Freeway about thirteen miles to Bell Road, then go east less than five miles to Scottsdale Road and north about twelve miles to el Pedregal at the corner of Carefree Highway.*

Several miles of northern Scottsdale Road and paralleling Cave Creek Road have been designated as Desert Foothills Scenic Drive. This is a thickly vegetated area backdropped by rugged mountains and dramatic piles of boulders that seem to have been scattered by some careless prehistoric giant. The Scottsdale Road section from el Pedregal south to Ashler Hills Road is a virtual desert garden and it has separate pedestrian paths on either side of highway. Signs identify the various plants along the way. Although they're canted toward the highway to give motorists a 55-mile-an-hour botany lesson, they can be read from the walkway as well. And of course, strollers and cyclists can admire this desert garden with much more detail.

Begin your walk by exploring ❖ **el Pedregal,** then stroll over to ❖ **The Boulders,** the area's most dramatically situated resort. To reach it, walk to the northern edge of el Pedregal and follow an extension of Cave Creek Highway east through a lift gate. Motorists need a code to activate the gate although there's room for pedestrians to walk through. Return to el Pedregal, cross to the west side of Scottsdale Road and start south along the pedestrian path, opposite **Terravita Shopping Center.** The path dips in and out of shallow dry washes, giving it pleasant contour as it travels south. Enjoy this nice stroll among the saguaro, ocotillo, palo verde and other desert plants, then cross Scottsdale Road—carefully, for the traffic's thick—and return on the other side. When we last strolled, the path ended at Ashler Hills Road, just over a mile from el Pedregal. However, it may have been extended by the time you arrive.

5 CHAPARRAL PARK • *Corner of Hayden and Scottsdale roads in north Scottsdale. Park hours are sunrise to 10:30. Level route with a one-mile par course. GETTING THERE: From Phoenix, take I-10 and Freeway Loop 202 east, then Loop 101 north about 4.5 miles to Chaparral (exit 46), and go west just over a mile to the park.*

A one-mile walking and running path circles a duck-busy lake in the center of this north Scottsdale park. This is a good place to do your morning workout, taking as many turns as needed to shed the pounds from last night's margaritas and burritos. And if you had too much dessert, you can work the par course as you circle the pond. On the lake's west side, the path merges with our Hayden Road bike route (page 134), then it peels away to complete its loop of the lagoon.

THE BEST BIKE ROUTES

The Valley of the Sun has few separate bike paths, although several of its major roads have marked bike lanes on the shoulders. Our favorite route is between Carefree and northern Scottsdale because it travels through an appealing swatch of desert. However, it's heavily trafficked so this route shouldn't be attempted by novice riders.

6 CAREFREE TO RAWHIDE • *On Scottsdale and Tom Darlington roads; flat with a few gentle rises, eighteen miles round trip.*

Start your ride at ❖ **el Pedregal Festival Marketplace** at the corner of Scottsdale Road and Carefree Highway. It has abundant parking and it's definitely worth a browse, with its many galleries and specialty shops. From here, pedal into the nearby ❖ **Boulders Resort** by following an extension of Carefree Highway east toward a lift gate. (See details in the "Desert Foothills Scenic Drive" walk on the previous page.)

Depart this elegant resort by following its main access road northwest, which takes you to Tom Darlington Drive, an extension of Scottsdale Road. Turn right and follow it about a mile into the cute little planned community of ❖ **Carefree.** There's no marked bike lane on this stretch, so ride with caution. At the center of town, turn right onto Wampum Way and follow it to Sundial Circle. Your destination is the ❖ **world's largest sundial,** with a 62-foot-long arm casting its shadow over a clock in an attractive circular garden.

From Carefree, follow Tom Darlington back to el Pedregal and pedal south on the pedestrian path alongside Scottsdale Road. (This is the route we walked above; it's marked as a pedestrian path although no signs prohibit bicycles.) Gentle dips through dry washes give this route a pleasing contour and thick vegetation shelters you from the traffic, although not from its noise. Signs along the way identify some of the desert plants, providing a linear botany lesson as you pedal. The separate path ends about a mile beyond el Pedregal at Ashler Hills Road, although a marked bike lane continues from here, on the shoulder of Scottsdale Road.

The bike lane ends at Pinnacle Peak Road, just short of the Western tourist town of ❖ **Rawhide.** Return north along Scottsdale Road, again picking up the separate pedestrian path. Watch on your right for Westland Road, a side street that leads to several subdivisions tucked into these thick desert gardens. We particularly like the classic Santa Fe adobe style homes along this route. The street, which is lightly traveled, extends about a mile eastward. Pedal to the end, then return to Scottsdale Road and complete your ride back to el Pedregal.

7 *CAVE CREEK ROAD* • *From Bell Road to Cave Creek and Carefree. About thirty miles round trip; gentle upgrade on the first leg. GETTING THERE: Take the Squaw Peak Freeway about thirteen miles north from downtown, then go west about a mile on Bell Road to Cave Creek Road.*

A marked bike lane follows Cave Creek Road from Bell Road into the town of Cave Creek. Much of this route isn't very interesting, despite being part of the Desert Foothills Scenic Drive. However, it provides a good workout if you just want to crank off a few miles. Avoid it during rush hours, since it's a busy commute route. We'd recommend an early morning weekend ride. You'll find plenty of parking in strip malls at the Cave Creek-Bell Road junction.

Initially, you'll pedal through a rather busy commercial district, then the road enters a residential area. It soon reaches beyond the spread of suburbia and travels through open desert, although it still isn't particularly scenic. As you approach Cave Creek, the desert scenery begins to improve. You'll pedal past rough, rocky hills that mark the distinct terrain around the Cave Creek-Carefree area. Note the homes notched into steep slopes, surrounded by saguaro cactus.

The bike lane ends shortly after you enter the rustic former mining town of ❖ **Cave Creek**, although traffic is relatively slow here. On the south side of town, follow signs to the ❖ **Cave Creek Museum**. Back on Cave Creek Road, you'll shortly encounter ❖ **Frontier Town**, a rustic cowboy-tourist shopping and dining complex. About a mile beyond, you can turn right at a stop sign onto Tom Darlington Drive and pedal east into ❖ **Carefree**, part of our "Carefree to Rawhide" trek above.

You can turn this into a semi-loop trip—more accurately, a tadpole shape—by continuing through Carefree and pedaling south to ❖ **el Pedregal Festival Marketplace**. Then take Carefree Highway west to Cave Creek Road and go south to your starting point. However, be cautioned that this section does not have a bike lane.

8 SCOTTSDALE'S HAYDEN ROAD ● Indian School Park to Scottsdale Country Club. About thirteen miles round trip, all level. GETTING THERE: From Phoenix, take I-10 and Freeway Loop 202 east, then Loop 101 north about four miles to Indian School Road (exit 47). Go west about a mile to Hayden Road.

Nicely landscaped Hayden Road passes several Scottsdale parks, several planned communities and shopping complexes. Most of this cycling route is on separate bike paths or wide sidewalks. Unleash your bikes at a shopping center near Indian School and Hayden roads, then start peddling northward on the east side of Hayden through **Indian School Park**. After half a mile, cross to the west side to avoid the Villa Monterey Golf Course. (Players frown on cyclists using their golf cart roads.) Follow a recreational path called Indian Bend Wash, which travels through a shallow landscaped ravine paralleling Hayden. At Chaparral Road, cross back to the east side and pedal along the edge of a lawn-rimmed lake in **Chaparral Park**. (A path around this lake is one of our designated walks on page 132.)

More parklands flank Hayden Road, extending north along Indian Bend Wash to the Arizona Canal near Indian Bend Road. At Jackrabbit Road, cross again to the west side to stay with the park. At Villa de Ventura, you'll encounter the **Village at Hayden**, a Spanish style shopping center. You might want to peddle through the complex and perhaps take a break at one of its restaurants or cafes. North of here, you'll pass a pleasantly planned community called Las Palmas just beyond San Lorenzo Drive. Its lake and golf course are visible from Hayden Road's landscaped sidewalk. As you continue northward, you might want to peddle about some of the very attractive residential communities along here.

At Shea Boulevard, you'll encounter **Scottsdale Country Club**. After pedaling alongside it for about half a mile, you'll run out of sidewalk at Cholla Road, which is a logical turnaround.

9 McDOWELL MOUNTAIN REGIONAL PARK • *Four miles east of Fountain Hills on McDowell Mountain Road; (480) 471-0173. GETTING THERE: From downtown, take I-10 and then Freeway 202 north and east; the route becomes the Beeline Highway. About eleven miles from the end of the freeway, follow Shea Boulevard west past Fountain Hills. Go north on Fountain Hills Road to McDowell Mountain Road, which takes you four miles to the park.*

McDowell Mountain Park is the valley's best haven for serious cyclists, since it's relatively level. This 21,000-acre desert preserve has several miles of mountain biking and hiking trails. Further, it's rich with desert gardens and it offers grand views of surrounding rough hills. The fourteen-mile McDowell Mountain Competitive Path is a dirt course through rolling desert terrain, designed for cyclists and runners seeking a serious workout. It's often used for bike races. The trail twists and winds through thick desert gardens, so it's a great place for a walk—as long as it isn't being used for a race. And you must stay alert for those in a hurry. Come early on a weekday morning when the path isn't very busy. To reach it, take a road to the left just after passing through the park's main gate.

In addition to this path, the preserve has several other cycling and walking trails. Or you can pedal on the park's asphalt roads. They don't have bike lanes, although speed limits are low and traffic is light. The park also has a campground and several picnic areas.

On your way to or from McDowell Mountain Park, you might like to pause in Fountain Hills to see the ❖ **world's highest fountain**. Jutting more than 500 feet skyward, this Old Faithful of the desert is visible for miles around. It squirts for fifteen minutes at the top of each hour, from 10 to 9, except when it's too windy. If you want to pedal to the fountain from the park, McDowell Mountain Road has marked bike lanes. However, they're rather narrow and traffic often exceeds the road's 45-mile-per-hour speed limit, so it might be best to drive. When you reach town, turn left onto Saguaro Boulevard and follow it a mile to the fountain.

10 AHWATUKEE FOOTHILLS • *A loop trip from Ray Road at Ranch Circle into South Mountain's residential foothills. About eleven miles round trip; moderately hilly with some grades. GETTING THERE: Drive south from Phoenix on I-10, then go west on Ray Road (exit 159) just over two miles.*

A fast-growing suburb called Ahwatukee is spreading its tile-roofed planned communities into South Mountain's southern foothills. Many of its roads have bike lanes. A good starting point is **Mountain Park Pavilion** at the corner of Ray Road and Ranch Circle. It's a shopping center with plenty of parking space and a Fry's Food and Drug, if you need grub or drinks for the ride. There's also a bike shop here—**Fun Sports**—handy if your cycle needs a tune-up. It's open weekdays 10 to 7, Saturday 10 to 6 and Sunday 11 to 5; (480) 706-0858.

From the shopping center, pedal west on Ray Road. It's fairly busy since this is a commercial area, although the road does have designated bike lanes. You'll clear this section after about a mile and pass through a residential area, where the traffic begins to thin out. Most of the homes here are tucked behind walls, set back from landscaped sidewalks. You may be tempted to use those sidewalks, although the bike lane continues.

A mile and a half from your starting point, fork to the right onto Chandler Boulevard West. You'll begin an uphill climb as you enter appealing foothill country that's a mix of desert flora and housing developments. After a mile or so, the road levels and then drops down toward a new shopping area. At its western edge, about three miles from your starting point, turn right up Desert Foothills Parkway. And we do mean *up*; the street climbs steeply into South Mountain's flanks, passing more nice homes. There's no bike lane, although it's relatively wide and lightly traveled, and it has a wide sidewalk.

At the crest of a brief climb, you can switch from biking to hiking by turning right into South Mountain Park's **Desert Foothills Trailhead**. The parking area has a water fountain, potties and places to lash your bikes. Or you can ride up the trail briefly—particularly if you're on mountain bikes—since the first part is paved. At the end of pavement, the route splits into a pair of trails. The Desert Classic Trail rambles along the foothills through a nice display of native flora. The Telegraph Pass Trail climbs steeply up a South Mountain ravine and ends at a scenic drive which comes up from the other side. This trail, about a mile long, is too steep for mountain bikes unless you're willing to carry them.

Back in the bike saddle again, you'll have an easy downhill run on Desert Foothills Parkway, which loops back to Chandler Boulevard. Turn left and you'll soon return to that new shopping center. En route, you'll pass a nice slice of desert in the undeveloped **Foothills Park**. Beyond the shopping center, the scenery becomes more deliberate—a planned community bordered by a fake lake. Pressing eastward, fork to the left to rejoin Ray Road and return to your starting point.

THE TEN BEST VIEWPOINTS AND PHOTO ANGLES

The Valley of the Sun's striking blend of desert and mountains provides some impressive vista points and photo angles. However, the best viewpoints don't always produce good photos. Our eyes provide us with three-dimensional vision and a near 180-degree angle of sight.

A camera, unless it's equipped with a fisheye lens, has a much narrower field of view and the resulting photos are two-dimensional. Thus, we offer separate lists of five each, starting with our favorites.

THE BEST VIEWPOINTS

1 COMPASS RESTAURANT ● *24th floor of the Hyatt Regency at 122 N. Second St; (602) 252-1234. GETTING THERE: The Hyatt Regency is downtown between First and Second streets.* ❖

You don't have to have an expensive dinner to enjoy Phoenix's best overview. For the price of a drink in the Compass cocktail lounge, you can sit and sip for fifty-five minutes while this rotating sphere unravels the entire tapestry of the sprawling metropolis. From this aerie, you realize that the Salt River Valley is remarkably flat, with its desert mountains creating a rough-hewn perimeter. The best time to arrive is just before sundown, although you may find the lounge full during the peak tourist season. With luck, you'll see one of those spectacular Arizona sunsets, followed the gradual twinkling-on of a zillion lights, like a carelessly scattered carpet of diamonds.

2 DIFFERENT POINTE OF VIEW ● *At the Pointe Hilton Tapatio Cliffs Resort, 11111 N. Seventh St., Phoenix; (602) 866-7500. (www.pointehilton.com) GETTING THERE: The resort is about twelve miles north of downtown on the southeast corner of Seventh Street and Thunderbird Road.* ❖

Different point of view, indeed! Sitting dramatically on a high cleft above the Pointe Hilton resort, this restaurant offers an imposing vista of downtown Phoenix, framed in rough-hewn foreground mountains. Plan on a sunset dinner to watch the dramatic transition from sunlight to city lights. Or if you don't want to commit to a meal, stop by for a drink. Both the restaurant and a lower-floor cocktail lounge have outside decks. When you drive into the resort, don't park below but continue up to the restaurant. Its narrow access road has no sidewalks.

3 SQUAW PEAK SUMMIT ● *From the end of the Squaw Peak Summit Trail. GETTING THERE: See the Squaw Peak Recreation Area hike above, on page 130.*

The vista from the rocky double crest of Squaw Peak is almost as imposing as that from the Compass cocktail lounge. Although the Compass vantage point places you closer to the ground and thus provides more detail, this much higher aerie offers a wider view of the valley. For more descriptive adjectives, see the Squaw Peak Recreation Area listing above.

4 *LOBBY BAR AT FOUR SEASONS RESORT* • *10600 E. Crescent Moon Dr., Scottsdale; (480) 515-5700. (www.fourseasons.com) GETTING THERE: From downtown, take the Squaw Peak Freeway north fourteen miles to Bell Road and go east less than five miles to Scottsdale Road. Drive north to Pinnacle Peak Road (just beyond Rawhide) and go east briefly, then go north on Pima Road and east on Alma School Parkway. Shortly after passing the turnoff to Pinnacle Peak Patio, turn left onto Crescent Moon Drive.* ❖

The oddly-named Four Seasons Resort Scottsdale at Troon North has one of the best viewpoints of any resort in the area. Perched dramatically among massive boulders in north Scottsdale, it provides splendid vistas of the rugged desert and two rocky spires, Pinnacle Peak and Troon North—and now you know where the odd name comes from. The best views of these stony monoliths, with a slice of faraway Phoenix on the horizon, are from the resort's lobby bar or its outdoor veranda. This vista is best enjoyed—margarita in hand—around sundown. The Crescent Moon restaurant has a similar vantage point, should you like Italian fare with your vista. See chapters three and four for more on Troon North and its restaurant.

5 *THE BEST AQUATIC VIEW: Encanto Park* • *Fifteenth Avenue and Encanto Boulevard, Phoenix; (602) 261-8993. GETTING THERE: The park is about two miles northeast of downtown. Take any main street north, then go west on Encanto Boulevard and turn north into the park.*

There's not a lot of water in the Valley of the Sun since this is, after all, a desert. However, Encanto Park provides a pleasant aquatic view of Phoenix. This is the valley's only park with a large lagoon and it's so close to downtown that you can get a nice vista of the highrises from here. The best view—or photo, if you prefer—is from a concrete deck on the east side of a brick building near the boathouse. This composite view includes the lagoon and a rocky island busy with palm trees, and several downtown office towers beyond.

THE BEST PHOTO ANGLES

6 *SQUAW PEAK SUMMIT TRAIL* • *Squaw Peak Recreational Area northeast of downtown. GETTING THERE: See the Squaw Peak Summit Trail hike above.*

Although the views from atop Squaw Peak are impressive, the best photo, which captures the feel of this city rising from a rough-hewn desert, is from a low point on the trail. Start up the trail from the Summit parking lot. After a short distance, you'll get a nice view of the city skyline on the left and a slice of Squaw Peak on the right, with hikers zig-zagging up the steep switchbacks. Your lens can capture a slice of the mountain's rugged flanks and some saguaro cactus in the middleground. All of this can be framed in the overhanging branch of an ocotillo for the ultimate Valley of the Sun photo. The format is horizontal, with a medium to slightly wide angle lens. Shoot it early in the morning while shadows on the buildings and the mountain crevices are still sharply defined.

7 *THE BEST SHOT OF DOWNTOWN HIGHRISES ● In front of the East Court Building at 101 West Jefferson near First Avenue. GETTING THERE: This picture spot is just southwest of downtown.*

If you stand in front of the east wing of the Maricopa County Court and Government Complex, just west of the corner of Jefferson and First Avenue, you can capture a fine panorama of downtown highrises. It will require a wide angle lens to take in the entire sweep, which includes the copper colored Ernst & Young building, the new Phelps Dodge Center, a surrealistic "tent" above the outdoor stage of Patriots Square and the curving Bank of America Tower. You can frame all of this in the twiggy limbs of a sidewalk tree. Shoot it in early morning to capture shadows on the buildings.

8 *THE BEST SHOT OF NEW AND OLD PHOENIX ● St. Mary's Basilica and Arizona Center office tower, from the top of the stairway of the second level of Collier Center. GETTING THERE: Collier Center is at the base of the Bank of America Tower, bounded by Washington, Second, Third and Jefferson.*

St. Mary's Basilica is one of downtown Phoenix's oldest buildings and Arizona Center is one of its most modern. You can get a nice shot of the basilica's twin towers with the Arizona Center office tower in the background from the Collier Center. By standing at the top of a stairway leading from the sidewalk at the corner of Third and Washington, you can capture the basilica and the highrise, with a slice of Phoenix Civic Plaza on the right. Your position above the sidewalk permits you to shoot over foreground signs and traffic lights. This is a square format, best captured in late afternoon with a medium lens. For more drama, take a tripod and shoot it at night, since the basilica is floodlighted.

9 *BEST SHOT OF PUBLIC NUDITY: Forecourt of the Herberger Theater ● Corner of Monroe and Second streets downtown.*

Several life-sized bronze nudes scamper in frozen dance around the forecourt of the Herberger Theater complex. Perfectly decent and artistic, they offer nice elements to a photo of the theater facility. It's best as an early morning or late afternoon shot, and you can work any of several interesting angles. For an overall photo, stand near the corner of Monroe and Second and you'll get some of the dark bronze dancing forms, the beige theater building with its red tile roof and—for a dash of color—a yellow flower bed in front of the building. The chocolate-bronze glass office tower of Arizona Center rises in the background. The format is squarish, with a normal to slightly wide angle lens.

10 THE BEST SCOTTSDALE PHOTO: City Hall reflec-
tion pool ● *In the Scottsdale Civic Center Mall. GETTING THERE: Go north about twelve miles on the Squaw Peak Freeway and then east on Indian School Road about seven miles to Scottsdale Road. Continue two more blocks to Second Street and go south two blocks. You'll be adjacent to the mall.* ❖

For a fine photo composite of Scottsdale's Civic Center Mall, position yourself and your Canon southwest of city hall beside a reflection pool. The spot is between city hall and the library. You can catch a brilliant swatch of bedding plants in the foreground and the reflection pool with a rusty-modern sculpture of Don Quixote in the middle-ground. The beige pueblo style city hall with American and Arizona flags a-flying in the background completes the picture. This is a horizontal format, using a medium wide angle lens.

THE TEN BEST SPECIALTY GUIDES TO PHOENIX & ARIZONA IN GENERAL

We assume that you aren't copping a free read in the book store and have purchased *The Best of Phoenix & Tucson* for your very own. If you've done so, we can recommend some specialty guides that will provide more specifics about your destination, or about the state. Most are available only in bookstores in the Valley of the Sun, or they may be ordered directly from the publisher. We've listed addresses where they're available. However, don't just send them a check; there'll be shipping charges and the prices may have changed, so inquire first.

Many of these books can be ordered on line from *amazon.com*, *bn.com* or *borders.com*. ❖ Barnes & Noble Booksellers and Borders Books and Music stores have the best selection of regional guides.

We have no favorite guidebooks other than our own, so our choices are listed alphabetically by title. (Note that we do include our relocation guide, *Arizona In Your Future*.)

1 ARIZONA: AN ILLUSTRATED HISTORY ● By Patrick
Lavin. Hippocrene Books, 170 Madison Ave., New York, NY 10016; 252 pages; $14.95. (www.hippocrenebooks.com)

Thorough and comprehensive, this is a highly readable treatment of the state's past, with lots of old black and white photos.

2 *ARIZONA HIKING: URBAN TRAILS* • *Published by Arizona Highways, 2039 Lewis Ave., Phoenix, AZ 85009; (602) 712-2200; 120 pages; $16.95. (www.arizonahighways.com)*

Illustrated with 120 color photos, this book outlines "easy paths and overnight treks in the Valley of the Sun and other urban areas.

3 *ARIZONA IN YOUR FUTURE* • *By Don & Betty Martin. Dis-coverGuides, P.O. Box 231954, Las Vegas, NV 89123-0033; $17.95.*

Is Arizona in your future? This comprehensive relocation guide covers everything from job prospects to retirement communities to the best nests for winter "Snowbirds."

4 *BEST EASY DAY HIKES: PHOENIX* • *By Steward M. Green. Falcon Guides, Globe-Pequot Press, P.O. Box 480, Guilford, CT 06437; 114 pages; $6.95. (www.globepequot.com)*

This small pocket-sized book features directions and maps for several of the Phoenix area's short, easy to follow trails.

5 *DAY HIKES AND TRAIL RIDES IN AND AROUND PHOENIX* • *By Roger and Ethel Freeman. Gem Guides, 315 Cloverleaf Dr., Suite F, Baldwin Park, CA 91706; (626) 855-1611; 280 pages, $14.95. (www.gemguidesbooks.com)*

Feel like a good workout, a leisurely stroll or a few hours in the saddle? This guide features a variety of trails in the Valley of the Sun.

6 *DAY TRIPS FROM PHOENIX, TUCSON AND FLAG-STAFF* • *By Pam Hait. Globe-Pequot Press; 324 pages; $14.95. (www.globepequot.com)*

The lengthy title says it all. This guide to outings from Arizona's metropolitan areas is handy for visitors with spare time and residents seeking weekend getaways.

7 *FIFTY GREAT WEEKEND ESCAPES IN ARIZONA* • *By Ray Bangs and Chris Becker. Northland Publishing, P.O. Box 1389, Flag-staff, AZ 86002; 200 pages; $19.95. (www.northlandpub.com)*

This book offers a year's worth of weekend outdoor escapes from Arizona's urban areas, featuring a variety of activities, with maps and even discount coupons.

8 *PHOENIX FOR FAMILIES* • *By Michelle Burgess. Hot to Go Publishing, 4123 N. Longview, Phoenix, AZ 85014; (602) 996-7129; 240 pages; $14.95. (www.phoenixpublishinggroup.com)*

Got the rug-rats in tow? This book tells you where to take the kids in the Valley of the Sun, covering such lures as attractions, farmers markets, boys and girls clubs, parks, family camps and miniature golf courses.

9 *PHOENIX: THE HISTORY OF A SOUTHWESTERN METROPOLIS* • *By Bradford Luckingham. University of Arizona Press, Tucson; 316 pages; $15.95. (www.uapress.arizona.edu)*

A professor of history at Arizona State University, Luckingham writes a comprehensive study of the Valley of the Sun, from the ancient Hohokam to the urbanization of Phoenix. The latest copyright we found was 1989, although the book offers a very thorough and readable treatment up to that date.

10 *ROADSIDE GEOLOGY OF ARIZONA* • *By Halka Chronic. Mountain Press Publishing, P.O. Box 2399, Missoula, MT 59806; (406) 728-1900; 322 pages; $18. (www.mountain-press.com)*

How were the Grand Canyon and Picacho Peak formed? This well-written book explains the geological features along the state's highways and back roads.

EASY LISTENING:
THE TEN BEST RADIO STATIONS

As you cruise about the valley's sprawl of streets, freeways and highways, you may want to surf your car radio dial for your favorite sounds. Our choices are rather broad-based and they're listed in no order of preference, since one person's music is the next person's noise.

1 *KFOL—94.5-FM* • This station plays "cool favorites," which translates as top hits and soft rock from previous decades.

2 *KDAQ—89.5-FM* • This National Public Radio station plays classical music, plus the usual NPR news, talk and features. (A second NPR station, KJZZ at 91.5, plays jazz.)

3 *KYOT—95.5-FM* • This smooth-sounding station features jazz and other easy listening music.

4 *KEZ—99.9-FM* ● It's Phoenix's best soft rock venue, playing old and new pops, with no hard rock.

5 *KNIX—102.5-FM* ● Need your daily Loretta Lynn fix? This is one of the valley's stronger country stations.

6 *KOOL—94.5-FM* ● Feeling oldish? This station features pops oldies of the 60s through 80s.

7 *KTAR—620-AM* ● It's one of the area's more popular news, talk and sports stations, with a strong local focus.

8 *KFYI—550-AM* ● This is a news, talk, traffic and sports station.

9 *KMVP—860-AM* ● So what's happening with the Suns, Cardinals, Diamondbacks and Coyotes? This ESPN all-sports station will keep you posted.

10 *KOY—1230-AM* ● One of the area's oldest stations, it plays classic oldies, interspersed with traffic reports, plus CNN news and sports.

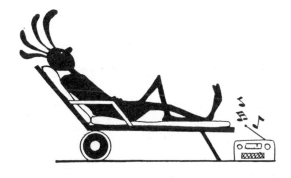

*The traveler sees what he
sees; the tourist sees what
he has come to see.*
— **Gilbert K. Chesterton**

Chapter Ten

BEYOND PHOENIX
WHAT TO SEE AFTER YOU'VE SEEN
THE VALLEY OF THE SUN

By the time you get through with Phoenix, you may want to visit
some of the rest of the Grand Canyon State. Since we've divided this
book's focus between Phoenix and Tucson, we're suggesting ten interesting side trips from each. For geographic practicality, our Ten Best
Phoenix side trips cover northern and western Arizona. Tucson gets
the southern and eastern parts.

Our listings—while covering most of the best that Arizona offers—
aren't necessarily obvious. While pointing you toward the Grand Canyon and Sedona from Phoenix and Tumacácori National Historical
Park and Tombstone from Tucson, we'll also suggest some roads less
traveled.

These are by no means comprehensive listings; they're brief descriptions intended to whet your travel appetites. We've given sources
for further information in each listing and you'll likely want to seek additional material from a detailed statewide guidebook. Our *Arizona
Discovery Guide* comes to mind. Before starting one of these side trips,
trace the route on the map, based on our brief descriptions. It will sim-
plify your navigation.

We'll end this introduction with the obvious. If you've purchased this book prior to departing for Phoenix or Tucson, you may want to take some of these side trips en route.

THE TEN BEST SIDE TRIPS

Our favorite detour from Phoenix is not just to the Grand Canyon, but to the North Rim. The Grand Canyon is Arizona's most popular attraction, drawing about eight million visitors a year, so to suggest it as a side trip is to belabor the obvious. However, only about a tenth of these folks go to the North Rim. And it's not that much farther from Phoenix than the heavily impacted South Rim.

1 *GRAND CANYON NORTH RIM* ● *For information: Superintendent, Grand Canyon National Park, P.O. Box 129, Grand Canyon, AZ 86023; (928) 638-7888. For lodging: Amfac Parks & Resorts, 14001 E. Illiff, Suite 600, Aurora, CO 80014; (303) 297-2757. For Jacob Lake lodging and camping: Jacob Lake Inn, Jacob Lake, AZ 86022; (928) 643-7232.*

The Grand Canyon of the Colorado River, the inspiration for Arizona's nickname, is perhaps the most splendid geological spectacle on the planet. To best appreciate this spectacle, we usually head for the North Rim, less crowded and even more awesome than the South Rim. While the South Rim suggests a long, irregular cliff edge, the North Rim is comprised of peninsulas thrusting far out into the main chasm. They were formed by deep side canyons cut by centuries of erosion. Vista points at the edges of these peninsulas provide splendid views—across to the South Rim eleven miles away, down into the heart of the main chasm and into smaller yet spectacularly rugged canyons on either side. A twenty-mile drive—one of the most scenic in Western America—takes visitors to the North Rim's several viewpoints, ending at Cape Royal. Forest fires in 2000 and 2001 blackened portions of this drive, although the views are as grand as ever.

Lodging facilities here are much more limited than at the South Rim, which we feel is just fine. If you plan to visit either or both rims, make your reservations as early as possible. North Rim camping is available both within the park and in adjacent Kaibab National Forest. The pleasantly rustic settlement of Jacob Lake has commercial lodging and campgrounds.

At 9,000 feet elevation, the North Rim is about 2,000 feet higher than the South Rim, since the Colorado Plateau through which the Grand Canyon is carved tilts from northeast to southwest. Winter snows close access to the North Rim, generally from the first serious storm in November or December until mid-May. If you're visiting Phoenix during winter or early spring, head for the South Rim, which is kept open the year around. It's not nearly as crowded in winter and it's quite beautiful then, since patches of snow accent the spectacular canyon vistas.

The North Rim is about 350 miles from Phoenix. Take I-17 north to Flagstaff, then continue north on U.S. 89 through the Navajo Indian Reservation. Fork left onto 89-A, follow it about fifty miles north and west to Jacob Lake, and then take State Route 67 forty miles south.

2 *GLEN CANYON AND THE ARIZONA STRIP* • *For information: Page-Lake Powell Chamber of Commerce, 644 N. Navajo, Suite C. (P.O. Box 727), Page, AZ 86040; (888) 261-7243 or (928) 645-2741.*

Page and Glen Canyon are about 275 miles north of Phoenix. Follow directions to the North Rim (above), but stay on U.S. 89 to Page. Sitting on a red rock plateau, the town began life as a construction camp for the Glen Canyon Dam project in the 1960s. It now serves as gateway to Glen Canyon National Recreation Area. While the damned dam flooded a chasm that was nearly as awesome as the Grand Canyon, the resulting Lake Powell is a major water recreation area. House-boating is particularly popular as floating vacationers explore the many arms and inlets of the lake. It extends 186 miles upstream like a gnarled, mutilated hand. Most of the recreation area and its reservoir are in neighboring Utah.

West of Page and Glen Canyon lies the remote, almost mystical Arizona Strip. Cut off from the rest of the state by the Grand Canyon, this vast high prairie rimmed by red rock cliffs is one of Arizona's least populated areas. Only a few settlements—mostly Mormon and some still secretly practicing polygamy—dot this lonely landscape. Socially and economically, the Arizona Strip relates more to Utah, since the fair-sized town of St. George and smaller Hurricane are just across the border. To explore this intriguing region, head south from Page on U.S. 89, then swing north and cross the lofty Navajo Bridge over the Colorado River's **Marble Canyon.** Just north are historic exhibits concerning a Mormon river crossing called **Lee's Ferry,** now part of Glen Canyon National Recreation Area. Navajo Bridge is the last Colorado River highway crossing for about 300 miles, and this is a popular put-in spot for river runners.

Head west on Highway 89-A along the base of the gorgeous Vermilion Cliffs. You'll cross the lonely prairie of the Arizona Strip, then climb into ponderosa pinelands of Kaibab National Forest to **Jacob Lake.** Continue northwest on 89-A to **Fredonia** and then head southwest on State Route 389 into the Moccasin Indian Reservation and **Pipe Springs National Monument.** It preserves an historic Mormon cattle ranch. If you press northwestward from here, you'll reach **Colorado City,** a traditional Mormon settlement at the Utah border. Not far away are St. George and Zion National Park.

3 *APACHE JUNCTION TO ROOSEVELT DAM* ● *For information: Apache Junction Chamber of Commerce, 112 E. Second Ave. (P.O. Box 1747), Apache Junction, AZ 85219-1747; (480) 982-3141.*

The historic Apache Trail, built during the construction of Roosevelt Dam early in the last century, is a popular weekend recreation route for Valley of the Sun residents. As visitors, you might prefer to drive it on less-busy weekdays. To begin this tour, head east from the Valley of the Sun on the Superstition Freeway, then take Idaho Road (exit 196) north **Apache Junction,** a Valley of the Sun bedroom community and retirement town.

From here, the highway winds into the cactus-busy foothills of the **Superstition Mountains,** alleged home to the Lost Dutchman mine. According to legend, a local prospector—German, not Dutch—supposedly found a treasure trove of gold in the 1860s. He never revealed its whereabouts and died with his secret. According to legend, several people who've gone looking for his mine have disappeared, or have been found dead.

You can learn more about the Dutchman's gold at **Lost Dutchman State Park,** a few miles northwest of Apache Junction. From here, the highway winds into excessively scenic Salt River Canyon. **Canyon Lake,** backed up by Mormon Flat Dam, offers the usual reservoir water sports. Just beyond is deliberately rustic **Tortilla Flat.** It pretends to be an old Western town but in fact, it was built as a construction camp for Roosevelt Dam at the turn of the last century. Pavement ends just beyond Tortilla Flat, although the twisting dirt road through the upper reaches of the strikingly beautiful **Salt River Canyon** is well maintained. Carefully driven family sedans and *very* carefully driven small to mid-size RVs can make it. Trailer rigs or RVs approaching forty feet long shouldn't try.

The twisting route rejoins pavement at **Roosevelt Dam,** which was the world's largest masonry structure when it was completed in 1911. Its height was increased by several feet and a new bridge was built across the dam in the 1990s. Facilities here include a visitor center and marina. Just beyond the dam is **Tonto National Monument,** sheltering a nicely preserved cliff dwelling on a steep saguaro-studded hillside.

To turn this drive into a loop trip, go southeast on State Route 88 to **Globe** and **Miami,** a pair of old mining towns. They're described below, on page 151. From here, follow U.S. 60 back to Phoenix.

4 *INDIAN COUNTRY* ● *For information: Office of Public Relations, The Hopi Tribe, P.O. Box 123, Kykotsmovi, AZ 86039, (928) 734-2331; and Navajoland Tourism, P.O. Box 663, Window Rock, AZ 86515; (928) 871-6436, extension 7371.*

The northeastern corner of Arizona is occupied by two quite different native nations. Their lands cover 29,000 square miles, an area nearly as large as New England. The Hopi Nation, made up of closely packed pueblo communities dating back more than a thousand years, occupies a series of terraced plateaus. The much larger Navajo Nation surrounds the Hopi reservation—much to the Hopis' irritation. It's comprised mostly of scattered small communities and sheep camps. The Hopi, probably descended from the ancient Anasazi, are communal villagers. The Navajo, descended from Canadian Athabascan tribes, migrated here within the last few centuries and are much more nomadic. Visits to these two Indian nations provide many rewards, both to study their diverse cultures and to admire the beautiful high desert landscape they occupy.

To reach this area Phoenix, go north on I-17 to Flagstaff. Continue north on U.S. 89 and then U.S. 160 to Tuba City, the largest Navajo town. Then take State Route 264 southeast toward the Hopi mesas.

The Hopi Nation

The Hopi are more tolerant than friendly as far as visitors are concerned, although most individuals we've met have been very cordial. When you visit the Hopi villages, do so with respect, and avoid being too intrusive. Bear in mind that all photography is strictly prohibited, as is tape recording of any ceremonies.

Driving east from Tuba City, you'll encounter the terraced Hopi villages in quick succession. You can work on your pronunciation as you pass through these ancient pueblos—**Hotevilla** (*HOAT-vih-la*), **Old Oraibi** (*Oh-RYE-bee*), **Kykotsmovi** (*Kee-KOTS-mo-vee*) and **Shungnopavi** (*Shung-O-PO-vee*). You'll finally reach a place you can pronounce, **Second Mesa,** which is home to the fine **Hopi Cultural Center and Museum.** Here, you can learn much about Hopi culture, and buy some of their fine handicrafts. The complex includes a gift shop, restaurant and motel. You also may be able to learn if a Hopi ceremonial dance has been scheduled somewhere on the reservation.

Continuing east on Route 264, you'll pass through the more contemporary village of **Keams Canyon** with a small shopping center, restaurant and motel. Beyond, you'll re-enter the Navajo Nation.

The Navajo Nation

East from Hopi Land, State Route 264 travels through several miles of high prairie and eventually reaches **Ganado** and **Hubbell Trading Post National Historic Site.** It's a still-active example of the trading posts that formed early links between native people and whites. East of here, the highway climbs a high tableland, then drops down to **Window Rock,** home to the **Navajo Arts and Crafts Center** and adjacent **Navajo Tribal Museum.** Ask directions to the unusual hole-in-a-rock formation that gives the town its name. Head northward from here on Navajo Route 12 through imposing red rock formations to **Tsaile Lake**. Just beyond is the campus of **Navajo Community College** with its **Hatathli Museum** of tribal lore.

From Tsaile Lake, follow Navajo Route 64 west to the most imposing attraction in this corner of Arizona, **Canyon de Chelly National Monument** (*du-SHAY*). The reserve contains two dramatic, sheer-walled canyons, de Chelly and del Muerto. Press southwestward on Route 64 to the Canyon de Chelly visitor center at **Chinle**, then follow U.S. 191 north to **Mexican Water**. From here, head east, following signs to the **Four Corners Monument** where Arizona, Utah, Colorado and New Mexico converge. It's more novelty than substance, although you can get Indian tacos, jewelry and T-shirts from vendor stalls. Return to Mexican Hat, go southwest to **Kayenta** and then north to the famous **Monument Valley Tribal Park** on the Arizona-Utah border. Return to Kayenta and head southwest on U.S. 160 to **Navajo National Monument** with its impressive Betatakin Ruin. From here, Highway 160 returns to Tuba City to complete your loop.

5 *FLAGSTAFF AND SURROUNDS* • *For information: Flagstaff Visitor Center, 1 E. State Route 66, Flagstaff, AZ 86001; (800) 842-7293 or (928) 774-9541.*

The largest city outside the Phoenix and Tucson metropolitan areas, Flagstaff sits not in the desert but in the pines, at the base of the San Francisco Peaks. The city and its surrounds offer a grand mix of attractions. The Arizona Snowbowl is one of the state's best ski areas, and the San Francisco Peaks provide summer hiking, camping and fishing. And if you're really serious about hiking, you can grunt to the top of Arizona's highest mountain, 12,663-foot **Humphreys Peak**.

Back in Flagstaff, **Northern Arizona University** and the excellent **Museum of Northern Arizona** provide cultural offerings. This city of 50,000 has several smaller museums and historic sites and it's home to **Lowell Observatory,** one of America's leading astronomical facilities. Nearby are **Walnut Canyon National Monument,** preserving an ancient Sinagua cliff dwelling; **Sunset Crater National Monument**, a fascinating area shaped by volcanism; and **Wupatki National Monument,** one of Arizona's most extensive prehistoric ruins.

6 *SEDONA AND SURROUNDS* • *For information: Sedona-Oak Creek Canyon Chamber of Commerce, Forest Road at State Route 89-A (P.O. Box 478), Sedona, AZ 86339; (800) 288-7336 or (928) 282-7722.*

Sedona and Oak Creek Canyon are easily reached from Flagstaff by heading south on State Route 89-A. From Phoenix, take I-17 north to exit 287, go northwest on State Route 260 to Cottonwood, then follow 89-A north. You'll then run the below-suggested route in reverse.

Sitting at 7,700 feet, Sedona is a popular retreat for Phoenicians when summer starts to sizzle. It enjoys one of the most dramatic settings of any city in America, at the base of lower Oak Creek Canyon's striking red rock formations. Several posh resorts are tucked among these awesome shapes and Sedona can be a rather expensive vacation retreat. However, mere mortals can afford to visit as well—particularly mortals who enjoy camping and hiking among the red rock shapes. Several scenic drives take visitors through these formations.

South of Sedona, the small town of **Cottonwood** offers more affordable lodgings, and it's the gateway to **Tuzigoot National Monument,** a Sinagua ruin on a high ridge. Just west of Cottonwood is **Jerome,** a scruffily-historic town that once was a bawdy mining camp. Displays at **Jerome State Historic Park** trace its lusty history. Other attractions in the Sedona-Cottonwood area are **Red Rock State Park,** a riparian section of lower Oak Creek; **Dead Horse Ranch State Park** on the site of an old homestead; **Fort Verde State Historic Park,** a former army post in the town of Camp Verde; and **Montezuma Castle National Monument** and **Montezuma Well,** two Sinagua ruins off I-17.

7 **PRESCOTT** • *For information: Prescott Chamber of Commerce, 117 W. Goodwin St., Prescott, AZ 86302; (800) 266-7534 or (928) 445-2000; www.visit-prescott.com.*

Prescott is about 135 miles northeast of Phoenix. Take I-17 north to exit 262 (Cordes Junction), then go northwest on State Route 69. First, you may want to check out **Arcosanti** by going briefly northeast from the turnoff. It's a futuristic town being built by visionary Paolo Soleri and it hosts public tours. (Soleri's studio, called Cosanti, is in Scottsdale; see Chapter Two, page 34.)

Then head for Prescott, and pronounce it *PRESS-kit,* please. Once you've gotten that right, you'll discover that this is one of Arizona's most appealing small towns, sitting between the high desert and the cool pines of Prescott National Forest. Although Prescott's roots go deeply into Arizona's history—it served briefly as the territorial capital—it has the look of a prim New England town. Despite that eastern look, it offers a kind of cowboy-cultural mix, with several Western art galleries and museums, a large fine arts center, two colleges and even an aeronautical university. Its Frontier Days is said to be America's oldest continuous rodeo, dating from 1888.

Downtown's focal point is **Courthouse Square** with the doric column Yavapai County Courthouse. Nearby **Whiskey Row** was the site of several wicked saloons during Prescott's bawdy days. Among other Prescott attractions are the excellent **Sharlot Hall Museum** that includes the territorial governor's house; the **Smoki Museum,** focusing on native art and culture; and the **Phippen Museum of Western Art.**

8 *NORTH CENTRAL ARIZONA • For information: Greater Globe-Miami Chamber of Commerce, 1360 N. Broad St. (P.O. Box 2539), Globe, AZ 85502, (800) 804-5623 or (928) 425-4495; Show Low Chamber of Commerce, 951 W. Deuce of Clubs (P.O. Box 1083), Show Low, AZ 85902, (888) 746-9569 or (928) 537-2326; Holbrook Chamber of Commerce, 100 E. Arizona St., Holbrook, AZ 86025, (800) 524-2459 or (928) 524-6558; and Rim Country Regional Chamber of Commerce, 100 W. Main St. (P.O. Box 1380), Payson, AZ 85547, (800) 672-9766 or (928) 474-4515.*

This area is ignored by most Arizona visitors although it contains an impressive mix of attractions. Start by heading east from Tempe on U.S. 60. Your first stop should be **Superior,** with its fine **Boyce Thompson Arboretum State Park.** About seventeen miles beyond, you'll encounter **Miami** and **Globe,** two rustically appealing mining towns with several historic sites. Globe is home to the fine **Besh-Ba-Gowah Archeological Park.** From here, follow U.S. 60 northeast through the **San Carlos** and **Fort Apache** reservations. The Fort Apache reservation is noted for its **Sunrise** winter-summer mountain resort.

Continue from the Fort Apache Reservation to **Show Low,** a forest-rimmed town noted mostly for its silly name. (It was based on a low-ball poker game.) **Pine Top** and **Lakeside** just southeast of Show Low are popular summer retreats. Head north on State Route 77 to **Holbrook,** where you might want to pause for a look at the **Courthouse Museum.** Then go southeast on U.S. 180 to the south entrance of **Petrified Forest National Park.** Amble northward through the park to Interstate 40 and return to Holbrook. (If you've already seen Petrified Forest, drive northeast from Show Low to Heber on State Route 260.)

From Holbrook, head southwest on State Route 377 to **Heber** and follow routes 277 and 260 through the attractive woodlands of Tonto National Forest to **Payson.** Scattered over juniper-covered hills, it's a retirement community and a popular weekend retreat for Phoenicians. Famous Western author Zane Grey once lived near here, and his life and works are featured in the **Zane Grey Museum.** The **Museum of the Forest** has more exhibits on the author, plus displays about Payson. From here, return to Phoenix via State Route 87. As you near the Valley of the Sun, you'll recognize it as the Beeline Highway.

9 *WICKENBURG TO KINGMAN • For Information: Wickenburg Chamber of Commerce, 216 N. Frontier St., Wickenburg, AZ 85390, (800) 942-5242 or (928) 684-5479; and Kingman Powerhouse Visitor Center, 120 W. Andy Devine St., Kingman, AZ 86401, (928) 753-6103.*

These two communities are on a northwest diagonal line from Phoenix. Take Grand Avenue (U.S. 60) to Wickenburg, fifty-two miles from Phoenix. Then shift to U.S. 93 for Kingman. Anyone coming to the Valley of the Sun from California or Nevada can run this route in reverse.

The Old West survives out **Wickenburg** way—at least in architecture and attitude. Its main streets are lined with old fashioned storefronts, and half a dozen guest ranches host assorted dudes. The excellent **Desert Caballeros Western Museum** recalls the days when Wickenburg was serious ranching country and the trade center for several area mines. One of these, the **Vulture Mine,** hosts public tours. Just southeast of Wickenburg is the **Hassayampa River Preserve,** operated by the Nature Conservancy. It's an excellent example of a riparian woodland and a fine bird watching area.

Are there really interesting attractions in Kingman, a weathered town that's famous mostly as the home of Andy Devine? Surprisingly so. Kingman was an important stop on old **Route 66** and its downtown has been preserved as a kind of historic monument to that famous highway. The fine **Mojave Museum of History and Arts** traces the town's history as a mining and ranching center, and it has a major exhibit on Mr. Devine, everybody's favorite Western sidekick. **Railroad Park** exhibits steam trains and several homes in the old town area feature historic displays. Nearby **Hualapai Mountain Park** offers pine tree respite from Kingman's arid high desert.

North of Kingman off U.S. 93 is the near ghost town of **Chloride,** Arizona's longest-surviving silver mining camp. Its main lure, other than a few shops and galleries, is contemporary artist Roy Pursell's **rock murals** in a nearby canyon. If you continue northwest on U.S. 93, you'll reach **Hoover Dam** and then America's greatest party town, **Las Vegas.**

Another interesting drive is southwest from Kingman on the **Oatman Highway,** one of the few untouched sections of historic Route 66. It winds steeply over rock-ribbed **Sitgreaves Pass.** Displays along the way tell of the westward migration during the Great Depression when Dustbowl fugitives struggled up the steep grade in their wheezing Model-T's. Just down the other side is **Oatman.** It's an old mining town that has become a delightfully tacky tourist attraction, with saloons, curio shops and free-thinking burros th streets. If you press westward, you'll wind up at the and our final side trip.

10 COLORADO RIVER CORRIDOR •

*Bullhead Area Chamber of Commerce, 1251 State Rou
City, AZ 86429, (928) 754-4141; Lake Havasu City
314 London Bridge Rd., Lake Havasu City, AZ 86403,
or (928) 453-3444; Parker Area Chamber of Commer*

nia Ave., Parker, AZ 85344, (928) 669-2174; Quartzsite Chamber of Commerce, 1490 Main Event Lane (P.O. Box 85), Quartzsite, AZ 85346, (928) 927-5600; and Yuma Convention and Visitors Bureau, 377 Main St., Suite 102, Yuma, AZ 85364; (800) 293-0071 or (928) 783-0071.

The Colorado River corridor marks Arizona's lowest elevation and hottest region—even hotter than Phoenix. This is primarily a winter haven and a major lure for Snowbirds who flock south to escape northland blizzards. The river along here is actually a chain of reservoirs, backed up by a succession of dams. It thus lends itself to boating, fishing, waterskiing and other flatwater sports.

From the tail end of our previous side trip, you can drive north briefly on State Route 95 to **Bullhead City,** an inelegant scatter of a community. More interesting is **Laughlin, Nevada,** just across the water, with several riverside casinos. Heading south from here on Route 95, you'll hit—after a brief I-40 interruption—**Lake Havasu City,** home to the **London Bridge.** It was moved stone by numbered stone and reassembled here in the late 1960s. South of here, Route 95 skims **Lake Havasu State Park,** offering water sports, picnicking and camping, then **Parker Dam,** with self-guiding tours. You'll next encounter **Parker** on the Colorado River Indian Reservation, offering lots of RV parks and the **Colorado River Indian Tribes Museum.**

Below Parker, the highway shifts inland to cross I-10 at **Quartzsite,** possibly the ugliest town in America. It is mostly a sprawl of RV parks on scraped-off patches of desert. It's also home to a series of winter swap meets and gem and mineral shows. They're attended by hundreds of thousands, most of whom arrive in RVs. Below Quartzsite, State Route 95 gets promoted to U.S. 95 and leads to **Yuma,** a town more interesting than most folks think. Among its attractions are **Yuma Territorial Prison** and **Yuma Crossing,** both state historic parks. This was a major fording point on the Colorado river. Yuma Crossing State Historic Park recalls the days of wandering Spanish missionaries (who gave the river its name here), paddlewheel steamers and California-bound goldseekers. From Yuma, I-8 will hurry you eastward across southern Arizona for a reunion with I-10. Go north and you're back in Phoenix; head south and you're in the next section of this book.

PART II
TUCSON & SURROUNDS
OUR FAVORITE SUN

Since this book is highly opinionated, we'll confess to liking Tucson a little better than Phoenix. Actually, we're fond of both since we're urban desert rats with a penchant for Southwestern cities, which is one of the reasons we live in Las Vegas. (If you don't know the other reasons, you've never been to America's greatest party town.)

We prefer Tucson to Phoenix because it has more of a sense of history and it's simply more charming. The Old Pueblo is more rooted to its past while Phoenix gallops furiously toward tomorrow. To quote from our *Arizona Discovery Guide:* "Tucson is large enough to provide all the cosmopolitan essentials, yet small enough to be familiar and friendly. With a population just under half a million, it offers a great mix of indoor culture and outdoor recreation."

There are many similarities between Tucson and Phoenix. They are the two largest cities in Arizona and both occupy desert basins rimmed by rough-hewn mountains. Both have a mix of cultural facilities and desert preserves to provide a versatile leisure base. Both lure winter visitors to posh resorts and both can get hotter than the hinges of Hades in summer, although Tucson is slightly cooler.

The cities have differences as well. Tucson began as a mission settlement and is closer to its Hispanic roots. Phoenix was and still is mostly Anglo, demographically and sociologically. Tucson is rich in history, with its El Presidio Historic District and Mission San Xavier, while Phoenix is just rich, more preoccupied with growth than with preservation. Some Tusconans regard Phoenicians as more uptight and avaricious; a few Phoenicians say Tusconans are more provincial and less sophisticated.

Some of the jealousies between the two cities are rooted in their respective universities. Tucson's University of Arizona is the oldest, although the Valley of the Sun's ASU is much larger. A friend in Phoenix, more kind than many of his brethren in either city, summed things up this way:

"Tucson probably has the better university, with its schools of medicine, law and architecture. So people get their educations there, then they come to Phoenix to make their money."

But never mind all that. We come here to praise Tucson, not to bury Phoenix.

Tucson's mystique has a way of permeating every person who stays here—for even a little while. And the longer you stay, the more you want to know.

— Charles W. Polzer,
Tucson: A Short History,
© 1986 by Southwest
Mission Research Center

Chapter Eleven

THE OLD PUEBLO
FINDING ARIZONA'S SPANISH ROOTS

It might be unkind to call our favorite Arizona city Los Angeles with cactus. And then again, it might not. Metropolitan Tucson covers 550 square miles, an area larger than greater Los Angeles. Thankfully, the resemblance stops there.

Several million people are jammed into the Los Angeles Basin, along with several trillion cubic yards of smog. Tucson's population is half a million, and desert breezes blow the smog away. Further, the Old Pueblo isn't hemmed in by other cities, like Los Angeles or Phoenix. Once you reach Tucson's edge, you're in open desert.

That desert is the Sonoran, which forms an irregular oval through southern Arizona, the northern part of Mexico's state of Sonora and a small swatch of Baja California Norte. A relatively "wet" desert with about eleven inches of rainfall a year, it's noted for its lush plant growth and it is particularly famous for the giant saguaro cactus. Tucson's outstanding Arizona-Sonora Desert Museum is devoted to the study of this fascinating desert.

Four mountain ranges cradle the city—the lofty Santa Catalinas and Rincons and the lower elevation Santa Ritas and Tucson Mountains. The Santa Catalinas and Rincons are so high that their crests are thatched with evergreens. While only hiking trails reach the Rincon forests, a scenic highway climbs high into the Santa Catalinas, providing woodsy recreation and imposing views back down to the sprawling Tucson Basin.

The Santa Catalinas' Mount Lemmon Recreation area even has a small ski facility. Tucson is one of only two cities in America where winter visitors can ski in the morning and work on their suntans at poolside in the afternoon. Should you wonder, the other suntan-and-ski city is Las Vegas, although its winters are cooler than Tucson's.

You WANT THE TRUTH? AN UNAUTHORIZED HISTORY

Tucson is not the oldest continuously inhabited city in America, as stated by its convention and visitors bureau. One can't really fault the bureau for stretching the truth. It is, after all, in business to stir interest in the Old Pueblo.

The city is more or less descended from a Tohono O'odham village. The word "Tucson" was first found on a map drawn in 1695 by that peripatetic Jesuit missionary, Father Eusebio Francisco Kino. It translates either as "black spring" or "at the foot of a black hill," and it referred to a mountain-rimmed basin occupied by several Tohono O'odham villages. The word originally was spelled *Stjukshon* (STOOK-shon), then it was altered to Tucson and initially pronounced "TUK-son."

The year before Kino drew his map, his associate Padre Agustín de Campos named the largest of the Tucson Basin settlements San Agustín del Oiaur, or "Saint Augustine of the Fields." Later it became St. Agustín de Tucson. In 1700, Kino founded a mission several miles south at the village of Bac, naming it for St. Xavier. St. Agustín de Tucson also came under the care of padres, although not as a full-fledged mission.

Historians don't know the true ages of Tohono O'odham villages, and to suggest that one of them is America's oldest city is a stretch. Most were rather casual and impermanent settlements, unlike the sturdy pueblo villages of other Southwest tribes. By the time Bac and Tucson were occupied by the Spanish, New Mexico's Santa Fe had thrived for nearly a century, established in 1609 as a colonial capital. Florida's St. Augustine is even older. And if we compare Bac or Tucson with other native communities in America, the Hopi pueblo village of Old Oraibi in northeastern Arizona has existed for more than 800 years. That undoubtedly puts Tucson and Bac at the back of the pack.

Whatever its age, St. Agustín de Tucson continued to grow, luring more natives and Spanish ranchers, miners and merchants. By the mid-1700s, it had about 800 residents living in 180 adobes. Other settlements in the area thrived as well.

Alarmed at the growing numbers of settlers and angered by harsh Spanish rule, a Tohono O'odham group revolted in 1751. Ironically, the uprising was led by a native who had once served with the Spanish, Luis Oacapigua. The revolt was short-lived, mostly because many native people had grown comfortable with the good life of the missions. However, nervous settlers demanded the construction of a military fort in case of another uprising. In response, the government of New Spain built Arizona's first presidio at Tubac in 1752.

Nearly half of St. Agustín de Tucson's native and Spanish residents had left during the revolt, and a full-scale mission was established 1757 to lure them back. Settlers continued flowing into the basin. In 1775, Irish-born Hugo O'Conor, the newly appointed commander of Spain's interior provinces, urged that the presidio be moved from Tubac to Tucson. It was accomplished the following year, and the presidio's walls were extended to protect the city's adobes.

Tucson, Mexico?

Thus, Tucson became America's first walled city—except that it was still part of Spain. In fact, if it hadn't been for Mormons and the Gadsden Purchase, we might need a Mexican tourist card to visit the Old Pueblo. Mexico won its independence from Spain in the 1820s. Then Americans, greedily eying Mexican territories that are now Texas, New Mexico, Arizona and California, provoked the new nation into war. Mexico lost and was forced to cede its northern holdings to the United States in the 1848 Treaty of Guadalupe Hidalgo.

However, the lower third of present-day Arizona—including Tucson—remained Mexican territory. To further complicate matters, the Mormon Battalion, which had marched south from Utah to help fight the Mexican War, had occupied Tucson. Despite the treaty, the Mormons refused to yield it. In 1854, cash-strapped Mexico agreed to sell 30,000 square miles of southern Arizona to the U.S., and Old Glory remained flying over the Old Pueblo.

After this problem was resolved, Tucson continued growing as a ranching and provisioning center. A Butterfield Stage stop was opened in 1857 and Tucson's cantinas became notorious hangouts for drifters, outlaws and randy cowpokes. Folks said the outpost was so primitive that stage passengers who spent the night had to sleep in a "Tucson bed"—using their stomach for a mattress and their back for a blanket.

The Old Pueblo suffered the indignity of capture by rebel Texas troops during the Civil War. They were evicted by a pro-Union California battalion in 1862, following the Battle of Picacho Pass. That battle, which occurred between Tucson and Phoenix, was the Civil War's westernmost conflict.

Tucson lured the territorial capital from Prescott in 1867, only to lose it ten years later to Phoenix. Still, it continued to grow. By the turn of the last century, the Old Pueblo was a busy town of 10,000, the largest city in Arizona. Then Phoenix—nurtured by the Roosevelt Dam

Project that irrigated its fertile desert, and apparently better at self-promotion—soon exceeded Tucson's population.

Tucson experienced a growth surge as World War II brought thousands of servicemen to Davis-Monthan Army Air Corps Base. Many of them liked the idea of January suntans and returned. However, since Phoenix had its own returning servicemen, its citrus groves and its status as the state capitol, Tucson couldn't hope to catch it.

Now, of course, the Old Pueblo doesn't want to.

GETTING THERE

While not as centrally located as Phoenix, Tucson is still easy to reach. It's served by major highways, rail and a busy airport.

By highway • Dropping southeast from Phoenix, Interstate 10 cuts through Tucson just west of the downtown area, providing quick access from west and east. Interstate 8, originating in San Diego and entering Arizona through Yuma, intersects I-10 at Casa Grande, between Tucson and Phoenix. I-19, America's only all-metric freeway, drops south from Tucson, leading to the Mexican border at Nogales.

By air • Tucson International Airport is served by Aero California, Alaskan Airlines, America West, American, Continental, Delta, Northwest, Southwest, United and United Shuttle. The Tucson Airport Authority number is (520) 573-8100; the paging and information number is (520) 573-8000. *(www.tucsonairport.org)* All major **rental car** agencies serve the airport and several **cab and limo** companies provides airport transfers to downtown and elsewhere. See the *Tucson Official Visitor Guide* (referenced below) for lists of companies.

By rail • Amtrak's Sunset Limited provides service three days a week, west to Los Angeles and east to Orlando. Tucson's Amtrak station is at 400 E. Toole St.; (520) 623-4442 or (800) USA-RAIL.

By bus • Greyhound gallops from its station at 2 S. Fourth Avenue; (800) 231-2222 or (520) 792-3475. It has service north to Phoenix and east to the rest of the country on I-10, with connections west to Yuma and San Diego on Interstate 8.

GETTING ABOUT

Like Phoenix, Tucson is laid out in a large, simple grid, so it's easy to navigate. It doesn't have the complex local freeway system of the larger city. However, several primary streets will get you from one end of the city to the other relatively quickly. The main east-west routes are Grant Road, which runs eastward from I-10 and blends into Tanque Verde Road and the Catalina Highway leading into the Santa Catalina mountains; Speedway Boulevard, which runs west to Tucson Mountain Park and east to Tucson's desert outskirts; and Broadway Boulevard, which splits off from Congress Street downtown and heads east to the Old Spanish Trail and Saguaro National Park. River Road follows the contours of the dry bed of the Rillito River in north Tucson, providing nice views of the city.

Major north-south arteries are Oracle Road, the former main highway to Phoenix, leading north to the resort areas of Oro Valley and Catalina; Alvernon Road, which leads from Tucson International Airport north into the Santa Catalina foothills; and Kolb Road which runs north and links with a road into scenic Sabino Canyon.

Tucson's small urban core is just east of I-10, reached by the Congress Street offramp (exit 258). Street patterns of the downtown area are a bit complex, since they were laid out during the city's Spanish colonial period. It's best to park and explore this area by foot; see the suggested walking tour in Chapter Eighteen, page 240. The downtown area includes the Tucson Convention Center, the multi-colored La Placita Village where the visitor center is located, and the adjacent El Presidio Historic District, where the Old Pueblo began.

Local bus service ● Sun Tran provides transit service throughout the greater Tucson area; call (520) 792-9222.

Resort, hotel and motel shopping ● Most of Tucson's major resorts are tucked into the foothills of the Santa Catalinas, particularly northwest of town around Oro Valley. Its dude ranches are south and west beyond the Tucson Mountains and in the deserts to the east of town. Tucson doesn't have many downtown hotels or motels; most are near the airport or at freeway interchanges. Most of its inexpensive motels are along Oracle Road, once the main north-south highway. These are older lodgings and some—but not all—are rather scruffy.

Sightseeing ● Tucson's attractions are widely scattered so a rental car is essential if you're flying in. Many are in Tucson Mountain Park, a huge desert recreation area west of town and reached by Speedway Boulevard. Among the lures out there are Old Tucson Studios, the Arizona-Sonora Desert Museum and the western section of Saguaro National Park. Deserts east of Tucson shelter the other element of Saguaro National Park, Colossal Cave and Pima Air Museum. Other lures are north of downtown and in the Santa Catalinas.

Visitor services ● Contact the Metropolitan Tucson Convention & Visitors Bureau, 110 S. Church Ave., Suite 9100, Tucson, AZ 85701; (800) 638-8350. (*www.visittucson.org*) The bureau operates a visitor center in La Placita Village, adjacent to the Tucson Convention Center at the corner of Church Avenue and Broadway Boulevard. It's open weekdays 8 to 5 and weekends 9 to 4. **GETTING THERE:** From I-10, take the Congress Street exit east into downtown. After a few blocks, fork to the right onto Broadway, then turn right onto Church Street and you'll see the brightly painted La Placita Village. Park and follow signs to the visitor center. There's metered parking in front of La Placita and a large public garage just beyond, with a pedestrian overcrossing leading into the complex.

Our ten favorite Tucson moments

We've been visiting the Old Pueblo for decades, and it has given us many fine moments and good memories. We recall talking with Ted de Grazia about his philosophy of painting and life; of encountering a torch-lighted religious ceremony at Mission San Xavier del Bac; of overeating at El Charro Café. While researching this book, we've had new experiences and made new discoveries, so we picked our ten old and new favorites. You'll find further mention of these places and activities in upcoming chapters; check the index for their listings.

1 *VISITING THE WHITE DOVE OF THE DESERT AT NIGHT* • *Mission San Xavier del Bac, San Xavier Road; (520) 294-2624. GETTING THERE: Drive south from Tucson on I-19, take exit 92 and go west briefly to the mission.*

Mission San Xavier is one of Tucson's most splendid sights, with its twin octagonal towers, Moorish dome and whitewashed adobe walls. It attracts hundreds of daytime visitors, although we prefer coming at night, when this "White Dove of the Desert" is bathed in spotlights like a ghostly vision from Tucson's past. And indeed it is, for the area's first permanent mission settlement was established here by Father Eusebio Kino in 1700. The present mission building, completed in 1778, is more than an historical shrine. It still serves its original purpose, ministering to Tohono O'odham people of the surrounding San Xavier Indian Reservation.

2 *HAVING POOLSIDE BREAKFAST AT THE ARIZONA INN* • *2200 E. Elm St.; (520) 325-1541. (www.arizonainn.com) GETTING THERE: From downtown, drive north on Campbell past the University of Arizona campus, turn right onto Elm Street and go about three blocks. The inn is on the right, with parking on the left.*

The Arizona Inn is the most exquisite small resort in Tucson, and it's one of the most historic, dating from 1930. We often start our day there, having breakfast on a deck at poolside. Admiring the resort's lush landscaping, listening to birds chirp in the palms and orange trees, we feel as if we're in a world apart. And indeed we are. Although the inn is within minutes of busy downtown Tucson, it's sheltered in a fourteen-acre walled compound. Even traffic noise fails to disturb the quiet of this elegant retreat.

3 *WATCHING THE SUNSET FROM GATES PASS* • *Tucson Mountain Park; eight miles west of Tucson. GETTING THERE: Take I-10 exit 257 and drive west on Speedway Boulevard. It becomes Gates Pass Road after about five miles.*

A fine way to end a Tucson day is to watch the sunset from a vista point at Gates Pass, the rugged mountain gateway to Tucson Mountain Park. Enjoying the sunset from here is a local tradition and one might be hard pressed to find a spot in the vista point parking lot on a weekend. Actually, the best place to watch the sunset is from a rocky slope to the left of the vista point, where the view is better. Dozens of folks clamber up a rough trail, select a perch and sit like happy rockchucks, waiting for The Moment. Some evenings, they even break out in applause when Ole Sol disappears.

However, the real drama is not the sun slipping behind a distant mountain range. It's the light and shadow show it casts on the surrounding ridges, and the halos it creates on the silhouettes of saguaro cactus below.

4 RELAXING AT VENTANA FALLS • Loew's Ventana Canyon

Resort, 7000 N. Resort Dr.; (520) 299-2020. GETTING THERE: The resort is northeast of Tucson, just off Kolb Road in the Santa Catalina foothills. Take Grant Road east about eight miles, go northeast half a mile on Tanque Verde Road, then about two miles north on Sabino Canyon Road. Fork left onto Kolb Road and continue north another three miles. After crossing Sunrise Drive, continue about a mile and turn right into the resort.

This is one of the most appealing and romantic spots in the Tucson Basin. Ventana Falls is a silver wisp of water spilling down a sheer eighty-foot cliff into a stone-walled basin. Causal visitors to the resort often miss it, for there are no signs. It's reached by a short walk alongside Ventana Creek, on a riparian desert-woodland trail canopied with mesquite and palo verde trees. In spring, this desert garden trail is enhanced by flame-tipped ocotillo, cactus blooms and the yellow blossoms of the green-limbed palo verde.

5 HAVING DRINKS OR DINNER AT SOLEIL RESTAU-

RANT • 3001 E. Skyline Dr.; (520) 299-3345. Lunch and dinner daily, fall through spring; closed Mondays in summer. GETTING THERE: The restaurant is on the east side of El Cortijo Plaza, at Campbell Avenue and Skyline. Drive eight miles north from downtown on Campbell, then turn right into the complex immediately after crossing Skyline.

This appealing restaurant is part of El Cortijo Plaza, an art gallery complex. It's tucked into the foothills of the Santa Catalinas, offering pleasing views of the Tucson Basin. As its name says, Soleil is a sunny place, done in fall colors, with lots of windows to admit the ever-present Tucson sun. We like to browse about the nearby galleries, then adjourn to the restaurant just before sundown for a drink or dinner, watching the sky darken and the lights of Tucson brighten.

6 **WANDERING THE DESERT MUSEUM'S PATHS** • *Arizona-Sonora Desert Museum, 2021 N. Kinney Rd.; (520) 883-2702. (www.desertmuseum.org) Daily 7:30 to 5 March-September (plus Saturday evenings until 10 from June through September), and 8:30 to 5 the rest of the year. GETTING THERE: It's in Tucson Mountain Park, about eight miles west of downtown. Go west on Speedway Boulevard, spiral up through Gates Pass then down the other side to Kinney Road, turn right and follow signs.*

This is one of the finest indoor-outdoor museums in America, an extensive complex dedicated to the flora, fauna, geology and human history of the Sonoran Desert. There is so much to see here that we often spend hours wandering its trails. We peer at the pumas and bobcats in Cat Canyon, walk through bird-busy aviaries and study the almost humanoid shapes of the saguaro cactus. When the sun's too toasty, we retreat to the cool underground Earth Science Center and learn how this desert—and indeed the earth itself—was formed.

7 **VISITING DE GRAZIA'S GALLERY IN THE SUN** • *6300 N. Swan Rd.; (800) 545-2185 or (520) 299-9191. Daily 10 to 4. GETTING THERE: Follow Swan Road several miles north from downtown, cross Sunrise Road, then turn right into the complex after less than a mile, just short of Skyline Drive.*

The late Ted De Grazia was Arizona's most famous artist, developing a big following for his impressionistic, whimsical style of painting. Simple, quick brush strokes created color-splashed pictures of native people, Mexicans, roadrunners and other Southwestern subjects. We met De Grazia a few years before he died and I recall Betty haggling with him over the price of an artist's proof of one of his serigraph. Called "Prancing Horse," it hangs in our home in Las Vegas. Every time we look at that picture, we think of the talented, maverick painter who built his studio complex by hand, gave much to charity and once burned $250,000 worth of his paintings in a tax protest. And every time we come to Tucson, we stop by to pay our respects to his spirit, and to browse among the displays in his gallery.

8 **HAVING A CHICKEN BURRITO AT EL CHARRO** • *311 N. Court St.; (520) 622-1922. Lunch and dinner daily. GETTING THERE: It's in El Presidio Historic District near the corner of Franklin and Court.*

Started in 1922, the cheerfully decorated El Charrro Café is America's oldest Mexican restaurant still operated by the founding family. It is said that the chimichanga—essentially a deep-fried burrito—was first served here. This legendary café has been written up in *Gourmet* magazine, and *USA Today* once praised its chicken chimichanga as one of the "fifty best plates in America." However, we prefer the less greasy burrito version (some call it a burro). We accompany our meal with tortilla soup and a margarita on the rocks (no salt), made with 100 percent blue agave tequila. This is our traditional first supper when we come to town, and often our last upon departing.

9 *HIKING THE HUGH NORRIS TRAIL* ● *Saguaro National Park West on Kinney Road; (520) 733-5158. Park gates open daily 6 to dusk; visitor center 8:30 to 5. GETTING THERE: Follow directions to the Arizona-Sonora Desert Museum (above) and continue on Kinney Road to the park turnoff. The trailhead is less than a mile up Bajada Loop Drive, about two miles from the visitor center.*

This is our favorite desert hike because it passes through striking cactus gardens and rocky mountainous terrain. The trail is more than five miles long, leading along ridgelines to Wasson Peak, the Tucson Mountains' highest point. However, unless we're feeling particularly masochistic, we hike only the first mile or so, following a switchback up through some of the finest desert flora in the Tucson Basin. The trail is steep, although it's easy to negotiate since it was carefully engineered by the Civilian Conservation Corps during the Depression. They obviously did a fine job because it's still in good shape nearly seventy years later.

10 *DRIVING THE CATALINA HIGHWAY* ● *For information: Santa Catalina Ranger District, 5700 N. Sabino Canyon Rd.; (520) 749-8700. GETTING THERE: Follow any major street north to Grant Road and drive several miles east to Tanque Verde Road. Go northeast and east on Tanque Verde about two miles, then fork left onto the Catalina Highway.*

This is one of the most beautiful drives in Arizona and certainly the most spectacular in the Tucson area. The Catalina Highway spirals gently yet quickly from saguaro-busy foothills to the piney forests of the Santa Catalinas' Mount Lemmon Recreation Area. It passes through several climate zones before reaching the forests 8,000 feet above sea level. Fantastic rock formations line the roadside, resembling Easter Island statues or broken columns of Greek temples. We like to escape to Mount Lemmon on a hot day, lounge beneath cool pines, then start back near sunset. We then pause at the Windy Point lookout to watch the great sprawl of Tucson slowly light up like an upside-down canopy of stars.

This desert can speak to us in many ways...and we must meet it on its own terms, with patience and alertness of the senses. It is here for all of us to share and for each of us to protect.

— Narration from "Voices of the Desert" slide show at the Saguaro National Park West visitor center; © 1997 by the Finlay-Holiday Film Corp.

Chapter Twelve

DISCOVERING TUCSON

SAGUAROS, MUSEUMS AND A MISSION

Although greater Tucson's population is less than a third that of the Valley of the Sun, it has nearly as many attractions. They come in a variety of shapes and subjects, from a world-famous desert museum to a large aviation museum; from a beautiful Spanish mission to a national park dedicated to a cactus.

Tucson's attractions are widespread and a visitor with one or two weeks may have difficulty giving all of them quality time. To assist you in making some agonizing choices, we've compiled "A" and "B" lists. And to help you find your way, we provide driving directions to the area's various lures, either from downtown or from freeway exits.

A detailed map will be helpful—nay—essential in steering you to these assorted attractions. The *AAA Tucson CitiMap* is particularly useful, although it's available only to Triple-A members. Similar versions are sold in book stores and many tourist shops.

THE WAY THINGS WORK ● If you've skipped directly to the Tucson section of this book, having dismissed the Phoenix area as a potential place to visit, we'll review briefly the way our Ten Best lists work. We begin each with our favorite choice, followed by the next nine in alphabetical order. Thus, we have no losers in *The Best of Phoenix & Tucson,* only winners and runners up.

☺ **KID STUFF:** This little grinning guy marks attractions that are of particular interest to pre-teens.

NOTE: Items marked with ❖ are listed elsewhere in this book; check the index for page numbers.

PRICING: We use dollar sign codes to indicate the price range of adult admissions to various attractions and activities: *$* = under $5; *$$* = $5 to $9; *$$$* = $10 to $14 ; *$$$$* = $15 to $19; *$$$$$* = $20 or more.

THE TEN VERY BEST ATTRACTIONS

The Sonoran Desert is the most complex of all the world's arid zones, with more plant variety and more dramatic landforms than any similar region. This desert also can be regarded as the Tucson area's major tourist attraction. Although Phoenix is surrounded by the same desert, the Sonoran is the center of attention here.

Equally famous is a cactus that grows only in this desert, the giant saguaro (*sa-WHAR-oh*). Botanists and other fans of desert flora regard it as the monarch of cactus. With arms extending from thick trunks, it almost suggests human form. Indeed, early peoples regarded saguaros as departed spirits and treated them with great respect. They get less respect from people today. Some carve initials into their thick green hides, and illustrators turn them into comic figures and advertising icons. Indeed, their classic form often is used to represent generic cactus, although their range is very limited. They grow only in southern Arizona, northern Mexico and a small area of southeastern California.

Four of our Ten Best attractions focus on the fascinating Sonoran Desert and its famous cactus—Saguaro National Park, Sabino Canyon, Tucson Botanical Gardens and our favorite—a remarkable museum devoted to the study of this region:

1 ***ARIZONA-SONORA DESERT MUSEUM*** ● *2021 N. Kinney Rd.; (520) 883-2702. (www.desertmuseum.org) Daily 7:30 to 5 March-September (plus Saturday evenings until 10 from June through September); and 8:30 to 5 the rest of the year. MC/VISA; $$$. GETTING THERE: It's in Tucson Mountain Park, about eight miles west of downtown. Go west on Speedway Boulevard, which becomes Gates Pass Road after about five miles. Spiral up through Gates Pass then down the other side to Kinney Road, turn right and follow signs.* ☺

The finest natural history museum in Arizona just keeps getting better. The *New York Times* once called it "the most distinctive zoo in the United States." Yet to call it a zoo is a simplification. The Arizona-Sonora Desert Museum is a multi-faceted indoor-outdoor life sciences center devoted to the study of the Sonoran Desert. Deservedly, it's Tucson's most visited attraction. The museum takes its name from the American state of Arizona and the Mexican state of Sonora. Its primary focus is ecological, telling the story of the plants, animals and geology of the Sonoran Desert that spreads into these two states. Plan most of a day to walk its paths, viewing desert creatures in typical habitats, learning about desert flora and strolling through bird-busy aviaries. Over-under exhibits allow you to watch beavers and river otters at play above and below the surface of streams; or to see bobcats or pumas exploring their enclosures or napping in their dens. Museum exhibits cover all the climate zones of the Sonoran Desert, from cactus country to grasslands to mountain woodlands. Several activities are scheduled daily, from animal encounters in Cat Canyon to basket weaving demonstrations.

Our favorite exhibit is the Earth Sciences Center, an elaborate grotto featuring a realistic limestone cave, a jewel-like mineral display and a graphic explanation of the formation of our four-billion-year-old planet. Among the museum's other features are a walk-in humming-bird aviary and a desert grassland that demonstrates the biodiversity of a community of plants and animals, right down to micro-organisms. The facility also has an art gallery, coffee bar, terraced indoor-outdoor café and a dining room. Under preparation when we last visited was a major burrowing animal exhibit, which may be completed by the time you arrive.

2 **ARIZONA STATE MUSEUM** ● *University of Arizona campus at Park Avenue and University Boulevard; (520) 621-6302. (w3.arizona.edu/~asm) Monday-Saturday 10 to 5 and Sunday noon to 5. Free; donations accepted. GETTING THERE: From downtown, go north on Sixth Avenue to Sixth Street, and east about ten blocks to Euclid Avenue at the corner of the university campus. Drive north to the Main Gate parking garage between First and Second streets. It offers validated parking for the museum, and the garage cashier will give you a campus map.*

Tucson's finest archive after the Arizona-Sonora Desert Museum, this facility has an outstanding exhibit called "Paths of Life: American Indians of the Southwest." Actually, the focus is on ten tribes of Arizona and northern Mexico. Excellent displays depict the origins, history and present-day lives of these groups. To better appreciate the exhibit, watch a fifteen-minute introductory film, then follow a path past nicely done displays of artifacts, old photos, costumes, weapons, ceremonial items and present day folk arts. Many of the displays focus on creation legends and clashes with whites, such as the torment of the Yaquis by Mexico, and the tragic "Long Walk" when Arizona's Diné (Navajo) were marched to a barren reservation in New Mexico. At several video stations, tribal members present oral histories and discuss their current lives. The museum also has the world's largest collection of Southwestern native pottery. It has been acquiring pots since the late 1800s and the collection now includes more than 20,000 pieces spanning 2,000 years of history. You'll frequently see many of these items displayed in the museum's changing exhibits.

3 *MISSION SAN XAVIER DEL BAC* • *San Xavier Road; (520) 294-2624. Daily 7 to 5; donations appreciated. MC/VISA accepted at the gift shop. Daily mass at 8:30 a.m., Saturday vigil at 5:30 p.m. and Sunday masses at 8, 11 and 12:30. GETTING THERE: Drive south from Tucson on I-19, take exit 92 and go west briefly to the mission.*

After an extensive renovation completed in 1998, Tucson's splendid "White Dove of the Desert" is more beautiful than ever. A team of local and European restoration experts worked several years to restore its gleaming white exterior and the lavish Baroque décor inside. Sacred paintings on the chapel walls emerge with more vivid colors and the complex altar, with its many saintly statues, has been repaired and retouched.

The mission's museum contains relics from the past, and visitors can watch a 25-minute PBS video about the restoration. A gift shop occupies one end of the mission complex and a nearby path leads to a rugged volcanic hilltop with a cross and a fine view of the surrounding countryside. (There's no path up to the cross, although folks don't seem to mind if visitors scramble over the rocks to reach it.) From here, one sees a striking contrast—the gleaming whitewashed mission in its simple dirt compound below, and the highrises of modern Tucson in the distance.

Located on the 17,000-acre San Xavier Reservation, the mission still serves the Tohono O'odham people. Best time to visit is on weekends, when they set up a market on the mission grounds, selling crafts and tasty cinnamon-dusted Indian fry bread, along with other native and Mexican foods. Native dances often are conducted.

Construction of the present church was completed by Franciscan friars around 1778, although records of its architect and the creator of its splendid statuary have been lost. Not lost is the mystery of why the mission has only one bell tower. Local *rancheros* who had been supporting the construction project simply stopped providing funds.

4 *MOUNT LEMMON RECREATION AREA* • *For information: Santa Catalina Ranger District, 5700 N. Sabino Canyon Rd.; (520) 749-8700. (www.fs.fed.us/r3/coronado/scrd) Per-car entry fee $$; half-price for holders of Golden Age and Golden Access passes. Lodging and* *dining available at Alpine Lodge, (520) 576-1544. Mount Lemmon Ski Valley phone is (520) 576-1400 or (520) 576-1321. Lift tickets $$$$$; scenic lift rides $$. GETTING THERE: Follow any major street north to Grant Road and drive several miles east to Tanque Verde Road. Go northeast and east on Tanque Verde about two miles, then fork left onto the Catalina Highway.*☺

The Catalina Highway spirals quickly from the saguaro-thick foothills of the Santa Catalina mountains to the piney forests of Mount Lemmon. It passes through several climate zones and tops out at more than 8,000 feet. Along the way, you'll see fantastic roadside rock formations that suggest Easter Island statues or eroded temple columns. Several viewpoints provide impressive vistas of the Tucson Basin's vast carpet of civilization. The best view is from ❖ **Windy Point**. It's best to avoid the Mount Lemmon Recreation Area on weekends, since it's very popular with Tusconans, particularly in summer when thousands flee the desert heat.

If you're a winter visitor, you can hit the slopes at Mount Lemmon Ski Valley. The small facility has three lifts and twenty-one runs, from bunny to advanced. Skiing generally continues through Easter weekend, if there's sufficient snow. The main lift operates spring through fall for sightseers; it runs weekdays 11 to 5 and weekends 10 to 5. Nearby Summerhaven is an alpine community with a couple of restaurants, shops, a general store and rooms and dining at Alpine Lodge. A-frame homes tucked among the ponderosa pines provide summer solace for desert dwellers. The region is part of Coronado National Forest, with the typical recreational opportunities of camping, picnicking, hiking, backpacking and fishing. You can get information at the Palisades Ranger Station, a few miles below Summerhaven. Hiking is best in summer and fall. April through May is "mud season" with melting snow making a mess of most of the trails.

5 *OLD TUCSON STUDIOS* ● *201 S. Kinney Rd.; (520) 883-0100. (www.oldtucson.com) Daily 10 to 6. Major credit cards; $$$$. GETTING THERE: Follow directions to the Arizona-Sonora Desert Museum (above), but turn left on Kinney Road.* ☺

Like the phoenix bird of Tucson's big sister city, Old Tucson Studios has risen from its ashes. It's again functioning as a Western style amusement park and location site for movies and TV shows. Its story began in 1939 when Columbia Pictures produced one of the first big Western movie epics, *Arizona*, starring young William Holden and Jean Arthur. Seeking authenticity, producers built a life-sized model of early day Tucson, complete with adobe buildings, corrals and hitchin' rails. When filming was completed, the company left Old Tucson to wither in the desert sun. Twenty years later, entrepreneur Bob Sheldon bought the crumbling ruin, added more buildings and created a permanent set for Western movies. Since then, more than 150 movies and TV shows have been filmed here. Then in 1995, a fire swept through the grounds and destroyed nearly half of the complex. It re-opened a year later.

However, it was rebuilt more with tourism in mind than movie-making. With this shift of focus—and the loss of soundstages and props in the fire—few movies are filmed here these days. It's more of a Western style amusement park, with train rides, a stage coach ride, gold panning, stunt shows, shootouts on main street and lots of country and cowboy music—both live and recorded. The most interesting attraction is the Town Hall Museum, with memorabilia about the many oat-baggers filmed here. They include classics such as John Wayne's *Rio Lobo* and forgettables such as *The Last Outpost* with Ronald Reagan and *I Married Wyatt Earp* with Marie Osmond.

6 *PIMA AIR & SPACE MUSEUM* • *6000 E. Valencia Rd.; (520) 574-0462. (www.pimaair.org) Daily 9 to 5; MC/VISA, AMEX; $$. Guided walking tours at 10:15 and 1:15. GETTING THERE: Head south on I-10, take exit 267 and go east on Valencia Road; the museum appears on your right after about two miles.* ☺

This place is thick with aircraft, with more than 150 displayed inside several hangars and on a large sandy field. Some are impeccably restored; others have weeds growing around their landing gear. Most are combat, cargo and training craft from World War II through the Vietnam War, although a few civilian planes are in the collection.

The main building has several exhibits on the history of flight, including a replica of the 1903 Wright brothers Flyer. Among interesting aircraft outside and in the hangars are five Russian MiGs, a jeep-carrying Sikorsky Mojave helicopter complete with jeep, completely restored B-19 and B-29 World War II bombers and a Marine F4U Corsair. One of the oddest looking planes is a "Super Guppy" whose inflated and bulbous fuselage was designed to carry space vehicle components. Tours are conducted through a DC-6 that served as Air Force One from 1961 to 1965 for presidents Kennedy and Johnson. One building is devoted to space exploration, with a mockup of an Apollo command center, a Mercury capsule and a robotic exhibit.

7 *SABINO CANYON* • *5700 N. Sabino Canyon Road; (520) 749-8700. (www.fs.fed.us/r3/coronado/scrd or sabinocanyon.com) Visitor Center open 8:30 to 4:30 weekdays and 8 to 4:30 weekends. Per-car entry fee $$; half-price for holders of Golden Age and Golden Access passes. Trams depart every half hour from 9 to 4 for Sabino Canyon and hourly 9 to 4 for Bear Canyon; (520) 749-2327 or (520) 749-2861; $$; no credit cards. GETTING THERE: The canyon is about fifteen miles from downtown Tucson. Drive east on Grant Road, swerve left onto Tan-*

que Verde Road then—after a few blocks—go left again onto Sabino Canyon Road. Follow it four miles north and turn right into the parking area shortly after crossing Sunrise Drive. ☺

This Coronado National Forest recreation area encompasses two desert canyons, Sabino and Bear. They're immensely popular with locals—particularly Sabino Canyon on weekends—so the area is best visited on weekdays. Bear Canyon is less crowded. Just minutes from downtown, these steep-walled chasms cut deeply into the flanks of the Santa Catalinas. Forests of saguaro march from the banks of the two creeks up rugged canyon walls. Ultimately, they give way to forests of pines. Hiking trails lead into the more remote heights, although it requires quite a grunt to reach the evergreens.

Because of congestion on the narrow canyon roads, vehicle access is limited to trams. The Sabino tram takes visitors on a 45-minute round trip, with stops at picnic areas and trailheads along the way. The driver describes the canyon's geology, flora and fauna as the tram trundles along. One ticket is good all day, and visitors can hop on and off the tram at will, as long as they don't leave the canyon area. The Bear Canyon tram, used mostly by hikers, goes directly a trailhead for hikes to Seven Falls and other areas.

Sabino Creek is the most appealing part of Sabino Canyon as it splashes merrily down through rocky gorges, providing great places to swim and soak on hot days. However, it's a seasonal creek, subject to the whims of July-August "monsoons" and snowmelt from the Santa Catalinas. The best time to visit is in the spring, when the runoff is strong and desert plants are in bloom.

8 SAGUARO NATIONAL PARK • *The park comes in two parcels about thirty miles apart—Rincon Mountain Section (Saguaro East) which contains park headquarters, and Tucson Mountain Section (Saguaro West). Mailing address: 3693 Old Spanish Trail, Tucson, AZ 85730-5601; (520) 733-5153. The Saguaro West phone number is (520) 733-5158.* ☺

RINCON MOUNTAIN SECTION • Park gates open daily 7 to 10; visitor center 8:30 to 5. Per car fee $$; MC/VISA accepted in gift shop. GETTING THERE: For the most direct approach, drive east on Broadway about twelve miles, then fork right (south) onto Old Spanish Trail, which leads to the park.

Saguaro East is the larger of the two sections, covering 62,499 acres. This handsome preserve reaches through five climate zones from the desert to the conifer ramparts of the Rincon Mountains. Its saguaro forests are older and less dense than those of Saguaro West. At the visitor center, you can learn more than you probably ever wanted to know about this strange plant. It can reach a height of fifty feet, although it takes its time getting there. A seedling grows only a quarter of an inch the first year and it takes fifteen years to reach a foot; the familiar arms don't appear until it's more than fifty years old.

A desert garden in front of the visitor center helps you identify desert flora. Inside, an exhibit gallery has a topo map of the park, plus a few nature displays. Picture windows provide pleasing vistas of the desert and the distant Santa Catalinas. The best way to sample a cross-section of this park is to follow the paved eight-mile ❖ **Cactus Forest Drive** through the Rincon foothills. There are picnic areas and hiking trails along the way. If you're in good shape, get an early start and hike 17.5 miles to the top of 8,666-foot Mica Mountain. Several other less strenuous trails amble through the park, including our recommended ❖ **Cactus Forest Trail** in Chapter Eighteen.

TUCSON MOUNTAIN SECTION ● *Park gates open daily 6 to dusk; visitor center 8:30 to 5. Free entry; MC/VISA accepted at the gift shop. GETTING THERE: Follow directions to the Arizona-Sonora Desert Museum and continue west a couple of miles.*

Covering 21,152 acres, this section has more bountiful cactus gardens than its eastern counterpart, although it doesn't have the elevation range. The six-mile Bajada Loop Drive will take you through a dense thicket of saguaro and other desert flora, scattered over rough foothills of the Tucson Mountain. The road is rough, too. It's graded dirt and washboardy although navigable by patiently-driven cars. Our favorite short desert walk, the Valley View Trail, spurs off this road, offering an excuse to pause from the bumps. Less than a mile long, it travels through two dry washes and up to a low ridge that has nice views of the desert basin. Signs along the way provide brief descriptions of desert flora, so you can finally tell the difference between a mesquite and a palo verde, and you can learn how the teddy bear cactus got its name.

Although Saguaro East's visitor center is larger, Saguaro West's is more attractive, done in a classic Southwest pueblo style. It features a small diorama of Sonoran Desert fauna and some nice photos of the park's terrain. A fifteen-minute slide show, "Voices of the Desert," is beautifully photographed and more poetic than informative. We won't reveal the ending, although almost no one leaves after the final slide.

9 *TUCSON BOTANICAL GARDENS* ● *2150 N. Alvernon Way; (520) 326-9255. (www.tucsonbotanical.org) Daily 8:30 to 4:30; $. GETTING THERE: It's northeast of downtown, near the southeast corner of Alvernon and Grant Road.*

Once the estate of a local nurseryman and his wife, the garden rambles over more than five acres, with pleasant paths leading through lush plant life. It's thick with mature trees and plant-entwined trellises, so it's a nice retreat on a hot day. Among its displays are an Australian garden, herb garden, historical garden with English ivy and such, and a Tohono O'odham garden with crops typical of those tilled by native peoples. We were particularly interested in the Xeriscape Demonstration Garden which exhibits water-conservation methods essential to a desert environment. Solar energy is used to irrigate and illuminate this water-sipping garden.

10 *TUCSON MOUNTAIN PARK ● Eight miles west of downtown. Open for day use from 7 a.m. to sunset. The Pima County Parks and Recreation number is (520) 749-2690. For the Gilbert Ray campground, call (520) 883-4200. GETTING THERE: Go west on Speedway Boulevard, which becomes Gates Pass Road as it cuts through the Tucson Mountains and enters the park. This route isn't recommended for large RVs or trailers; they should take exit 99 from I-19 and follow Ajo Way (State Route 86) about six miles west, then go north into the park on Kinney Road.* ☺

Although several attractions within or adjacent to this huge preserve are listed elsewhere in this chapter, Tucson Mountain Park deserves a place of its own. This Pima County park sprawls over 17,000 acres of the rough-hewn Tucson Mountains and a desert basin to the west. It provides instant wilderness for Tucson residents and visitors. Park facilities include picnic areas, miles of hiking and riding trails and the Gilbert Ray Campground. A viewpoint at the top of Gates Pass provides nice vistas of the sweeping cactus-busy basin below. From here, one can see—with the aid of lenses—the telescopes of Kitt Peak Observatory, thirty-one miles away. The vista point, which is a popular place for sunsets, also has several exhibits on the geology, flora and history of the park.

Tucson Mountain Park was born of the Great Depression when Pima County and National Parks officials utilized men of the Civilian Conservation Corps to build its first stone structures, roads and trails.

THE NEXT TEN BEST ATTRACTIONS

These "B" list lures are certainly worthy of a pause if you have sufficient time. In the case of the Biosphere, you can catch it inbound or outbound if you're traveling between Tucson and Phoenix.

1 *COLUMBIA UNIVERSITY BIOSPHERE 2 ● 32540 S. Biosphere Rd. (P.O. Box 698), Oracle, AZ 85623; (520) 896-6200. (www.bio2.edu) Visitor center open daily 8:30 to 5. Campus tours on the hour from 9 to 3; $$$. "Under the Glass" tours weekdays at noon and 2, and weekends at 11:30, 1:30 and 3; $$$$$. Major credit cards. GETTING THERE: Biosphere 2 is about twenty-five miles north of Tucson near the town of Oracle. Head north on Oracle Road, which becomes State Route 77.*

A grand survival experiment started by a visionary billionaire now has university credentials. In the early 1990s, Texas oilman Edward P. Bass financed construction of a five-acre airtight ecosystem under glass. He wanted to demonstrate that humans could survive for years in a completely isolated, self-sustaining environment. And if one could succeed here, could the moon or Mars be next? Four men and four women remained sealed inside for two years, although they were plagued with problems. A second group stayed in scientific solitary only six months before voting themselves out of their "island." The two experiments became embroiled in controversy and lawsuits. There were charges that oxygen, food and insecticides had been smuggled in, and that animals essential to sustain the "bionaughts" had died and had to be replaced. Pigs intended to provide pork ate the baby chicks, so there went the future breakfast omelettes.

Then in 1996, Columbia University agreed to take over the facility, intending to practice real science and not survivalist gimmickry. The primary purpose of its ongoing experiments is the sustainability of our own planet, not a space bubble on Mars. The biosphere has become an important environmental teaching center, with several students taking courses and living on campus.

Since it's no longer used as a long-range survivalist lockup, it's open to public tours. Visitors are conducted through its five "biomes"— rainforest, savannah, ocean, desert and marsh. The Biosphere's growing campus includes an astronomy observatory, ocean reef gallery and an exhibit sponsored by Volvo to study the impact of cars on the environment. The facility also has a restaurant and even a hotel for those wishing to stay longer.

2 ARIZONA HISTORICAL SOCIETY MUSEUM ● *On the University of Arizona campus at 949 E. Second St.; (520) 628-5774. (w3.arizona.edu/~azhist) Monday-Saturday 10 to 4, Sunday noon to 4. Free; contributions encouraged. GETTING THERE: See directions for the Arizona State Museum on page 166.*

This nicely-done facility picks up where the Arizona State Museum leaves off, covering the settlement of Arizona from the arrival of the Spanish to the development of a modern society. Uncluttered, informative exhibits tell the state's story with a focus on Tucson. Displays change frequently, although three are more or less permanent. "Exploring 1870s Tucson" features replicas of Mexican-American, Anglo and Tohono O'odham homes of that era. The Transportation Exhibit traces the development of Arizona transport from bull carts and an ill-fated attempt at a camel corps to paddlewheelers on the Colorado River to horseless carriages. The Arizona Mining Hall has a realistic mockup of a hard-rock mine, plus a gem and mineral exhibit, a miner's tent cabin, a huge ore crusher and old photos of life in Arizona's mining communities.

3 COLOSSAL CAVE • *In Colossal Cave Mountain Park at 16711 E. Colossal Cave Rd.; (520) 647-7275. (www.colossalcave.com) Daily 8 to 6 in summer and 9 to 5 the rest of the year; open an hour later on Sundays and holidays. Cave tours leave frequently. MC/VISA; $$ plus a small per-car park admission. GETTING THERE: Go south on I-10 to exit 279 and follow State Highway 83 east through the small town of Vail. Continue eastward to the junction of Old Spanish Trail and Colossal Cave Road and turn north.* ☺

Colossal Cave isn't quite. And it's not a cave but an extensive cavern. This is a huge complex, possibly the world's largest dry cave; the end has never been found. It may have been colossal once, although earlier decades of misuse destroyed many of its formations. One operator would break off stalactites and stalagmites and sell them to his customers for $2 apiece. The cave is now part of a Pima County park and it is run by concessionaires who—of course—are quite careful about its preservation. However, because the cave is dry, it's not as interesting as "wet caves" where the formations are still growing. It does have some impressive limestone displays in several rooms, which were connected by tunnels and steps during the 1930s by CCC workers. Tours last forty-five minutes and cover about a mile. This is only the tip of the—well—stalactite. It's estimated that the complex has more than forty miles of tunnels.

Another interesting element of this Pima County park is the historic La Posta Quemada Ranch. Among its facilities are a museum, two cafés, a picnic area, gift shop, playground, riding stables, butterfly garden, tortoise enclosure and several ranch exhibits. The park also has camping areas and hiking trails.

4 DE GRAZIA GALLERY IN THE SUN • *6300 N. Swan Rd.; (800) 545-2185 or (520) 299-9191. Daily 10 to 4; free. GETTING THERE: Follow Swan Road several miles north from downtown, cross Sunrise Road, then turn right into the complex after less than a mile, just short of Skyline Drive.*

The late Ted De Grazia developed a big following for his impressionistic, whimsical style of painting. His simple brush strokes created color-splashed pictures of native people, Mexicans, roadrunners and other Southwestern subjects. An earthy individual, he used local adobe and other materials to build his studio and an adjacent chapel called "Mission in the Sun." This is an appealing and rustic retreat, tucked into thick desert foliage that shelters it from encroaching suburbia.

Since his death in 1982, a foundation continues operating his rustic gallery and gift shop. Some exhibits are permanent while others are changed periodically, drawn from an extensive collection. De grazia did not shy from commercialism. Throughout Arizona and the West, you'll see his works replicated on everything from greeting cards to refrigerator magnets. In fact, he may be the world's most published artist. He donated much of his time and his art to charitable causes, allowing his images to be used on millions of UNICEF cards to raise funds for that organization. The gallery's gift shop sells ceramics, enamel work, note cards and inexpensive prints of his art—and refrigerator magnets. The adjacent "Little Gallery" displays and sells works of other Arizona artists.

5 *EL PRESIDIO HISTORIC DISTRICT • Just north of downtown, bordered by Sixth Street, Ninth Avenue, Alameda Street and Granada Avenue. Old Town Artisans is at 210 Court Ave., Monday- Saturday 9:30 to 5:30 and Sunday noon to 5; (800) 782-8027 or (520) 623-6024. (www.oldtownartisans.com) Saguaro Artisans is at 215 N. Court Ave., Monday-Saturday 9:30 to 5:30 and Sunday 10:30 to 5:30; (520) 792-3466.*

This is where Tucson began, when a walled garrison was established in 1776. Patterns of the original walls are marked on a walking tour map in the *Tucson Official Visitors Guide,* although little physical evidence remains. The area does contain Tucson's oldest surviving adobe buildings. A few of these house professional offices, restaurants and inns, although most are still private homes. Two of the largest adobes contain gift, crafts and souvenir shops—❖ **Old Town Artisans** and **Saguaro Artisans.** Old Town Artisans and its adjacent Old Town Pot Shop cover an entire block, with more than a dozen shops built around an attractively landscaped patio. ❖ **La Cocina Restaurant** is part of this complex, and its Wilde Rose Coffee Company takeout offers snacks and designer coffees. Other area restaurants are ❖ **El Charro**, a block north of Old Town Artisans at 311 N. Court Avenue, and ❖ **El Minuto**, two blocks west of Old Town Artisans at 354 S. Main Avenue.

A few of the historic buildings display signs marking their vintage and significance. The ❖ **Tucson Museum of Art** is on El Presidio's southern edge near Alameda Street. It's in a modern building, although the complex shelters several ancient adobes in its Historic Block; see page 177 below.

6 *FLANDRAU SCIENCE CENTER, PLANETARIUM & MINERAL MUSEUM • University of Arizona campus at 1601 E. University Blvd.; (520) 621-STAR. (www.flandrau.org) Monday-Saturday 9 to 5 and Sunday noon to 5; plus Wednesday-Saturday evenings 7 to 9 for stargazing; $; theater tickets $$. Call for schedules of shows and public telescope viewings. MC/VISA accepted in the science shop. Mineral Museum is included in the Science Center admission; (520) 621-4227. GETTING THERE: The center is at the corner of University and Cherry Street* *on the university campus. Closest parking is in the McKale Garage, reached by turning north from Sixth Street onto National Championship Drive near Arizona Stadium, between Park and Campbell avenues.* ☺

The Flandrau facility seems preoccupied with minerals, both from outer space (meteorites) and as a part of the earth's environment. Perhaps it's because the Mineral Museum is downstairs from the science center. The facility's most interesting offerings are its "Theater of the Stars" astronomy shows, laser light shows and public access to its observatory. Start your visit by standing on a "human sundial" out front to check the hour; it's always accurate because Arizona doesn't go on daylight saving time. Inside, you'll see exhibits concerning the mineral composition of the earth's crust, and displays of crystal symmetry and fluorescent minerals. Videos discuss our planet's composition and our uses of minerals, and the center has a nice collection of meteorites gathered from various parts of the world.

Downstairs, the **Mineral Museum** displays hundreds of specimens from around the world. Most are from Arizona, and from south of the border because a museum patron donated his huge collection of Mexican minerals. One exhibit shows gemstones both in their raw and finished states after they've been fashioned into jewelry.

7 INTERNATIONAL WILDLIFE MUSEUM ● *4800 W. Gates Pass Rd.; (520) 617-1439. (www.thewildlifemuseum.org or www.safari-clubfoundation.org) Weekdays 9 to 5 and weekends 10 to 6. Major credit cards; $$. GETTING THERE: Drive about five miles west on Speedway Boulevard; it becomes Gates Pass Road just short of the museum.* ☺

Calling itself "Tucson's Natural History Museum," this attractive facility is something of an anomaly. Behind a curious castle-like façade—complete with moat—is a huge collection of stuffed critters from around the world. It's a fine educational facility, with displays concerning wild animal characteristics and behavior. Yet the museum, which is privately funded by the Safari Club Foundation, seems out of step with current conservation practices. Many exhibits focus on wildlife preservation, while endorsing "regulated hunting." One large room—Wildlife of the World Gallery—is filled with more than a hundred hunting trophies. Bodyless Cape buffalo, rhinos, elephants and assorted antelopes stare morosely from the walls in this room, which has the look of a huge hunting lodge. Another exhibit extols several "hunter heroes," including Teddy Roosevelt, who was a big game hunter and yet one of the chief architects our national park system.

Several large dioramas are nicely done, yet the preoccupation with hunting continues—in this case by animals. Here, a pack of gray wolves chomps on a wild-eyed caribou; there a pride of lions is taking down an African buffalo; and over there, bears are pigging out on spawning salmon. Of course not all exhibits portray such savagery. And overall, this is a pretty impressive wildlife museum.

8 *REID PARK ZOO* • *1100 S. Randolph Way; (520) 791-4022. Daily 9 to 4. MC/VISA; $. GETTING THERE: The zoo is about four miles east and south of downtown. It's in Gene C. Reid Park, off 22nd Avenue between Country Club Road and Randolph Way. ☺*

Although it must share the limelight with the famous Arizona-Sonora Desert Museum, this fine little zoo has carved its own niche, with its impressive educational activities and endangered species programs. It leads the zoological world in the successful breeding of the rare giant anteater—which might suggest that it doesn't have an ant problem. Despite its sunbelt location, the zoo is home to a couple of contented looking polar bears. They must be happy here, since they became parents of a cub in 2001.

Reid Park Zoo is nicely landscaped and well kept, shaded by eucalyptus and palm trees. Its busy collection of more than 500 critters includes giraffes, lions, tigers, hippos, primates and more. Many of its occupants are housed in small but modern open air enclosures, allowing visitors close-up looks. The zoo shares large Reid Park with a baseball and soccer field, rose garden, duck pond, fishing and paddleboat lake, swimming pools, golf course, playground and picnic areas. It's also home to Hi Corbett Field, a baseball park used by the minor league Tucson Toros, and for spring Cactus League exhibition baseball by Denver's Colorado Rockies.

9 *TUCSON MUSEUM OF ART* • *140 N. Main Ave.; (520) 624-2333. (www.tucsonarts.com) Monday-Saturday 10 to 4 and Sunday noon to 4; $. MC/VISA accepted in gift shop. GETTING THERE: The museum is on the southern edge of El Presidio Historic District.*

One of Arizona's finest art museums, this facility presents a curious intrusion on the edge of El Presidio. Although the main museum is a dramatically modern building, the complex shelters five old homes in its Historic Block. They serve as extensions of the museum, containing galleries and other exhibits. The main museum is architecturally intriguing—low-rise and bunkered into the ground. Changing exhibits are arrayed along a "squared spiral" ramp that leads down to a lower gallery floor.

The Historic Block buildings are arrayed around a sculpture garden called the Plaza of the Pioneers. The Goodman Pavilion contains several galleries of Western art. The Stevens House has the museum's largest permanent exhibit—a fine collection of pre-Colombian artifacts, and religious and folkloric items from Spanish South America and Mexico. Its crucifix and ceremonial mask collections are particularly impressive. The Corbett House, built around the turn of the last century, is a classic Arts and Crafts bungalow. Its rooms exhibit the sturdy and stern wooden furniture of that era.

10 *UNIVERSITY OF ARIZONA CAMPUS* • *The Visitor Center occupies a small building in the heart of the campus near Cherry Street, across University Boulevard from the Flandrau Science Center. It's open Monday-Friday 7:30 to 5 and Saturday 9 to noon; (520) 621-5130. (www.arizona.edu) For information on free campus tours conducted during the academic year, call (520) 621-3641. For University of Arizona events, call the McKay Center ticket office at (520) 621-2287. (www.arizcats.com) GETTING THERE: From downtown, go north on Sixth Avenue to Sixth Street and follow it east to the campus. To reach the Visitor Center, turn north from Sixth onto National Champion Drive near Arizona Stadium, between Park and Campbell avenues. There's visitor parking near the center, or you can park in the McKale Garage.*

The University of Arizona is both a scholastic and a cultural center, with a fine academic reputation and eight museums and galleries. It was established in 1885 as Arizona's first institute of higher learning, with six faculty, six freshmen and twenty-six prep students. It now has an enrollment exceeding 35,000. You can visit its many museums and galleries, or just stroll about the handsome campus with its sturdy red brick buildings and mix of green lawns and desert flora. Grab a snack or an Arizona Wildcat souvenir at the Memorial Student Union and Bookstore. Among its attractions not listed elsewhere in this book:

Center for Creative Photography has one of the world's largest photo collections, with 60,000 prints by 1,400 photographers. Its changing exhibits are drawn from this collection and from elsewhere. The center is in the John P. Schafter Building at Olive Road and Second Street; (520) 621-7968.

University of Arizona Museum of Art has a fine collection of paintings from the Renaissance through the Nineteenth Century, and includes works by Picasso, Rodin and Andrew Wyeth. Changing exhibits often feature student art. The museum is at Park Avenue and Speedway Boulevard; (520) 621-7567.

The **Wildcat Heritage Gallery** is an essential stop for university alumni, with photos and other memorabilia of teams dating back to 1897. It's in McKale Memorial Center on Enke Drive just east of the Cherry Avenue Garage.

Also worth a visit is a two-block section of University Boulevard extending west from the campus between Park Avenue and Euclid Avenue. It's a typical collegiate street with coffee houses, small cafés, beer pubs, a couple of galleries, book stores and Wildcat logo shops. Several of its inexpensive diners are featured in Chapter Fifteen.

Chapter Thirteen

TUCSON DINING
HOLY FRIJOLES! IT'S MORE THAN TACOS

Tucson has a very active dining scene and even boasts a couple of celebrity chefs. Local foodies say that Tucson's Donna Nordon created contemporary Southwest cuisine at her Café Terra Cotta, although Mark Miller's Coyote Café fans in Santa Fe will argue that point. She recently moved her restaurant to a sleek new home in the desert slopes above the city. Also retreating to higher ground was another noted local chef, Janos Wilder. He shifted his upscale Southwest style restaurant from downtown to the opulent Westin La Paloma.

Few of the premiere restaurant chains have opened branches in Tucson. There is no McCormick and Schmick's seafood parlor or Morton's of Chicago. Neither LA's Wolfgang Puck nor Honolulu's Roy Yamaguchi have been seen lurking about. However, local entrepreneur Bob McMahon is ensuring that Tucson gets its share of trendy diners. His firm, Metro Restaurants, has opened several vogue cafés such as Firecracker Bistro, Metropolitan Grill and his own McMahon's Prime Steakhouse. McMahon also is a partner in the legendary Tack Room.

Tucson's restaurants, like the city itself, are rather scattered. There is no restaurant row here; no focused dining area. Some of the better restaurants are in the resorts; others are free-standing and rather randomly placed; a few are in shopping centers. Other than various versions of Hispanic restaurants, Tucson doesn't have a strong ethnic dining scene. There is no Chinatown here and no Italian neighborhood; Tucson is mostly Gringo and Mexican country. It does offer a few ethnic cafés, however. Some of the more interesting ones are around the University of Arizona campus, particularly along University Boulevard. Most are rather inexpensive and several make our budget dining scene in Chapter Fifteen.

NOTE: Items marked with ❖ are listed elsewhere in this book; check the index for page numbers.

PRICING: Dollar sign codes indicate the price of a typical dinner with entrée, soup or salad, not including drinks, appetizers or dessert: **$** = less than $10 per entrée; **$$** = $10 to $19; **$$$** = $20 to $29; **$$$$** = "Did you say you were buying?"

THE TEN VERY BEST RESTAURANTS

Tucson's finest restaurants are a predicable mix of upscale resort diners, old standards that have been around for decades and some interesting new culinary kids on the block.

1 **VENTANA ROOM** • *At Loew's Ventana Canyon Resort, 7000 N. Resort Dr.; (520) 299-2020. Contemporary American; full bar service. Dinner nightly. Major credit cards; $$$$. GETTING THERE: The resort is just off Kolb Road in the Santa Catalina foothills. From downtown, go north to Grant Road and follow it east about eight miles, go northeast half a mile on Tanque Verde Road, then about two miles north on Sabino Canyon Road. Fork left onto Kolb Road and continue north another three miles. Shortly after crossing Sunrise Drive at a traffic light, turn right onto Clubhouse Lane, passing through an entry gate.*

Local foodies and many others agree that the Ventana Room is Tucson's finest restaurant. It carries an AAA Four Diamond Award; *100 Best Restaurants in Arizona* gives it three stars, the book's highest rating; and the Zagat survey's *Southwest Top Restaurants* gives it the highest score in the entire Southwest.

An evening here will confirm all of this, assuming you're willing to pay for entrées starting in the thirties and reaching toward a hundred dollars for a tasting menu that includes matched wines. It is a handsome space, terraced above the resort's main lobby. A mix of rough-cut stone and glass brick walls give it a particularly striking look, and picture windows provide impressive views to the Tucson Basin far below. The frequently changing menu is a study in contemporary cuisine. Some entrées when we last visited were sea bass with apricot ginger glaze, grilled tenderloin of buffalo with a sweet potato pancake, prime sirloin with chanterelle roquefort bread pudding, and grilled veal with a casoulette of beans and sautéed Brussels sprouts.

2 ANTHONY'S IN THE CATALINAS • *6440 N. Campbell Ave.; (520) 299-1771. Contemporary American and continental; full bar service. Lunch weekdays and dinner nightly. Major credit cards; $$$$. GETTING THERE: Drive about seven miles north on Campbell Avenue, then turn right shortly after crossing Skyline Drive.*

Anthony's is Tucson's legendary special event restaurant, where anniversaries are celebrated, visiting Aunt Maudes are taken (if they're buying) and business associates are impressed. Service by the tuxedo-clad waitstaff is impeccable yet safely short of pompous. The restaurant's foothills perch affords a nice city view, but save it for evening since Tucson without night lights isn't that impressive from afar; see page 186. Housed in a pink stucco Spanish Colonial style building, Anthony's is handsome within, with polished tile floors, thick beam cathedral ceilings and modern beveled glass lighting fixtures. Two dining areas provide views—one of the Santa Catalinas and the other of the city. Menu offerings include chicken Francaise, pork tenderloin breaded in cornmeal, lamb with herbs and Dijon *demi-glace*, veal scaloppine and *Chateaubriand* in red wine sauce.

3 ARIZONA INN DINING ROOM • *2200 E. Elm St.; (520) 325-1541. (www.arizonainn.com) American and continental; full bar service. Breakfast, lunch and dinner daily, with Sunday brunch. Major credit cards; $$$ to $$$$. Jackets suggested for men. GETTING THERE: From downtown, drive north on Campbell Avenue past the University of Arizona campus, turn right onto Elm Street and go about three blocks. The inn is on the right, with parking on the left.*

The opulence of Tucson's most appealing small resort is reflected in its old world style dining room—truss beam ceilings, little lamp shade chandeliers and wall sconces, handcrafted ladderback chairs and tables set with fine silver and crystal. An antique sideboard, gilt-edge mirrors and classic artwork create an elegant dining setting. The menu is elegant as well, more classic than contemporary. It features handsomely presented entrées such as roast duck breast with red wine sauce; saffron grilled venison, New York steak, potato encrusted orange roughy, seared veal chops and beef *Bourguignonne*. The restaurant has an excellent wine list and it's noted for its in-house desserts.

4 CAFÉ TERRA COTTA • *3500 E. Sunrise Dr.; (520) 577-8100. (www.cafeterracotta.com) Southwest cuisine; full bar service. Lunch and dinner daily. Major credit cards; $$ to $$$. GETTING THERE: The café is on the southeast corner of Sunrise and Campo Ar-*

bieto. *Follow Campbell Avenue about seven miles north, then turn right onto Skyline Drive. Go east half a mile, veering to the right to blend onto Sunrise, and the restaurant is on your right, just beyond a traffic light.*

Donna Nordon's legendary café moved in early 2001 from St. Phillips Plaza to an impressive Santa Fe style building in the Santa Catalina foothills. Something puzzles us, however. Despite her new restaurant's lofty location, the main dining room faces north and most diners are denied the valley view. Nordon's menu offers both small plates and main courses. When we last visited, her menu featured entrées such as grilled Angus tip steak with Vermont cheddar cheese, marinated lamb with apple chutney, pork chops with mashed sweet potatoes, and chicken breast with roasted garlic and cheese sauce. These entrées seem more contemporary American than Southwest. However, Nordon also offers poblano chili relleno with rock shrimp or roasted pork, and a vegetable enchilada. The restaurant is severely modern with a step-down drop ceiling in blue, red and purple and—to prove that it's a place famous for Southwest cuisine—potted cactus.

5 **THE DISH** • *3200 E. Speedway Blvd.; (520) 326-1714. Contemporary American; wine and beer. Dinner Tuesday-Saturday. MC/VISA; $$ to $$$. GETTING THERE: This dish is just east of Country Club Boulevard, on the south side of Speedway.*

To find one of Tucson's most intimate restaurant, look first for the RumRunner wine shop with its bold purple entrance canopy. The Dish, a tiny place with a dozen tables, is tucked in behind the wine shop, which we rate as the best in Tucson in Chapter Seventeen, page 235. Remarkably tasty fare is served in the Dish's cozy space. The changing menu may—or may not, by the time you arrive—offer cioppino busy with fish, crab meat, mussels and shrimp; grilled pork chops with hard cider cinnamon demi-glacé; roast duck with port and mulatto chile glaze; and—for vegans—a vegetable torte of zucchini, squash, eggplant, tomatoes, mushrooms, spinach and havarti cheese. Lighter appetites can go for "small dishes" such as shrimp and scallops or saffron mussels. With subdued lighting and soft jazz whispering in the background, The Dish also is our choice as one of Tucson's most romantic restaurants; see Chapter Eighteen, page 250.

6 **¡FUEGO!** • *6958 E. Tanque Verde Rd.; (520) 886-1745. Southwest cuisine; full bar service. Dinner nightly. Major credit cards; $$ to $$$. GETTING THERE: The restaurant is about ten miles northeast of downtown, on the south side of Tanque Verde between Grant Road and Sabino Canyon Road. Go east on Broadway Boulevard just under six miles to Wilmot Road. Follow it north 1.5 miles and go half-right onto Tanque Verde Road, then follow it about a mile northeast and east to the restaurant.*

Alan Zeman's ¡Fuego! was a quick hit when it opened in the 1998, praised by Zagat as "Tucson's best new restaurant" and winner of the *Wine Spectator* Award of Excellence. Among Zeman's recent creations were pork tenderloin in barbecue glaze with apple chutney, grilled salmon cakes with chipotle aioli and salsa fresca, and the namesake Fuego—chorizo and jumbo shrimp flambé. Although most entrées range into the twenties, ¡Fuego! offers several "small plates" that provide filling repasts for around $10. The restaurant interior is as warmly contemporary as the menu, with wooden floors and booths, drop lamps and a fireplace. It's a large complex, with two dining areas, a separate cocktail lounge and a rear patio.

7 THE GOLD ROOM • *In the Westward Look Resort at 245 E. Ina Rd.; (520) 297-1151. (www.westwardlook.com) Southwestern nouveau with continental accents; full bar service. Breakfast, lunch and dinner daily, with Sunday brunch. Major credit cards; $$$ to $$$$. GETTING THERE: Take Oracle Road about nine miles north from downtown and turn right on Ina. Then within a few blocks, turn left up Westward Look Drive. From I-10 take Ina Road (exit 248) six miles east to Oracle Road.*

The gold is mostly in the menu in this AAA Four Diamond rated restaurant. The Gold Room has a Southwest modern look, with a pole beam and *lantilla* ceiling, potted cactus and scenic desert photos on the walls. Both the terraced dining room and an outside deck offer views of distant Tucson. The changing menu may feature savories such as sautéed seafood medley with garlic mashed potatoes, roasted game hen with wild mushroom risotto, buffalo sirloin with chipotle maple glacé, rack of lamb with truffle port sauce, and a vegetarian dish of sun dried tomato polenta with pan-seared mushrooms.

8 JANOS • *At the Westin La Paloma at 3800 E. Sunrise; (520) 615-6100. Southwest cuisine; full bar service. Dinner Monday-Saturday; closed Sunday. Major credit cards; $$$$. GETTING THERE: The restaurant occupies its own building just northwest of the main resort. To reach La Paloma, follow Campbell Avenue about seven miles north from downtown, then turn right onto Skyline Drive. Go east briefly then veer to the right onto Sunrise; turn south onto La Palomita and follow signs.*

Janos Wilder is perhaps Tucson's best known celebrity chef and cookbook author, and pronounce it *YAH-nos*, please. He moved his restaurant from an historic downtown building to the Westin a few years ago, where his guests enjoy the same creative cooking along with valley vistas. The restaurant foyer suggests a handsome Spanish drawing room, although the main dining area is almost spartanly elegant. If you seek ultimate opulence, bring thirteen friends and reserve the Wine Room, where you can dine among thousands of bottles of good vintages—and hope someone else is picking up the check. The main dining room is tiered to maximize the views, better at night than in daylight. Janos' entrées change frequently, often exhibiting Mediterranean and Asian accents among the salsas and tortilla shards. Some recent examples were *nori*-wrapped ahi with Dungeness crab and spring rolls, chicken in red wine with baby onions and mushrooms, Colorado lamb in two styles, grilled ribeye steak with potato grautin, and seared and roasted duck breast. Those seeking simpler and less expensive fare can dine at the J-Bar, a more casual café just below Janos.

9 *OVENS BISTRO & WINE BAR* • *In St. Phillips Plaza at 4280 N. Campbell Ave.; (520) 577-9001. Contemporary American; full bar service. Lunch Monday-Saturday, dinner nightly and Sunday brunch. Major credit cards; $$ to $$$. GETTING THERE: St. Phillips Plaza is about five miles north of downtown, between the Rillito River and River Road. The restaurant is on the south side of the plaza.*

Opened in the early 1990s, Ovens has been called Tucson's best bistro by local food fans. The look is softly Southwestern, with light colors, modern furnishings, beam ceilings and an open kitchen with a wood-fired oven. However, its most inviting dining area is a patio shaded by mesquite trees just off one of St. Phillips' landscaped plazas. The menu is creative American with Mediterranean and Asian accents. Frequently-changing entrées may include rotisserie chicken, grilled ahi tuna, salmon seared with spices, grilled tenderloin of beef, or rack of lamb. Ovens also offers specialty pizzas such as shrimp and smoked bacon, and an assortment of fresh pastas. The wine list is quite fine, with a couple dozen by the glass. For a fee, diners can try two-ounce samples of wine flights.

10 *THE TACK ROOM* • *7300 E. Vactor Ranch Trail off Sabino Canyon Road; (520) 722-2800. (www.metrorestaurants.com) Contemporary American; full bar service. Dinner Tuesday-Sunday; closed Monday. Major credit cards; $$$ to $$$$. GETTING THERE: It's about ten miles northeast of downtown. Go east on Grant Road, then northeast and east on Tanque Verde Road to Sabino Canyon Road. Drive north on Sabino Canyon about half a mile, then turn right onto Vactor Ranch.*

There was a time when this legendary Tucson restaurant sat on a lonely knoll with a view of the Santa Catalinas, far out in the desert. It hasn't moved an inch since it opened in 1965, although it's now surrounded by a modern subdivision. One must drive past the desert-landscaped homes to reach it. Once there, you'll find a classic "ranch house elegant" Santa Fe style adobe structure that was built as a private home sixty years ago. Rough cut wooden beams hold up lofty ceilings; walls are decorated with Western art and artifact. The waitstaff matches the setting—formally attired yet casual and friendly. Although the Tack Room once was a bastion of Western American cooking—which means mostly steak—it has shifted to American regional fare. Filet mignon and New York steak are still staples, although the menu also offers more contemporary dishes. Some examples are pistachio crusted roast duckling with orange fig chutney, breast of chicken with herb stuffing and garlic potatoes, garlic rack of lamb with sautéed spinach, and salmon with chili potato gratin.

THE TEN BEST SPECIALTY RESTAURANTS

What's your specialty? A Western style steak house or a modern one? Perhaps you prefer seafood or maybe just a good pizza. Our choices reflect the variety in Tucson's dining scene, and are listed in no particular order.

1 **THE BEST COWBOY STEAK: Pinnacle Peak** ● *In Trail Dust Town at 6541 E. Tanque Verde Rd.; (520) 296-0911. Full bar service. Dinner nightly. Major credit cards; $$ to $$$. GETTING THERE: Trail Dust Town is about eight miles northeast of downtown, on the north side of Tanque Verde between Wilmot and Kolb roads. Go east on Pima Street, then northeast briefly on Tanque Verde.*

Well, dang my britches! Git yourselves over to Trail Dust Town and sink your chompers into a cowboy steak. An institution for half a century, this is Tucson's unabashed Western tourist gimmick. It's similar to Scottsdale's Pinnacle Peak Patio, although Tucson's version is more extensive, part of the Western-style Trail Dust Town. Both pinnacles Peak have the same gimmick—anyone caught wearing a necktie will have it snipped off, and signs warn of this danger. Obviously, many have ignored these signs, since thousands of ties hang from the restaurant's walls and rafters. The menu in this huge Western style steak house is simple—mostly mesquite grilled loin steak. Other choices are ribs, salmon filet and hamburgers. Trail Dust Town is popular with families and it's the darling of the tour bus set, with dining halls large enough to accommodate bus loads, plus a big patio out back.

When not chomping down on cowboy steak, you can ride a miniature train, visit the Museum of the Horse Soldier and the Wagon Museum, and watch a shootout. Or just stroll along the remarkably detailed frontier town main street and poke into the boutiques and curio shops. This is an evening-only place, even in winter. Everything—including the steak house—opens at 5 p.m.

2 **THE BEST NON-COWBOY STEAK: McMahon's Prime Steakhouse** ● *2959 N. Swan Rd.; (520) 32-PRIME. (www.metrorestaurants.com) Full bar service. Lunch weekdays and dinner nightly. Major credit cards; $$$ to $$$$. GETTING THERE: The restaurant is near the southwest corner of Swan and Fort Lowell, northeast of downtown.*

When Metro Restaurants CEO Bob McMahon decided to create a stylish steak house for Tucson, he modestly named it for himself. McMahon's is at once clubby and sleek, with dim indirect lighting over dark curved booths, flagstone tile floors and a dramatic curving glass-walled wine cellar off the foyer. The menu is rather straightforward—no sun dried tomatoes or raspberry purée in this establishment. USDA prime Delmonico steak, New York strip and filet mignon are served in small and large slabs, with a choice of sauces. Other offerings include pork chops, beef short ribs, chicken Oscar and fresh seafood.

3 THE BEST SEAFOOD RESTAURANT: Kingfisher ● 2564

E. Grant Rd.; (520) 323-7739. Full bar service. Lunch weekdays and dinner nightly. Major credit cards; $$ to $$$. GETTING THERE: It's on the south side of Grant Road, half a block east of Tucson Boulevard.

This smart-looking seafood restaurant brings the ocean to Tucson, with fresh fish flown in daily. Its best offerings are simply prepared filets of whatever just got off the plane. Or try the raw and slippery offerings from the oyster bar. Among its menu items are pan fried soft shelled crabs, pecan crusted Atlantic salmon, bay scallop ceviche, halibut with steamed clams and grilled ahi tuna. Babyback ribs, pasta, filet and chicken are available for those who can't abide fish. In a town that favors Southwest adobe and Spanish colonial décor, Kingfisher has a decidedly eastern urban look, with tufted black vinyl booths, brick walls with glass brick insets, and dim lighting.

4 THE BEST BREAKFAST CAFÉ: The Good Egg ● 4775 E.

Grant near Swan in the Crossroads Festival Shopping Center, (520) 885-4838; 7219 E. Speedway east of Kolb Road, (520) 885-4838; and 5350 E. Broadway in William's Plaza, (520) 512-0280. Breakfast through lunch daily; no alcohol. Major credit cards; $.

The Good Eggs are styled like oversized little old ladies tearooms, only brighter. These deliberately homespun places feature drop lamps over patterned fabric booths, wainscotting and print wall paper. The focus obviously is on breakfast, with eggs prepared any style, including a large assortment of omelets, scrambles and Benedicts. The kitchen also issues French toast and pancakes. Incidentally, the Good Eggs aren't just cholesterol factories. They feature several "heart smart" options, using egg whites only or egg substitutes. The menu also has a Southwest side, with huevos rancheros, breakfast burritos and an egg and chorizo scramble.

5 THE BEST VIEW RESTAURANT: Anthony's in the

Catalinas ● 6440 N. Campbell Ave.; (520) 299-1771. *Contemporary American and continental; full bar. Lunch weekdays and dinner nightly. Major credit cards; $$$$. GETTING THERE: See listing on page 181.*

One of Tucson's Ten Best restaurants has no peer when it comes to the view. Since Tucson is rather flat and often hazy, views are impressive only at night. Anthony's lofty perch provides an awesome vista of the city's nighttime blanket of lights and its small downtown core of highrises. The restaurant has two dining areas—one overlooking the broad Tucson basin and another with a view of the rough-hewn crags of the Santa Catalinas. If you like to dine early, come before sunset and watch the dramatic play of light and shadow on the mountains. Then perhaps adjourn for after-dinner drinks on an outdoor patio for that night-light panorama of the basin.

6 *THE BEST BAKERY: Beyond Bread* • *3055 N. Campbell Ave.; (520) 322-9965. Breakfast through early dinner weekdays and breakfast through early evening weekends. MC/VISA, DISC; $ to $$. GETTING THERE: It's north of downtown, in Campbell Village on the west side of Campbell Avenue, between Glenn and Fort Lowell Road.*

"Beyond Bakery" might be a more apt name. Housed in a Southwest style stucco building, it's an attractive café and bakery with tables indoors and out. The menu offers hot and cold sandwiches, salads, quiche and breakfast rolls. Some of the sandwiches are quite intriguing, such as Maya's Market with roasted vegetables, provolone and *baba ganoush* on whole wheat; and Missy's Mania, with havarti dill, Swiss and brie cheese and tomatoes on white. This is a serious bake shop as well, and the luscious looking desserts in a cold case will catch your eye. The bakery posts a daily "bread line-up" listing the various specialty breads emerging from its ovens, and samples are available. Some of the creative varieties are parsley and Swiss, green chili and provolone, semolina-sesame and ancho-chipotle.

7 *THE BEST SUN LUNCH PLACE: La Cocina* • *In El Presidio's Old Town Artisans complex at 201 N. Court Ave.; (520) 622-0351. American and Mexican, full bar service. Lunch daily. Major credit cards; $ to $$. GETTING THERE: From downtown, take Alameda to Court Avenue and go a block north to Telles.*

La Cocina's landscaped, bougainvillea-splashed patio in El Presidio historic district is a fine place for an *al fresco* lunch and perhaps even a margarita. Relax to the sound of soft music and the chirping of sparrows, who may be on the lookout for spare crumbs. As you sit at an umbrella table beside a gurgling fountain, it's easy to pretend you're on a shady patio in old Mexico. The fare is essential *Latino*, such as burritos, enchiladas, quesadillas and tacos, or you can opt for Gringo chow—sandwiches, 'burgers and salads. If you're not in a luncheon mood, adjourn to the adjacent Old Town Artisans patio. You can get designer coffees and other drinks at the Wilde Rose Coffee Company takeout there.

8 *THE BEST PIZZA PARLOR: Zachary's • 1028 E. Sixth St.; (520) 623-6323. Wine and beer. Lunch through dinner Monday-Saturday; closed Sunday. MC/VISA; $ to $$. GETTING THERE: Zachary's is across from the University of Arizona Campus, just west of Fremont Avenue.*

Tucson's best pizza parlor is a bit hard to find because its owners haven't bothered to post a sign out front. It occupies an austere white masonry building adjacent to a parking lot, about half a block west of Fremont. Park in the lot, walk west and enter the first door that's unlocked. Zachary's battered paper menus list an interesting assortment of pizzas, such as Big Z with pepperoni, sausage, onion and mushroom; chicken Florentine with provolone, spinach and garlic; and the Super Veggie with mushrooms, green peppers, olives and spinach. The pizzas are huge—great ponds of cheese buried by toppings and settled onto thick crusts. Since the large version is almost the size of a garbage can lid, most munchers order pizza by the slice. A single wedge with a beer, glass of wine or soft drink is more than adequate for a meal. The faithful flock to Zachary's for its memorable pizzas, not for the décor. This place is so basic that calling it spartan would be an overstatement. Diners munch their giant wedges of pizza at Formica tables in a couple of bare rooms, or on a lattice-roofed patio out back.

9 *THE BEST VEGETARIAN CAFÉ: Blue Willow • 2616 N. Campbell Ave.; (520) 327-7577. Wine and beer. Breakfast through dinner daily. MC/VISA; $ to $$. GETTING THERE: It's on the east side of Campbell Avenue, about a block above Grant Road.*

Blue Willow is a charming gift and card shop and bakery, as well as a locally popular restaurant. It isn't strictly vegetarian, although its versatile menu has several meatless offerings among its breakfast items, sandwiches, soups, salads and Mexican specialties. Some examples are a breakfast tofu scramble; avocado, jack cheese and cucumber sandwich; vegetarian chili; and Blue Willow tostada, which comes in a vegetarian version with black olives and avocado. Meals are served in a couple of intimate dining areas and on an outside patio with a screened roof to dapple the sun.

10 *THE BEST BARBECUE: El Paso Bar-B-Que Company • 5510 E. Broadway Blvd.; (520) 745-2000. Full bar service. Lunch through dinner daily. Major credit cards; $$ to $$$. GETTING THERE: The restaurant is about six miles east of downtown, on the southeast corner of Broadway and Craycroft Road.*

This place is cowboy cool. It's a large and handsome Texas style restaurant trimmed in wrought iron, with polished floors, high-backed booths, Western paintings on the walls and a central bar with a wooden drop ceiling. Wrought iron "stars on sticks" add interesting decorator accents, and a pair of patios invite *al fresco* dining. The menu is identical to its Phoenix version (page 59), featuring spicy barbecued babyback ribs, brisket dinner, smoked chicken, pulled pork, Andouille sausage platter and slow-smoked beef ribs. From El Paso's mesquite grill emerges steak, prawns, salmon and pork tenderloin.

THE TEN BEST HISPANIC RESTAURANTS

Hispanic cooking here tilts toward Southwest cuisine—more than in Phoenix but less than in Santa Fe. Our choices range from trendy Southwest *nouveau* restaurants to simple mom and pop taco parlors.

Two local *Latino* restaurants achieved national note of sorts. *USA Today* once called El Charro's chimichangas "one of the fifty best plates in America." During a 1999 Tucson visit, former president William Jefferson Clinton lunched at Mi Nidito, ordering a shredded beef burrito. We tried them both and preferred Mi Nidito's burrito; the chimichanga was too greasy. Overall, However, El Charro is our favorite Mexican café.

Incidentally, there is no greater dining pricing extreme than in the city's Hispanic restaurants. You can get a full meal at El Charro or Mi Nidito for the price of an appetizer at a trendy Southwest *nouveau* diner. Check our $ ratings atop this chapter for your comfort zone.

Menu note: The terms *"burrito"* and *"burro"*—describing various fillings wrapped in large flour tortillas—are used interchangeably in Tucson. Although by definition, a *burrito* should be a small *burro*, we've been served some mighty large ones.

1 EL CHARRO CAFÉ ● 311 N. Court Ave.; (520) 622-1922.
Mexican-Southwestern; full bar service. Lunch through dinner daily. Major credit cards; $ to $$. GETTING THERE: From downtown, take Alameda to Court Avenue and go three blocks north to Franklin.

It's almost too obvious to pick El Charro as Tucson's best Hispanic restaurant. We'd have preferred to discover some undiscovered little jewel as our favorite. Yet, the reality is that Tucson's oldest and best known *Latino* diner also serves the best basic Mexican food in town, and at remarkably modest prices. Started in 1922, it's America's oldest Mexican restaurant still in the same family, currently operated by Chef Carlotta Flores, the great-niece of the founder. The ancient adobe it occupies is a National Historic Landmark. The café is a cheerfully gaudy place with splashy wall paintings, artifacts, photos of grim-faced banditos draped with cartridge belts, bright tapestries, sombreros and irreligiously displayed Catholic icons. One can dine indoors, on a porch or in a landscaped patio. *Mariachis* often serenade the diners.

Our favorite El Charro dinner begins with the house margarita over ice, with Herradura 100 percent blue agave tequila, no salt, please. Next comes tortilla soup with a big dollop of stringy melted cheese floating in a spicy broth. Tortilla chips are on the side, to be installed just prior to eating to ensure crispness. This is followed by a chicken burrito, called *pollo El Charro* on the menu. It's a huge thing with chunks of spiced chicken wrapped in a thick, crisp whole wheat flour tortilla. El Charro's entrées are accompanied by the usual smashed beans and rice and an interesting salad of corn, black beans, diced tomatoes and lettuce.

2 CAFÉ POCA COSA & LITTLE POCA COSA

● *Poca Cosa is at 88 E. Broadway Boulevard near Scott Avenue at the Clarion Hotel; (520) 622-6400. Southwest nouveau, wine and beer. Lunch and dinner Monday-Saturday. Major credit cards; $$. Little Poca Cosa is at 20 Scott Avenue near Congress Street; no phone. Mexican; wine and beer. Breakfast through lunch. No credit cards; $. GETTING THERE: Both are downtown near Broadway and Congress.*

Different in menu and price yet similar in gaudy décor, the two cafés Poca Cosa are favorites of the downtown crowd. The larger version at the Clarion changes its menu whenever owner Suzana Davila changes her mind, which may be twice a day. The inventive regional Mexican fare may include picadillo chicken, beef strips with sun-dried chilies, chicken Sereno with cilantro and onions, or green corn quesadillas. For less than $20, you can get a sampler of whatever was created for the day. The menu at Little Poca rarely changes; the diner features huge servings of more traditional fare at modest prices, such as huevos rancheros and huevos chorizo for breakfast, and chili colorado or verde, and chicken molé for lunch. Both cafés are gaudily colored with bold splashes of red, yellow, green and blue. They're decorated with Oaxacan folk masks and other Mexican artifacts. Café Poca Cosa is rather roomy, with an outside patio; Little Poca Cosa is a tiny slot of a place.

3 EL MINUTO

● *354 S. Main Avenue in El Presidio Historic District; (520) 882-4145. Also at 8 N. Kolb Road in Circle Plaza at the corner of Broadway; (520) 290-9591. Mexican; wine and beer. The café in El Presidio serves lunch and dinner daily; the Kolb Road restaurant is closed Monday. MC/VISA; $ to $$.*

One of Tucson's oldest restaurants, El Minuto Café started in El Presidio in 1936. A newer version is in a small shopping center seven miles east of downtown. The older edition is more quaint, tucked into a weathered adobe, while the newer rendition is roomy and contemporary, in a pink stucco building with a bougainvillea-entwined patio. An El Minuto specialty is fried cheese crisps, which come in several versions, including green chilies, ground or shredded beef or chorizo. Other specials are chicken flautas, breaded shrimp and a Spanish rice and egg scramble. The balance of the menu is preoccupied with the usual tacos, tostadas, enchiladas, chimichangas and burros. Many items are quite inexpensive, qualifying El Minuto as one of our Ten Best cheap eats in Chapter Fifteen, page 215.

4 *EL TORERO* • *231 E. 26th St.; (520) 622-9534. Mexican; wine and beer. Lunch through dinner daily. MC/VISA; $. GETTING THERE: It's in South Tucson about 1.5 miles from downtown. Drive south on I-10, take Star Pass Road exit 259 and go east on 22nd Street, then south again on Fourth Avenue. Go right on 26th Street for a block and a half; the restaurant is on the right.*

El Torero and Mi Nidito (listed below), located in the predominately Mexican community of South Tucson, are popular with both Hispanics and Anglos. Both are longtime institutions, dating from the 1950s. El Torero generally is less crowded, so it's useful in absorbing Mi Nidito's overflow. It's rather spartan inside, although the building itself is appealing—a bougainvillea-splashed pink adobe set back off the street. The fare is tasty and very inexpensive—so much so that we also list it as the Tucson area's best cheap diner in Chapter Fifteen, page 214. It offers the usual burros, enchiladas, tacos and such, plus more elaborate entrées such as flounder and shrimp Vera Cruz.

5 *LA PARILLA SUISA* • *2720 N. Oracle Road between Kelso and Glenn Streets; (520) 624-4300. Also at 5602 E. Speedway Boulevard at the corner of Jefferson Avenue; (520) 747-4838. Mexican; full bar service. Lunch through dinner daily. Major credit cards; $$.*

The two Parillas Suisa specialize in Mexico City style fare, which means that the meats, seafood and poultry used in their various entrées are charcoal grilled in an open oven. Among the more tasty items are sirloin and chorizo with melted cheese, beef strips and cheese with green peppers, and beef sautéed with bacon and served with charro beans. The restaurants also serve the usual burros, fajitas and other tortilla-wrapped items. We particularly like the Oracle Road restaurant, housed in a cottage with a handsome interior of brick arches, tile floors and Tiffany style drop lamps over booths. The Speedway place, also attractive, occupies a more traditional adobe style building.

6 *LA PLACITA CAFÉ* • *In Plaza Palomino at Swan and Fort Lowell roads; (520) 881-1150. Mexican; full bar service. Lunch Monday-Saturday and dinner nightly. Major credit cards; $ to $$. GETTING THERE: La Placita is in the eastern end of Plaza Palomino, off Fort Lowell Road.*

This cheery café is dressed like a fiesta—in reds, greens and blues, decorated in Mexican folk art and bright prints. The large menu covers the full range of Mexican fare, from the usual enchiladas, chimichangas, burros, tacos and tamales to more elaborate dishes. Among them are gulf shrimp sautéed in garlic, marinated chicken with guacamole, chicken molé, and beef in green chili and onion sauce. It also has a few Gringo dishes such as hamburgers, filet of sea bass and tenderloin with grilled onions. There's an outdoor dining patio in back.

7 **MI NIDITO** • *1814 S. Fourth Ave.; (520) 622-5081. (www. minidito.net) Mexican; wine, beer and margaritas. Lunch through late dinner Wednesday-Sunday; closed Monday-Tuesday. Major credit cards; $. GETTING THERE: It's near the northeast corner of Fourth and 29th Street (Silverlake) in South Tucson. Go south on I-10, then east on 22nd Street at exit 259 and south again on Fourth Avenue.*

Mi Nidito—"My Little Nest"—rivals El Charro as one of the area's best Mexican cafés, with good food at modest prices. Owner Ernie Lopez' family established it in 1952. It's popular both with Mexicans and Gringos, so expect a wait on weekends. However, Ernie makes the wait more comfortable by offering you a margarita. Mi Nidito doesn't have a bar; the margarita simply appears from somewhere, and it shows up on your bill later. While waiting, you can study the decorous riot of ceramic tile, multi-colored striped booths, Mexican doodads, beaded lights and fake palms. Not one square inch of wall space has been spared. There's nothing distinctive about the menu, which lists the usual tacos, chimichangas, enchiladas, tostadas, burros and such. However, the food is fresh, nicely prepared and offered in large portions. Our favorite is not Bill Clinton's carne seca burro but a spicier chorrizo burro. Be wary of the warm, thick-cut tortilla chips that arrive the moment you sit; they're so good you may spoil your appetite.

8 **OLD PUEBLO GRILLE** • *60 N. Alvernon Way; (520) 326-6000. (www.metrorestaurants.com) Southwest and Mexican with American accents; full bar service. Lunch through dinner daily. Major credit cards; $ to $$$. GETTING THERE: It's on the east side of Alvernon, between Broadway Boulevard and Elmwood Street, about three miles east of downtown.*

Most local food critics overlook this very attractive restaurant, which is housed in one of Tucson's old adobes. The structure dates from 1928, and its renovators have preserved much of its early Southwest look. Dining happens in a bright, cheery space with heavy beam ceilings, and in a landscaped courtyard. The fare—while not leading edge Southwest *nouveau*—is quite tasty. The menu dances from one thought to another, offering stone roasted chicken with mild chiles, corn crusted salmon, chilies relleno, chicken with green chili sauce and

Monterey jack cheese, fish tacos, green chili crusted halibut served over seasoned rice, and barbecued pork ribs. Our favorite is Old Pueblo machada—shredded beef with tomatoes, cilantro, pico de gallo and poblano mashed potatoes.

9 PAPAGAYO MEXICAN RESTAURANT • 4717 E. Sunrise Dr.; (520) 577-6055. Mexican; full bar service. Lunch through dinner daily. Major credit cards; $ to $$. GETTING THERE: The restaurant is just east of Swan Road on the north side of Sunrise.

Papagayo has been issuing tasty Mexican fare to locals for twenty-five years. The fifth generation of an old Tucson family now runs the place. This attractive restaurant with color-splashed walls, hanging plants and comfortable cane-back chairs is nestled in the Catalina foothills. The kitchen produces traditional burros, enchiladas, quesadillas and beyond, plus several specialties. Among them are a spicy steak tampiqueño, molé poblano, and a Papagayo pizza with a choice of chicken, roast or shredded beef, topped with jalapeños and cheese.

10 VEGA'S MEXICAN RESTAURANT • 3156 E. Fort Lowell Rd.; (520) 322-0977. Mexican; wine and beer. Breakfast through early dinner daily, with a Sunday buffet. MC/VISA; $. GETTING THERE: It's is on the east side of the small Winterhaven Shopping Center at the southeast corner of Fort Lowell and Country Club roads.

Little Vega's café earns a spot on our Ten Best list for several good reasons. It's decidedly bright cute for a shopping mall restaurant, it serves hearty and very inexpensive fare, it offers vegetarian and other "heart smart" meals, and finally, it's one of the few small Mexican cafés that's open for breakfast. Start your day here with huevos rancheros, a chorizo and egg scramble or a spicy shrimp and cheddar omelet. The typical chimichangas, burritos, enchiladas, tacos, tostadas and tamales will take care of your lunch needs. For dinner, try inexpensive entrées such as chili lime chicken, Southwestern style sirloin, Sonoran steak skillet or chicken Vera Cruz with lime and salsa marinade.

THE TEN BEST OTHER ETHNIC RESTAURANTS

The Asian invasion hasn't reached Tucson, probably too busy with its friendly conquest of California. The Old Pueblo isn't much of a European melting pot either, so it doesn't offer a great mix of international fare. However, we did find a reasonably tasty assortment of cuisine from beyond our borders. We have no overall winner. How can one compare sushi with spaghetti? Our choices are listed alphabetically by cuisine.

1 CHINESE: Lotus Garden • *5957 E. Speedway; (520) 298-3351. Full bar service. Lunch through dinner daily. Major credit cards; $$ to $$$. GETTING THERE: It's about six miles east of downtown, on the north side of Speedway at the corner of Sonoita Avenue.*

Lotus Garden has been serving tasty Chinese fare since 1967. It's an attractive place, with soft gray booths and black lacquered furniture, pink nappery and a few Chinese ornaments on the walls. Frosted glass dividers separate the large dining room into more intimate spaces. The huge menu touches most Chinese culinary bases, from mild Cantonese to spicier Szechuan and Mandarin fare. In addition to individual dishes, it offers a variety of pre-selected family dinners, ranging from less than $10 to around $20 per person. Lotus Garden has a rather extensive wine list, unusual for a Chinese restaurant. Another pleasant oddity is a long list of Polynesian drinks, with South Pacific style appetizers called *pu pu* platters to accompany them.

2 EUROPEAN: Mountain View Restaurant • *1220 E. Prince Rd.; (520) 293-0375. Full bar service. Lunch through dinner daily. MC/VISA; $$. GETTING THERE: The restaurant is about 3.5 miles north of downtown, on the south side of Prince near Mountain Avenue.*

Although the food is mostly German and eastern European, Mountain View has more the look of a modern American restaurant, with light woods, potted plants, a pitched ceiling and big picture windows onto the Santa Catalinas. Locally popular, it's quite inexpensive, with many *ala carte* dinner entrées under $10. For an additional dollar or so, diners get homemade rye bread, soup or salad (including traditional German potato salad), and a choice of sweet and sour cabbage or vegetable, plus dessert. One does not leave Mountain View hungry. Its European dishes include *sauerbraten,* spicy meat loaf, Polish sausage or bratwurst combo, cordon bleu and assorted *schnitzels*—jaeger, wiener, pork or chicken. The large menu also lists American style chops, steaks and seafood.

3 FRENCH: Le Rendez-Vous Restaurant Français • *3844 Fort Lowell Rd.; (520) 323-7373. (www.lerendez-vous.com) Full bar service. Lunch Tuesday-Friday and dinner Tuesday-Saturday; closed Sunday. Major credit cards; $$$ to $$$$. GETTING THERE: The restaurant is northeast of downtown, near the southwest corner of Fort Lowell and Alvernon Way. Turn west from Fort Lowell onto Alvernon, then take an immediate left into the parking lot.*

This is indeed a charming place for a rendezvous—a cheerful yet sensuous little French dining room beneath a burgundy fabric canopy. Tables and brocaded booths are set with tiny lamps and fresh-cut flowers. The French charm of chef-owner Jean Claude Berger's restaurant is mostly inside; it occupies a Spanish style building in a light commercial area. Settle into a comfy booth, however, and you're in Paris. Berger doesn't tinker much with *nouveau* accents; his menu features standards such as half chicken with sherry, veal medallions with apple and calvados, duck *l'orange*, sweetbreads and veal *dijonnaise* and sole *meuniér*.

4 GREEK: Olive Tree • *7000 E. Tanque Verde Rd.; (520) 298-1845. Full bar service. Dinner nightly. Major credit cards; $$ to $$$. GETTING THERE: The restaurant is about eight miles northeast of downtown, in Santa Fe Square on the south side of Tanque Verde, opposite ¡Fuego! (page 182).*

This is no noisy Greek taverna with wriggling navels, but a rather elegant restaurant that been offering Grecian fare for more than two decades. The look is more Southwest, since the restaurant is housed in a pueblo style building. The main dining room has cozy tufted booths and ceiling fans, and old black and white photos of Greece give it a Mediterranean aura. An appealing landscaped patio is out back. If the look is Southwest, the fare is Greek—albeit with some interesting contemporary twists. Among recent entrées were braised stewed lamb shank, roast chicken Athenian with lemon sauce, and cinnamon chicken with caramelized onions, plus traditional *gyro* plates, *moussaka* and *dolmas*.

5 INDIAN: Delhi Palace • *6751 E. Broadway Blvd.; (520) 296-8585. Full bar service. Lunch buffet, plus dinner nightly. MC/VISA, AMEX; $$ to $$$. GETTING THERE: Delhi is about seven miles east of downtown, in a strip mall just west of Jessica Avenue.*

Although this restaurant occupies a small mall near a large Walgreen's, you'll be transported to the mysterious East when you step inside. The décor isn't elaborate, but rather simple and tasteful. A large mural of an east Indian palace fills one wall and a few choice Mideastern artifacts accent the main dining area. Owned by an Indian couple, Jas and Suky Khangura, the restaurant has been voted "Best of Tucson" in its category for more than a decade. Jas and Suky specialize in spicy clay oven *tandoori* chicken, shrimp, lamb and mixed grill, accompanied by warm *tandoori* breads. For peppier dishes, try the various curries, featuring chicken, lamb, shrimp or lobster. Vegetarians will like the wide choice of meatless dishes, served mild, medium or hot.

6 ITALIAN: Caruso's • *434 N. Fourth Ave.; (520) 624-5765. Southern Italian; full bar service. Dinner nightly except Monday. Major credit cards; $$ to $$$. GETTING THERE: From downtown, follow Sixth Avenue north under a railroad pass, then shift left onto Fourth Avenue. Caruso's is at the corner of Fourth and Sixth Street.*

In business since 1938, Caruso's is one of those sturdy' restaurants that serves fine and simple food in a pleasant atmosphere, offering ample portions at reasonable prices. It occupies a large cottage set back off the street and rimmed by patios in the Fourth Avenue shopping district. The interior look is predictable Italian with candle-lit tables and *raffia* bottles. There's a very appealing dining patio out back. Often overlooked by visitors, Caruso's is a favorite of locals and recently was voted Best Italian Restaurant in a *Tucson Weekly* readers' poll.

From the busy kitchen emerges Caruso's popular baked lasagna created from homemade noodles, plus veal Parmigiana, shrimp marinara and all of the usual fresh-cooked pastas—spaghetti, ravioli, linguine, manicotti and cannelloni.

7 *JAPANESE: Sakura ● 6534 E. Tanque Verde Rd.; (520) 298-7777. Full bar service. Lunch weekdays and dinner nightly. Major credit cards; $$ to $$$. GETTING THERE: It's about eight miles northeast of downtown, on the south side of Tanque Verde between Wilmot and Kolb roads. Go east on Pima Street, then northeast briefly on Tanque Verde.*

Tucson's best Japanese restaurant occupies a green tile-roofed structure with the vague suggestion of an Asian temple. The interior look is Japanese modern although—in pleasant contrast—its waitresses are wear traditional kimonos. Sakura has a serious sushi bar in addition to a large main dining room. You can choose from a long sushi list or opt for traditional teriyakis, tempuras and domburis. Sakura offers showy tableside cooking with spinning knives and judo-chopping thrusts made popular in America a few decades ago in Rocky Aoki's Benihana restaurants.

8 *PAN-ASIAN: Firecracker Bistro ● In Plaza Palomino at 2990 N. Swan Rd.; (520) 318-1118. (www.metrorestaurants.com) Full bar service. Lunch and dinner daily. Major credit cards; $$ to $$$. GETTING THERE: The restaurant is on the southeast corner of Swan and Fort Lowell roads, northeast of downtown.*

This trendy place forms a bright red cornerstone of Plaza Palomino, and the color may be symbolic of both its name and its often spicy cuisine. The interior is a pleasing study in South Pacific Island décor, with *faux* palm trunks, bamboo ceilings, wooden Venetian blinds and horizontal paddle fans. You expect Sydney Greenstreet to push through the bamboo curtains, except there aren't any. The Pacific Rim menu draws mostly from American, Chinese and Southeast Asian sources, offering fare that ranges from firecracker hot to Cantonese cool. Some examples are wok chicken, Szechuan orange peel chicken, and wok-charred salmon. Coconut créme brûlet is a dessert specialty. This tropical fusion fare is served in a large main dining room, a cozy bar and on an appealing patio off Plaza Palomino's courtyard.

9 THAI: **Karuna's Thai Plate** • *1917 E. Grant Rd.; (520) 325-4129. Wine and beer. Lunch and dinner Monday-Saturday (closed mid-afternoon to early evening), and dinner only on Sunday. MC/VISA; $. GETTING THERE: It's a couple of miles northeast of downtown, on the north side of Grant, just beyond Campbell Avenue.*

Although it's very spartan, Karuna's serves the best Thai plates in town. And it's so inexpensive that it also qualified for our Ten Best cheap eats list in Chapter Fifteen, page 216. Although this basic Formica restaurant is small, the menu is large, offering the full range of Thai dishes. Our favorite is *chuchee,* fillet of cod with curry and basil leaves, topped with coconut cream and lime leaves. Vegetarians will like this place because it offers a good selection of meatless dishes, some tame and some spicy. If you like things *really* spicy, try the hot curry dishes such as *gang kua,* which is chicken, beef, pork or duck with pineapple, simmered in coconut milk; *gang ped phed yang,* roast duck with red curry and bell pepper; or *pad ped,* pork, beef or chicken stir-fried in a red curry paste. Among dishes more gentle on the tongue are *kratiam prig thai,* beef, pork or chicken in garlic; and *guey teaw,* a rice noodle and bean sprout soup with pork or chicken, topped with cilantro. Karuna's also has a very modestly priced multi-item lunch buffet.

10 VIETNAMESE: **Hoa Mai Restaurant** • *2547 E. Broadway Blvd.; (520) 319-8420. Wine and beer. Lunch weekdays and dinner Monday-Saturday; closed Sunday. GETTING THERE: The restaurant is about 2.5 miles east of downtown, on the north side of Broadway, just beyond Tucson Boulevard.*

Hoa Mai, indeed! Tucson's best Vietnamese café is so cute and cozy that it also makes our list of the city's most romantic restaurants—particularly for those on a budget; see Chapter Eighteen, page 251. To find this tiny strip mall café, look for a bright green awning. Inside, you'll find a quiet and dimly lit dining room. The fare is traditional Vietnamese, served with spicy jasmine tea. Our favorites are steaming rice noodle stews simmering with bean sprouts, fresh mint and cilantro; they come with beef, pork, chicken or shrimp marinated in lemon grass. For something more spicy, try the curry chicken, five spice roast chicken, ginger chicken or beef, and Mongolian chicken or beef. Hoa Mai also serves Chinese style fried rice and several vegetarian dishes.

*Like many Western ranchers
of the era, the owners quickly
discovered that Easterners
were willing to pay...money
to play cowboy.*
**— Article by Nancy Sharkey
on Tanque Verde Ranch in
the *New York Times*, © 1998**

Chapter Fourteen

LODGING & DUDE RANCHING

TUCSON'S BEST RESORTS & GUEST RANCHES

Lodgings in Phoenix and Tucson have some major differences. The larger city has several downtown hotels while Tucson has very few. The desert resorts around Phoenix-Scottsdale tend to be larger and flashier. Those near Tucson are smaller although they're often quite elegant and frequently in stunning locations against the city's surrounding mountains. And finally, Phoenix has few dude ranches, while Tucson rivals Wickenburg as the dude ranch capital of Arizona. It also has many more bed and breakfast inns than Phoenix. The listings reflect these differences. After our Ten Best resorts, we follow with a combined list of the Ten Best dude ranches and small inns.

NOTE: Items marked with ❖ are listed elsewhere in this book; check the index for page numbers.

PRICING: Dollar sign codes indicate room price ranges for two people, based on high season (fall through spring) rates: *$* = a standard two-person room for $99 or less; *$$* = $100 to $149; *$$$* = $150 to $249; and *$$$$* = $250 or more. Rates often drop by more than half in summer.

TUCSON'S TEN BEST RESORTS

There are two basic types of desert resorts in and around Tucson—grand and spacious getaways with golf courses and other amenities, and smaller retreats that still offer many resort facilities. We've selected our favorite five in each category, starting with the very best and following with the rest in alphabetical order.

THE BEST LARGE RESORTS

1 *SHERATON EL CONQUISTADOR ● 1000 Oracle Rd., Tucson, AZ 85737; (800) 325-3535 or (520) 544-5000. (www.sheraton-conquistador.com) A luxury desert resort with 428 spacious rooms, suites and casitas; phones with dataports and voice mail, honor bars and TV movies; some patios, balconies and fireplaces. Major credit cards; $$$$.*
GETTING THERE: Take Ina Road (I-10 exit 248) six miles east to Oracle Road, then go north 4.5 miles to El Conquistadore Way and turn right. From downtown, follow Oracle Road about fourteen miles north.

One of the most striking aspects of this large resort is the dramatic backdrop of Pusch Ridge, a sheer promontory of the Santa Catalina mountains. The twin fins of the ridge rise in stony contrast to the lush desert and green landscaping of this 500-acre Spanish-modern retreat. El Conquistador is impressive within as well. Its lobby is the most imposing of any Tucson resort, with a three-story atrium ceiling, polished flagstone floors and an impressive copper and green Southwestern scene above the registration desk. A lobby bar with plush seating invites lingering to admire that mountain view

The resort's extensive facilities include forty-five holes of golf, a practice green, two fitness centers, four nicely landscaped pools and spas, lighted tennis and racquetball courts, riding stables, several gift shops and four restaurants. The most appealing, Dos Locos Latinos, has a curved, flower-rimmed outdoor dining deck with a view of the pool and the rugged mountains—an appealing place for lunch or dinner; see Chapter Eighteen, page 250.

2 *LOEW'S VENTANA CANYON RESORT ● 7000 N. Resort Dr., Tucson, AZ 85750; (800) 23-LOEWS or (520) 299-2020. (www.loewshotels.com) A luxury resort with 398 rooms and suites, featuring phones with dataports and voice mail, extended cable TV, honor bars; some units have video games. Major credit cards; $$$ to $$$$.*
GETTING THERE: From I-10 exit 256, take Grant Road east about eight miles, go northeast half a mile on Tanque Verde Road, then about two miles north on Sabino Canyon Road. Fork left onto Kolb Road and continue north about five miles; the resort is on the right. ❖

Loew's is a striking resort in a striking setting. Fashioned of rough-cut stone, it's built across Ventana Creek and terraced into a steep-walled canyon. Creeper vines spill over the craggy stone surfaces, creating the suggestion of an upscale Mayan temple. The stream has been terraced to form pools above and below this opulent retreat. A riparian woodland trail canopied with mesquite and palo verde leads up to a rock-walled basin, where the creek trickles down a sheer eighty-foot wall. Views from the resort are simply awesome—north into the Santa Catalinas and south over the sprawling Tucson Basin.

The main lobby is done in earth tones, with polished flagstone floors and rough-cut stones accented by glass bricks. A lobby bar has nice views across a large pool deck to the Catalinas. Golf course fairways cascade down the desert slopes. Loew's shares thirty-six holes with the Lodge at Ventana Canyon below. Other facilities include tennis courts, two pools and spas, a steam room, saunas, hiking trails and a kids' playground. The resort has five cafés and restaurants, including the Ventana Room, rated as one of the finest in Arizona; see Chapter Thirteen, page 180.

3 *SHERATON TUCSON HOTEL & SUITES • 5151 E. Grant Rd., Tucson, AZ 85712; (800) 257-7275 or (520) 323-6262. (starwood.com) An in-town resort hotel with 216 rooms and suites; extended cable TV with movies and videogames, phones with dataports and voice mail. Major credit cards; $$$. GETTING THERE: The hotel is just east of Rosemont Boulevard, on the north side of Grant Road, near the University of Phoenix and several medical facilities. From I-10, take exit 256 and go east just over six miles.*

The Sheraton is the closest thing to a resort in mid-town Tucson, handy if you want to near the city center and still enjoy many leisure amenities. The three-story Spanish colonial style hotel is built around a large, landscaped courtyard and swimming complex, providing sanctuary from the nearby streets. The hotel's facilities include a spa tub, steam room and exercise room, a small gift shop, two restaurants and a cocktail lounge.

4 *WESTIN LA PALOMA • 3800 E. Sunrise Dr., Tucson, AZ 85718; (800) WESTIN or (520) 742-6000. (www.westin.com) A full-service luxury resort with 487 units, featuring private balconies or patios, bars, refrigerators and multiple phones with dataports and voice mail. Major credit cards; $$$ to $$$$. GETTING THERE: Follow Campbell Avenue about eight miles north from downtown, then turn right onto Skyline Drive. Go east briefly then veer to the right onto Sunrise; turn south onto La Palomita and follow signs. From I-10, take Orange Grove Road (exit 250) east 6.5 miles until in ends at Skyline. Turn right and you'll cross the Campbell Avenue intersection in less than a mile.*

Occupying a high desert ridge, this large Spanish colonial style resort has views of the Santa Catalinas to the north and the sprawl of Tucson to the south. The impressive lobby is a three-level affair, terraced from the reception level and a comfortable sitting area down to a large cocktail lounge, then down again to the spacious Desert Garden Bistro restaurant. From all three levels of the atrium lobby, towering Spanish arch windows provide views of a pool complex and the Santa Catalinas. The resort has three swimming facilities, including a 177-foot waterslide and separate pools for kids and adults. The Tennis and Health Center has several tennis courts, indoor racquetball courts, a pro shop, workout room and a children's lounge. Guests have access to the adjacent La Paloma Country Club with a 27-hole golf course. Many rooms and suites have fireplaces and sunken spa tubs. The resort has a good selection of shops, plus several restaurants, including Janos, featured in Chapter Thirteen, page 183.

5 *WESTWARD LOOK RESORT • 245 E. Ina Rd., Tucson, AZ 85704; (800) 722-2500 or (520) 297-1151. (westwardlook.com) An appealing desert retreat with 224 large guest rooms with TV movies and video games, honor bars, phones with dataports and voice mail. Major credit cards; $$$$. GETTING THERE: From I-10 take Ina Road (exit 248) six miles east, cross Oracle Road, then within a few blocks, turn north up Westward Look Drive. From downtown, follow Oracle Road about nine miles north to Ina.*

Set on eighty acres of desert foothills at the base of the Santa Catalinas, the Westward Look is one of Tucson's oldest resorts, dating from 1912. However the look of the Look is quite contemporary, after a multi-million dollar remodeling. It has modern Southwestern décor while retaining its old adobe style charm. The lobby and many of the public rooms have traditional pole beam and *lantilla* ceilings. The resort's many facilities include a fitness center, wellness center, riding stable, eight tennis courts, three pools and spas, hiking and jogging trails, a gift shop and two restaurants. The Gold Room is featured in Chapter Thirteen, page 183.

THE BEST SMALLER RESORTS

6 *ARIZONA INN • 2200 E. Elm St., Tucson, AZ 85719; (800) 933-1093 or (520) 325-1541. (www.arizonainn.com) A luxurious 86-unit inn with beautifully decorated Southwest style rooms offering voice mail, extended cable TV and other amenities. Major credit cards; $$$ to $$$$. GETTING THERE: From downtown, drive north on Campbell Avenue past the University of Arizona campus, then turn right onto Elm Street and go about three blocks. The inn is on the right, with parking on the left.* ❖

This opulent pink stucco inn is our favorite retreat in all of Arizona. It's a charming place of quiet repose, tucked into fourteen lushly landscaped acres in the heart of Tucson. Stepping into the lobby is like passing through a time curtain—from a busy, modern city to a quiet and dignified yesterday retreat. Mature trees and bright flower beds rim cool green lawns; the hum of traffic is replaced by the cheerful chirp of birds. Established in 1930 by Arizona Congresswoman Isabella Greenway, it's as elegant today as it was when she hosted guests such as Eleanor Roosevelt and John D. Rockefeller, Jr. Yet, this is a casual elegance. With its warm and comfortable décor and its friendly staff, there is a sense of easy grace to this place, not stuffy refinement.

The library just off the small lobby is particularly inviting, a study in old world finery with its fireplace, dark wood truss beam ceiling, wall sconces, plush seats and shelves of books waiting to be read. The dining room is excellent, listed among the Ten Very Best restaurants in Chapter Thirteen, page 181. Another attractive spot is a swimming pool deck where breakfast is served each morning. The inn's accommodations, across a flower-bordered croquet court from the main lodge, are in cozy casitas tucked into lush landscaping. Resort amenities include two pools, saunas, tennis courts and a gift shop. The inn is listed on the National Register of Historic Places, and *Country Inns of America* recently rated it one of the country's ten best.

7 *CANYON RANCH SPA • 8600 E. Rockcliff Rd., Tucson, AZ 85750; (800) 742-9000 or (520) 749-9000. (www. canyonranch.com) An opulent health spa in a seventy-acre desert basin offering multi-day packages. Major credit cards; $$$$. GETTING THERE: The spa is northeast of Tucson at the end of Rockcliff Road. Follow Sabino Canyon Road north and east from Tanque Verde Road for about 3.5 miles to Snyder Road, take it briefly to Rockcliff Road and turn right. NOTE: The resort is not open to casual visitors, although tours are given periodically; call for hours.*

Canyon Ranch may be America's ultimate fitness resort, providing—at very high prices—an immersion program of workouts conducted by experts, proper diet and pampered relaxation. The Tucson version is one of two; the other is in the Berkshire Mountains near Lenox, Massachusetts. An abbreviated edition is in the Venetian Resort in Las Vegas. The Tucson retreat is set in a desert basin with awesome views of the Santa Catalinas. Its facilities include a complete spa facility, swimming pool, and hiking trails; plus tennis, racquetball and basketball courts.

Guests can indulge in every conceivable kind of workout—aerobics, yoga, *tai chi*, swimming, stretch training, cycling and hiking. Or if they prefer just to be pampered, the spa has massage, hydromassage, herbal and aroma wraps and various facial treatments. Three health-focused meals a day are part of the package.

8 *GOLF VILLAS AT ORO VALLEY* • *10950 N. La Cañada, Tucson, AZ 85737; (888) 388-0098 or (520) 498-0098. (www.the-golfvillas.com) A 67-unit luxury condo complex with full kitchens, extended cable TV with video library, multiple phones and dataports. Major credit cards; $$$$. GETTING THERE: The resort is about fifteen miles north of Tucson in the small town of Oro Valley. Drive north on I-10, take Ina Road (exit 248) east about five miles to La Cañada Drive and follow it north about 4.5 miles. It's on the right, on the northern edge of Oro Valley.*

This AAA Four Diamond Resort focuses primarily on two things—lots of golf and luxurious condo units. Guests have access to the links and other amenities of the adjacent Conquistadore Country Club, plus preferred tee times at some of the area's top courses, such as the Raven Golf Club at Sabino Springs (rated one of the ten best in the country) and the Tucson National (home to the Tucson open). The Golf Villas complex has a modern Santa Fe style reception center with an adjacent swimming pool that offers nice views of the Santa Catalinas, plus spa tubs and a 24-hour fitness center. The condo units have full kitchens with separate living rooms and bedrooms, washers and dryers, and private patios with golf course and mountain views. And should you really want to be spoiled, the resort's concierge staff can provide shopping services to stock your kitchen and even arrange for a personal chef to do the cooking.

9 *THE LODGE AT VENTANA CANYON* • *6200 N. Clubhouse Lane, Tucson, AZ 85750; (888) 472-6229 or (520) 577-1400. (www.wyndham.com/luxury) A golf and tennis resort with fifty efficiency units; oversized rooms and suites with refreshment centers, multiple phones with dataports and voice mail, extended cable TV and safes. Major credit cards; $$$$. GETTING THERE: The resort is northeast of Tucson, just off Kolb Road in the Santa Catalina foothills. From I-10, take Grant Road (exit 256) east about eight miles, go northeast half a mile on Tanque Verde Road, then about two miles north on Sabino Canyon Road. Fork left onto Kolb Road and continue north another three miles. Shortly after crossing Sunrise Drive, turn right onto Clubhouse Lane, passing through an entry gate.*

Part of a 600-acre golf and tennis club, the lodge is terraced into a desert slope at the base of the Santa Catalinas. The drive-up entry is quite pretty, with a lawn rimmed by desert plants and flower beds, accented by an ancient mesquite tree. Another focal point—in the otherwise modest lobby—is a massive flagstone fireplace. If the lobby is modest, the rooms are not. They're large and spacious, with Spanish colonial and Southwest décor. Some are two-story with spiral staircases leading to the upper bedrooms. Many have fine views of the

Santa Catalinas, a vista shared by window walls of the lodge's main dining room. This rather small resort is serious about golf and tennis. It shares two golf courses with the neighboring Loew's Ventana Canyon Resort. Lush green fairways on the desert upslope add dramatic contrast to the resort's cactus gardens. The facility has a dozen lighted tennis courts, a croquet court, plus a pool and spa, a large workout room and a jogging track.

10 OMNI TUCSON NATIONAL GOLF RESORT • *2727 W. Club Dr., Tucson, AZ 85742; (800) 528-4856 or (520) 297-2271. (www.omnihotels.com) Attractive 167-unit resort with TV movies, voice mail and honor bars; some suites, casitas and kitchen units. Major credit cards; $$$ to $$$$. GETTING THERE: From I-10 exit 246 and follow Cortaro Road about 3.5 miles east, then turn north onto Shannon Road. After less than half a mile, turn right into the resort complex.*

Both scratch golfers and hackers are drawn to this resort, which is home to the Tucson Open. Set among country estates, it has three eighteen-hole courses and a practice facility. Some of the resort's lodging-golf packages include private instruction. Omni has a pleasing Tuscan look, with brick walls and orange tile roofs. The grounds are handsomely landscaped and a large free-form swimming complex is particularly appealing, with a stone "island fountain" rising in the center. The resort's amenities include two pools, a health club, full service fitness center and a gift shop. The Catalina Grill features American contemporary fare and the Fiesta Room offers casual dining; both have indoor and outdoor seating with views of the distant Santa Catalinas.

THE TEN BEST DUDE RANCHES AND SMALL INNS

Tucson is particularly noted for its dude ranches, and it also has a good number of small B&Bs and other inns. Incidentally, the term "dude ranch" has fallen from fashion, and they're now called guest ranches or ranch resorts. Our favorite—one of America's first and most famous—is simply called a ranch.

THE BEST DUDE RANCHES

1 TANQUE VERDE RANCH • *14301 E. Speedway Blvd., Tucson, AZ 85748; (800) 234-DUDE or (520) 296-6275. (www.tanqueverderanch.com) Historic guest ranch with seventy-four units; private baths, phones and patios. Major credit cards; $$$$. Rates include all meals. GETTING THERE: The ranch is about seventeen miles east of downtown, at the end of Speedway.*

Bob Cote, manager of one of America's oldest ranch resorts, doesn't mind calling Tanque Verde a dude ranch. The word is even part of the reservation phone number. Cote seems very much the cowboy, with his jeans and bolo tie, his sun-weathered face and gentle drawl. The ranch, originally called Le Cebadilla (wild barley), was established by a Mexican cattleman in 1868. A later owner—cowman Jim Converse—converted it into one of America's first dude ranches in the 1920s, calling it Tanque Verde Cattle and Guest Ranch. Brownie Cote, Bob's father, bought it and greatly expanded its facilities in 1957.

Carrying a Mobil Four Star rating, Tanque Verde is at once rustic, comfortable and modern. Its Southwestern style casitas have baths, phones, private patios and air conditioning; many have fireplaces. One can slip easily into the ranching life here, with riding lessons in the morning, followed by a trail ride into the deserts near Saguaro National Park that afternoon, and perhaps a Western cookout in the evening. Not completely rustic, the resort has amenities such as indoor and outdoor pools, tennis courts, saunas, spa tubs, an exercise room and meeting facilities. Its many activities include breakfast trail rides, naturalist hikes, mountain biking, tennis lessons and catch-and-release fishing.

2 *HACIENDA DEL SOL GUEST RANCH RESORT* • *5601 N. Hacienda del Sol Rd., Tucson, AZ 85718; (800) 728-6514 or (520) 299-1501. (www.haciendadelsol.com) Historic inn with thirty-five Southwest style rooms, suites and casitas. Major credit cards; $$ to $$$$; rates include continental breakfast. The Grill, open to the public, serves lunch and dinner daily, with Sunday brunch; (520) 299-1501. GETTING THERE: From downtown, go north about eight miles on Campbell Avenue to River Road, head east just over half a mile and turn north up Hacienda del Sol Road. Follow it 1.5 miles to Via Alcalde and turn left, following signs to the resort.*

Once hidden high above Tucson in the Santa Catalina foothills, this "House of the Sun" is now surrounded by suburban homes. However, it's still buffered by thirty-four desert acres, as it was when the likes of Clark Gable and Spencer Tracy sought refuge here. Hacienda del Sol is an attractive retreat built around sheltering courtyards, with a mix of Spanish colonial and Santa Fe style architecture. It has a small swimming pool, riding trails, tennis and croquet courts, and a comfy library off the lobby. The Grill, one of Tucson's better restaurants, serves American-continental fare. It has earned a *Wine Spectator* Award of Excellence, and the resort was picked by *National Geographic Traveler* as one of the top fifty small lodges in the country.

Hacienda del Sol began life in 1929 as a prep school for "young women of prominence." In was converted to a ranch resort for the rich and famous in 1948, then it became a private club and finally, a neglected relic. Local investors reopened it as a ranch resort in 1995 and major restoration has returned it to its rustic glory. Stroll down its collonaded corridors and you'll see black and white photos of its earlier days when it hosted proper you ladies and then film stars.

3 *LA TIERRA LINDA GUEST RANCH RESORT* • *7501 N. Wade Rd., Tucson, AZ 85743; (888) 872-6241 or (520) 744-7700. (www.latierralinda.com) Fourteen casitas with TV, phones, refrigerators and private patios. Major credit cards; $$ to $$$$; rates are per-person with either breakfast only, or all meals. Ranch House Grill, open to the public, serves dinner Tuesday-Sunday; (520) 744-7200. GETTING THERE: The ranch is northwest of Tucson. Take Ina Road (I-10 exit 248) just under three miles west to Wade Road, then drive less than a quarter of a mile north on a dirt road to the ranch.*

Although it occupies its own personal thirty-acre patch of desert, this small ranch resort is only minutes off I-10 and thus within easy reach of Tucson. Tucson Mountain Park and Saguaro National Park West are nearby. This is a pleasantly rustic place, with stone and stucco buildings set in desert landscaping. Lodgings are in several Southwest style casitas. The resort's amenities include a riding stable, tennis courts, swimming pool, horseshoes, volleyball and a kids' playground. Walking and biking trails lead into the surrounding desert. The Ranch House Grill provides breakfast for guests and it's open to the public for lunch and dinner. The dining room is properly Western-rustic, with an outdoor patio adjacent. The menu features American and Mexican fare.

4 *LAZY K BAR GUEST RANCH* • *8401 N. Scenic Dr., Tucson, AZ 85743; (800) 321-7018 or (520) 744-3050. (www.lazykbar.com) A 23-unit guest ranch with private baths; no room TV or phones. Major credit cards; $$$$. Rates include meals. GETTING THERE: The ranch is about sixteen miles northwest of Tucson. Take I-10 exit 246, go a mile west on Cortaro Road, drive north just over a mile on Silverbell Road, then go west again 1.5 miles on Pima Farms Road to Scenic Drive.*

Tucked into the Tucson Mountains' cactus-busy foothills, this 23-unit retreat offers the typical dude ranch lures of trail rides, Western cookouts and hayrides. Cattle-cutting and penning demonstrations are conducted in the ranch arena. Facilities include a swimming pool, spa, horseshoes, shuffleboard, ping pong and billiards. Among the ranch's activities are breakfast and lunch rides, nature walks and even rock climbing and rappelling in the adjacent hills. The ranch's recently renovated rooms are Western-modern with "no telephones or televisions...to disturb you," says the brochure. If you can't stand the thought of missing the next episode of *Survivor,* the main lodge has a TV room.

5 **WHITE STALLION RANCH** • *9251 W. Twin Peaks Rd., Tucson, AZ 85743; (888) 977-2624 or (520) 297-0252. (www.ws-ranch.com) A large guest ranch with Western style rooms, all with private baths. GETTING THERE: From I-10, take Cortaro Road (exit 246) less than a mile and turn right onto Silverbell Road. It becomes Twin Peaks Road and leads to the ranch after about five miles. The entrance is on the left, just after Twin Peaks tops a small hill.*

If you're old enough to remember *The High Chaparral* TV series, you've seen White Stallion Ranch, since many episodes were shot here. Fortunately, the ranch hasn't changed much since. It sprawls over 3,000 acres in the foothills of the Tucson Mountains, not far from the western unit of Saguaro National Park. There's plenty of room to roam on the ranch's desert trails, either on horseback or afoot. The main ranch house was built as a homestead in 1939 and—while modernized—it retains its old Western charm. Facilities include a large library, billiard room and a bar with saddles as barstools. Among the ranch's many offerings are riding stables, a swimming pool, hot tub, ping pong and horseshoes; plus volleyball, basketball and tennis courts. The ranch even has a petting zoo, so it's a good family place.

THE BEST SMALL INNS

6 **THE ROYAL ELIZABETH** • *204 S. Scott Ave., Tucson, AZ 85701; (887) 670-9022 or (520) 670-9022. (www.royalelizabeth.com) Attractive six-unit inn with private baths, some with spa tubs and fireplaces. Major credit cards; $$ to $$$. Rates include full breakfast and daytime snacks. GETTING THERE: The inn is downtown near McCormick Street, just east of the Tucson Convention Center.*

Tucson's finest small inn is simply gorgeous—an impressive study in Victorian splendor, housed in an 1878 adobe mansion. Once the home of a wealthy judge, the Royal Elizabeth has been meticulously restored. The large foyer features ornately carved woodwork, elaborate arched doorways, Victorian furnishings and plush carpets over polished wood floors. Each of the six rooms is individually decorated, with oversized beds, satellite TV with VCRs, and refrigerators tucked into antique armoires. Two units have separate sitting rooms and one has a spa tub. A courtyard rimmed by elaborately landscaped grounds shelters a pool and spa.

7 **EL PRESIDIO BED & BREAKFAST** • *297 N. Main Ave., Tucson, AZ 85701; (800) 349-6151 or (520) 623-6151. Four units with TV, phones and private baths. No credit cards; $ to $$. GETTING*

THERE: It's in El Presidio Historic District at the corner of Main and Franklin. Take I-10 exit 257-A, go east briefly on Sixth Avenue, then south a block on Main to Franklin.

This is your choice if you want to stay right in the heart of the El Presidio. Although it's surrounded by other structures, the inn is rather isolated, cloistered behind wrought iron fencing and elaborate gardens with patios, pools and fountains. This large pitched-roof 1886 Arizona territorial adobe is rimmed by a traditional veranda and it's furnished with Victorian and early American antiques. Elaborate breakfasts are served in a formal dining room, with complimentary juices and wines available during the day. Two of the large units are suites with kitchens. The inn is within a sort walk of the Tucson Museum of Art, the galleries, shops and restaurants of El Presidio, the Visitor Center at La Placita and downtown Tucson.

8 CATALINA PARK INN ● *309 E. First St., Tucson, AZ 85705; (800) 792-4885 or (520) 792-4541. (www.bbonline.com/az/cpinn/) Six rooms with private baths. MC/VISA; $$. Rates include full breakfast. GETTING THERE: The inn is near the University of Arizona campus, about a mile northeast of downtown. It's on the northeast corner of First Street and Fifth Avenue, opposite Catalina Park.*

This inn occupies a nicely refurbished 1927 two-story Spanish colonial mansion with a wrap-around porch. The attractive retreat is rimmed by nicely landscaped gardens. The living room is quite handsome, with carved wood accents, comfortable overstuffed furniture and a fireplace. The large rooms have phones and TV sets; some have porches, fireplaces and private entrances. Furnishings are a mix of antique and modern and beds have thick down comforters. The Oak Room is quite nice, with a four-poster bed and a sitting area.

9 LODGE ON THE DESERT ● *306 N. Alvernon Way, Tucson, AZ 85711; (800) 456-5634 or (520) 325-3366. (www.lodgeonthedesert.com) Thirty-nine rooms and suites with private baths. Major credit cards; $$$ to $$$$. Cielo's Restaurant serves breakfast, lunch and dinner. GETTING THERE: The lodge is on the east side of Alvernon, two blocks north of Broadway Boulevard at the corner of Poe Street.*

This is another of those resorts hidden by adobe walls and thick shrubbery in the busy heart of town. These walls are a curious mauve color and they shelter a hideaway that first opened its doors in 1936. Its historic claim is that it's Arizona's oldest adobe resort still being used for its original purpose. Guest quarters are in haciendas landscaped with mature palms, orange trees and bright floral borders. The rooms feature southwest décor and many have *lantilla* ceilings, *kiva* fireplaces and tile patios. Cielo's Restaurant is open to the public, serving American-Southwest fare, with full bar service.

10 *PEPPERTREES BED & BREAKFAST INN* • *724 E. University Blvd., Tucson, AZ 85719-5045; (520) 622-7167. (www.peppertreesinn.com) Six units, all with private baths. MC/VISA, AMEX; $$ to $$$. Rates include full breakfast. GETTING THERE: The inn is near the university, about a mile northeast of downtown. It's on the south side of University Boulevard, between Fourth and Euclid avenues.*

This comfortable inn is ideal for families or extended-stay visitors, since some units have two bedrooms and some have kitchens. The complex consists of four buildings around a large lawn area; it's nicely landscaped with a central fountain. The main house dates from 1905 and a next-door annex was built in the 1920s; both feature a mix of antique and modern furnishings. A small studio apartment is decorated like a Mexican casita. One of two detached guest houses features Southwestern décor and the other is furnished with interesting African artifacts.

I wasn't born in a log cabin, but my family moved into one as soon as they could afford it.
— **Melville D. Landon**

Chapter Fifteen

AFFORDABLE TUCSON

SURVIVING & THRIVING ON A BUDGET

It is now Tucson's turn to cater to the budget minded traveler. The Old Pueblo is a bit less expensive than its big sister to the north. We had no trouble finding free attractions and inexpensive places to eat and sleep.

NOTE: Items marked with ❖ are listed elsewhere in this book; check the index for page numbers.

FRUGAL FUN: THE TEN BEST FREE ATTRACTIONS

Here's an interesting note. Although Tucson has less than a third the population of the Valley of the Sun and receives far fewer visitors, it has more free attractions. The list that follows will be useful to those who are down to their last nickels and want to keep them.

☺ *KID STUFF:* This indicates attractions that are of particular interest to pre-teens.

1 **MISSION SAN XAVIER DEL BAC** • *San Xavier Road; (520) 294-2624. Daily 6 to 7; donations appreciated. MC/VISA accepted at gift shop. Daily mass at 8:30, Saturday vigil at 5:30 and Sunday masses at 8, 11 and 12:30. GETTING THERE: Drive south from Tucson on I-19, take exit 92 and go west briefly to the mission.*

The beautiful "White Dove of the Desert" is one of our favorite Tucson places and it is certainly the area's best free attraction. After a multi-million dollar restoration late in the last century, it is even more striking than before. Its whitewashed exterior and lavish Baroque décor in the main sanctuary appear as they must have looked when the mission was completed more than two centuries ago. For more on San Xavier, see Chapter Twelve, page 167.

2 **ARIZONA HISTORICAL SOCIETY MUSEUM** • *On the University of Arizona campus at 949 E. Second St.; (520) 628-5774. (w3.arizona.edu/~azhist) Monday-Saturday 10 to 4, Sunday noon to 4. Contributions accepted. GETTING THERE: From downtown, go north on Sixth Avenue to Sixth Street, and east about ten blocks to Euclid Avenue at the corner of the university campus. Drive north and turn into Main Gate parking garage between First and Second streets.*

This archive covers Arizona's contemporary history, from the arrival of the Spanish to the present, while the Arizona State Museum is concerned with pre-Hispanic peoples. For a better understanding of the area's past, we suggest visiting the state museum first. The historical society museum has several changing exhibit galleries, plus three long-term displays—Tucson of the 1870s, a transportation exhibit and the Arizona Mining Hall. See Chapter Twelve, page 173.

3 **ARIZONA STATE MUSEUM** • *University of Arizona campus as Park Avenue and University Boulevard; (520) 621-6302. (w3.arizona.edu/~asm) Monday-Saturday 10 to 5 and Sunday noon to 5. Donations accepted. GETTING THERE: See directions for the Arizona State Historical Society Museum above. The Main Gate garage offers validated museum parking.*

The focal point of this outstanding museum is an exhibit called "Paths of Life: American Indians of the Southwest." It's an historical-sociological study of ten tribes of Arizona and northern Mexico. For more, see Chapter Twelve, page 166.

4 **DE GRAZIA GALLERY IN THE SUN** • *6300 N. Swan Rd.; (800) 545-2185 or (520) 299-9191. Daily 10 to 4. GETTING THERE: Follow Swan Road several miles north from downtown, cross Sunrise*

Road, then turn right into the gallery complex after less than a mile, just short of Skyline Drive.

This appealing complex was built by the late Ted De Grazia, Arizona's most famous artist. It includes his original studio with many of his paintings on display, a smaller gallery where works of regional artists are exhibited and a charming little chapel called "Mission in the Sun." See Chapter Twelve, page 174.

5 **EL PRESIDIO HISTORIC DISTRICT** ● *Just north of downtown, bordered by Sixth Street, Ninth Avenue, Alameda Street and Granada Avenue. Old Town Artisans is at 210 Court, open Monday-Saturday 9:30 to 5:30 and Sunday noon to 5; (800) 782-8027 or (520) 623-6024. (www.oldtownartisans.com) Saguaro Artisans is at 215 N. Court Ave., open Monday-Saturday 9:30 to 5:30 and Sunday 10:30 to 5:30; (520) 792-3466.* ❖

Little is left of the walled garrison where Tucson was established in 1775. El Presidio is primarily a residential area of ancient adobes either restored or in need of restoration. The weathered neighborhood does contain two large gift, craft and souvenir shops—Old Town Artisans and Saguaro Artisans. It costs nothing to browse their pleasantly cluttered aisles or explore the narrow streets of El Presidio. The former walled city also shelters the excellent Tucson Museum of Art (which has an admission fee) and the city's most popular Mexican restaurant, El Charro, plus a few other cafés. All of the above are featured elsewhere in the book; check their index listings.

6 **FORT LOWELL MUSEUM** ● *Craycroft and Fort Lowell roads; (520) 885-3832. Wednesday-Saturday 10 to 4. GETTING THERE: Fort Lowell is about six miles northeast of downtown. Drive east on Broadway and then north on Craycroft. The museum is on the right, between Glenn Street and Fort Lowell Road.*

Part of a large city park and recreation center, Fort Lowell Museum is a reconstruction of a military camp established in 1873 to quell Apache uprisings. The facility includes the commanding officers quarters with period furnishings and historical displays, the "kitchen building" with exhibits concerning the fort's development and excavations of early native sites. Like most of Arizona's frontier forts, this was not a walled stockade like Tucson during its Spanish era, but a garrison from which troops set forth to do battle with the Geronimo, Cochise and friends. When the soldiers weren't chasing Apaches, they were socializing with the folks of Tucson, attending dances and raising a little Saturday night hell.

"The boys in blue raked over the dry embers of the town in pursuit of life and sport," the *Tucson Citizen* reported on May, 1874.

7 *SAGUARO NATIONAL PARK WEST* ● *The park comes in two parcels, about thirty miles apart with Tucson between them—Rincon Mountain Section (Saguaro East) which contains park headquarters, and Tucson Mountain Section (Saguaro West). Mailing address: 3693 Old Spanish Trail, Tucson, AZ 85730-5601; (520) 733-5153. The Saguaro West phone number is (520) 733-5158.* ☺

The Tucson Mountain section of Saguaro National Park is free, and only a token fee is collected at the Rincon section. For more on these fine cactus gardens and their visitor centers, hiking trails and other lures, see Chapter Twelve, pages 170-171.

8 *SOSA-CARILLO-FRÉMONT HOUSE* ● *151 S. Granada Ave.; (520) 622-0956. Wednesday-Saturday 10 to 4. GETTING THERE: This historic adobe is between El Presidio Historic District and the Tucson Convention Center.*

The elongated name identifies the original builders of this 1860s adobe, the family that lived here for decades and the famous frontiersman who briefly rented it. The adobe was built by José María Sosa, occupied for many years by the family of Jesús Suárez de Carillo and rented briefly to pathfinder and former Arizona territorial governor John C. Frémont. However, he apparently rented it for family members and never occupied it himself. Now nearly enveloped by the Tucson Convention Center, this Mexican-American style structure has been restored by the Arizona Historical Society. Several rooms are furnished with artifacts from the 1880s.

9 *TOHONO CHUL PARK* ● *7366 N. Paseo del Norte; (520) 575-8468. (www.tohonochulpark.org) Park open daily 7 to sunset; Tea Room 8 to 5 and gift gallery 9:30 to 5. Plant Interpretation Center and Greenhouse open 10 to 4 Labor Day through May, and 9 to noon the rest of the year. Donations encouraged; credit cards accepted at the Tea Room and gift shops. GETTING THERE: Drive north about seven miles on Oracle Road, turn left onto Ina Road, then right onto Paseo de Norte at the traffic light and right again into the park.*

Arizona's finest privately endowed park, Tohono Chul preserves a patch of desert in northern Tucson. Nature trails, patios, shade ramadas, gift shops, an exhibit gallery and a charming Southwest style tea room provide refuge from the growing city. The park was created by Richard and Jean Wilson, fashioned from two old estates. They purchased the land to rescue it from developers, then formed a non-profit foundation to operate the park. The exhibit center has changing displays focusing on Arizona arts, crafts and lifestyles. Two attractive gift shops—one in the exhibit center and another in the Tohono Chul Tea

Room—sell crafts, curios, artwork and native handicrafts. The tea room, set in a serene courtyard with a ceramic tile fountain, offers breakfast croissants and light meals of sandwiches and soups. Desserts are a specialty, and high tea is served with scones and pastries.

10 UNIVERSITY OF ARIZONA MUSEUM OF ART • On

the University of Arizona campus at Park Avenue and Speedway Boulevard; (520) 621-7567. GETTING THERE: See directions for the Arizona Historical Society and Arizona state museums above. If you park in the Main Gate Garage between First and Second streets, you're close to the art museum and the garage cashier will give you a campus map.

The museum has an impressive collection of European and American paintings and some sculptures from the Renaissance through the Nineteenth Century, including works by Picasso, Rodin and Andrew Wyeth. Changing exhibits often include student art and works by local and regional professional artists. For more on this and other UofA campus attractions, see Chapter Twelve, page 178.

THE TEN BEST CHEAP EATS

As we noted in Chapter Five, we define "cheap eats" as places where you can get filling dinners for less than $8 including a side dish and beverage. We don't include the major fast food chains.

Most inexpensive restaurants tend to be ethnic. Tucson doesn't offer many ethnic communities other than Mexican, so Hispanic cafés dominate our list. The closest thing to an international settlement—by café type, not by population—is a two-block stretch of University Boulevard just west of the university campus. We found several inexpensive restaurants there.

1 EL TORERO • 231 E. 26th St.; (520) 622-9534. Mexican;

wine and beer. Lunch through dinner daily. MC/VISA; $. GETTING THERE: It's in South Tucson about 1.5 miles from downtown. Drive south on I-10, take Star Pass Road exit 259 and go east on 22nd Street, then south again on Fourth Avenue. Go right on 26th Street for a block and a half; the restaurant is on the right.

Look for this popular café in a small alley, occupying a bougainvillea-splashed pink adobe. It's a local institution, serving inexpensive Mexican grub since 1956. El Torero also makes our list as one of the Ten Best Hispanic restaurants in Chapter Thirteen, page 191. It earns the top spot in this list because its dishes are remarkably inexpensive for their quality. Most of its enchiladas, burros, chimichangas, tacos and such come in "little plate" and "big plate" versions. The smaller ones are around $5, yet they're still very filling. Even the more elaborate entrées such as shrimp or flounder Vera Cruz are modestly priced, although they do exceed our arbitrary limit somewhat. The look of El Torero is rather austere, but who cares at these prices? Its single large room is dominated by an L-shaped bar, with basic Formica tables filling the rest of the space.

2 **EL MINUTO** • *354 S. Main Avenue in El Presidio Historic District; (520) 882-4145. Also at 8 N. Kolb Road in Circle Plaza at the corner of Broadway; (520) 290-9591. Mexican; wine and beer. Lunch through dinner daily at El Presidio's El Minuto; the Kolb Road restaurant is closed Monday. MC/VISA.* ❖

Among Tucson's Hispanic restaurants, the two El Minutos fall into the medium price range. However, some combination plates qualify for our budget list, and they're full meals. Among items priced well under $8 are chorizo and eggs with rice and beans, huevos rancheros with beans and a tortilla, and an enchilada casserole with rice and beans. They also have individual items within our budget range. This isn't unusual for small Mexican cafés, although the two El Minutos offer interesting environments as bonuses. El Presidio's café is in an ancient adobe while the Kolb Road version occupies a cute pink tile-roofed Southwest style building with a pleasing interior. For more, see Chapter Thirteen, page 190.

3 **EPIC CAFÉ** • *745 N. Fourth Ave.; (520) 624-6844. Mideastern-American eclectic; no alcohol. Breakfast through late afternoon Sunday-Tuesday; open later Wednesday-Saturday. GETTING THERE: The Epic is at the southwest corner of Fourth Avenue and University Boulevard. It's on the edge of the university campus, at the northern end of the Fourth Avenue shopping district.*

This appealing little café suggests a bit of California's Berkeley in Tucson. It has a casual coffee house look and the fare is whole earth and frequently vegetarian, with strong Mediterranean accents. Prices are geared to a university student's budget. For a few dollars, you can get a hearty hummus plate, quiche with salad, *spanakopita* or assorted sandwiches. Epic also features specialty coffees and bakery goods.

4 **THE FAT GREEK** • *970 University Ave.; (520) 206-0246. Greek; no alcohol. Lunch through early evening weekdays. MC/VISA. GETTING THERE: It's just west of the university campus, near the corner of Park Avenue. From downtown, go east on Broadway and then north on Sixth Avenue about seven blocks to University Boulevard and go right, toward the campus.*

You probably can afford to get fat at this second-floor walkup, where hungry students gather for inexpensive *dolmas*, gyro sandwiches and baklava for dessert. A specialty for a mere $6 is the Fat Greek Sampler of a gyro with meat, feta cheese, *kalamata* olives and three *dolmas* (stuffed grape leaves). For a curious Greek-American treat, try the Greek hot dog in pita bread with feta and onion sauce.

5 KARUNA'S THAI PLATE • *1917 E. Grant Rd.; (520) 325-4129. Thai; wine and beer. Lunch and dinner Friday-Saturday (closed mid-afternoon to early evening), and dinner only Sunday. MC/VISA. GETTING THERE: It's a couple of miles northeast of downtown, on the north side of Grant, just beyond Campbell Avenue.*

This spartan place is not only inexpensive; some local foodies say it's the best Thai restaurant in town and we agree. All but a few of the entrées are less than $6, leaving ample room for a drink. Entrées are served with a bowl of steamed rice, so these are very filling meals. Among the budget choices are *kratiam prig Thai* (beef, pork or chicken sautéed in garlic and black pepper sauce); *pat khing sod* (beef, pork or chicken with fried onions, fresh ginger, bell peppers and black mushrooms); and several hefty noodle dishes. Karuna's also has a multi-item lunch buffet, which was only $5 when we last checked. For more on this little cafe, see Chapter Thirteen, page 197.

6 LA SALSA FRESH MEXICAN GRILL • *Ina at Oracle in a Safeway shopping center, (520) 531-1211; Grant and Swan roads in Crossroads Festival, (520) 425-2200; and Campbell Avenue and Fort Lowell Road in the Blockbuster center, (520) 325-0082. Mexican; no alcohol. From 11 daily; various closing times. Major credit cards.*

The only franchise restaurant on our budget list, La Salsa earns a spot because its food is freshly made, health-oriented and quite modestly priced. This is no heat lamp Taco Bell; La Salsa's serving area is an open kitchen where food is prepared on order. You can get several combinations within the budget, such as a taco and quesadilla, taquito and quesadilla, two enchiladas or a chicken platter with avocado and tortillas. The chicken, steak, shrimp or fish tacos are so inexpensive that you can get two within our price limit. Hefty burritos are a specialty and most are priced under $5.

7 ORIENTAL EXPRESS • *982 E. University Blvd.; (520) 624-5798. Chinese; no alcohol. Lunch and dinner daily. MC/VISA. GETTING THERE: It's just west of the university campus, near the corner of Park Avenue. See directions for the Fat Greek above.*

This is another inexpensive university district café, sharing the same second-story deck with the Fat Greek. Most of its entrées are less than $5 and with steamed rice, they're sufficient for a full meal. The small café offers a several spicy or mild chicken, beef, pork, shrimp and vegetable dishes. It also features several combination platters, including sweet and sour pork, beef and broccoli, mixed vegetables, twice cooked pork and teriyaki chicken, all within our budget. The combo platters are served with fried rice and an egg roll. The café has seating indoors and out.

8 *SAMURAI SAM'S • 944 E. University Blvd.; (520) 792-0404. Japanese; no alcohol. Lunch through dinner Monday-Saturday; closed Sunday. MC/VISA, AMEX. GETTING THERE: It's just west of the campus of the University of Arizona, at the corner of Park Avenue. See directions for Andalus above.*

This neat little corner café opposite the university campus can fill you up with a variety of teriyaki bowls, most for less than $6, leaving budget room for a soft drink. They're served over a bed of rice with sautéed vegetables. A teriyaki wrap with a bowl of noodles also stays within our price limit. Sam's is a takeout, with seating indoors and at a single table on the sidewalk.

9 *TOKYO RICE BOWL • 2807 N. Campbell Ave.; (520) 324-0800. Chinese and Japanese; no alcohol. Lunch through dinner daily. No credit cards. GETTING THERE: The café is northeast of downtown on the northwest corner of Campbell and Glenn Street.*

Despite its name, nearly everything on the menu at this small walkup café is Chinese, except for teriyaki chicken and a sushi and salad offering. The food is served to order, not drying and dying on a steam table and most of the entrées are under $5, with drinks less than a dollar extra. Further, it's relatively healthy, prepared with vegetable oil, and no MSG. Most of the inexpensive entrées are rice plates, quite filling for lunch or dinner. Among them are chicken broccoli, cashew chicken, beef broccoli, Mongolian beef, barbecued pork, shrimp chop suey and spicy shrimp. Some combination plates, such as teriyaki chicken with barbecue pork, also fall within our price range. This tiny café has indoor seating and a couple of tables outside.

10 *WORLDWIDE WRAPS • Northeast corner of Fourth Avenue and Sixth Street, lunch through early dinner daily, (520) 884-7070; and 942 E. University Boulevard at Park Avenue, lunch through late afternoon, (520) 884-9787. International fare; no alcohol. MC/VISA.*

These tiny takeouts earn a spot on our budget list because they offer large and tasty "wraps"—assorted ethnic foods that are chopped and stuffed into large tortillas. And they are indeed large, enough for a filling meal. Some examples are Louisiana Cajun chicken or shrimp, teriyaki chicken with steamed vegetables, and Greek shrimp with vegetables. Tortilla wrapper choices are white, whole wheat, spinach with herb tomato basil and jalapeña-cheese. If you're not a tortilla fan, you can order the same fare in a bowl over jasmine or Spanish rice. The wraps and bowls can be accompanied by herbal and mint teas, fresh juices and fruit smoothies. The smoothies will put you over budget, although they're quite tasty.

THE TEN BEST CHEAP SLEEPS

Overall, Tucson motels are less expensive than those in Phoenix and most other major Western cities. As our criteria for cheap sleeps, we sought motels with high season (fall through spring) rates of $60 or less per couple—although prices are subject to change. We chose only those that were well maintained and clean, and reasonably close to downtown. Some of our selections are members of budget chains.

Several inexpensive motels are clustered along Oracle Road, which once was Tucson's main north-south highway. Most are between Grant Road and Speedway Boulevard, with a few more just east of Oracle on Drachman Street, off a traffic circle. These are older lodgings; some are well-kept and some are not. Four units on our list were drawn from this rather weather-worn motel row. They were reasonably tidy when we inspected them and they offer weekly rates. They also have refrigerators and microwaves or kitchenettes, convenient for extended stays. And they're close to I-10 and within blocks of downtown. Our other choices—including our Number One—are elsewhere in the basin, although not too far out.

1 STUDIO 6 TUCSON • *4950 Outlet Center Rd., Tucson, AZ 85706; (800) 4-MOTEL-6 or (520) 746-0030. Major credit cards. GETTING THERE: The motel is in South Tucson. From southbound I-10, take exit 264-B to Palo Verde Road, then go west on Irvington to Outlet Center. Northbound, take exit 264 to Irvington and go left under the freeway.*

Topping our list of best budget lodgings, this is one of the new extended stay properties operated by Motel 6. Its weekly rates are well within our price range. This AAA Two Diamond rated facility has 120 units with fully equipped kitchens, cable TV and room phones with voice mail, plus a swimming pool and coin laundry.

2 ECONO LODGE • *1136 N. Stone Ave., Tucson, AZ 85705; (877) 229-4271 or (520) 622-6714. Major credit cards. GETTING THERE: The motel is between Speedway Boulevard and Helen Street, just east of the Oracle Road motel row.*

A rather well-kept motel close to downtown, the Econo Lode has cable TV with HBO, room refrigerators, phones and a pool. Non-smoking units are available.

3 FRONTIER MOTEL • *227 W. Drachman St., Tucson, AZ 85705; (520) 798-3005. Major credit cards. GETTING THERE: The motel is on the south side of Drachman, half a block east of the Oracle-Drachman traffic circle.*

Although it's a little scruffy, the Frontier is an attractive old brick-walled and tile-roofed motel. It has a pool and rooms have cable TV and phones; kitchen units are available.

4 KNIGHTS INN • *720 W. 29th St., Tucson, AZ 85712; (520) 624-8291. Major credit cards. GETTING THERE: The inn is about 1.5 miles south of downtown. Take I-10 exit 259, follow the westside frontage road half a mile south, then go west briefly on 29th.*

This tidy 94-unit AAA-approved motel has room phones, cable TV, a pool, spa and guest laundry.

5 LA QUINTA INNS • *La Quinta West, 665 N. Freeway, Tucson, AZ 85745; (520) 622-6491. La Quinta East, 6404 E. Broadway, Tucson, AZ 85710, (520) 747-1414. Reservations for either: (800) 221-4731. Major credit cards. Rates include continental breakfast. GETTING THERE: For La Quinta West, take Mary's Road exit 257-A, then go briefly west. To reach La Quinta East, take southbound I-10 exit 258 and follow Congress and then Broadway 7.5 miles east, or take northbound I-10 exit 270 and go north 7.5 miles on Kolb Road, then east a mile on Broadway.*

Although most of their rates are above our limit, these La Quinta Inns have a few inexpensive rooms, and the price includes continental breakfast. The inns are much nicer than most budget lodgings; La Quinta East even has an AAA Three Diamond rating. Both inns have room phones, pools and guest laundries; La Quinta East also has a spa, voice mail and extended cable TV with video games.

6 LAZY 8 MOTEL • *314 E. Benson Hwy., Tucson, AZ 85713; (520) 622-3336. Major credit cards. Rates include continental breakfast. GETTING THERE: The motel is just under two miles south and east of downtown. Take I-10 exit 261 and go south along the frontage road; the motel is just east of Sixth Avenue.*

This 48-unit AAA-approved motel has TV, room phones and a coin laundry. Weekly rates are available.

7 MOTEL 6 • *Five in the Tucson area: 755 E. Benson Hwy., (520) 622-4614; 1031 E. Benson Hwy. (near the airport), (520) 628-1264; 960 S. Freeway near Congress Street, (520) 628-1339; 4630 W.*

Ina Rd., (520) 744-0300; and 1222 S. Freeway near 22nd Street, (520) 624-2516. For reservations: (800) 4-MOTEL-6. (www.motel6.com) Major credit cards.

These motels offer the usual spartan but clean and comfortable rooms with TV movies and phones with dataports. All Tucson locations have swimming pools and all except the 775 E. Benson Highway motel have coin laundries.

8 *OASIS MOTEL • 1701 N. Oracle Rd., Tucson, AZ 85705; (520) 622-2808. Major credit cards. GETTING THERE: The Oasis is at the corner of Elm Street, three blocks north of the Oracle-Drachman traffic circle.*

The Oasis has fair-sized rooms with phones and extended cable TV with HBO; kitchenettes are available. Facilities include a pool and guest laundry.

9 *QUAIL INN MOTEL • 1650 Oracle Rd., Tucson, AZ 85705; (520) 6722-8757. Major credit cards. GETTING THERE: The Quail Inn just north of Lee Street, two blocks north of the Oracle-Drachman traffic circle.*

This rather spartan but clean motel has extended cable TV with HBO, and phones. Kitchenettes and non-smoking rooms are available.

10 *TRAVEL INN • 1510 S. Freeway (I-10 exit 259), Tucson, AZ 85713, (520) 623-0521; and 6161 E. Benson Hwy. (I-10 exit 269), Tucson, AZ 85706, (520) 574-0191. Major credit cards.*

These modest, fairly well-kept motels have extended cable TV with HBO, room phones and laundry facilities.

*They talk about the
dignity of work.
Bosh. The dignity is
in pleasure.*
— **Herman Melville**

Chapter Sixteen

NIGHTFALL

AFTER DARK IN THE OLD PUEBLO

Tucson has most of the same kinds of nighttime lures as Phoenix, to lesser degrees but certainly not of lesser quality. It's one of the smallest cities in America to have a professional symphony orchestra, theater group, opera and ballet. Some are shared with Phoenix, performing in both communities.

In addition to offering nightlife options ranging from music and drama to lively clubs and pubs, the city has a very active creative arts scene. The grandly ornate 1927 Temple of Music and Art was restored several years ago as the catalyst for an ambitious program to create a Tucson Arts District downtown. It's focused around the Scott Avenue and Congress Street area, with many galleries, studios, cafés and artists lofts.

NIGHTLIFE SOURCES ● Two weekly tabloid-sized newspapers keep Tusconans and visitors up to date on what's happening where. *¡Caliente!*, published as an insert in the Friday *Arizona Daily Star,* tells you what's hot in the local entertainment scene. *Tucson Weekly,* an independent tabloid, hits the streets on Thursdays, and is available free at news racks throughout the area. It's also on the internet at *www.tucsonweekly.com.* Both publications provide comprehensive listings of the performing arts, movie, cultural and club scenes, along with book and restaurant reviews and listings. *Tucson Weekly,* definitely more liberated than the *Star's* entertainment tab, also has a large classified section that includes frisky personal ads.

GETTING TICKETED ● Tucson's major tickets-by-phone sources are Ticketmaster, (520) 321-1000 for performing arts and sporting events; Tucson Convention Center ticket office for events at the Music Hall, (520) 791-4836; Tucson Symphony box office, (520) 882-8585; and Centennial Hall ticket office for University of Arizona performing arts, (520) 621-3341.

NOTE: Items marked with ❖ are listed elsewhere in this book; check the index for page numbers.

THE TEN BEST PERFORMING ARTS GROUPS

Tucson's performing arts season tends to correspond with the tourist season—September through May. This has more to do with the weather than trying to sell tickets to tourists, although it's certainly convenient for high-season visitors seeking cultural offerings.

The city has three major venues for its performing arts activities, plus several smaller theaters. The **Temple of Music and Art** at 330 S. Scott Avenue is home base for the Arizona Theater. It hosts a wide variety of other events in its two theaters, and it also has an art gallery; (520) 884-8210. The 2,177-seat **Music Hall** in the Tucson Convention Center is home to the Tucson Symphony and Ballet Arizona; (520) 791-4836 or (520) 791-4266. A smaller showplace in the building, the 503-seat **Leo Rich Theater,** is used for dramas, recitals, chamber music and such. The University of Arizona's **Centennial Hall**, on the campus at 1020 E. University Boulevard, hosts many UofA performing arts events, with seating for 2,500; (520) 621-3341.

1 ARIZONA THEATER COMPANY ● *In the Temple of Music and Art at 330 Scott Ave.; (520) 884-8210 or (520) 622-2823.*

This highly regarded professional group started here as the amateur Arizona Civic Theater in 1967, then it went professional in 1972. Six years later, it opened a second company in Phoenix. ATC mounts six productions a year in both venues, ranging from Shakespeare to *avant garde* to Broadway musicals.

2 ARIZONA OPERA COMPANY ● *3501 N. Mountain Ave.; (520) 293-4336. Performs at the Music Hall.*

This is another performing arts company that began in Tucson and then expanded to Phoenix. It was started here in 1971 and now presents five productions a year. Its Tucson season is October to March and it's the only opera company in the nation that performs regularly in two cities.

3 ARIZONA REPERTORY THEATER • *University of Arizona; (520) 621-1162. Performs at the UofA Fine Arts Complex at Park Avenue and Speedway Boulevard.*

Professional and faculty actors, directors and drama coaches have been shaping shows for the UofA Theatre Arts Department for more than half a century. ART is one of the oldest university-based drama companies west of the Mississippi. The group presents half a dozen dramas, comedies and musicals a year, from November through April.

4 BALLET ARIZONA • *Offices and rehearsal facilities at 3645 E. Indian School Rd., Phoenix; (602) 381-0184; tickets (520) 206-6988. Performs at the Pima Community College Center for the Arts, 2202 W. Anklam Road.*

Based in Phoenix, Ballet Arizona presents six productions at the Center for the Arts' Proscenium Theater from September through May. It features mostly classic ballets, with some contemporary dance productions, and it mounts a *Nutcracker* production in both cities during the holidays. (For more on the company, see Chapter Six, page 99.)

5 GASLIGHT THEATRE • *7010 E. Broadway Blvd.; (520) 886-9428. The theater is just under eight miles east of downtown, at the southwest side of Broadway and Kolb Road.*

Do you like to hiss the villain and cheer the hero, or perhaps the other way around? Gaslight Theatre presents old fashioned "meller-drammers"—fun, all-family musicals, written and produced by local talent. You can nosh while you jeer or cheer, since Little Anthony's Diner is located in the theater. Shows are presented throughout the year.

6 ORTS THEATRE OF DANCE • *121 E. Seventh St.; (520) 624-3799. Performs at the Temple of Music and Art and Pima Community College Center for the Arts.*

This innovative company, which sometimes mixes trapeze work with its choreography, stages a variety of modern, traditional and folk dance productions. It was started in 1985 and its warehouse studio also conducts dance classes for the public. In addition to shows at the Temple and Pima College, it presents an annual program at DeMeester Outdoor Performing Center at Reid Park, East 22nd Street and Country Club Road.

7 **TUCSON BOYS CHORUS** • *5770 E. Pima St.; (520) 296-6277. Performs at various venues.*

Although it's locally based, this sixty-voice youth choir has performed throughout the United States and Europe. Its Tucson season consists of about a dozen programs, including a series of pops concerts, plus the annual Musicale Regale and Winter Holiday program. The season is October through may.

8 **TUCSON POPS ORCHESTRA** • *P.O. Box 14545, Tucson, AZ 85732; (520) 722-5853. Performs at Reid Park's Outdoor Performance Center.*

If you like your music free and on the lighter side, Tucson Pops presents a series of ten "Arizona Under the Stars" concerts in Reid Park in May, June and September. It's one of the city's oldest musical groups, established in 1954.

9 **TUCSON SYMPHONY ORCHESTRA** • *2175 N. Sixth Ave.; (520) 882-8585. Performs at the Music Hall and Pima Community College Proscenium Theater.*

The Tucson Symphony presents a busy and versatile season of classical and popular music from September through April, often featuring top guest artists. It's the oldest symphony orchestra in the Southwest, dating from 1929.

10 **UNIVERSITY OF ARIZONA SCHOOL OF MUSIC & DANCE** • *Crowder Hall, University of Arizona; (520) 621-1162.*

Students and faculty of the UofA have been presenting a versatile program of music and dance for more than a century. They give an amazing 300 performances a year, so there's almost always something happening in Crowder Hall. Instructors—all accomplished musicians—present their Faculty Arts Series, and they join with students in offering everything from jazz to opera to Top Forty pops.

THE TEN BEST NIGHTSPOTS

While not exactly a wild party town, Tucson has a lively nightlife scene. Much of it happens along ❖ **Fourth Avenue**. Simply called "The Avenue" by locals, it's a shopping and club district northeast of downtown between Ninth Street and University Avenue at the edge of the UofA campus. Tucson's nightlife really jumps during the "Club Crawl" held each spring and fall, featuring as many as a hundred bands at twenty different nightspots. For dates and information on the

"Crawl" and other nightlife events, contact the visitors bureau at (800) 638-8350; or check with the Visitor Center in La Placita Village.

Our choices of the Ten Best nightspots are a mixed musical bag and we begin with Tucson's most popular downtown club, housed in an historic hotel:

1 **CLUB CONGRESS** • *In the Congress Hotel at 311 E. Congress St.; (520) 622-8848. Dance club with a mix of live and deejay music most nights. GETTING THERE: It's downtown at the corner of Congress Street and Fifth Avenue.*

The venerable Congress Hotel has become downtown's most popular hotspot in recent years. Its Club Congress lures a wide cross-section of patrons and music. Theme nights feature everything from hard rock to Latin. The quiet ones can retire to the Cyber Café for an intense evening with the internet.

2 **BERKY'S BAR** • *5769 E. Speedway Blvd.; (520) 296-1981. (www.berkeys.com) Live music Monday-Saturday. GETTING THERE: It's about six miles east of downtown between Craycroft and Wilmot.*

If you liked rock before heavy metal and rap, you'll like this nightspot. It features live music six nights a week, from jazz to blues to rock, with local and touring bands. Sunday is karaoke night.

3 **BOONDOCKS LOUNGE** • *3660 N. First Ave.; (520) 690-0991. Live blues, jazz and rock Friday- Sunday. GETTING THERE: The lounge is about three miles north of downtown, near the corner of First and Fort Lowell Road.*

This comfortable, dimly-lit lounge and dance club presents live music Friday through Sunday, with recorded sounds the rest of the week. It's a large place, with two service bars and a pool room.

4 **LAFF'S COMEDY CLUB** • *2900 E. Broadway Blvd.; (520) 323-8669. (www.thirdrockshop.com) GETTING THERE: It's about three miles east of downtown, between Tucson Boulevard and Country Club Road.*

The comedy club presents assorted stand-up mike-clutchers Thursday through Sunday nights. It's also a restaurant, serving Mexican fare most evenings.

5 **NIMBUS BREWING COMPANY** • *3850 E. 44th St.; (520) 745-9175. Live rock and pops music Friday through Sunday. GETTING THERE: It's about five miles southeast of downtown Tucson. Take the*

Maclovivo-Barraza-Aviation Parkway about four miles southeast, go south briefly on Palo Verde Boulevard, turn east on 44th Street and follow it three blocks to its end.

This large brewpub in a converted warehouse features local rock bands three nights a week. It's a popular nightspot the rest of the week as well, often featuring free movies.

6 **O'MALLEY'S ON FOURTH** ● *247 Fourth Ave.; (520) 623-8600. Rock and pops bands several nights a week. GETTING THERE: It's at the southwest corner of Fourth Avenue and Eighth Street in Fourth Avenue shopping and nightlife district. From downtown, follow Sixth Avenue north to Sixth Street, then go east to Fourth Avenue.*

This large hangout hosts groups several nights a week in a back room especially rigged for live bands. The acoustics are good and the beat is heavy. It's also a popular local bar (page 229), particularly for UofA students.

7 **PLUSH** ● *340 E. Sixth St.; (520) 798-1298. (www.plushtucson.com.) Live music five to seven nights a week. GETTING THERE: It's in the heart of the Fourth Avenue shopping and nightlife district, at the corner of Fourth Avenue and Sixth.*

This upbeat, comfortable and somewhat plush nightspot books local, regional and national touring groups most nights of the week. It features lounge entertainment Sunday-Tuesday, then rock, pops, jazz and Dixie on the main stage Wednesday-Saturday. It's a lively cocktail lounge as well, with the usual libations and a good choice of wines by the glass.

8 **RIALTO THEATRE** ● *318 E. Congress St.; (520) 740-0126. Live music for dancing several nights a week. GETTING THERE: It's downtown between Fifth and Toole avenues.*

A grand old movie theater has been restored and converted into a live entertainment venue, booking a variety of bands from jazz to rock. There's room for dancing or you can just sit back in comfortable theater seats and listen.

9 **SMUGGLERS INN** ● *6330 E. Speedway; (520) 296-6111. (www.smugglersinn.com) A mix of live and recorded music six nights a week, mostly classic pops and light rock. GETTING THERE: It's about 6.5 miles east of downtown at Speedway and Wilmot.*

The attractive Caribbean style Smugglers Inn resort shelters a lively nightclub adjacent to its restaurant. It features mostly pops and rock from the fifties through the eighties.

10 SPEAK EASY • *Wilmot Road and 22nd Street; (520) 519-0355. Neighborhood pub with music several nights a week. GETTING THERE: From downtown, go east on Broadway just over 5.5 miles to Wilmot, then go south less than a mile. Turn right into the parking area behind Lucky Wishbone Shrimp and Chicken, just short of 22nd.*

If you like a good old boy redneck bar that features live oldies, Latin and Motown dance music Friday and Saturdays and karaoke most other nights, Speak Easy is your place. And you don't even have to say: "Joe sent me." This speakeasy is a sprawling joint spread through several rooms with a dance floor, large main bar, multiple TV monitors, pool tables, couches and a few booths with food service.

THE TEN BEST WATERING HOLES

The bar scene it Tucson is similar to that in Phoenix. Most of the more elegant and quiet lounges—the kind we like—are in the area's resorts and inns. For something a bit livelier, check out the pubs downtown, particularly along Congress Street, and north along Fourth Avenue toward the university campus.

1 AUDUBON BAR • *At the Arizona Inn, 2200 E. Elm St.; (520) 325-1541. (www.arizonainn.com) GETTING THERE: From downtown, drive north on Campbell past the University of Arizona campus, turn right onto Elm Street and go about three blocks. The inn is on the right, with parking on the left.*

The Audubon is the most quietly elegant cocktail lounge in the city, with a carved mahogany main bar, European antiques and an unusual octagonal drop ceiling. Plush chairs are set before little marble-topped tables and comfy couches are tucked into quiet corners. The bar gets its name from original Audubon prints on the walls—not of birds but of small mammals. For birds, one simply adjourns to an outdoor deck beside a floral-bordered croquet court, and listens. (John James Audubon painted both birds and animals, unfortunately shooting them first to ensure that they held still.)

2 EL CONQUISTADOR LOBBY BAR • *At the Sheraton El Conquistador Resort, 1000 Oracle Rd., (520) 544-5000. GETTING THERE: Take Ina Road (exit 248) six miles east to Oracle Road, then go north 4.5 miles to El Conquistadore Way and turn right. From downtown, follow Oracle Road about fourteen miles north.* ❖

El Conquistador's lobby bar is a most appealing space, with deep cushion chairs and couches, museum-quality artifacts placed about, and a high ceiling with a crown style wrought iron chandelier. Picture windows provide one of the best resort bar views in the area—an imposing vista of the ramparts of the Santa Catalina mountains that loom over this opulent foothills resort.

3 **FIRECRACKER BISTRO** • *In Plaza Palomino at 2990 N. Swan Rd.; (520) 318-1118. (www.metrorestaurants.com) Full bar service. Lunch and dinner daily. Major credit cards. GETTING THERE: The restaurant is on the southeast corner of Swan and Fort Lowell roads.* ❖

If you're an aficionado of the film *Casablanca*, you'll like the tropical bar at Firecracker Bistro. Although *Casablanca* was set in North Africa and Firecracker has a Pacific Rim theme, the setting is similar—bamboo bar stools, wooden Venetian blinds and rattan fans. The restaurant, which features Pan-Asian cuisine, has two bars, one adjacent to the main dining room and a more intimate enclave off to one side. We prefer the smaller one, where we can relax on a curving settee with a proper tropical drink in hand.

4 **FROG & FIRKIN** • *874 E. University Blvd.; (520) 623-7507. Lunch through dinner daily. Major credit cards. GETTING THERE: It's just west of the UofA campus between Park and Tyndall avenues. From downtown, go east on Broadway, then north on Sixth Avenue about seven blocks to University Boulevard and turn right, toward the campus.*

This vaguely English style pub is a lively and upbeat hangout for university students. The faithful simply call it "The Frog." The small interior is decorated mostly with beer bottles, a single pool table and—oddly—not many Wildcat logo items. A cozy seating area is in the rear, although most of the action takes place on a large two-level patio up front. Here, shapely coeds and their guys—usually waited on by other shapely coeds—drink pitchers of beer and munch thick-crust pizzas, hamburgers and assorted other sandwiches. "You always feel better after the first beer," states the Frog's motto.

5 **HOOTERS** • *6335 E. Tanque Verde Road near Wilmot, behind Capin Car Care Center, (520) 722-8500; and 4385 Ina Road at Camino Martin, just east of I-10 exit 248, (520) 744-7744.*

If you've been to a Hooters, you know the story. They're upbeat sports bar restaurants where amply endowed lasses wearing scoop T-shirts and orange hotpants serve pitchers of beer, spicy food and Colgate smiles. While they're the kinds of places that draw collective frowns from the National Organization for Women, we feel that they're just harmless fun. The Hooters' motto is "Delightfully tacky yet unrefined." The fare is typical sports bar—Philly cheese steak, 'burgers, pizzas, buffalo wings and such, with a long list of beers and wines by the glass. The décor consists mostly of the girls and their pin-ups and logo items, plus TV sets tuned to the latest games. The Pima Road Hooters is part of a nightlife complex called New West and Gotham.

6 MALONEY'S ON FOURTH • *213 N. Fourth Ave.; (520) 388-9355. MC/VISA. GETTING THERE: The pub is on the lower end of "The Avenue" district, near the corner of Ninth Street.*

This large, pleasant pub seems transplanted from Chicago's South Side, with its brick walls, dark friendly interior and warm paneled woods. One expects a smiling barkeep—mopping the plank with his damp cloth—to ask: "What's yours?" Except that most of the servers are pretty young women in shorts and the bar's walls are covered with hundreds of old black and white photos of film stars. This is popular hangout is huge, with several serving bars and seating areas, including tables on a front deck. A specialty is grinders—sandwiches served on sliced baguettes.

7 O'MALLEY'S ON FOURTH • *247 Fourth Ave.; (520) 623-8600. GETTING THERE: It's at the southwest corner of Fourth Avenue and Eighth Street in "The Avenue" district.*

This sturdy and rather austere-looking pub is a popular hangout for university students, and it often presents live music for a small cover charge. It's also a serious drinking establishment, with a large central serving bar and lots of places to sit and sip, including a spacious covered patio. The décor is simple—open beam ceilings, wooden tables, ladder-back chairs, neon beer signs and a few shamrocks on the walls. It's not really an Irish pub, despite the name. It's mostly a lively saloon that caters to the young and the restless. The patrons probably drink more Corona the Guinness.

8 PINNACLE PEAK SALOON • *In Trail Dust Town at 6541 E. Tanque Verde Rd.; (520) 296-0911. Open nightly. GETTING THERE: Trail Dust Town is about eight miles northeast of downtown, on the north side of Tanque Verde between Wilmot and Kolb roads. Go east on Pima Street, then northeast briefly on Tanque Verde.*

If you've ever wanted to push through batwing doors—just like the Duke or Hoppy or Roy or Gene—step into this wonderfully contrived saloon at Pinnacle Peak Steakhouse. It's much more interesting than the watering holes at Old Tucson (Chapter Thirteen, page 185) and there's no admission charge. Belly up to the bar, order a brew and check out the ornate mirrored backbar, pot bellied stove, patterned wallpaper, old wild west show posters and round poker tables. However, no poker is played here, so don't expect one of those "B" Western movie scenes when the cowboy tips the table over and draws down on the card sharp.

9 *THUNDER CANYON BREWING COMPANY* ● *In Foothills Mall at 7401 N. La Cholla Blvd.; (520) 797-2652. GETTING THERE: From downtown, go north on Oracle Road about nine miles, turn left on Ina Road and follow it three miles to La Cholla Boulevard. Foothills Mall is on the northwest corner and Thunder Mountain is on the east side.*

Tucson's most appealing brewpub occupies a large, open space with the usual beam ceilings, exposed utility ducts and stainless steel brewing tanks. Earthy brown walls are decorated mostly with beer trays. However, its most appealing space is outside, where misters keep patio suds-sippers cool on the hottest days. The pub brews an assortment of beers with predictably cute names such as Flash Light, Windstorm Wheat, Thunderhead IPA and Blackout Stout. The brewpub also is a locally popular restaurant, with an open kitchen issuing fare such as 'burgers, sandwiches, steak, meat loaf, fajitas and fish & chips. Wood-fired pizzas are a specialty.

10 *WESTIN LA PALOMA LOBBY BAR* ● *3800 E. Sunrise Dr.; (520) 742-6000. (www.westin.com) GETTING THERE: Follow Campbell Avenue about eight miles north from downtown, then turn right onto Skyline Drive. Go east 1.3 miles, veering to the right to blend onto Sunrise; turn south on Via Palomita and follow signs.*

The dramatic atrium lobby of this luxury resort in the Santa Catalina foothills steps down three levels, with the center terrace occupied by a spacious lobby bar. Settle into a comfortable captain's chair or onto couch—margarita in hand—and enjoy one of the best views in the Tucson basin. The vista, through thirty-foot arched windows, takes your eyes across a large swimming lagoon to desert foothills and the craggy ramparts of Mount Lemmon. After finishing your margarita, you can stroll down another level to the Desert Garden Lounge and have lunch or dinner—still enjoying that spectacular view.

Chapter Seventeen

BEING SPENDY

SHOPPING AND BOUTIQUE HOPPING

Like Phoenix, downtown Tucson isn't a serious shopping area. The small highrise urban core is geared more to office buildings, restaurants, theaters and pubs. For really ambitious shopping, most folks head for the suburbs of this spread-out city.

NOTE: Items marked with ❖ are listed elsewhere in this book; check the index for page numbers.

THE TEN BEST MALLS AND SHOPPING AREAS

Our choices are a mixed shopping bag. Tucson has the usual large malls—many covered in deference to summer heat—plus some interesting specialty shopping areas. Our top choice is the Tucson Basin's largest mall, where you can be spendy to your heart's content.

1 TUCSON MALL ● *4500 N. Oracle Rd.; (520) 293-7330.* *(www.thetucson-mall.com) Most stores open Monday-Saturday 10 to 9 and Sunday 11 to 6. GETTING THERE: The mall is at the southeast corner of Oracle and Wetmore roads, about four miles from downtown.*

Tucson's largest and most attractive mall, this complex has more than 200 shops and restaurants, all under cover in an oddly staggered layout. Its anchors are Sears, JCPenny, Macy's, Mervyn's, Robinsons-May and Dillard's. Greenhouse-style skylights admit sunshine to keep the mall's potted plants, trees and other flora happy. Shops are on a main level and a mezzanine that runs the full length of the mall.

Because of the mall's rather staggered layout, it's easy to get lost. A map, available at a customer service counter on the ground floor near Macy's, will keep you oriented. The Carousel Court has about a dozen food stalls and a merry-go-round for the kiddies. Particularly appealing at this large mall is Arizona Avenue, a festively decorated corridor lined with open-front shops that sell Southwest artifacts, art, collector items and specialty foods.

2 BROADWAY VILLAGE ● *Southwest corner of East Broadway Boulevard at Country Club Drive. Most shops open Monday-Saturday from 10 and Sunday from noon; various closing hours. GETTING THERE: The complex is about 2.5 miles east of downtown.*

This is not a shopping mall but a small specialty store center. With tile roofs, brick arches and walls spilling with vines, it has an appealing Tuscan look. Its tenants are a interesting mix—art galleries, a shop specializing in Mideastern carpets, a mystery book shop, a perfume shop, a charming bakery café and an indoor-outdoor café called Elle Wine Country Restaurant. The largest tenant is Zôcalo Fine Colonial Furniture, a virtual museum of Mexican and Spanish colonial decorator items; (520) 320-1236. It sells hand-carved furniture, hammered tin and wrought iron goods, colorful pottery and carved masks. Another shop, the second-floor Primitive Arts Gallery, specializes in pre-Colombian native and ethnographic art; (520) 326-4852.

3 CROSSROADS FESTIVAL ● *Northeast corner of Grant and Swan roads. Various hours for stores. GETTING THERE: It's about seven miles northeast of downtown.*

Not a shopping mall in the normal sense, Crossroads is a collection of shops and stores, many fronting on a long, continuous façade. It stretches for nearly a block along Grant and wraps around to Swan. Although this isn't a covered mall, a colonnaded overhang extends its full length, shading patrons and window shoppers. Crossroads has no major anchors; it's a collection of about thirty-five large and small specialty shops and several restaurants, including Outback Steak House, Buddy's Grill and ❖ **The Good Egg**. Among the stores are a bed & bath shop, beauty parlor, several clothing stores, two card and gift shops, a large jewelers, Blockbuster video, Starbucks, Fry's Food and Drug and Super Cuts, should you need shearing.

4 **EL CON MALL** • *3601 E. Broadway Blvd.; (520) 327-8767. (www.shopelcon.con) Most stores open Monday-Saturday 10 to 9 and Sunday 11 to 6. GETTING THERE: The mall is on the north side of Broadway, between Jones and Dodge boulevards, about three miles east of downtown.*

Opened in 1960, Tucson's first covered shopping complex is undergoing a mall-to-wall renovation and major expansion, with a handsome Spanish Colonial look. With Robinsons-May and JCPenney as its anchors and a new Home Depot adjacent, the growing facility will have more than a hundred shops. Among national chains represented are Target, Millers Outpost, Radio Shack, Foot Locker and Payless ShoeSource. The mall's facilities include a large food court, farmers market, restaurant plaza and multi-screen Century 20 El Con Theatres. The interior features what developers call a "main street cityscape."

5 **EL CORTIJO PLAZA & FINE ART GALLERIES** • *Campbell Avenue and Skyline Drive. Most galleries open Monday-Saturday 10 to 6 and Sunday noon to 5. GETTING THERE: This dual gallery complex is at the northeast corner of Campbell Avenue and Skyline Drive, just below Anthony's restaurant. Follow Campbell about eight miles north from downtown, then turn right into the complex after crossing Skyline.*

This complex contains Tucson's largest collection of Southwest theme art galleries and gift shops. It comes in two sections—El Cortijo Plaza and a courtyard complex simply labeled Fine Art Galleries. El Cortijo's galleries are housed in attractive Santa Fe adobe style structures just above Skyline. When you aren't shopping, you can enjoy a fine view of Tucson. The lineup includes Victoria Boyce, Barbara Schaefer Designs, Rosequist Galleries, Wilde Meyer Gallery, El Presidio Gallery and Antoine's Jewelers.

The Fine Art Galleries, in a shaded courtyard just above El Cortijo, features mostly Southwestern and native peoples' paintings and sculptures. Within the complex are Neice Kimpton Gallery, Sanders Galleries, Settlers West Galleries and Gallery West.

6 **FOOTHILLS MALL** • *Ina Road at La Cholla Boulevard; (520) 219-0650. Various hours for stores. GETTING THERE: From downtown, go north on Oracle Road about nine miles to Ina Road, then turn west and follow it about three miles to La Cholla Boulevard. The mall is on the northwest corner.*

Foothills is a single-level outdoor-indoor mall that targets budget to mid-range credit card clutchers. Its larger stores are specialty places such as a Nike Factory Store, Ross Dress for Less, Mikasa, a Sak's Fifth Avenue outlet called Off Fifth, a designer shoe outlet and a large Barnes & Noble book store. Several smaller shops and boutiques line the mall's interior corridors, and a multi-screen theater is out back. Foothills also is home to Tucson's most appealing brewpub, Thunder Canyon; see Chapter Sixteen, page 230.

7 *FOURTH AVENUE SHOPPING DISTRICT* • *Fourth Avenue Merchants Association; (520) 624-5004. (www.avefun.com) Old Pueblo Trolley runs Friday 6 to 10, Saturday noon to midnight and Sunday noon to 6. GETTING THERE: The area extends along Fourth from Ninth Street to University Boulevard. From downtown, follow Sixth Avenue north under a railroad underpass, then shift east to Fourth Avenue.* ❖

Locals call it "The Avenue." Influenced in part by the youthful and trendy tastes of the nearby university, a six-block string of mid-twentieth century low-rise stores has evolved into a specialty shopping and entertainment area. To add additional charm, Tucson's transit agency runs old fashioned trolley cars from Eighth Street up "The Avenue" to University Boulevard and on to the west campus area. The Avenue's 1950s style storefronts house an interesting assortment—small cafés, coffee houses, pubs, hip apparel shops, thrift stores, pottery and crafts shops and music stores. A few murals dress up old brick walls.

8 *PARK PLACE* • *5870 E. Broadway Blvd.; (520) 748-1222. (www.malibu.com) Most stores open Monday-Saturday 10 to 9 and Sunday noon to 6. GETTING THERE: The mall is six miles east of downtown, on the south side of Broadway between Craycroft and Wilmot roads.*

Park Place is the city's second largest covered shopping complex after Tucson Mall. Built on a single level, it's anchored by Macy's, Sears and Dillard's, with more than a hundred smaller specialty stores and boutiques. Added in late 2001 were a large food court and a twenty-screen movie theater. Park Place is an inviting space, shaped as a large cross with barrel-arched roofs and skylights, and accented with potted palms and other flora. A customer service counter is conveniently located at the center of the cross. Plush couches and chairs invite shoppers to take a break from credit card abuse.

9 *PLAZA PALOMINO* • *2970 N. Swan Rd. (www.dotucson.com) Most stores open Monday-Saturday 10 to 6 and Sunday noon to 5. GETTING THERE: Plaza Palomino is on the southeast corner of Swan and Fort Lowell roads, about six miles northeast of downtown.*

This small Spanish colonial style center is built along a landscaped courtyard and a narrower side corridor; it has about twenty shops and several restaurants. The trend here is trendy, with most stores featuring contemporary clothing, giftwares and artwork. The plaza hosts a

Gourmet Food Fair every Saturday from 10 to 3, in addition to assorted other events. Two of its restaurants, La Placita and Firecracker Bistro, are featured in Chapter Thirteen, pages 191 and 196.

10 *ST. PHILLIPS PLAZA* • *4380 N. Campbell Ave.; (520) 529-2775. Various hours for stores and restaurants. GETTING THERE: This stylish center is about five miles north of downtown, on the right side of Campbell between the Rillito River and River Road.*

Although rather small with only about twenty stores, St. Phillips Plaza is one of Tucson's most attractive shopping areas. This Spanish colonial style open air center is nicely landscaped with large sycamores, native plants, terra cotta pots bursting with blooms and fountains trimmed in colored tile. Most of the shops are specialty boutiques and galleries, offering designer clothing, jewelry, and Southwestern and native peoples art. A couple of appealing restaurants are here— Ovens (Chapter Thirteen, page 184) and Vivace (795-7221); both offer indoor and outdoor dining. More shopping and dining facilities are in the adjacent Windmill Suites hotel. A farmers' market is held at St. Phillips on Sunday mornings.

THE TEN BEST SPECIALTY STORES

This list is intended to help folks find essential items such as a good book, authentic native crafts, healthy groceries or a good bottle of wine—which of course is a healthy grocery item. Our choices are listed in no particular order, not even alphabetical.

1 *THE BEST WINE SHOP: The RumRunner* • *3200 E. Speedway Blvd.; (520) 326-0121. Monday-Saturday 10 to 10 and Sunday 10 to 7. GETTING THERE: The shop is just east of Country Club Boulevard, about three miles northeast of downtown.*

Selling considerably more wine than rum, this small yet well-stocked shop has Tucson's best selection of California and European wines. However, it leans more toward pricey French wines than equally good and less expensive California varietals. It also has a good choice of Ports, Cognacs, single malt Scotches and designer bourbons, plus a large assortment of imported and limited edition American beers. Like any decent wine shop, it has a nice gourmet food section, focusing mostly on cheeses, plus a choice of patés, caviar and condiments. *Food and Wine Magazine* calls the RumRunner one of America's best wine shops. Stock more California wines, guys, and we'll agree.

Tucked behind the RumRunner is the Dish, one of Tucson's better restaurants. See Chapter Thirteen, page 182.

2 THE BEST SHOP FOR NATIVE CRAFTS: Bahti Indian Arts • *In St. Phillips Plaza at 4300 N. Campbell Ave.; (520) 577-0290. (www.bahti.com) Open daily; various hours. Major credit cards. GETTING THERE: See the St. Phillips Plaza listing above.*

The Bahti family has been selling high quality native peoples' arts and crafts and writing books on this subject for more than half a century. The handsome store in St. Phillips Plaza offers a fine assortment of top quality items, including traditional and contemporary paintings and sculptures, silver and turquoise jewelry, hand-woven rugs, carved masks and books on native lore. The selection isn't limited to native people of the Southwest. Bahti carries items from other American tribal groups, including some fine brightly colored masks carved by Northwest tribes.

3 THE BEST TOURIST SHOP: Old Town Artisans • *201 N. Court Ave.; (800) 782-8072 or (520) 623-6024. Monday-Saturday 9:30 to 5:30 and Sunday noon to 5. LaCocina Restaurant and Two Micks Grill & Cantina serve lunch daily and dinner Tuesday-Sunday. GETTING THERE: It's in El Presidio Historic District, immediately northwest of downtown.* ❖

To call Old Town Artisans a tourist shop is a little unfair, since this block-square complex also sells nice quality folk arts and crafts. Housed in a fused-together complex of several former adobe homes, it has a dozen galleries and shops and a pair of restaurants. Whatever your needs in Southwest treasures or trinkets, you'll find them here—turquoise and silver jewelry, T-shirts, Kokopelli in every possible configuration, hand-woven carpets, refrigerator magnets, books on the Southwest, paper flowers, wrought iron and hammered tin decorator items, lots of pottery, and some serious oils and watercolors plus inexpensive prints. Old Town Pot Shop, the facility's largest tenant, has a serious selection of pots, plus sculptures, paintings and blown glass and metalworks.

4 THE BEST NEW BOOK STORE: Barnes & Noble • *In Foothills Mall at Ina Road and La Cholla Boulevard, (520) 742-6402; and at 5130 E. Broadway at the northeast corner of Rosemont Boulevard, (520) 512-1166. Daily 9 to 11. Major credit cards.*

Barnes & Nobles are what bookstores should be—very large with an extensive selection, and comfortable and inviting with lots of places to sit, like well-stocked libraries. These outlets carry tens of thousands of books—including our **DiscoverGuides**—plus many regional guidebooks a good selection of music on CDs and tapes. And unlike public libraries, they have pleasant cafés that invite lingering.

5 THE BEST USED BOOK STORE: Bookman's • 1930 E. Grant Road at the corner of Campbell Avenue, (520) 325-5767; and 3733 Ina Road at Thornydale, opposite Frye's, (520) 579-0303. Daily 9 to 10; Major credit cards.

One of the West's largest used book stores, Bookman's has hundreds of thousands of titles on every conceivable subject. The stores have rare book sections, large "Kid's Corners" with juvenile titles, and extensive collections of used magazines. This is where you go for your pre-1900 editions of National Geographic. Keeping pace with the times, these long-established stores have software sections with video games and computer books, plus music departments with hundreds of CDS, cassettes and even old 78s.

6 THE BEST HEALTHY FOOD STORES: Wild Oats Community Market • Three Tucson locations: 7133 Oracle Road at Ina Road, (520) 297-5394; 3360 E. Speedway Boulevard near Country Club Road, (520) 795-9844; and 4751 E. Sunrise Drive at the northeast corner of Swan Road, (520) 299-8858. Daily 7 to 10. Major credit cards.

As noted in the Phoenix listing, we call these healthy food stores instead of health food stores because they're full service supermarkets that feature mostly organic and pesticide-free groceries. The stores also have books and magazines on nutrition and natural living, whole grain bakeries, build-it-yourself salad bars and health-conscious delis. Most Wild Oats stores have a few tables near the deli and outside, in case you want to take a healthy lunch break. Serious vegans come here for their soy yogurt, brown rice and couscous.

7 THE BEST OUTDOOR STORE: Summit Hut • 5045 E. Speedway Blvd.; (800) 499-8696 or (520) 325-1554. Monday-Friday 9 to 8, Saturday 10 to 6:30 and Sunday 11 to 5. Major credit cards. GETTING THERE: It's about five miles northeast of downtown, near the northwest corner of Speedway and Rosemont.

Did you forget your fanny pack or hiking shorts? Tucson doesn't have an REI store, although the Summit Hut fills that void just fine. Like REI, it's a large store devoted to outdoor types—hikers, backpackers, campers, skiers, kayakers and climbers. It has extensive selections of hiking shoes, outdoor clothing, backpacks, fanny packs, assorted tents and serious climbing gear.

8 THE BEST ANTIQUE WAREHOUSE: Antique Center of Tucson • 5001 E. Speedway Blvd.; (520) 323-0319. Monday-Saturday 10 to 6 and Sunday 11 to 5. MC/VISA. GETTING THERE: The complex is *on the north side of Speedway at the corner of Santa Rosa Avenue, just west of the Summit Hut.*

If you like to browse for antiques, plan most of a day here. This isn't a shop but a block-long collection of dozens of shops and stalls under one roof. You'll find every kind of collectible—old *Life* and *National Geographic* magazines, books and records, knickknacks, yesterday logo items, glassware, old prints and photos, postcards—whatever you need to clutter up your habitat. You also can pick up a free brochure listing more than fifty other antique dealers around Tucson.

9 BEST COWBOY STORE: Corral West Ranchwear ●

4525 E. Broadway Blvd.; (520) 322-6001. (www.corralwest.com) Monday-Saturday 9 to 8 and Sunday 11 to 5. Major credit cards. GETTING THERE: It's about 4.5 miles east of downtown. Look for the adobe style store in a strip mall on the north side of Broadway. It's between Columbus and Swan, near the corner of Belvedere Avenue.

This isn't a rhinestone cowboy place with gaudy silver belt buckles and pearl button shirts, but a contemporary store for the modern rancher and ranch hand. It's abrim with wide-brimmed hats (mostly straw, which is what modern cowboys prefer when they aren't wearing truckers' caps), boots, denims (mostly Wranglers, not Levi's), long sleeved shirts, belts and more. The store also sells sportswear like denim shorts and polo shirts that still suggest a Western look. This is part of a large chain, with outlets in every Western state, plus Georgia. There are cowboys in Georgia?

10 THE BEST IMPORT COMPLEX: Lost Barrio ●

200-350 S. Park Avenue. Most stores open 10 to early evening. GETTING THERE: This misplaced Barrio is just southeast of downtown. Go east on Broadway about half a mile, then south on Park Avenue two blocks to Twelfth Street.

Looking for handmade Mexican or South American furniture, African tribal masks or hand-blown glass objects? Several old brick warehouses stretching for two city blocks have been converted into large import shops specializing in folk art and crafts. One can spend hours browsing through these weathered old cargo barns, which are stacked wall to wall with fascinating objects from around the world. The major shops are Magellan Trading, featuring African tribal art and masks, (*www.magellantraders.com*); Colonial Frontiers, with handmade imported furniture, pottery and folk art; Explorations, offering ornate mirrors, international folk art and decorator wares; and ¡Aqui Esta!, focusing on Mexican folk art and decorator pieces, including custom furniture made in its own shop, (*www.aquiestaaz.com*). Across the way are two more home decorator shops—Sunset on Park and La Bohemia, plus Tooley's indoor-outdoor cafe.

A place for everything;
everything in its place.
— **Benjamin Franklin**

Chapter Eighteen
BITS & PIECES
ASSORTED ODDS AND ENDS

Feeling the need to work off all those burritos? Or perhaps you're feeling romantic as you relax under the Tucson sun. Maybe you'd prefer just to lie at poolside and listen to some cool sounds on a local radio station, or read a specialized guidebook about Tucson. This chapter presents assorted lists useful to both visitors and residents.

GETTING PHYSICAL: THE TEN BEST HIKES, WALKS AND BIKE ROUTES

Greater Tucson has more interesting hiking trails than walking paths, since it's rimmed by four mountain ranges—the Santa Catalinas, Rincons, Santa Ritas and Tucson Mountains. It's also a serious cycling city, with many miles of marked bike routes.

THE BEST WALKING AND HIKING ROUTES

One of the appeals of this area is that you can reach any of several hiking trails within minutes of downtown. However, we begin our walking/hiking list by staying downtown. You may want to take this walk early in your visit to familiarize yourself with the Old Pueblo.

NOTE: Items marked with ❖ are listed elsewhere in this book; check the index for page numbers.

1 **DOWNTOWN TUCSON ●** *Starting at the Tucson Visitor Center in La Placita Village. About two miles, all level. The center is open weekdays 8 to 5 and weekends 9 to 4. GETTING THERE: La Placita is at the corner of Church Avenue and Broadway Boulevard just north of the Tucson Contention Center.*

Tucson has a surprisingly small urban core for a city of half a million residents. Most of its businesses, people and attractions are widely spread over the Tucson Basin. The few lures that draw visitors downtown can be seen by strolling through parks, along streets and on a couple of pedestrian overcrossings. This stroll is best taken on a weekend, since traffic is lighter, the parking meters needn't be fed and you may encounter a festival or art fair in one of the parks or plazas.

We recommend starting at the Visitor Center in **Placita Village** because you can pick up a copy of the free *Tucson Visitors Guide* which has a detailed downtown map and a suggested walking tour. However, that walking tour will take you all over hell's half acre. It leads throughout the city center, El Presidio Historic District and other neighborhoods, passing scores of old adobe buildings. Our route is much shorter, hitting only the highlights. Trace it onto the city center map in the visitors guide, which you can then tear out and stuff into pocket or purse.

Incidentally, Placita Village is easy to find; it's so gaudily multicolored that it would put a rainbow to shame. From the Visitor Center, angle northward across La Placita's main plaza, past the right side of the **Pima County Sports Hall of Fame** (Monday, Wednesday and Friday 10 to 2). Cross Congress Street on the **Garcés Footbridge**, named in honor of Francisco Garcés, the first pastor of Mission San Xavier. Continue north through a landscaped park beside the **Government Center of Pima County.** Another pedestrian crossing will take you into **Plaza de las Armas** in Presidio Park, on the west side of the Pima County Courthouse.

Ignore the courthouse for the moment and continue north across the plaza, crossing Alameda Street into ❖ **El Presidio Historic District,** the birthplace of Tucson. A garrison was established here in 1776. Its former walls have since melted back into the dirt, although this area shelters some of Tucson's oldest buildings. A few contain shops and restaurants. Crossing Alameda into El Presidio, you'll see the ❖ **Tucson Museum of Art** on your left, at Alameda and Main Avenue. You'll want to explore two large curio shop complexes, ❖ **Old Town Artisans** at 201 N. Court Avenue, and **Saguaro Artisans** at 215 N. Court. Two popular Mexican restaurants are here as well—our favorite ❖ **El Charro** at 311 N. Court, and ❖ **La Cocina** in the Old Town Artisans complex.

After finishing with El Presidio Historic District, return to Plaza de las Armas and visit the **Pima County Courthouse.** Admire its columns, arches, busy façade and distinctive Moorish dome. Follow a breezeway through the courthouse, cross Church Avenue and walk a block through a small sculpture plaza and park beside the **Tucson Public Library** at Stone Avenue and Pennington Street. This park often is the scene of crafts fairs, musicales and other events. Note the really strange red steel sculpture standing before the library entrance. Across from the library is the **Arizona Historical Society Museum Downtown** at 140 Stone Avenue, open weekdays 10 to 4.

Walk south on Stone Avenue through the heart of downtown. The ten-story brick front **Bank One building** at the corner of Stone and Congress was the first highrise in Tucson. Step inside the lofty lobby—if it's open—to admire murals tracing the area's history from dinosaurs to territorial days. Walk a block west to the city's newest and tallest highrise, the **UniSource Energy Tower**, at the corner of Congress and Church. Across Church is a wedge-shaped park stretching between Congress and Broadway called ❖ **Viente de Agosto**, with a "kissing bench" and a larger-than-life bronze of General Francisco "Pancho" Villa astride his horse.

After strolling through the park, follow Stone a couple of blocks south to the imposing twin-towered 1896 **St. Augustine Cathedral** at the corner of Ochoa Street. Step inside to admire its lofty vaulted ceiling and stained glass windows. Then stroll west along the cathedral's left side and cross Church Avenue to the **Tucson Convention Center**. Walk to the right of the center's main building, following signs to the Music Hall; you'll pass through an attractive park behind La Placita. Veer to your left and you'll approach the back side of the ❖ **Sosa-Carillo-Frémont House.** Walk around to the front to explore this historic museum. Dating from the 1860s and now almost swallowed up by the convention center, it's one of Tucson's oldest surviving adobes. Museum hours are Wednesday-Saturday 10 to 4; (520) 622-0956.

From the adobe, angle northeast back into the convention center grounds, through a pretty garden with a blue-painted fountain behind the **Music Hall** and you'll see the gaudy colors of La Placita, your starting point.

2 *HUGH NORRIS TRAIL* ● *Saguaro National Park West on Kinney Road; (520) 733-5158. Moderately difficult, with a rather steep climb at the start; just under ten miles. Park gates open daily 6 to dusk; visitor center 8:30 to 5. GETTING THERE: The trailhead is less than a mile up Bajada Loop Drive, about two miles from the visitor center.*

We like this hike because it passes through striking cactus gardens and rocky mountainous terrain. Although it begins with a steep climb, most of the route is rather level as it follows a series of ridgelines to the highest spot in the Tucson Mountains, Wasson Peak. The most interesting part of this hike is that steep beginning, as it switchbacks and stairsteps up a rocky canyon thick with desert vegetation. If you lack the time or energy to trudge the trail's entire length, you can see the best of this route by hiking up to the first saddleback ridge and back, a distance of less than two miles. At the ridge, you can scramble over some huge boulders for an impressive panorama of the Tucson Mountain Park basin below.

The trail up to that ridge is nicely engineered with stepping stones and switchbacks, the work of Civilian Conservation Corps boys back in the thirties. Once you achieve the ridgeline, the saguaro stands are thinner and the terrain is less dramatic, although you'll still see a good variety of cactus growth. From this point, it's a rather easy stroll, with a few gentle switchbacks as the trail follows a series of other relatively level ridges.

There's a final moderately steep climb a third of a mile before trail's end, and then another easy hike to your goal, 4,687-foot Wasson Peak. The vista takes in most of the Tucson Basin, with the city far below. Unfortunately, it's almost always hazy and sprawling Tucson isn't that interesting from the air. The rocky knoll of Wasson Peak would be a nice place for a mountain finder or other graphics, yet there's nothing manmade up here, not even a place to sit.

3 SABINO CANYON ● *5700 N. Sabino Canyon Road; (520) 749-8700. (www.fs.fed.us/r3/coronado/scrd) West fork of Sabino Canyon to Hutch's Pool. Moderately difficult 8.2-mile round trip, with a half-mile switchback up to a ridge at the beginning. The trailhead is at the final stop on the Sabino Canyon tram.* ❖

SABINO SPECIFICS: Visitor Center is open 8 to 4. Per-car entry fee **$$**; *half-price for holders of Golden Age and Golden Access passes. Trams depart every half hour from 9 to 4 for Sabino Canyon and hourly for Bear Canyon; (520) 749-2327 or (520) 749-2861; **$$**; no credit cards. GETTING THERE: The canyon is about fifteen miles northeast of downtown Tucson. Drive east on Grant Road, swerve left onto Tanque Verde Road then after a few blocks, go left again onto Sabino Canyon Road. Follow it four miles north and turn right into the parking area shortly after crossing Sunrise Drive.*

Several trails extend into Sabino and Bear canyons, and our favorite is the hike to Hutch's Pool, perhaps the prettiest sylvan glen in all of Tucson's mountains. It's a deep pond cupped in steep canyon walls and partly shaded by oaks and sycamores. The beginning of the hike to the pool is a well-graded switchback up a steep canyon wall. After half a mile, you'll see the Phoneline Trail branching to the right. It leads back down through lower Sabino, staying above the canyon bottom. It makes a nice round trip for those who want to ride the tram or hike up the canyon, then take a different route back.

However, our route continues upward. Shortly beyond the Phone-line junction, you'll reach the top of the switchback. From here, it's a rather easy trail, notched high on the brow of upper Sabino Canyon, occasionally dipping in and out of creek ravines. After another mile, the route drops down to creekside—a good place to soak your shirt or blouse—then it veers away from the creek and passes through a moun-tain meadowland. The trail goes through a thin forest of mesquite trees which, because of their tiny leaves, unfortunately don't shed much shade. After about a mile, you'll encounter Sabino Creek again. Rock-hop to the other side and continue up the west bank another half mile or so. Shortly after the trail veers away from the creek, a cairn near a large oak will direct you on a spur trail down to the pond.

4 *CACTUS FOREST TRAIL* • *Saguaro National Park East, 3693 Old Spanish Trail; (520) 733-5153. Park gates open daily 7 to 10; visitor center 8:30 to 5. Easy walk through cactus foothills, with frequent dips in and out of dry washes. Varying distances. GETTING THERE: For the most direct approach, drive east on Broadway about twelve miles, then fork right onto Old Spanish Trail, which leads to the park.*

If you feel up to hiking ten miles round trip through undulating de-sert terrain, you can walk the full length of the Cactus Forest Trail. It roughly parallels Old Spanish Trail, stretching from Broadway to the Rincon section of Saguaro National Park and beyond. If you prefer a lesser challenge, start your walk in the park, which contains the trail's most interesting section. Drive past the visitor center, go through the park's entry kiosk and you'll hit a stop sign at the Cactus Forest Drive. Go right for less than a mile and you'll see a parking area where the trail crosses the road. Park and start walking to your left.

This stroll will take you through a sampler of desert foliage, al-though it lacks the thick saguaro forests of the park's Tucson Mountain section. You'll walk through thinner stands of saguaro and thatches of mesquite, palo verde, prickly pear, cholla and barrel cactus. It's mostly open country, with the Rincon Mountains looming above and the Santa Catalinas in the far distance. Along the route, you'll encounter ruins of cone-shaped adobe kilns constructed in the 1880s to leach lime from limestone. You can continue along this gently undulating trail until you grow weary of undulating, then return to your car.

5 *RILLITO RIVER PARK* • *East from St. Phillips Plaza along Rillito River Park to Country Club Road. Level, about three miles round trip. GETTING THERE: Drive north about five miles on Campbell Avenue, cross the dry Rillito River and turn right into Phillips Plaza.*

The Pima County Parks and Recreation Department has developed two "liner parks," essentially multiple use trails extending several miles along the dry beds of the Rillito and Santa Cruz rivers. The Santa Cruz parkway roughly parallels I-10 opposite downtown Tucson, while the more rural Rillito River Park is on the city's northern edge, below the Santa Catalina foothills. These are nicely developed parkways, with picnic areas, potties and occasional grassy swatches. For most of their lengths, the two long and skinny parks have paths on both banks of their rivers. We've selected both for bike trails, since their separation from traffic, level grades and extended lengths are ideal for cyclists.

A section of the Rillito parkway between Campbell Road and Country Club Road also is pleasant for walking. Its sandy and thus easy on the Nikes, and it provides nice views of the Santa Catalinas. Other than the mountains, there's not much to see along this route, except the sandy and brushy bed of the Rillito River. It's just a pleasant, quiet place for a stroll.

We chose St. Phillips Plaza as our starting point because there's plenty of parking on the back lot of the Windmill Inn here. Perhaps more important, before our after your walk, you can relax with an iced caffé latte or other designer beverage with a pastry or sandwich from Paula's Café in the plaza. This pleasant little place has outdoor seating.

THE BEST BIKE ROUTES

Tucson is a serious cycling city, and has been rated by *Bicycling Magazine* as the second best city in America for bike riders. It has more than fifty miles of bike lanes and even has its own cycling coordinator. Signs around town proclaim this to be a "bicycle friendly community," and a local ordinance requires that all new street construction include bike lanes. The Pima Association of Governments publishes the *Tucson Bicycle Map*. It's available free at local bike shops, or call the Pima County Parks and Recreation Department at (520) 740-2690.

Most of Greater Tucson's bike routes are marked lanes along streets and highways, although several are independent of traffic, including those two "linear parks" mentioned above.

6 *THE OLD SPANISH TRAIL* • *Pedaling either direction from Saguaro National Park East. Varying lengths and moderately difficult; mostly rolling with some hill climbs and occasional dips. GETTING THERE: See directions for the Cactus Forest Trail hike above.*

The Old Spanish Trail is a street of several personalities. Starting at Broadway Boulevard in eastern Tucson, it rambles for about sixteen miles, first through a commercial area, and then past fancy rural homes and finally through open cactus country before it ends near Colossal Cave. Virtually all of its length has a marked bike lane and some sections have bike paths separated from traffic. Our suggested starting point is Saguaro National Park East. The route southeast is more difficult—a gradual incline with lots of dips and hills, although it's more scenic and you'll be going mostly downhill on the return. The northwest route is shorter and easier, taking you on a gentle downslope toward Tucson. Of course, the return will be a gradual upgrade.

If you go southeast, you can pedal eleven miles to its end, near the Colossal Cave turnoff. The route travels through mostly open desert country busy with saguaro and other cactus; the landscape is dotted here and there with country homes.

Heading northwest from the park, the Old Spanish Trail has both marked bike lanes and a separate bike path, which parallels its east shoulder. Like the southeast leg, it meanders through desert vegetation, although you'll pass more homes in this direction. Your views are across the wide Tucson Basin to the distant Santa Catalinas. After just over five miles, you'll enter Tucson suburbs and the route T-bones into Broadway.

7 *CACTUS FOREST DRIVE* • *Saguaro National Park East, 3693 Old Spanish Trail; (520) 733-5153. Park gates open daily 7 to 10; visitor center 8:30 to 5. Moderately difficult with several steep climbs and lots of dips. Eight-mile loop. GETTING THERE: See "The Old Spanish Trail" route above.*

This driving route through the Rincon section of Saguaro National Park is popular with cyclists—at least those in good shape. The Cactus Forest Drive is all asphalt, yet it's very hilly. Although cyclists must share this rather narrow route with cars, it's mostly one-way and the speed limit is twenty-five mph.

Start at the visitor center parking lot and follow signs to the scenic drive. It undulates through the Rincon Mountain foothills, passing through thick cactus gardens. If you've brought lunch, you can take a break at the Mica View picnic area, which provides splendid vistas of surrounding cactus lands, the Rincon Mountains to the east and the distant Santa Catalinas to the northwest. Shortly beyond the picnic area, the Desert Ecology Trail provides another excuse to stop. Signs along this brief loop trail discuss the interrelationship between the plants, animals, terrain and weather of the Sonoran Desert.

8 *TUCSON MOUNTAIN PARK* • *Round trip from Old Tucson Studios on Kinney and McCain Loop roads. Gently undulating route with some dips and a few steep climbs; about fourteen miles. GETTING THERE: Go west on Speedway Boulevard, which becomes Gates Pass Road after about five miles. Spiral up through Gates Pass then down the other side to Kinney Road, turn left and follow signs to Old Tucson.*

This route provides a pleasing panorama of Tucson Mountain Park with its lush desert growth and the ruggedly handsome profile of the mountains as a backdrop. It also takes you to the park's three main attractions—Old Tucson, the Arizona-Sonora Desert Museum and the west section of Saguaro National Park. Although Kinney and McCain Loop roads don't have separate bike lanes, they aren't usually heavily traveled and there's a 35-mile-per hour speed limit. It's best to do this ride on a weekday morning, since traffic can get busy on weekends.

PRECAUTIONARY NOTE: Not everyone keeps to the speed limit and there are some blind corners on the route. Only accomplished and alert cyclists should take this ride.

Starting from Old Tucson Studios and pedaling northwest, you'll reach the Arizona-Sonora Desert Museum after about three miles. The traffic gets thinner beyond here, since the museum is the destination of many motorists. Kinney Road goes through some steep dips beyond the desert museum. Stay alert because some of them conceal blind corners. You'll shortly see the turnoff for Saguaro National Park; go right and pedal into the visitor center parking lot. Don't turn around quite yet, however. Continue past the visitor center, pedaling just under two miles through more lush desert gardens to the entrance of the Bajada Loop Drive. If you're on a mountain bike, you might pedal this unpaved six-mile loop although it's very rough and steep in places. Otherwise, use the entrance to the drive as your turn-around point.

Back on Kinney Road, before you reach the Arizona-Sonora Desert Museum, turn right onto McCain Loop Road. This will take you on a merry rollercoaster ride through the lumpy desert basin. It's narrower than Kinney Road although it has less traffic. Shortly after you pass Gilbert Ray Campground, you'll return to Kinney, and a right turn will take you to your starting point at Old Tucson Studios.

9 SANTA CRUZ RIVER PARK • *Speedway Boulevard to Silverlake Road. All level; six to ten-mile round trip or loop trip, depending on your route choice. GETTING THERE: Go west briefly on Speedway Boulevard from I-10, cross the Santa Cruz River and turn left on Riverside Avenue. You'll see a small park with potties and picnic tables, and access to the bike trail.*

Santa Cruz River Park encloses the one of the two multi-use trails we discussed above. Although it begins at Grant Road farther north, we suggest starting at Speedway because a small park here offers ample parking. If you pedal north from here, you'll reach the end of the bike route at Grant Road within a mile. En route, you'll pass a larger recreation area that's essentially a widening of Santa Cruz River Park.

Heading southeast from your Speedway starting point, the trail eventually swerves away from the riverbed to wrap around **The Garden of Gethsemane,** at the corner of Bonita Avenue and Congress Street. This fenced enclosure contains several religious scenes done by Tucson sculptor Felix Lucero in 1945, including Jesus on the cross and the Last Supper. If you go up to Bonita Avenue which borders the park and follow it to briefly Congress Street, you'll see the **largest tree in Tucson,** a huge eucalyptus with a trunk thirteen feet around and four feet in diameter. To continue on the bikeway, go past the garden and pedal beneath the Congress Street bridge. The riverside trail ends less than a mile beyond, at Silverlake Road.

For variety, you can return to your starting point by surface streets, most with curbside bike lanes. To do so, pedal west about half a mile on Silverlake, then head north on Mission Road, which has a marked bike lane. It travels through open country on the edge of Tucson, along the base of ❖ **Sentinel Peak**. Locals call it "A" Mountain because University of Arizona students built a huge stone and plaster letter "A" on its brow several years ago. To the north, you can see the distant skyline of downtown Tucson. For a more dramatic view—requiring a tough 1.7-mile uphill pedal—turn left onto Congress Street, then left again onto Cuesta Avenue, which becomes Sentinel Peak Road. This spirals up into Sentinel Peak Park, wraps around the north side of the peak and finally levels out to provide a nice aerial view of the city's highrise clump. For more on Sentinel Peak, see "The Ten Best Viewpoints and Photo Angles" below.

Back on the bike route, Mission Road changes its name to Grande Avenue as it crosses Congress. It passes through a modest residential area and has no bike lane. However, the driving lane is rather wide, or you can retreat to the sidewalk. After a mile, you'll hit Speedway Boulevard, and a right turn will take you back to your starting point.

10 *RILLITO RIVER PARK* • *The park follows the dry bed of the Rillito River in north Tucson. Its recreational paths extend from La Cholla Boulevard east to Campbell Avenue. Completely level; about nine miles round trip. GETTING THERE: Our access point is St. Phillips Plaza; see the Rillito River Park walk on page 243.*

This route is longer than the Santa Cruz River parkway and it's more rural, since it follows Tucson's northern border. This is a pleasant path, with picnic areas and potties and attractive gently arched bridges over side washes. The northern side is designated for cyclists and pedestrians while the south bank is intended for equestrians and pedestrians. This doesn't seem to be taken seriously, however. We noted evidence of horse passage on the north and cyclists using the south side. However, the trail is rarely crowded, even on weekends.

You can pick up the parkway at several points where street bridges cross the riverbed. We prefer starting from St. Phillips Plaza, which has direct access to the trail, and Paula's Café, where you can fuel up for the trip. The route the east is hardpacked sand, nice for fat-tired bikes, and the westward trail is asphalt.

TUCSON'S TEN MOST INTIMATE PLACES

There is something innately romantic about the desert, and about desert resorts—cloud-painted sunsets, quiet walks among the cactus, swimsuit clad bodies basking at poolside; nighttime burbles in a hot tub or an in-room spa for two; dinner on a patio under the stars. The Old Pueblo itself is romantic, with its beautiful mission, charming plazas and ancient adobes whispering the history of colonial Spain.

And so, are you ready for romance? Here are the Old Pueblo's five best places to snuggle with your sweetie, followed by its five most romantic restaurants.

THE BEST PLACES TO SNUGGLE WITH YOUR SWEETIE

1 VENTANA FALLS AT LOEW'S VENTANA CANYON RE-

SORT • *7000 N. Resort Dr.; (520) 299-2020. (www.loewshotels.com) GETTING THERE: The resort is just off Kolb Road in the Santa Catalina foothills. From downtown, go north to Grant Road and then east to Tanque Verde Road. Follow it northeast half a mile, then drive about two miles north on Sabino Canyon Road. Fork left onto Kolb Road and turn right onto Resort Drive after about 2.5 miles. From I-10, take Grant Road exit 256 and head east, then follow the directions above.* ❖

This is the most romantic spot in the Tucson area. A gentle little waterfall slips down the craggy face of an eighty-foot cliff and spills into a rock basin. Saguaro cactus cling tenaciously to steep canyon walls above. You and your lover can snuggle on a bench fashioned from stone, enjoying this scene and listening to the doves and cactus wrens. It's not a soft seat, although you may be too preoccupied with this peaceful glen—and with one another—to notice. A riparian desert-woodland trail, canopied with mesquite and palo verde trees, leads from the resort to this spot.

2 WESTIN LA PALOMA LOBBY BAR • *3800 E. Sunrise Dr.;

(520) 742-6000. (www.westin.com) GETTING THERE: Follow Campbell Avenue about eight miles north from downtown, then turn right onto Skyline Drive. Go east 1.3 miles, veering to the right to blend onto Sunrise; turn south on Via Palomita and follow signs.*

The terraced lobby bar at the Westin La Paloma offers a stunning view of the rugged Santa Catalina mountains through the resort's 30-foot arched windows. To enhance the romance of the view, come at sundown to watch light and shadows play on the hills. Comfy couches provide ideal spots for snuggling and enjoying this visual drama.

3 VIENTE DE AGOSTO PARK • *Downtown at Church Avenue

and Congress Street.*

What? Snuggling right in the middle of downtown Tucson? This is too cute to ignore. There's a "kissing bench" in the middle of a small wedge of public park called Viente de Agosto, across Church Avenue from the highrise UniSource Energy Tower. The park also contains a large statue of General Francisco "Pancho" Villa, presented to Arizona several years ago by a Mexican president. And what's a kissing bench? It's designed with opposite-facing seats so that people occupying the bench are facing one another. Actually, the bench has room for four people, but let's not get strange...

4 HUTCH'S POOL • *On the West Sabino Canyon Trail in Sabino Canyon Recreation Area, 5700 N. Sabino Canyon Road; (520) 749-8700. GETTING THERE: The canyon is about fifteen miles from downtown Tucson. Drive east on Grant Road, swerve left onto Tanque Verde Road then after a few blocks, go left again onto Sabino Canyon Road. Follow it four miles north and turn right into the parking area shortly after crossing Sunrise Drive.*

This snuggle spot requires a four-mile tram ride up lower Sabino Canyon, followed by a four-mile hike into the upper canyon. And isn't it worth the effort to be alone with your significant other? Hutch's Pool is a pretty sylvan glen shaded by oaks and sycamores and cupped between steep canyon walls. This is a popular hike and you may not have the pool to yourselves, so stay alert if you're tempted to skinny dip. The odds of privacy are better on weekdays. For details on the hike to the pool, see above on page 242.

5 VALLEY VIEW OVERLOOK • *Tucson Mountain section of Saguaro National Park. Gates open daily 6 to dusk. GETTING THERE: Valley View Overlook trailhead is about midway through the Bajada Loop Drive.*

A short nature trail leads through gorgeous cactus gardens and ends at an overlook with pleasing views of a desert basin and distant mountains. Few people use this trail and those who do don't stay long at this viewpoint. Two benches invite lingering, snuggling and enjoying the views. One faces west over the above-mentioned desert basin. Another faces east, offering an inviting study of the rugged saguaro-studded ramparts of the Tucson Mountains.

THE MOST ROMANTIC RESTAURANTS

PRICING: Dollar sign codes indicate the price of a typical dinner with entrée, soup or salad, not including drinks, appetizers or dessert: *$* = less than $10 per entrée; *$$* = $10 to $19; *$$$* = $20 to $29; *$$$$* = "Did you say you were buying?"

6 LE BISTRO • *2574 N. Campbell Ave.; (520) 327-3086. French-European; full bar service. Lunch Monday-Friday and dinner Tuesday-Sunday. Major credit cards; $$ to $$$. GETTING THERE: This* *charming bistro is on the east side of Campbell, a block north of Grant Road, about 2.5 miles northeast of downtown.*

The charm begins outside—a tiny building painted with a Paris street scene mural—and continues within. Intimate booths are practically inundated with planters of fishtail palms strung with twinkling lights. Etched glass mirrors, satin tablecloths and lace curtains complete a cozy picture. You and your lover could practically lose yourselves in these small jungle-clad booths, emerging only to have your wine glasses refilled. The fare is mostly French, with a few continental dishes. Some recent examples were filet of salmon with ginger and honey crust, pork tenderloin with *herb de Provence* crust, and chicken breast *roulade* stuffed with mushrooms and artichoke hearts.

7 **DOS LOCOS LATINOS** • *At the Sheraton El Conquistador Resort • 1000 Oracle Rd.; (520) 544-5000. (www.sheratonconquistador.com) Southwestern with Pan Pacific accents; full bar service. Lunch and dinner daily. Major credit cards; $$$ to $$$$. GETTING THERE: From downtown, follow Oracle Road about fourteen miles north.*

The name certainly isn't romantic. However, the "Two Crazy Latins" outdoor dining patio is quite appealing, rimmed by a curving planter wall spilling with bright blooms. The view will kindle any romantic soul—across a landscaped swimming lagoon and golf greens to cactus slopes and bold granite walls of the Santa Catalinas. At night, table candles and glittering stars add another level of intimacy. The interesting menu features entrées such as sizzling fajitas with chicken or flank steak, chimichangas, smoked tenderloin fillet with whipped potatoes and demi-glacé, mahi mahi steamed in banana leaves with coconut jasmine rice, corn crusted salmon, and pork tenderloin with coconut rice and black beans.

8 **THE DISH** • *3200 E. Speedway Blvd.; (520) 326-1714. Contemporary American; full bar service. Dinner Tuesday-Saturday. Major credit cards; $ $$ to $$$. GETTING THERE: This dish is just east of Country Club Boulevard, on the south side of Speedway, behind the Rum-Runner wine shop. It's about three miles northeast of downtown.*

The Dish has to be one of Tucson's most romantic restaurants. It's so tiny that it's impossible *not* to be close to your lover. This little hideout is sleekly modern, done in browns and blacks with pink walls. A couple of ceiling fans waft from above and soft jazz whispers from somewhere. And if you want to ply your lover with wine, there's an unlimited supply, since The Dish is a satellite of Tucson's best wine shop (page 235). Wine by the glass is rather pricey, however, as it is in most better restaurants. Better to order a bottle; obviously, the selection's great. The Dish also earned a spot as one of Tucson's Ten Best restaurants; see Chapter Thirteen, page 182, for menu details.

9 *HOA MAI RESTAURANT* • *2547 E. Broadway Blvd.; (520) 319-8420. Vietnamese; wine and beer. Lunch weekdays and dinner Monday-Saturday; closed Sunday. GETTING THERE: The restaurant is about 2.5 miles east of downtown, just beyond Tucson Boulevard.*

If you're feeling romantic but also feeling financially pinched—maybe you're saving for that honeymoon cottage—take your lover to this remarkably cute little café, where most entrées are less than $10. It's quite cozy—windowless and dimly lit with intimate booths for two along one wall. Each booth is decorated by a charming red-tasseled wall lantern that sheds just enough light to bring sparkle to your significant other's eyes. It's also our favorite Southeast Asian restaurant; see Chapter Thirteen, page 197.

10 *SOLEIL* • *3001 E. Skyline Dr.; (520) 299-3345. French-Mediterranean; full bar service. Lunch and dinner daily, fall through spring; closed Mondays in summer. Major credit cards; $$$ to $$$$. GETTING THERE: It's on the east end of ❖ El Cortijo Plaza, at Campbell Avenue and Skyline. Drive eight miles north on Campbell, then turn right into the complex immediately after crossing Skyline.*

Do you prefer your romantic dining with a view, or do you really want to be alone? Soleil has the same view as Anthony's in the Catalinas (above), with tables set along window walls. It also has a decidedly charming triangular shaped dining room in back, with a few intimate tables for two. One is tucked into a narrow alcove at the tip of the triangle—a decidedly private space.

As its name says, Soleil is a sunny place, done in fall colors, with lots of windows to admit the ever-present Tucson sun. We prefer this to Anthony's for romantic dining because it's more cheerful and upbeat, without the tux-clad waitstaff. And it's less expensive, with dinner entrées starting in the high teens. Among its offerings are saffron ravioli, braised lamb shanks with a ragout of French green lentils, grilled sea scallops with saffron rice, and roast breast of chicken stuffed with spinach and herbs. Soleil has a large wine list, with more than eighty wines by the glass.

THE TEN BEST VIEWPOINTS AND PHOTO ANGLES

Since the Tucson Basin is rimmed by mountains, impressive vista points and "picture spots" are easy to find. However, as we pointed out in Chapter Nine, the best viewpoints don't always produce good photos. We have three-dimensional vision and cameras have only two-dimensional sight. Views from Mount Lemmon down to the Tucson basin are impressive to the eye but rather flat to the camera lens. However, some vantage points look good both to the eye and the lens.

THE BEST VIEWPOINTS

1 *WINDY POINT* ● *Mount Lemmon Recreation Area, reached via the Catalina Highway from northeast Tucson. For information: Coronado National Forest, (520) 576-1542. Per-car entry fee $; half-price for holders of Golden Age and Golden Access passes. GETTING THERE: Follow any major street north to Grant Road and drive several miles east to Tanque Verde Road. Go northeast and east on Tanque Verde about two miles, then fork left onto the Catalina Highway and follow it about fifteen miles to the viewpoint.*

The Catalina Highway provides imposing views of the Tucson Basin as it climbs into the piney heights of Mount Lemmon Recreation Area. There are several vista points along the way and the best is Windy Point. It offers an unobstructed view of the basin, and it's surrounded by awesome standing rock formations and dramatic ridges. This isn't a good picture stop, because the basin is too flat and hazy from this elevation. However, it's a nice place for studying the great sprawl of Tucson, preferably through strong lenses.

2 *DOWNTOWN FROM SENTINEL PEAK* ● *Sentinel Peak Park; open 7 to 10 Monday-Saturday and 7 to 6 Sunday. GETTING THERE: Follow Congress Street west across I-10 for less than a mile. Turn on Cuesta Avenue, which becomes Sentinel Peak Road, and follow it about 1.5 miles up to the park. The vista point is just below the large stone and plaster "A."*

Sentinel Peak provides the best overview of urban Tucson since it's less than a mile away and you can see detailed features of the downtown core. This cone-shaped mountain is fun to explore as well. If you continue around the loop drive past the vista point, you'll find a parking area on the peak's backside. A cross here is the site of Easter sunrise services and its base is sometimes festooned with brilliantly colored paper flowers.

If you follow a trail that passes beyond the cross, you'll rim the mountain and bump into the side of the giant "A." Clamber uphill beside it and you'll soon be king of the mountain, standing atop Sentinel Peak. You'll get a 360-degree sweep of the Tucson Basin and the land to the south toward Nogales. Several trails lead back down to the parking area from here. Unfortunately, Sentinel Peak is marred with litter, graffiti and broken glass. Just ignore the blight around you and enjoy the views.

3 *LA PLACITA VILLAGE FROM THE TUCSON CONVEN-TION CENTER GARDENS* • *The Convention Center is downtown. rimmed by Church Avenue, Cushing Street, Granada Avenue and Broadway Boulevard.*

An attractive garden behind the Music Hall provides a nice vantage point for viewing the wild colors of La Placita Village and Tucson highrises. This is an interesting "compound view" that also works well as a photograph. Relaxing on a bench in this shady desert landscaped garden, you can look across a blue-painted reflection pool and fountain marked by large stones. The brilliantly painted La Placita complex is just beyond. And beyond that, you'll see some of Tucson's downtown office towers.

4 *THE WEST SANTA CATALINAS FROM THE SHERA-TON EL CONQUISTADOR* • *1000 Oracle Road; (520) 544-5000. (www.sheratonconquistador.com) GETTING THERE: See Dos Locos Latinos restaurant listing above on page 243.*

The most dramatic geological feature of the Santa Catalina mountains' western edge is a twin finned promontory called Pusch Ridge. Sheraton El Conquistador is built into the foothills just below this sheer promontory and the mix of green landscaping, desert gardens and sheer cliffs create a very dramatic view. The vista is grand from any of several points around this 500-acre resort, including a large lobby bar and Dos Locos Latinos restaurant.

5 *THE SANTA CATALINAS FROM UPPER KOLB ROAD* • *About a dozen miles northeast of downtown. GETTING THERE: Take Broadway Boulevard east just under six miles to Wilmot Road, then go north 1.5 miles and take a half right onto Tanque Verde Road. Follow it northeast and then east just over a mile to Sabino Canyon Road. Go north about two miles, then turn left onto Kolb Road.*

Upper Kolb and Sabino Canyon roads shelter some of Tucson's most expensive and exclusive homes and desert estates, along with some of its most opulent resorts. And for good reason. The rolling desert foothills are lush with cactus gardens and the area offers splendid views of the Santa Catalina mountains above, as well as vistas back down to the Tucson Basin. There are several good vantage points along Kolb Road. If you continue north on this gently winding route, you'll encounter the area's two most opulent retreats—the ❖ **Lodge at Ventana Canyon** and ❖ **Loew's Ventana Canyon Resort**. The grounds, lounges and restaurants of both have fine views up Ventana Canyon and into the Santa Catalinas.

THE BEST PHOTO ANGLES

6 DOWNTOWN FROM SENTINEL PEAK ● *Sentinel Peak Park; open 7 to 10 Monday-Saturday and 7 to 6 Sunday. GETTING THERE: See Sentinel Peak vista point listing above.*

The small highrise cluster of Tucson's urban core photographs nicely from this vista point. It's only about a mile away, and Sentinel Peak is several hundred feet higher than downtown, providing a good angle. Shoot it early in the morning or late in the afternoon to get shadow accents on the buildings to give them depth and dimension. To add a little green to the scene, you can frame your photo in the limbs of paloverde in the foreground. This is best as a horizontal shot, with a medium-range telephoto.

7 LA PLACITA VILLAGE ● *Downtown at the corner of Broadway Boulevard and Church Avenue.*

With its vivid colors, square shapes and shadows, La Placita Village makes you want to reach for your camera. If you'd like to get interesting "wild and mild" shots, there are two good vantage points for capturing the wildly painted buildings with more conservative highrises in the background. The first is from the top deck of a public parking garage—equally brightly painted—just beyond La Placita at the southeast corner of Church and Jackson Street. Step out of the elevator onto the fifth floor and walk straight ahead to the corner of a low, mauve concrete wall about three feet high. You'll have a nice shot down to the Technicolor complex, with office towers beyond. This is a horizontal with a medium range lens.

The second photo angle is the same one we suggested above for best view of La Placita, from a public park behind the Music Hall in the Tucson Convention Center complex. Shoot it as a vertical, framed in one of the park's pepper trees, with a blue-painted boulder-studded reflection pool and fountain the foreground and Tucson's tallest building—the UniSource Energy Tower—in the background. It's best as an afternoon shot, to get sun and shadow on La Placita's multicolored buildings.

8 PIMA COUNTY COURTHOUSE DOME ● *From Plaza de las Armas just south of the courthouse. The plaza is rimmed by Alameda and Pennington streets and Church Avenue.*

The venerable Pima County Courthouse, as we noted above, is topped with a glossy multicolored dome, a favorite target of photographers. For even more color, shoot from a vantage point between the main fountain and a rose garden at Plaza de las Armas. To add drama to the photo—if you have a wide-angle lens—hunker down to bring a couple of roses well into the foreground, with the dome appearing to float above them. You'll be facing northward with the sun behind you, so shoot it early in the morning or late in the afternoon. You'll get a nice shadow effect on one side of the courthouse dome, like a waning or waxing moon.

9 *MISSION SAN XAVIER DEL BAC* ● *San Xavier Road; (520) 294-2624. Daily 6 to 7. GETTING THERE: Drive south from Tucson on I-19, take exit 92 and go west briefly to the mission.*

Thousands of photographers have taken tens of thousands of pictures of the splendid "White Dove of the Desert." With its graceful lines, soft curves and whitewashed complexion, it photographs well from almost any angle, like a beautiful woman. If you'd like some nice overview shots, walk up to a rugged volcanic hill topped by a cross. A path circles its rocky girth and you can get some high angle shots of the mission and its surrounding fields. There's no path up to the cross itself, although people don't seem to object if you scramble over the basaltic boulders to reach it. You can get even higher angle photos from here, including some contrasting shots of the old mission with modern Tucson in the distance.

10 *THE CATALINAS FROM UPPER KOLB ROAD* ● *About a dozen miles northeast of downtown. GETTING THERE: See "The best viewpoints" listing above.*

Keep your camera handy as you follow upper Kolb Road through a neighborhood of cactus gardens and fancy homes. You'll find several places to capture this scene, with the dramatic ramparts of Mount Lemmon and the Santa Catalinas in the background. If you continue up to the ❖ **Lodge at Ventana Canyon** and ❖ **Loew's Ventana Canyon Resort**, you can get shots with cool green golf fairways or resort facilities in the foreground. Our favorite angles are from Loew's, either from its large lobby bar across a pool complex to the Catalinas, or from a riparian woodland trail canopied with desert trees. It leads up to a sheltered rock basin, where Ventana Creek trickles down a sheer eighty-foot wall.

Tucson's Ten Best Specialty Guides

Some of these books are statewide and some are repeats from the Phoenix-Scottsdale listing in Chapter Nine. We've selected only those with a fair amount of material on Tucson.

We listed addresses when we were able to find them, but contact the publishers before sending a check, since there likely will be shipping charges, and prices may have changed. Most of these books also can be ordered on line from *amazon.com, bn.com* or *borders.com.* Barnes & Noble Booksellers (Chapter Seventeen, page 236), Borders Books and Music and the two Bookmans stores in the Tucson area have the best selection of regional guides. Our choices are listed in alphabetical order.

1 DAY TRIPS FROM PHOENIX, TUCSON & FLAGSTAFF •

By Shifra Stein; current edition by Pam Hait. Globe-Pequot Press, P.O. Box 480, Guilford, CT 06437; 324 pages; $14.95. (globe-pequot.com)

This comprehensive guide to outings from Arizona's metropolitan centers is handy for visitors with spare time and for residents seeking new getaways.

2 EL CHARRO CAFE: The Tastes and Traditions of Tucson •

By Carlotta Flores. Fisher Books, c/o Da Capo Press, 11 Cambridge Center, Cambridge, MA 02142; 144 pages; $27.50. (www.dacapopress.com)

The owner-chef of America's oldest family-owned Mexican restaurant spins tales of old Tucson and offers scores of her favorite recipes.

3 FIFTY GREAT WEEKEND ESCAPES IN ARIZONA •

By Ray Bangs and Chris Becker. Northland Publishing, P.O. Box 1389, Flagstaff, AZ 86002-1389; 200 pages; $19.95. (www.northlandpub.com)

This book lists a year's worth of weekend outdoor escapes from Arizona's urban areas, featuring a variety of activities, with maps and even discount coupons.

4 HIKING ARIZONA'S CACTUS COUNTRY •

By Erik Molvar. Falcon Guides, Globe-Pequot Press, P.O. Box 480, Gilford, CT 06437; 320 pages; $15.95. (www.globepequot.com)

This guide to nearly a hundred hikes focuses on Southern Arizona's Saguaro National Park, Organ Pipe National Monument, the Chiricahua Mountains and Coronado National Forest.

5 SAN XAVIER: THE SPIRIT ENDURES •

By Kathleen Walker. Published by Arizona Highways; eighty pages; $14.95. (www.arizonahighways.com)

This is a sensitively written portrait of the "White Dove of the Desert," beautifully illustrated by photographer-contributors to various *Arizona Highways* publications. Although it touches on San Xavier's history, it is more of a contemporary look at Arizona's most famous mission.

6 SOUTHERN ARIZONA NATURE ALMANAC ● *By Roseann and Jonathan Hanson. Pruett Publishing Company, 2928 Pearl St., Boulder, CO 80301; 324 pages; $21.95. (www.pruettpublishing.com)*

This is a book with a rather interesting format. It's a detailed month-by-month guide to the best times for visiting natural areas of Tucson, Pima County and beyond, focusing on natural habitats.

7 TUCSON: A SHORT HISTORY ● *Sections by Charles W. Polzer, Thomas H. Naylor, Thomas E. Sheridan and others. Published by the Southwest Mission Research Center in Tucson; 152 pages; $8.95.*

Busy with historic and contemporary photos—many in color—this highly readable book focuses on the people native to the area, the Spaniards who came and the people who are here today.

8 TUCSON: THE LIFE AND TIMES OF AN AMERICAN CITY ● *By C.L. Sonnichen. University of Oklahoma Press; $22.95.*

For the more serious student of Tucson's past, this is a scholarly, comprehensive and in depth history.

9 TUCSON: THE OLD PUEBLO ● *By Lisa Schembley Heidinger, with photography by Rick and Suzie Graetz and Larry Meyer. American World Geographic Publishing, P.O. Box 5630, Helena, MT 59604; 104 pages; $15.95.*

This is a very pretty picture book, featuring color photos of Tucson and the surrounding areas of Pima County.

10 TUCSON HIKING GUIDE ● *By Betty Leavengood. Pruett Publishing Co., 2928 Pearl St., Boulder, CO 80301; 212 pages; $15.95.*

Calling Tucson a "hiker's heaven," the author describes thirty-four hikes in the area, with maps and elevation charts.

EASY LISTENING: THE TEN BEST RADIO STATIONS

Here's where to tune in your favorite sounds while driving about the Tucson Basin.

1 KUAZ—89.1-FM ● This University of Arizona public broadcast station has the usual NPR features, with a jazz format. A second NPR station, KUAT, plays classical music at 89.7 and 90.5.

2 *KMNT—94.9-FM* ● It plays light rock and current hits, with news, sports and traffic.

3 *KWFM—92.9-FM* ● This "Coyote Country" station plays current and past country hits.

4 *KRQ—93.7-FM* ● This station features contemporary and older pops and rock.

5 *KHYT—107.5-FM* ● Classic rock—some soft, some not—is this station's format.

6 *KFAZ—580-AM* ● It plays classic adult pops, from the sixties forward.

7 *KCUB—1290-AM* ● "The Cub" plays present and past country favorites.

8 *KTUC—1400-AM* ● Miss the days of Der Bingle, The Voice and Frankie Laine? KTUC plays old standards, swing and big band sounds, with hourly news and sports.

9 *KNST—790-AM* ● This is one of Tucson's stronger news and talk stations.

10 *KGBY—1080-AM* ● Real oldies emanate from this station, going back to the era of big bands and golden voice vocalists.

Chapter Nineteen

BEYOND TUCSON
VISITING THE OLD PUEBLO'S NEIGHBORS

Southern Arizona offers an interesting mix of attractions, all within a few hours' drive of Tucson. They include the familiar, such as Tombstone and Organ Pipe National Monument; and the lesser known, like the recently opened Kartchner Caverns State Park and a scenic byway named in honor of a famous conquistador who never traveled it.

These aren't comprehensive listings, but brief descriptions intended to give you basic route outlines. Trace them on a state map and set forth. For guidance, each listing begins with sources for further information. Where practical, we've strung two or more of these side trips together. As noted in Chapter Ten, you'll want to embellish these skeletal listings with additional material from a comprehensive state-wide guidebook. Like our *Arizona Discovery Guide*, for instance.

THE TEN BEST SIDE TRIPS

We begin by heading west to a famous observatory and a preserve that—like Saguaro National Park—is named in honor of a cactus. We then take an interesting route to Phoenix, and then explore "Cowboy country," Arizona's fascinating yet little-visited southeast corner. And finally, we head down Mexico way to visit its border towns.

1 **TUCSON TO ORGAN PIPE** • *For information: Kitt Peak National Observatory, (520) 318-8726; Ajo District Chamber of Commerce, 400 Taladro St., Ajo, AZ 85321; (520) 387-7742; and Superintendent, Organ Pipe Cactus National Monument, Route 1, Box 100, Ajo, AZ 85321; (520) 387-6849.*

The region west of Tucson is one of the least populated and least visited areas of the state. It offers miles and miles of nothing except miles and miles, consisting mostly of greasewood desert in the 2.5-million acre Tohono O'odham Indian Reservation. It's the second largest in America after the Navajo reservation. However, three attractions make this drive worthwhile—a world famous observatory, an interesting desert hamlet and a national monument dedicated to a specific kind of cactus.

To begin, head south from Tucson on I-19, then take exit 99 and go west on Ajo Way, which is State Route 86. After thirty miles, you'll see the turnoff to **Kitt Peak National Observatory.** With more than twenty-four telescopes and other research instruments, it's the largest observatory on the globe. Press westward on State Route 86 through the empty sprawl of the Tohono O'odham reservation. You can get provisions at the small town of **Sells,** which is home to tribal headquarters. Continue west through more emptiness to the oddly-named hamlet of **Why** and head south on State Route 85.

The desert terrain improves dramatically as you climb toward **Ajo,** a cute Spanish colonial style town set among rough-hewn lava peaks. Check out the **Ajo Historical Museum** and the open-pit **New Cornelia Mine.** Continue south to **Organ Pipe National Monument,** a splendid desert garden that rivals anything in the Tucson Basin. It's named for a large cactus that sends heavy limbs upward from a common base. Just south is the tiny town of **Lukeville** and, across the Mexican border, dusty little **Sonoita**; see page 266.

2 **THE SCENIC ROUTE TO PHOENIX** • *For information: Pinal County Visitors Center, 330 E. Butte (P.O. Box 967), Florence, AZ 85232, (888) 469-0175 or (520) 868-4331; Superintendent, Casa Grande Ruins National Monument, 1100 Ruins Dr., Coolidge, AZ 85228, (520) 723-3172; and Greater Casa Grande Chamber of Commerce, 575 N. Marshall, Casa Grande, AZ 85222; (800) 916-1515 or (520) 836-2125.*

Most travelers dash quickly and sometimes madly between Tucson and Phoenix on I-10. A more leisurely and scenic approach is up state routes 77 and then 79; they roughly parallel Interstate 10 just to the east. Head north from Tucson on Oracle Road (State Route 77), which skims the rugged western edge of the Santa Catalinas and takes you to

Oracle Junction. If you haven't yet visited **Columbia University Biosphere 2** (Chapter Twelve, page 172), follow Route 77 east to **Oracle.** Otherwise, continue north from Oracle Junction on Route 79, the **Pinal Pioneer Parkway,** which travels through an area of rich desert flora. Signs along the route identify various plants. About twenty-five miles north of Oracle Junction, watch on your left for the **Tom Mix Monument,** marking the site where the 1930s cowboy movie star died in the crash of his Cord sports car in 1940.

Seventeen miles beyond the marker is the handsome old fashioned town of **Florence,** with a Western style downtown area and several historic buildings. It also has a pair of specific lures—**McFarland State Historic Park,** which chronicles the life of Senator Ernest W. McFarland, author of the G.I. Bill of Rights; and **Pinal County Historical Museum.** Head west from Florence on State Route 287 and you'll encounter **Casa Grande Ruins National Monument,** where a giant carport style roof keeps the rain off America's largest adobe ruin. The multi-story structure was the centerpiece of a Hohokam village and may have been used for ceremonial purposes.

From the ruin, take State Route 387 west to I-10, from where you can cruise quickly north to Phoenix. Or make this a round trip by heading south. In the town—not the ruin—of Casa Grande, the **Casa Grande Valley Historical Museum** is worth a stop. Pressing southward, you'll see a dramatic pinnacle—the centerpiece of **Picacho Peak State Park.** It was the site of the westernmost battle of the Civil War, fought between troops from California and Texas in 1862. The park has hiking trails, picnic areas and campsites.

3 *KARTCHNER CAVERNS TO SIERRA VISTA* ● *For information: Kartchner Caverns State Park, P.O. Box 1849, Benson, AZ 85602, (520) 586-4100 for information and (520) 586-CAVE for tour reservations; Sierra Vista Convention & Visitors Bureau, 21 E. Wilcox Dr., Sierra Vista, AZ 85635, (800) 288-3861 or (520) 417-6960; and Superintendent, Coronado National Memorial, 4101 E. Montezuma Canyon Rd., Hereford, AZ 85615, (520) 366-5515.*

Arizona's newest natural attraction wasn't opened to the public until 1999, yet it's millions of years old. Thus, the 2.4-mile-long limestone cave in **Kartchner Cavern State Park** has been spared vandalism and poor management suffered by many other caves. It can be toured only by reservation by calling the number above. From Tucson, drive east on I-10, then take exit 302 just short of **Benson** and head south on State Route 90 to the caverns.

After visiting the caves, continue south on Route 90 to **Sierra Vista,** a retirement community that's growing surprisingly fast despite its isolation. This town of 35,000 is gateway to **Fort Huachuca,** Arizona's oldest still active military base and the state's largest single employer. Its **Fort Huachuca Museum** is definitely worth a visit.

Just south of here, reached via State Route 92, is **Coronado National Memorial,** sitting on the Mexican border. It honors that peripatetic *conquistadore* Francisco Vásquez de Coronado, who roamed the Southwest in 1540 in a futile search for cities of gold. He never passed this way, although the visitor center focuses on his trek. The memorial also preserves a nice swatch of the wooded Huachuca Mountains.

4 **OLD TOMBSTONE** ● *For information: Tombstone Office of Tourism, P.O. Box 248, Tombstone, AZ 85638; (800) 457-3423 or the Tombstone Chamber of Commerce at (520) 457-9317.*

Tombstone has been called "the town too tough to die." It can't die of course, because Hollywood would never permit it. The famous shootout at the O.K. Corral involving the Earps and Clantons has been given more film footage than the invasion of Normandy.

Tombstone was born in the rocky desert after a gold strike in 1877; it was to become one of the wildest mining towns in the American West. It's now one of Arizona's best known tourist towns, abrim with lures such as **Boot Hill Cemetery** (complete with a gift shop), and reenactments of the **O.K. Corral shootout.** Its assorted historic sites and museums include the **Birdcage Theater, Crystal Palace Saloon, Tombstone Epitaph** newspaper office, **Museum of the West** and—if you must—the **Tombstone Historama.**

The most legitimate attraction here is **Tombstone Courthouse State Historic Park,** preserving the 1882 Cochise County court building. It's busy with displays concerning the town's lively history including—of course—The Shootout.

You can reach Tombstone from the previous tour by returning to Sierra Vista from Coronado National Memorial and following an unnumbered highway northeast.

5 **BISBEE TO DOUGLAS** ● *For information: Greater Bisbee Chamber of Commerce, 31 Subway St. (P.O. Drawer BA), Bisbee, AZ 85603, (520) 432-5421; and Douglas Visitors Center, 1125 Pan American Ave., Douglas, AZ 85607; (520) 364-2478.*

Once one of Arizona's richest mining towns, Bisbee is now one of its most appealing historic sites, with none of the tourist gimmickry of Tombstone. It's a pleasing collection of old brick and masonry, cantilevered into the steep slopes of Mule Pass Gulch and landscaped with tailing dumps. Among its attractions are the **Bisbee Mining and Historical Museum,** the gaping **Lavender Pit** open pit mine and the very interesting underground **Queen Mine Tour** that's conducted in old ore cars.

To reach Bisbee from the end of the previous tour, follow State Route 80 southeast from Tombstone. After your visit, continue east on Route 80 along the Arizona-Mexico border to **Douglas.** It's another old mining town although it lacks the dramatic hillside perch and historic allure of Bisbee. Its most interesting attraction is the downtown 1907 **Gadsden Hotel,** restored to its copper baron splendor. Two visitor lures are just outside town—the small **Douglas Wildlife Zoo** and **San Bernardino Ranch National Historic Landmark.** It preserves the fancy ranch house and some outbuildings of a huge cattle spread created by John Slaughter in the late 1800s. Just across the border from Douglas is the much larger Mexican town of **Agua Prieta**; see page 265.

6 *CHIRICAHUA TO WILLCOX* • *For information: Chiricahua National Monument,13063 E. Bonita Canyon Rd., Willox, AZ 85643, (520) 824-3560, ext. 104; and Willcox Chamber of Commerce, 1500 N. Circle Rd., Willcox, AZ 85643, (800) 200-2272 or (520) 384-2272.*

Chiricahua National Monument preserves a wooded area of fascinating rock formations and Willcox is a small but busy cowtown with a couple of interesting museums. Continuing from the previous tour, take U.S. 191 north from Douglas, then follow State Route 181 through **Sunizona** to **Chiricahua National Monument.** Called the "Wonderland of Rocks," it preserves wildly eroded volcanic rhyolite deposits on the wooded slopes of the Pendregosa Mountains. A steep, winding eight-mile drive takes visitors past these formations.

From Chiricahua, follow State Route 186 northwest and—if you don't mind a few bumps—take a dirt and gravel road about nine miles northeast to **Fort Bowie National Historic Site.** One of the most remote units of the national park system, it preserves the crumbling adobe walls of an 1862 army fort. Soldiers rode out from here in pursuit of Apache warriors Geronimo and Cochise. Return to State Route 186 and continue northwest to **Willcox** on Interstate 10. It's the hometown of a real cowboy who became a Hollywood cowboy—the late Rex Allen. His story is told in the **Rex Allen Arizona Cowboy Museum.** Willcox's other archive, the excellent **Museum of the Southwest** chronicles the history of this "cowboy corner" of Arizona.

7 *THE CORONADO TRAIL* • *For information: Graham County Chamber of Commerce, 1111 Thatcher Blvd., Safford, AZ 85546, (928) 428-2511; Greenlee County Chamber of Commerce, P.O. Box 1237, Clifton, AZ 85533, (928) 865-3313; and Round Valley Chamber of Commerce, 318 E. Main St. (P.O. Box 31), Springerville, AZ 85938, (928) 333-2123;*

There's no evidence that Coronado ever took this route, although a section of U.S. 191 along Arizona's eastern edge is called the Coronado Trail. This highway travels through little-visited yet very interesting country. Begin from the end of the previous tour by driving east from Willcox on I-10, then heading north on U.S. 191. After about thirty-five miles, you'll encounter **Safford**. It's an ordinary agricultural town with a couple of fine attractions, **Discovery Park** science center and **Mount Graham**, a wooded recreation area and home to **Mount Graham International Observatory**. A scenic highway winds high into the flanks of Mount Graham, offering pleasing vistas. The observatory isn't open to the public, although it operates a planetarium and other astronomical exhibits at Discovery Park.

Follow Highway 191 northeast and then north from Safford, and you'll see multi-colored tailing dumps of the **Clifton-Morenci** copper mining region. The two towns, tucked into a strange moonscape of tailing dumps and open mining pits, are quite different. Morenci is a prim, well-planned company town of the Phelps-Dodge Corporation, one of Arizona's largest mining firms. Clifton, just to the north, is a scruffy old town established in 1873 when copper was first discovered in the area. It's the seat of remote Greenlee County and home to the small **Greenlee Historical Museum,** with exhibits on the area's mining past.

North of here, U.S. 191 winds through scenic **Apache-Sitgreaves National Forest**. This is the section of the highway that's been labeled the Coronado Trail. It's also a National Forest Scenic Byway, climbing nearly 9,000 feet into the Blue Range Primitive Area.

The highway drops down to the twin communities of **Eagar** and **Springerville**. Just west of Eagar is the **Little House Museum** on the historic Diamond-X Ranch. Springerville has two very interesting lures—the archeological sites of **Casa Malpais Pueblo** and **Raven Site Ruin,** where archeological digs are still active.

8 *TUBAC-TUMACÁCORI CORRIDOR* • *For information: Green Valley Chamber of Commerce, 270 W. Continental, Suite 100, Green Valley, AZ 85622, (800) 858-5872 or (520) 625-7575; Tubac Chamber of Commerce, P.O. Box 1866, Tubac, AZ 85646, (520) 398-2704; and Superintendent, Tumacàcori National Historical Park, (520) 398-2341.*

The first thing you'll notice about Interstate 19 headed from south Tucson to Nogales is that the highway signs are metric. It's the only all-metric route in America. Beyond that novelty, it leads to some interesting towns and lures. **Green Valley** is a retirement community and home to the **Titan Missile Museum**. It's the only museum of its kind in America—a missile silo with the missile still in place.

Just to the south is **Tubac,** where Arizona's first Spanish presidio was built in 1752. Its history is preserved at **Tubac Presidio State Park,** with a museum, restored buildings and fragments of the original presidio walls. Tubac also is an art colony, with several galleries and shops. Below here, you'll encounter **Tumacàcori National Historical Park**, where mission-builder Eusebio Francisco Kino erected a simple mud chapel in 1691. The present church—the focal point of the historic park—was started around 1800. It houses several nicely done exhibits concerning Arizona's Spanish colonial legacy.

9 **DOS NOGALES** • *For information: Nogales-Santa Cruz County Chamber of Commerce, 123 W. Kino Parkway, Nogales, AZ 85621; (520) 287-3685.*

Nogales, which means "walnuts," is a twin city—a town of 20,000 on the Arizona side and a Mexican edition ten times larger. The size differential stems from the role of Mexico's Nogales as an "offshore" manufacturing center, with factories funded by American corporations and using inexpensive Mexican labor.

Nogales, Arizona, is an ordinary blue collar town, with an interesting museum in its downtown area—**Pima Alta Historical Society.** Exhibits tell the stories of both cities during their Spanish, Mexican and American periods. There was only one Nogales until the boundary line set by the Gadsden Purchase cut it in half.

It's an easy walk from downtown Nogales, Arizona, across the border to the colorful if somewhat dusty Nogales, Mexico. Several car lots on the American side provide inexpensive parking. In fact, it's best to walk across since the border crossing often becomes quite jammed with vehicles, particularly during rush hour and whenever the U.S. Border Patrol starts getting picky about illegal aliens. For more on Mexico's Nogales, see the listing below.

If you drive two miles east of Arizona's Nogales on State Route 82, you'll encounter the tasting room of **Arizona Vineyard**, the state's only winery.

10 **SOUTH OF THE BORDER** • *American citizens can visit Mexican border towns with no formal documents if their stay is brief. For visits longer than seventy-two hours or for trips more than sixteen miles beyond the border, Mexican Tourist Cards are required, and they're easily obtained at the border if you have proof of citizenship. If you drive into Mexico, you must get Mexican auto insurance which—again—can be purchased at the border.*

Arizona has six border crossings with Mexico and you may want to slip over to sample the wares, food and atmosphere of our good neighbors to the south. Here are those crossings:

Agua Prieta • Across from Douglas, this is a busy industrial town with about 80,000 residents. It offers a fair variety of shops, although not as many as Nogales. Downtown here is more of a conventional mix of businesses, with gift shops tucked among department stores, *farmacias* and professional offices. Paved highways lead into the interior; it's the most direct driving route to Mexico City.

Naco • A hamlet south of Bisbee, this is one of our favorite border towns. If there's such a thing as scruffily cute, this is it. Naco is more like an interior village—uncrowded, with little Mexican shops behind dusty pastel store fronts. You won't find much of a shopping selection here, but there's one good-sized liquor store, with very modest prices. Some of the wide but pot-holed streets have center dividers, giving the place a nice colonial charm.

Nogales • Opposite Nogales, Arizona, it's the largest of the border towns, with a population exceeding 200,000. Predictably, it's also the best place to shop. Scores of curio shops and liquor stores are crowded into the Calle Obregon, a shopping area that starts just a block from the border. Narrow arcades are stuffed with stalls, carrying everything from curios and general junk to leather goods, fabric, folk crafts and glassware.

San Luis • South of Yuma, San Luis is an agricultural community of 50,000 or so. Its weathered old business district offers several shops within two blocks of the border. Selections are fairly good, although it's a distant second to Nogales for variety. You can park free in Friendship Park on the American side; the lot closes at 9 p.m.

Sasabe • At the bottom of Highway 286 southwest of Tucson, this is the smallest, least crowded and most typically Mexican of the border towns. A handful of residents occupy its weathered buildings and its matching Arizona twin, and there are no tourist shops or other facilities. Only dirt roads lead south from here, so Sasabe obviously gets very little through traffic. Incidentally, the border station is closed between 8 p.m. and 8 a.m.

Sonoita • This little town is about three miles south of the border, opposite Lukeville and Organ Pipe Cactus National Monument. A few shops are within walking distance of Lukeville, although there isn't much of a selection. You might like to drive sixty-three miles south to **Rocky Point** (Puerto Peñasco), where you can swim, snorkel and fish in the clear waters of the Gulf of California. It has several tourist hotels and restaurants. Remember that you need a Mexican Tourist Card and vehicle permit to go south of Sonoita. The Sonoita-Lukeville border station is closed between midnight and 8 a.m.

INDEX: Primary listings indicated by bold face italics

A Jewel of the Crown restaurant, 69
Actors' Theater of Phoenix, 98
Agua Prieta, 263, *265*
Ahwatukee, 135
Ajo & Ajo Historical Museum, 260
America West Arena, 129
American Museum of Nursing, 49
Amtrak, 19, 158
Anthony's in the Catalinas, *181*, 186
Anthropology Museum, 46
Antique Center of Tucson, 237
Apache Junction, 147
Arcosanti, 150
Area codes, 20
Arizona Biltmore Resort & Spa, 74
Arizona Cardinals, 38
Arizona Center, 21, *117*, 128, 139
Arizona Cowboy College, 41
Arizona Diamondbacks, 38
Arizona Doll and Toy Museum, 29
Arizona Hall of Fame Museum, 33
Arizona Historical Society Museum, *45*, 85, 173, 211
Arizona Inn, 160, *181*, 201
Arizona Mills, 118
Arizona Mining/Mineral Museum, 33
Arizona Opera Company, 99, 222
Arizona Public Lands Center, 127
Arizona Repertory Theater, 223
Arizona Science Center, *27*, 128
Arizona State Capitol Museum, *27*, 85
Arizona State Museum, *166*, 211
Arizona State University, *45*, 128
Arizona Strip, 146
Arizona Theater Company, 99, 222
Arizona-Sonora Desert Museum, 162, *165*
Arriba Mexican Grill, 64
Audubon Bar, 227
AZ 88 club, 103

Bacchanal Greek Restaurant, 69
Bahti Indian Arts, 236
Baja Fresh, 89
Ballet Arizona, 99, *223*
Bank One Ballpark, *39*, 129
Battle of Picacho Pass, 157
Bavarian Point Restaurant, 69
Bead Museum, The, 49, *86*
Benson, town of, 261
Berky's Bar, 225
Beyond Bread, 187
Biltmore Fashion Park, 117
Bisbee, 262

Black Mountain Brewery, 47
Blue Burrito Grille, *64*, 89
Blue Willow, 188
Bookman's, 237
Boondocks Lounge, 225
Borgata, The, 118
Boulders Resort, 23, 47, 56, *73*, 110
Bouvier-Teeter House, 29
Broadway Village, 232
Budget Inn Motel, 93
Budget Lodge Motel, 92
Bullhead City, 153

Cactus League baseball, 22, *40*
Caesar Chavez Plaza, 128
Café Poca Cosa, 190
Café Terra Cotta, 181
Camelback Inn Marriott, 75
Canyon de Chelly National Monument, 149
Canyon Ranch Spa, 202
Carefree, town of, *46*, 132, 134
Caruso's, 195
Casa Grande Ruins, 261
Casino Arizona, 42
Catalina Highway, 163
Catalina Park Inn, 208
Cave Creek, *46*, 132, 134
Cave Creek Museum, 47, 134
Centennial Hall, 222
Center For Creative Photography, 178
Center For Meteorite Studies, 46
Central Gardens, 21, *108*, 128
Champlin Fighter Museum, 48
Chaparral Park, *132*, 134
Chaparral Suites, 80
Chinese Cultural Center, 43
Chinle, town of, 149
Chiricahua National Monument, 263
Chloride, town of, 152
Clifton, town of, 264
Club Level, 100
Club Congress, 225
Colorado City, 146
Colorado River Corridor, 152
Colossal Cave, 174
Columbia University Biosphere 2, 172
Comfort Inn, 93
Commemorative Air Force Museum, 48
Compass Restaurant, 24, *60*, 137
Convivo, 112
Coronado, Francisco Vásquez de, 262
Coronado National Memorial, 262
Coronado Trail, 263
Corral West Ranchwear, 238

Cosanti, 34
Cottonwood, town of, 150
Coup Des Tartes, 68
Crazy Ed's Satisfied Frog, 47
Crescent Moon, 54
Crossroads Festival, 232

De Grazia Gallery, 162, *174*
Dead Horse Ranch State Park, 150
Deer Valley Rock Art Center, *34*, 86
Delhi Palace, 195
Desert Botanical Garden, *28*, 11
Different Pointe of View, *54*, 100, 137
Discovery Channel Store, 124
Dish, The, *182*, 250
Dobbin's Lookout, 21, 88, *109*, 130
Dos Locos Latinos, 250
Doubletree Guest Suites, 80
Doubletree Paradise Valley Resort, 81
Douglas, 262

Eagar, town of, 264
Econo Lodge, 218
El Charro Café, 162, 175, *189*, 241
El Con Mall, 233
El Cortijo Plaza, 161, *233*
El Minuto, *190*, 215, 241
El Paso Bar-b-que, 59, 188
el Pedregal Festival Marketplace, 23, 46, *118*, 132, 134
El Presidio Bed & Breakfast, 207
El Presidio Historic District, *175*, 212, 240
El Torero, *191*, 214
Eli's Bar & American Grille, 103
Encanto Park, *35*, 86, 109, 138
Epic Café, 215

Fairmont Scottsdale Princess, 76
Fat Greek, The, 215
Field of Dreams, 123
Fiesta Mall, 119
Filito's Café, 44, *89*
Fine Art Galleries complex, 233
Firecracker Bistro, *196*, 228
First Watch cafés, 61
Flagstaff, 149
Flandrau Science Center, 175
Florence, town of, 261
Foothills Mall, 233
Fort Bowie Nat'l Historic Site, 263
Fort Lowell Museum, 212
Fort Verde State Historic Park, 150
Fountain Hills, 88
Four Corners Monument, 149
Four Seasons Resort Scottsdale, 76, 104, *138*

Fourth Avenue District 224, 227, *234*
Fredonia, 146
Friday's Front Row, *104*, 129
Frog & Firkin, 228
Frontier Motel, 219
Frontier Town, 47, 134
¡Fuego!, 182

Ganado, 148
Garden of Gethsemane, 246
Gaslight Theatre, 223
Gates Pass, 160
Gilbert Ortega Arts and Gifts, 38, *122*
Glen Canyon NRA, 146
Glendale, 49
Globe, town of, 147, 151
Gold Room, The, 183
Golden Swan, The, *55*, 112
Golf Villas at Oro Valley, 203
Good Egg, The, *186*, 232
Grady Gammage Auditorium, 46, *96*
Grand Canyon North Rim, 145
Greater Phoenix Convention & Visitors Bureau, 20
Green Leaf Café, 63
Green Valley, 264
Greenhouse Grille, 104
Greyhound buses, 19, 158
Guadalupe, 43

Hacienda del Sol Guest Ranch, 205
Hall of Flame Museum of Firefighting, 29
Harrah's Ak-Chin Casino Resort, 1011
Harris' Restaurant, *59*, 105
Hassayampa River Preserve, 152
Heard Museum, 26
Herberger Theater, *97*, 128, 139
Heritage and Science Park, 127, 129
Heritage Square, *29*, 128, 85
Hermosa Inn, 81
Hilton Scottsdale Resort & Villas, 81
Hoa Mai Restaurant, *197*, 251
Hohokam Canals, 30, 36
Hohokam Tribe, 12, 15, 87, 142, 261
Holbrook, 151
Hooters, 105, 228
Hoover Dam, 152
Hopi Indian Reservation, 147
Hopi Learning Center, *36*, 86
Hotevilla, 148
Hualapai Mountain Park, 152
Hubbell Trading Post Historic Site, 148
Humphreys Peak, 149
Hyatt Regency Phoenix, *82*, 108, 128
Hyatt Regency Scottsdale Resort, 23, 35, *77*, 87, 102, 110

Improv, The, 101
Indian Gaming, 42
International Wildlife Museum, 176

Jacob Lake, 146
Jacquee's Espresso, 62
Janos, 183
Jerome and Jerome State Historic Park, 150

Kartchner Cavern State Park, 261
Karuna's Thai Plate, *197*, 216
Kayenta, 149
Kingfisher, 186
Kingman, 152
Kino, Father Eusebio Francisco, 156
Kirin Wok, *90*, 129
Kitt Peak National Observatory, 260
Knights Inn, 219
Kokopelli Mexican Grill, 90
Kykotsmovi, 148

La Cocina, 187
La Hacienda, 63
La Paloma Mexican Food, 90
La Parilla Suisa, 191
La Placita Café, 191
La Placita Village, 253, *254*
La Quinta Inns, 219
La Salsa Fresh Mexican Grill, 216
La Tierra Linda Guest Ranch, 206
Lacocina Restaurant, 175
Laff's Comedy Club, 226
Lake Havasu City & state park, 153
Lantilla Restaurant, *55*, 112
"Largest tree in Tucson," 246
Laughlin, Nevada, 153
Lazy 8 Motel, 219
Lazy K Bar Guest Ranch, 206
Le Bistro, 249
Le Rendez-vous Restaurant, 194
Lee's Ferry, 146
Liquor laws, 20
Little Poca Cosa, 190
Lodge at Ventana Canyon, *203*, 253
Lodge on the Desert, 208
Loew's Ventana Canyon Resort, 161, *199*, 240, 248, 255
London Bridge, Lake Havasu, 153
Lon's at the Hermosa, 24, *113*
Los Dos Molinos, 65
Lost Barrio shopping area, 238
Lost Dutchman State Park, 147
Lotus Garden, 194
Lucky Chinese Restaurant, 91
Lukeville, 260

Macayo's Mexican Kitchen, 65
Mad Hatter's, 49
Malee's On Main, 71
Maloney's on Fourth, 229
Marble Canyon, 146
Marco Polo Supper Club, 100, 113
Maria's When in Naples, 70
Marquesa, The, *56*, 114
Martini Ranch, 1011
Marty Robbins Glendale Exhibit, 49
Mary Elaine's, *53*, 114
Mason Jar night club, 101
Matador restaurant, 66
Maverick King of Clubs, 226
McDowell Mountain Park, 88, *135*
McFarland State Historic Park, 261
McMahon's Prime Steakhouse, 185
Mercado Mexico, 44
Mesa Southwest Museum, 44
Metropolitan Tucson Convention and Visitors Bureau, 159
Mi Nidito, 192
Mia Amigo's Mexican Grill, 66
Miami, Ariz., 147, 151
Mineral Museum, UofA, 176
Mission San Xavier Del Bac, 156, 160, *167*, 211, 255
Montezuma Castle National Monument, 150
Monument Valley Tribal Park, 149
Morenci, town of, 264
Motel 6, 93, 219
Mount Lemmon Rec. Area, *167*, 252
Mountain View Restaurant, 194
Mr. C's Restaurant, 68
Mr. Lucky's, 102
Museo Mexicano, 128
Museum of Contemporary Art, 38
Museum of Geology, 46
Museum of the Southwest, 263
Music Hall, Tucson, *222*, 241
Mystery Castle, 36

Naco, 266
Navajo Arts and Crafts Center, 148
Navajo Indian Reservation, 147
Navajo National Monument, 149
Nimbus Brewing Company, 225
Nogales, 265

Oasis Motel, 220
Oatman, 152
O.K. Corral shootout, 262
Old Oraibi, 148
Old Pueblo Grille, 192
Old Town Artisans, 175, *236*, 240
Old Town Scottsdale, *37*, 121

Old Town Tortilla Factory, *66*, 114
Old Tucson Studios, 168
Olive Tree, 195
O'Malley's on Fourth, 226, **229**
Omni Tucson Nat'l Golf Resort, 204
Organ Pipe Cactus National Monument, 260
Oriental Express, 216
Orpheum Theatre, **97**, 128
Orts Theatre of Dance, 223
Our Lady of Guadalupe Church, 44
Out of Africa, 30, **50**
Ovens Bistro & Wine Bar, 184

Paola's Wine Bar, 106
Papagayo Mexican Restaurant, 193
Paradise Valley Mall, 119
Park Place, 234
Parker and Parker Dam, 153
Pastabilities, 91
Patriots Square, 129
Payson, 151
Pepin Restaurante Español, 67
Peppertrees Bed & Breakfast, 209
Peter's European Café, 68
Petrified Forest National Park, 151
Phoenician, The, 77
Phoenix Art Museum, 32
Phoenix City Hall, 128, 129 (historic)
Phoenix Civic Plaza, 129
Phoenix Convention & Visitors Bureau, 20
Phoenix Convention Center, 129
Phoenix Coyotes, 38
Phoenix Museum of History, **30**, 128
Phoenix Sky Harbor Int'l Airport, 18
Phoenix Symphony Hall, 97
Phoenix Symphony Orchestra, 98
Phoenix Zoo, 30
Picacho Peak State Park, 261
Pima Air & Space Museum, 169
Pima County Sports Hall of Fame, 244
Pinal County Historical Museum, 261
Pinal Pioneer Parkway, 261
Pinnacle Peak, Tucson, **185**, 229
Pinnacle Peak Patio, Scottsdale, 58
Pioneer Arizona History Museum, 50
Pipe Springs National Monument, 146
Pizzeria Uno, 62
Plaza De Las Armas, 240
Plaza Palomino, 234
Plush lounge, 226
Pointe Hilton Squaw Peak Resort, 78
Pointe Hilton Tapatio Cliffs Resort, 78
Poncho's, 91

Prescott, 150
Pueblo Grande Museum & Archeological Site, **31**, 87

Quail Inn Motel, 220
Quartzsite, 153

Rancho Pinot, 56
Rawhide, 22, **39**, 134
Red River Music Hall, 102
Red Rock State Park, 150
REI, 124
Reid Park Zoo, 177
Renaissance Square, 128
Restaurant Hapa, 57
Rhythm Room, 102
Rialto Theatre, 226
Rillito River Park, 243, 247
Ristorante Sandolo, 115
Ritz-Carlton, 80
Rocky Point, 266
Roosevelt Dam, 17, **147**
Rosson House, 29
RoxSand, 57
Royal Elizabeth, The, 207
Royal Palms Hotel, **82**, 110
Roy's of Scottsdale, 71
Rumrunner, The, 235

Sabino Canyon, **169**, 242
Safford, 264
Saguaro Artisans, 175, 240
Saguaro National Park, **170**, 213
St. Augustine Cathedral, 241
St. Mary's Basilica, 129, 139
St. Phillips Plaza, 235
Sakura, 196
Salt River Canyon, 147
Salt River Project History Center, 36
Samurai Sam's, 217
Sam's Café, 61
San Luis, 266
San Xavier Indian Reservation, 160
Santa Cruz River Park, 246
Sasabe, 266
Scott, Winfield, 16
Scottsdale Center for the Arts, 38, **98**
Scottsdale Civic Center Mall, 22, 38, **109**, 140
Scottsdale Fashion Square, 120
Scottsdale Museum of Contemporary Art, 37
Scottsdale Pavilions, 120
Second Mesa, 148
Sedona, 149
Select Suites, 93
Sells, town of, 260
Sentinel Peak, 247, **252**, 254

Sheraton El Conquistador, 227, **253**
Sheraton Tucson Hotel & Suites, 200
Show Low, 151
Shungnopavi, 148
Sierra Vista, 261
Smugglers Inn, 226
Soleil restaurant, 161, **251**
Sonoita, 260, **266**
Sosa-Carillo-Frémont House, **213**, 241
South China Buffet, 92
South Mountain Park, **87**, 130
Southwest Inn at Eagle Mountain, 83
Speak Easy, 227
Sports Hall of Fame, 46
Sportsman's Fine Wines & Spirits, 123
Springerville, 264
Squaw Peak, **130**, 138
Steamers Genuine Seafood, 60
Studio 6 motel, 93, 218
Summit Hut, 237
Sunrise Resort, 151
Sunset Crater Nat'l Monument, 149
Super 8 Motel, 94
Superior, town of, 151
Superstition Mountains, 147
Superstition Springs Center, 121
Sushi on Shea, 70
Symphony Hall, Phoenix, 128

Tack Room, The, 184
Taliesin West, 32
Tanque Verde Ranch, 204
Tee Pee cafés, 67
Tempe Town Lake, **41**, 111
Temple of Music and Art, 222
Tequila Grill, 106
Terravita Shopping Center, 132
Thunder Canyon Brewery, 230
Time zones, 20
Tohono Chul Park, 213
Tohono O'odham tribe, 15, 45, 156, 157, 160, 171, 260
Tokyo Rice Bowl, 217
Tombstone and Tombstone Courthouse State Historic Park, 262
Tonto National Monument, 147
Top of the Rock, 115
Tortilla Flat, 147
Travel Inn, 220
Travel Inn Nine Motel, 94
Travelers Inn, 94
Tubac and Tubac Presidio, 264
Tucson Botanical Gardens, 171

Tucson Boys Chorus, 224
Tucson Convention & Visitors Bureau, 159
Tucson Convention Center, 241
Tucson International Airport, 158
Tucson Mall, 231
Tucson Mountain Park, 160, **172, 245**
Tucson Museum of Art, 175,**177**, 240
Tucson Pops Orchestra, 224
Tucson Public Library, 241
Tucson Symphony Orchestra, 224
Tumacàcori Nat'l Historical Park, 264
Tuzigoot National Monument, 150
T. Cook's, 58

University of Arizona, 178
University of Arizona Museum of Art, 178, 214
University of Arizona School of Music & Dance, 224

Vega's Mexican Restaurant, 193
Ventana Room, 180
Victoria's Secret, 124
Viente De Agosto Park, 241, **248**
Virgin Megastore, 125
Visitor centers: Phoenix, 20; Tucson, 159

Walnut Canyon National Monument, 149
Westin La Paloma, **200**, 230, 248
Westward Look Resort, 201
White Stallion Ranch, 207
Wickenburg, 152
Wigwam Resort, 79
Wild Oats markets, 123, 237
Wildcat Heritage Gallery, 178
Wildlife World Zoo, 30, **51**
Willcox, 263
Window Rock, 148
Worldwide Wraps, 217
World's highest fountain, 88, 135
World's largest sundial, 47, 133
Wupatki National Monument, 149
Wyndham Buttes Resort, 83

YMCA, 94
Yuma, 153

Zachary's, 188
Zane Grey Museum, 151

Remarkably useful DISCOVERGUIDES
By Don & Betty Martin

Critics praise the "jaunty prose" and "beautiful editing" of travel, wine and relocation guides by authors Don and Betty Martin. They are winners of a gold medal for best guidebook of the year in the prestigious Lowell Thomas Travel Writing Competition. Their remarkably useful *DISCOVERGUIDES* are available at bookstores throughout the United States and Canada, or you can order them on the internet; see details below.

ARIZONA IN YOUR FUTURE — 272 pp; $15.95

THE BEST OF DENVER & THE ROCKIES — 248 pp; $16.95

THE BEST OF PHOENIX & TUCSON — 272 pp; $16.95

THE BEST OF THE WINE COUNTRY — 352 pp; $17.95

THE BEST OF SAN FRANCISCO — 280 pp; $16.95

CALIFORNIA-NEVADA ROADS LESS TRAVELED — 336 pp; $15.95

HAWAII: THE BEST OF PARADISE — 296 pp; $16.95

LAS VEGAS: THE BEST OF GLITTER CITY — 310 pp; $16.95

NEVADA IN YOUR FUTURE — 292 pp; $17.95

SAN DIEGO: THE BEST OF SUNSHINE CITY — 248 pp; $16.95

SEATTLE: THE BEST OF EMERALD CITY — 236 pp; $15.95

THE ULTIMATE WINE BOOK —194 pp; $10.95

WASHINGTON DISCOVERY GUIDE — 464 pp; $17.95